𝔑orthern 𝔄ntiquity

THE POST-MEDIEVAL RECEPTION
OF EDDA AND SAGA

Northern Antiquity

THE POST-MEDIEVAL RECEPTION
OF EDDA AND SAGA

Edited by Andrew Wawn

Hisarlik Press
1994

Published by Hisarlik Press, 4 Catisfield Road, Enfield Lock, Middlesex EN3 6BD, UK. Georgina Clark-Mazo and Dr Jeffrey Alan Mazo, publishers.

British Library Cataloguing-in-Publication data available.

ISBN 1 874312 18 4

10 9 8 7 6 5 4 3 2 1

Jacket illustration: 'Frithiof woos Ingibiorg'. From G.C. Allen, trans. [1912]. *The Song of Frithiof*. London.

Printed in Great Britain by Redwood Books Ltd.

Contents

Part IV. Afterword

Foreword

Of Herculean height and strength, with his long black beard descending to his waist, he resembled a Viking of old, and such I conceive he at times supposed himself to be. In fact, so deeply was he imbued with the spirit of antiquity, that a continual antagonism between the past and the present, or rather, I should say, between the imaginary and the real existed in his breast. He was two gentlemen at once. Though a sincerely religious man, still I cannot help suspecting that in his heart of hearts he looked on Christianity as a somewhat *parvenu* creed, and deemed that Thor, Odin, Freya, etc., were the proper objects of worship. In dull fact, he was an excellent citizen, a householder, paying rates and taxes, an affectionate husband, and the good father of a family; but in the dream, the fancy [...] he was a Berserker, a Norse pirate, ploughing the seas in his dragon-beaked barque, making his trusting falchion ring on the casques of his enemies, slaying, pillaging, burning, ravishing, and thus gratifying a laudable taste for adventure. I fear he preferred the glorious dream to the sober reality. I think he inwardly pined at his own respectability.[1]

Not every post-medieval enthusiast of Edda and saga featured in this volume would have sought to match either the length of Sir George Webbe Dasent's Viking-style beard or his dreams of berserk service in a dragon-beaked barque. Many, however, would have identified readily enough with other features of this wry but affectionate portrait of one of Victorian Britain's greatest Northern antiquaries. They would have empathised with the sense of vivid imaginative engagement, and perhaps also with that persistent itch of romantic irresponsibility which no amount of scratching by the fingers of civic or academic probity could entirely alleviate. They would certainly have been unsurprised by the extent to which personal and political commitment to the values of the ancient North could create a level of scholarly energy every bit as Herculean as Dasent's height. The Englishman was an editor and translator of sagas; a publicist and projector in all matters Northern; and, even by the standards of the age, an intensely politicised philologist. And, no disadvantage to a still marginal subject area in need of influential friends,

---

[1] [Charles Cavendish Clifford], *Travels by 'Umbra'* (Edinburgh, 1865), pp. 3–4.

he was for many years assistant editor of *The Times*.[2]

Many aspects of Dasent's mercurial career are mirrored in the scholarly figures highlighted in this collection of essays. European enthusiasm for the medieval North has, since the early seventeenth century, taken many forms and been driven by many impulses, both learned and 'lewed'— aesthetic, antiquarian, anthropological, archaeological, mythological, philological, nationalistic, political, and (every bit as important) private and personal. It is these impulses which find recurrent expression in essays whose governing theme is the post-medieval rediscovery and reception of Edda and saga in the lands bordering and the islands surrounded by the North Atlantic. Seven of the papers (Malm, Hagland, Lundgreen-Nielsen, Boyer, Glauser, Clunies Ross and Quinn, Kennedy) were first delivered as lectures at the International Saga Conference in Gothenburg in August 1991, as contributions to a workshop on the reception of Old Icelandic literary texts; three further essays are also the work of conference members (Byock, Driscoll, Wawn), though the topics differ from those originally presented in Sweden; the remaining three contributions (Helgason, Haraldsson, D'Arcy) represent the work of other scholars currently engaged in this now happily flourishing area of study.

Medieval monk, Enlightenment sage and modern advertising executive have constructed their versions of the Viking past with strikingly dissimilar priorities in mind. The ridiculous has thus had its place alongside the sublime, the sensual alongside the cerebral. In the papers which follow we move from heated debates about sagas in the wartime Alþingi to decadent depictions of Viking life in the Edwardian theatre; our gaze shifts from heroic statues of Óðinn to horned-helmeted Vikings glaring fiercely at prospective purchasers from the top of sardine tins. Theoretical interest in the generalities of 'reception' is properly balanced by attention to the idiosyncrasies of individual receivers as colourfully dissimilar as Olaf Rudbeck, N.F.S. Grundtvig, Halldór Laxness, and W.H. Auden. We find the medieval saga tradition covertly but successfully renewing itself in Enlightenment Iceland, whilst, elsewhere, we observe the emergence of a saga canon very different from that which obtains today, with times when and places in which works like *Bósa saga* and *Friðþjófs saga* towered in popular esteem over the likes of *Brennu-Njáls saga*. Reflecting the tension already noted between Dasent's glorious dream and his sober reality, the essays register other clashes, controversies and contradictions which have found expression through the

---

[2]Andrew Wawn, 'The Victorians and the Vikings: George Webbe Dasent and *Jómsvíkinga saga*,' in Janet Garton, ed., *Proceedings of the Ninth Biennial Conference of the British Association of Scandinavian Studies, April 1991* (Norwich, 1992), pp. 301–15.

cultivation and promotion of Northern antiquity—the uncertain Norse challenge to Graeco-Roman educational, cultural and imaginative hegemony; the battle between purism and innovation fought as translators seek to do stylistic justice to their spikily evasive primary texts; the fruitful and intriguing interplay between orature and literature which took place within the cultural space established by the Icelandic *kvöldvaka*; the bumpy transition from script to print which in Iceland postdated Gutenberg by several centuries; the political promotion of saga which could polarise radicals and conservatives of every age and nation; the images of trenchant nationalism which sagas encoded for readers in Iceland, mainland Scandinavia, the British Isles and Normandy; and, not least, the extent to which armchair reveries sometimes crumbled in the face of raw and dispiriting realities which travel to the saga-steads could reveal. It is surely appropriate, moreover, that the volume concludes with a mordant modern 'rime', that 'harmonie of words' which for so long was held to be the distinctive voiceprint of the Northern muse.

In the preparation of this volume I have been greatly helped by the patience and cooperation of my far-flung contributors. In the preparation of my own contribution, I am very happy to acknowledge the help afforded by research grants from the British Academy, and from the School of English, University of Leeds. If the reception of Edda and saga in the United States is one of several topics not treated in this essay collection, it can at least be said that much of the proof-reading was done in the library of St Mary's College of Maryland, and by the shores of Chesapeake Bay, one of many sites eagerly and erroneously promoted in the nineteenth century for the coveted title of Vínland. Not for the first time I am very conscious of how much I owe to the warm hospitality and good humour of my bayside host Dr John Richowsky.

A final word on two matters—one typographical, the other editorial—in which the synchronisation of ancient and modern has proved troublesome. Firstly, throughout this volume it has been necessary to represent Old Icelandic hooked *o* by Modern Icelandic *ö*. Secondly, in three of the following essays (Haraldsson, Kennedy, Wawn) there are repeated references to the life and works of the nineteenth-century Icelandic scholar Eiríkur Magnússon. On the title-pages of his publications and in correspondence Eiríkur used the older form 'Eiríkr', whereas his friends and his biographer Stefán Einarsson favoured the more modern spelling 'Eiríkur'. Editorial attempts 'að sigla milli skers og báru' in dealing with this tiny but teasing problem seem destined to end in tears and inconsistency. Accordingly the modern form has been adopted throughout.

Andrew Wawn
Adel, Leeds
June 1994

Part I:

Scandinavia and Europe

Olaus Rudbeck's *Atlantica* and Old Norse Poetics

MATS MALM

During the Renaissance, interest in language, particularly European vernaculars, grew significantly. Theories of language and interpretation were advanced and elaborated, and the major texts of Greek and Latin antiquity were published in thorough and often extensively annotated scholarly editions. In the wake of the rising prestige of contemporary European languages major editions of important vernacular texts began to appear. In the Nordic countries, several such editions and translations were published during the sixteenth century, but it was in the seventeenth century that this scholarly activity flourished. Snorri Sturluson's *Edda*, together with *Hávamál* and *Völuspá*, was published in Petrus Johannis Resenius's 1665 edition; there were Danish and Swedish translations of *Heimskringla*; whilst an edition of the original Icelandic text also appeared during the century. Whereas twentieth-century readers have exhibited a consistent enthusiasm for *Íslendingasögur* and been relatively disdainful towards *fornaldarsögur*, the seventeenth century placed a high priority on the publication of *fornaldarsögur*.

Amongst the explanations for the early prominence of these sagas may lie the fact that the *fornaldarsögur* first published were those set largely in Sweden, where the editions were prepared: *Gautreks saga*, *Herrauðs ok Bósa saga* and *Hervarar saga* were published between 1664 and 1672. A major priority with these editions was, of course, to provide scholars with further source material to add to that already available for historical research at this time. Firstly, and most importantly, there was the Bible, whose overall historicity was regarded as beyond question even though the literal level of individual texts often had to be decoded and interpreted in order to reveal underlying truths. Secondly, there were the major authors of classical antiquity, whose works were highly respected, but considered to be less useful than the third type of source—old 'Gothic' texts such as Snorri's *Edda*; Swedish scholars such as Johannes Bureus, Georg Stiernhielm, Olaus Verelius and Olaus Rudbeck would argue that Old Norse texts were older—and thus more accurate—sources than the Greek and Latin classics. These new editions of Old Norse texts certainly reflected the latest advances in philological understanding (see, for example, Olsson 1974, 202–209; Nordström 1924, CLXVI–CLXVII; Johannesson 1968, 261–274).

Much seventeenth-century antiquarian research lies neglected today, regarded merely as a preliminary episode in a greater subsequent tradition. But there is one major Swedish work of the time which has resisted the inevitable forces of oblivion, having long been viewed with both astonishment and a degree of horrified admiration. That work is the monumental *Atlantica*, which Olaus Rudbeck wrote during the last part of the seventeenth century. Even at that time, *Atlantica* was variously considered to be preposterous, ingenious, or ingeniously preposterous.

Atlantica consists of four volumes, the last one unfinished. The arrangement of the material is confusing, with many lengthy quotations and unexplained digressions. This tendency is especially prominent in the later volumes: the first volume is relatively lucid. This was not the first time that Swedish historians had sought to relate their native history to the broader history of the world, maintaining that Sweden was the home of the powerful Goths, who came from Götaland in Sweden and who helped to shape world history. During this period many such patriotic attempts were made in various countries to reveal the major role played by this land or that people in the development of the civilised world. Olaus Rudbeck, however, pursues his case to an extreme degree, offering an entirely new theory: he claims that Sweden is the lost land of Atlantis, the great civilisation described by Plato and about which many legends had developed. Rudbeck's interpretations of genuinely historical sources, and of other sources which he regards as historical, have a grandeur that surpasses the works of his contemporaries. Rudbeck's claims are more elaborate, more exact and more specific. In the first volume of *Atlantica*, Rudbeck addresses the vexed questions of the confusion of languages that took place at the tower of Babel, and the subsequent movement of peoples across the continents. Shortly after Babel, he argues, a powerful people settled in Sweden before dispersing over the world, laying the foundations of civilisation. Rudbeck then seeks to show how the vocabulary and names in Egyptian, Greek and Roman sources derive from the old 'Gothic' language. He suggests that these apparently dissimilar mythologies are in reality one and the same: classical mythology and other sources depict events that took place in Sweden, with the names and incidents distorted in various ways. Rudbeck's first volume thus offers material about words, myths and stories; supplementary discussion is to be found in the subsequent volumes.

While Rudbeck is now best known for the bizarre nature of his conclusions, the soundness of many of the scientific principles on which those conclusions were based has lately been increasingly acknowledged.

In his theoretical and methodological discussion, he displays a surprisingly rational critical sense, which seems strange in the light of his
conclusions. New light has recently been thrown on the historical method
of Rudbeck by Gunnar Eriksson. Relating *Atlantica* to a broader
European tradition of philosophy and science, Erikson demonstrates the
modernity of Rudbeck's methodology. Rudbeck played his part in the
introduction of Cartesian philosophy which emerged in opposition to neo-
Aristotelianism; but above all his methodology resembles closely that of
Francis Bacon, with its emphasis on the empirical compilation and
examination of facts, and the importance of allowing that factual evidence
to structure its subsequent interpretation. With Descartes reason shapes
the paradigm; with Bacon reason is subordinate to facts. Instead of
starting from some given Cartesian paradigm, Bacon allows the assembled data to shape the paradigm. Eriksson has shown how this (for its
time) well-developed empirical method underlies Rudbeck's works on
medicine and natural science, as well as *Atlantica* itself.[1] The principles
underlying his archaeological studies, for example, seem in many ways
quite sensible even to modern scholars (Eriksson 1984, 92-95).

Rudbeck's views on the interpretation of literary sources also resemble
those of Bacon. Bacon argues that after the Fall of man, there was a
period when man lost all knowledge about the world, later re-acquiring
it in the form of truth-veiling myths. There were two explanations for
this: either people were incapable of grasping such knowledge in any
other form, or those commanding that knowledge did not want it
divulged to the common people. This description fits that period which
Rudbeck calls *gåtetiden*, *tempus mytologicum*. Myths are thus enigmas
awaiting allegorical interpretation. It is only possible to interpret a myth
correctly by viewing it in its appropriate historical and intellectual
contexts—against the background of other myths, for example. Here
especially, in his allegorical and etymological interpretations, Rudbeck's
far-fetched conclusions are at their most provocative, as he claims to be
able to read the book of nature. Bacon maintains that allegory is still a
useful pedagogical instrument, and even writes a philosophical treatise in
allegorical form (Eriksson 1984, 107; 1981, 157–158). Rudbeck's style
is in fact extraordinarily concrete and visualised; he shows no interest in
allegorical abstraction. Often using examples and illustrations to render
the abstract comprehensible, he does not use allegory as a mode of
representation.

Rudbeck's interpretations are closely related to Medieval and Renais-

---

[1]See the attitudes of Bacon and Stiernhielm regarding etymologies; Agrell
1955, 95; Swartling 1909, 76–81.

sance symbolism, a mode of interpretation which reached Rudbeck through emblems and emblem books. As Renaissance interest in language grew, great attention was paid to the symbolic meaning of hieroglyphs and pythagorean enigmas, and to their connections with moral philosophy. This was the origin of emblems, in which visual art and poetry combined in ways that exercised an important influence on seventeenth-century culture (Friberg 1945, 9–38). Eriksson shows how Rudbeck's mythological interpretations relate to baroque symbolism, where the relationship between sign and referent can be distant and mystifying. Eriksson also shows how closely Rudbeck's association with myth corresponds with the relation of emblematist to emblem, or rather to that which is portrayed in an emblem. Rudbeck creates a method of research out of the enigmatical baroque style, Eriksson suggests (1984, 101, 104–5). It is primarily in his scholarly methodology, and his faith in its capacity to structure a paradigm, that Rudbeck comes close to Baconianism. As to the greater questions of life, however, he seems to adhere to no particular tradition. Eriksson quotes from a letter in which Rudbeck shows how a clock could be examined in many different ways, depending on the angle from which it is viewed; he notes that even if the clock's internal construction seems comprehensible, it is impossible to understand where the clockmaker began. So it is with Rudbeck's view that one can never find 'the first point' when examining worldly phenomena. Eriksson suggests that the clock image may reflect Rudbeck's belief that the lack of appropriate intellectual instruments had created areas of research inaccessible to man, and best left to religion. In his preface, Rudbeck says that he is offering 'something old new and new old', which, Eriksson suggests, should be taken as a description of Rudbeck's own work. *Atlantica* combines established interpretative models with the modern scientific examination of nature; it links the Middle Ages with the modern world (Eriksson 1984, 87–89, 109).

Rudbeck's conclusions are spectacular; but his theory of interpretation is no less interesting. It would be hard to assess whether Rudbeck took the theoretical discussion as his starting point, or whether he constructed the theoretical discussion in order to justify his conclusions; and the answer does not seem particularly important. Instead, in this essay I want to show how Rudbeck uses Old Norse texts not only as historical sources, but also as theoretical guides which supplement the Latin theory of interpretation.

THE AUTHORITY OF SOURCES

Rudbeck begins by stating that, short of being eye-witnesses to particular events and conditions, readers must make use of the secondary sources of information available. These are: I *tale* (sägn); II *saga* (saga); III *geography* (jordennes beskrifning); IV *convenience of the place* (ortens beqwämligheet); V *the buildings of a country* (et lands fullkomliga bebyggnad); VI *runestones* (stenar med gambla bokstäfwer eller okiände märken huggne). *Tales* are the oral traditions, Rudbeck explains. They are especially well preserved in Sweden, a land never subject to invasion by a foreign power which could have imposed its alien language on Swedish culture and corrupted native traditions. Neither has Swedish culture been influenced to any significant extent by commercial connections. When a tale is written down, it becomes *saga*.[2] Sweden does not have many sagas, but this is actually an advantage, claims Rudbeck, because in writing about one's own nation, the tendency is to make the portrait more beautiful than reality can justify. The historical descriptions of Sweden which Rudbeck finds in foreign authors are accordingly seen as more reliable. *Geography* shows how peoples have moved about and how the world has changed. This is important not least in the interpretation of words and names, since it appears that as nations and individuals change their environment, they also change their languages and names. Convenience is a major factor in attracting people to particular places. *Buildings* can also be a major source of knowledge: the more primitive and rough the ruins, the older they are. It thus becomes clear that the ruins of Sweden are older than those more elegant ruins to be found in Rome and elsewhere. *Runestones*, too, can be used as witnesses to the age of a country (*Atlantica* I 14).

Tale and saga convey truths either openly and literally, or in a veiled way, that is allegorically or 'förblommerat', as Rudbeck puts it. When compared such sources may seem contradictory, but their relationship may rather resemble that of the gospels—dissimilar narratives of the same, true events. History becomes distorted through transmission, but truth is recognisable at the point where the sources agree. If the interpreter knows what he is doing, it can actually be an advantage if the sources are not wholly in agreement: similarity would suggest common origin, with multiple sources effectively counting as just one. With

---

[2]'Historia' is the Latin term Rudbeck (and his tradition) uses for *saga*.

sources offering different descriptions of the same thing, each source may be taken as an autonomous witness. Rudbeck cites the example of the story of the Flood: the phenomenon has been described in many documents from different parts of the world, but the primary source is the Book of Moses. If all sources had agreed with the biblical version, there would only have been a single effective proof of the truth of the Flood. But, in fact, the sources differ greatly and require interpretation in order to be understood correctly; this suggests that they are indeed independent witnesses and that there is thus ample evidence to sustain belief in the veracity of the Flood story. It is this theoretical position which Rudbeck recommends to his contemporaries. Even historians of his own time offer distorted pictures of reality; even their statements must be interpreted critically (*Atlantica* I 12). The wisdom of previous ages was laid down in myth, and now lies obscured. To interpret the myths one needs to be familiar with their language, and with that language from which the vocabulary and names originally derive. Language is thus at the heart of many misunderstandings, Rudbeck concludes.

As is well known, the main purpose of the *Atlantica* was to prove that Sweden was in fact the lost civilisation of Atlantis. According to this theory, it was in Atlantis that the nation which founded most of the cultural centres of the world originated. When Christianity brought Latin culture to the North, it was simply returning to its place of origin. Rudbeck uses etymological and allegorical interpretations to show that Greek and Roman mythology in particular corresponds to the mythology of the North. Names and descriptions had changed, events had been obscured, but they were fundamentally the same. The mythologies tell of real events that had taken place in the North, in Atlantis. Rudbeck elaborates this argument by comparing Old Norse sources with the classical authors of Greece and Rome, with later European sources, and not least with the Bible. To Old Norse sources is thus attributed the same authority as the classics; indeed the Norse documents could claim greater authority because of the greater antiquity which Rudbeck ascribes to them. His major historical sources are Snorri Sturluson's *Edda* and *Heimskringla*, together with the *fornaldarsögur* which were collected and edited in Sweden.[3] As for his method, part seems to be entirely his own,

---

[3]According to the editor, *Atlantica* III 763, *Heimskringla* was available to Rudbeck in *Snorre Sturlesøns Norske Kongers Chronica. Vdsat paa Danske, aff Peder Claussøn* (Kiøbenhafn, 1633) and in Swedish translation by Jón Rugman in *Norlandz Chrönika och Beskriffning* (Wijsingzborg, 1670). In 1697 the first volume of Peringskiöld's Stockholm edition, with a Swedish translation by Guðmundur Ólafsson appeared: *Heims Kringla eller Snorre Sturlusons*

and part clearly derives from European philosophic and scientific movements. The seventeeth century is generally the starting-point for and main subject of the history of ideas in Sweden, and many detailed investigations of the influence of European learning on Swedish seventeenth-century culture have been made. Yet the nature of Rudbeck's use of Old Norse works as methodological and theoretical sources and models has not been examined.

RUDBECK'S THEORY OF INTERPRETATION

Rudbeck explains that most of the early events of world history, the great historical conflicts and figures, have been described in what he calls 'enigmas, and above all skaldic poems'.[4] He argues that the form of the enigma was supposed to render events memorable and stimulating to people. He quotes classical and patristic authors in support of the veracity of heathen mythology, but emphasises that mythology really tells us not about gods, but about historical figures. The skalds, as Rudbeck calls the poets and wise men, embellished the stories, sometimes in order to soften posterity's censure of kings and other powerful men. However, while the descriptions may have been changed, the actual events were often accurately related. After this period, the *tempus mytologicum*, people began describing the world in other ways and it became increasingly difficult to understand the old poems and enigmas. Additional problems arose during the transmission of poems: frequent repetition led to distortion and subsequent misunderstanding. This, and the phenomenon of language change itself, made the truths embodied in these poems more or less unintelligible to later generations.

When the kings left the North to subjugate the world, the tales about them and their deeds went with them, and spread throughout the world.

Nordländske Konunga-sagor. Snorri Sturluson's *Edda* was available to Rudbeck in the manuscript known as Codex Upsaliensis, and in P.H. Resen's 1665 edition with Danish and Latin translations.

[4]'genom gåtor, och hellst uti Scaldewijsor [poëtiske verser] och dichter', *Atlantica* II 29, in the chapter 'Huru de gamble Scribenter fordom de sanferdige och wisse Gudarnas och Konungarnas bedriffter hafwa genom förblomerade gåtor och dichter beskrifwit, och huru de swårligen eller intet råkat paa deras uttydningar, och huru man skal dem rätt igenfinna' [How the old authors once described the achievements of the truthful and certain gods and kings, and how they found their explanations with difficulty or not at all, and how they are to be found correctly].

These stories in turn became even more obscured and distorted as they reached different cultures and interpreters. This is why Rudbeck claims that it is essential for a modern interpreter to understand the entire corpus of material, the narratives in all their different refractions, so that the setting and meaning of each separate enigma can be carefully assessed, and the underlying truths decoded. Rudbeck warns us not to exaggerate our interpretations. For example, he says, it is not possible to identify Jewish history with classical or Gothic history and mythology. Whilst he admits that there may be some points of correspondence, identifications of Jesus with Apollo, or Mary with Venus are too far-fetched. On the other hand, such names are entirely suitable as metaphors, when comparing someone to a classical or Biblical figure in order to emphasise certain characteristics, as when calling someone a Hercules (*Atlantica* II 36).

In any initial examination of material, the scholar must also consider a work's beginning and end; its cause and purpose. This is essential if the object examined, the enigma, is to be viewed in its correct context. Rudbeck illustrates how differently the same thing may be interpreted, depending on the point of view from which it is regarded. The task of the historian is to be acquainted with all circumstances if the correct interpretation is to be made. As an example of how the topic or area may determine the interpretation, Rudbeck offers the following: 'I have consumed the sea god Neptune, the corn goddess Ceres and the garden goddess Venus'. This sounds absurd unless one takes Neptune, Ceres and Venus as metonymic references to wine or water, bread and lettuce respectively.[5] Rudbeck proceeds to describe the frame of reference in which an object may be interpreted. He says that when a king is spoken of, different referents are meant in different situations. Among celestial bodies, the sun is king; among metals, gold is; the king of the animals is either the lion or the bear, whilst the eagle or hawk is king of the birds. Rudbeck's observations up to this point are of a fairly general nature, but the discussion soon becomes more specialised.

AN OLD NORSE MODEL OF INTERPRETATION

Up to this point, Rudbeck has been using current theories from Latin tradition, referring to classical authorities. But he proceeds to show more precisely how poetic similes should be interpreted, and in order to

---

[5]'Jag hafwer förtärt siöguden Neptunum, korngudinnan Cererem och trägårdzgudinnan Venerem' (*Atlantica* II 40).

support his case he adduces an entirely new kind of evidence never previously used:

> Kan man intet få igen Begynnelsen och Endan på ett Wärck, uthan man kommer allenast til at see någre Ordh, så måste man grant achta hwart ord: som til Exempel. Konungen sitter å handa Fiällum o Fiäll, dhet är Bergh, och hwadh handh är, är noghsampt allom bekant. Nu kan ingen Konungh sittia på eens handh, icke heller kan en handh wara berg. Men tänk nu effter hwad för Diuur är, som wistas på bergen, och bäras på ens Handh och kallas Kung; intet Leyonet och Biörnen, ty dhe äro för stoora at sittia på Handen, icke heller Hwaalfisken, ty han fins ey på Bergen, icke heller Solen, uthan Hööken, den sitter på handa Fiollum. (*Atlantica* II 41)

> [If one cannot recover the beginning and the end of a work, but can only get to see a few words, then one must carefully examine each word, as for example: The king sits on the alps of the hand[s]. An alp is a mountain, and everyone knows what a hand is. Now no king can sit on someone's hand, nor can a hand be a mountain. But consider, what kind of animals dwell on mountains, and can be carried on one's hand and be called king: not the lion or bear, because they are too big to sit on the hand, nor the whale, because it does not dwell on the mountains, nor the sun, but the hawk sits on the alps of the hand.]

In this way, Rudbeck underlines the importance of the frame of reference. He sees the world as divided into a number of systems or spheres, in which a metaphor or any other figure of speech changes its meaning as it changes its context. We recognise Rudbeck's empirical method here, too: the collection of material is the starting-point. Just as we must know all myths in order to be able to interpret any individual myth correctly, so we must know each individual myth well to be able to interpret any of its single tropes or paraphrases. In this case, the myth itself is the original frame of reference.

Handa Fiällum, 'the mountain of the hand', seems to derive from Old Norse. 'The king of the mountain of the hand' appears to be a good kenning for 'hawk'. Whilst I know of no instance of exactly this kenning, it closely resembles kennings such as 'the mountain of the hawk' for 'hand'.[6] The whole discussion seems to derive from Old Norse tradition. This becomes even clearer as we continue the quotation:

---

[6]I have not found 'The mountain of the hand' in Meissner 1921, but whether interpreted as 'the back of the hand' or 'the mountain that is the hand', this circumlocution is close to well-established kennings for 'hand' listed in Meissner, pp. 141–2.

Dherföre är såsom Edda tahlar om wåre gamble Scalder, at en får gifwa alle Gudar, Konungar, Förstar, Diuur, Foglar, Fiskar, Örter och Trään etc. andras Nampn, allenast han något tillägger, genom hwilket han kiennes igen, antingen aff dhess serdeles gierningh, eller Slächt, eller Fäderneslandh, eller något annat: såsom om man säger dhen Eenögde Nicudur, då förstås Oden, ty han war eenögd, nemner man om Siökrijg och kallar en Siöwarg, då förstås om Siöröfware, talar man om Fiskar, så är det Geddan. (*Atlantica* II 41.)

[Therefore, as the Edda says about our old skalds, one may assign the names of others to all gods, kings, princes, animals, birds, fishes, herbs and trees etc., as long as one adds some feature whereby they can be recognised, either by virtue of a special achievement, or family, or country, or something else: as when one says the one-eyed Nicudur, then Othin is meant, because he was one-eyed. If one speaks of sea-war and calls someone a sea-wolf, then a pirate is meant; if one speaks of fish, it is the pike.]

This description of how to specify a paraphrase by the addition of a descriptive attribute clearly derives from Snorri's *Edda*. It is expressed as follows in the Danish translation available to Rudbeck in Resenius's edition:

Asianernis Naffne mue retteligen saaledis modificeris, at neffne den eene Asian med den andens Naffn, oc giffve hannem Øgge-Naffn udaff hans eigintlig Gierning eller Slect. Ligesom naar vi kallede Odin eller Thor, enten Tyr eller med en anden Asians eller Alffes Naffn, da tager jeg med det fremmede Naffn Hanon eigentlig, oc icke den anden som det ellers hørde til med rette. Ligesom E.G. der som vi neffne den hengendis Tyr, den lade Tyr, da ere de Odens Naffne, thi at være hengendis, oc ladit, ere de Naffne som beqvemmer Oden selff. (*Edda Islandorum*, Dd 1r–v.)

[The names of the Asians may correctly be altered so that one Asian is called by the name of another, and given an additional name/word [nickname] by virtue of some special achievement or family. As when Othin or Thor was called by the name of Tyr or of some other Asian or elf, so I take a strange name that is appropriate to him, and not really to the individual whose name it was. So, for example, when we speak of the hanging Tyr or the laden Tyr, those are names for Othin, because to be hanging and laden are appropriate terms for him.]

Rudbeck has extended the applicability of Snorri's discussion considerably: instead of its applying only to Scandinavian gods and mythological creatures, this form of description is now shown to be possible for virtually any conceivable phenomenon. The description of the kenning, that characteristic feature of Old Norse poetry, points Rudbeck towards a more concrete and exact method of interpretation than Latin tradition could supply. The name of any one god may refer to any other provided that there is some attribute indicating in what context the name, in Snorri's example Tyr, should be understood. When described as 'hanging', Tyr becomes the name of Odin in 'Hangatyr'. It is thus that Rudbeck shows how words and names can change their meaning as soon as they change their context. The principle is also illustrated by the structure of Snorri's *Edda*, in which mythological episodes are related in order to explain the background for numerous poetic expressions and paraphrases. There are lists of circumlocutions and synonyms for all kinds of phenomena—deities, weapons, animals and the like.[7] All this suits Rudbeck perfectly. Here, in the Gothic records that express to him fundamental truths, he has found sanction and justification for doing what he could not otherwise have done: for interpreting apparitions and events of history and myth as freely as he does. In this way, Rudbeck feels able to retain the concrete reference of metaphors such as 'king' for the eagle when interpreting myths that were normally considered to refer to abstract concepts or virtues. He thus makes historical sources out of ethical and religious ones. With his 'Old Norse' theory and method of interpretation, Rudbeck seems to have pushed Gothicism further than any other scholar. It is unlikely that he learnt this method from Snorri's *Edda*, but that is where he learnt to justify it.[8]

There is one further complication. In Snorri's description of the construction of the kenning, the attribute is of great importance, since it is that which indicates the context in which the symbol or the paraphrase is to be understood. When using this model of interpretation, Rudbeck of course generally lacks a descriptive attribute pointing to the true meaning of a word. He should have one, strictly speaking, and he readily solves this problem by referring to a passage from the *Edda* when explaining how to interpret Plato's claim that there were elephants in Atlantis. He must account for the demonstrable absence of elephants in Sweden in the face of Plato's contradictory claim:

> Elephanter äro ofta införde i Swerige, men aldrig här i myckenheet sedda, och derföre förstås här genom Elephanter Ulfar, ty man lär af Edda uti Diurens namn, at man må kalla det ena diuret med det

[7]This character is especially significant in the edition of Resenius, where Magnús Ólafsson had structured and numbered first the mythic narratives, and then the catalogues of poetic expressions.

[8]The importance of the frame of reference in itself is of course not a new invention. Even Aristotle in his *Art of Rhetoric* speaks of it when he shows how the goblet is to Dionysos what the shield is to Ares, with the shield of Dionysos becoming a metaphor for goblet and vice versa (III iv 4; Aristotle also treats this kind of metaphor in his *Poetics*, chapter 21).

andras namn, allenast det skal igenkiennas wid sina åthäfwor och
natur, eller wid sit boo och hemwist [...]. Att nu här af Platone Ulfar
kallas Elephanter på Skaldeart, wiises strax af Platonis efterföljande
ord, i hwilka han kallar det Diuret det snålesta. Det är nu hela
werlden bekandt, at intet Diur är snålare af alla grymma och snåla,
såsom Leyon, Biörnar, Parder, och sådana, än som Ulfwen. (*Atlantica*
I 184)

[Elephants have often been brought to Sweden, but they have never
been seen in any great numbers here, and therefore by elephants
wolves are meant here, because one learns from the animal names in
the Edda, that one animal may be called by the name of another, as
long as it is recognised [signified] by its habits and nature, or by its
dwellings and origin [...]. That Plato refers poetically to wolves as
elephants, is shown by his subsequent discussion, where he calls that
animal the greediest. Now, as the whole world knows, of all cruel and
greedy creatures, such as lions, bears, leopards and the like, none is
more greedy than the wolf.]

The nub of this argument is that the description prescribed for a kenning
does not necessarily have to be directly and syntactically tied to the main
word. Instead of an attribute, it is enough for the frame of reference to
be explained in some manner in the narrative. From this position, one
may easily choose the most suitable context from the surrounding text or
from one's own previous experience. Thus, individual readers can decide
the point of departure for themselves, with the sanction of one of the
oldest Gothic literary records behind them. As with so many scholars
after him, Rudbeck is not satisfied with Snorri's treatment of older
traditions, believing him often to have misunderstood the wisdom
concealed in the stories he tells. But Snorri, whether consciously or not,
had provided a most original and ingenious way of understanding the
culture and history of the world. Among seventeenth-century scholars,
Snorri's *Edda* was often considered to be a redaction of the poetic *Edda*,
which in turn derived from some original *Edda*, made by the Æsir.
Where such fundamental wisdom is presented, where so many comprehensive myths are related, instructions may also be found as to how the
hidden levels of reality can be penetrated.

RUDBECK'S FRAME OF REFERENCE

Rudbeck's research and conclusions are, as we have noted, extraordinary;
but no more remarkable than his methodology. He abandons traditional
theories of interpretation where they prove inadequate, and turns instead
to older documents offering a higher wisdom. Old Norse poetics becomes

a theory to be utilised in the interpretation of history. From the time when mythical and allegorical interpretations and exegesis were first disseminated, moral philosophy and ethics had been their main focus: the Church Fathers and philosophers paved an important path. Ethical implications were taken seriously in seventeenth-century antiquarian research: Resenius prefaces the first edition of Snorri's *Edda* with a lengthy discussion of the ethical and moral philosophy of different nations, and he presents the Eddic poems *Völuspá* and *Hávamál* as *Philosophia Antiqvissima Norvego-Danica* and *Ethica Odini*. Heathen mythologies had also been interpreted in a more worldly manner, as signifying laws of nature and physical entities (Lemmi 1933, 1–5). The referent of the allegory or symbol had mostly been an abstraction or some kind of concept.

Historical scholarship, on the other hand, whilst leaning on philology and other disciplines, had primarily used specific documentary sources—often much 'corrected'—in the search for solid historical facts. Of course, historical works of the seventeenth century often promote the idea that pieces of information must be understood as circumlocutions, albeit never very elaborate ones. So, for instance, in the preface to the 1633 edition of *Heimskringla* (b3v–b4r), Olaus Wormius speaks of giants, dwarves and wolves as circumlocutions for commanders, warriors and other normal creatures. If someone is said to have the power to become invisible, this means only, Wormius explains, that the individual in question was good at moving around without being discovered. Rudbeck's scholarly method involves use of both these ways of examining the world, whatever kind of source he is interpreting. Whilst he has no faith in any form of truth other than historical facts, and shows no interest in ethics and moral philosophy, he nevertheless makes use in his historical research of sources and methods that had previously been more or less the exclusive preserve of theological and moral/allegorical interpretation.

History had often been considered important because it conveyed ethical values, supplying edifying *exempla* of virtues and vices. But history according to Rudbeck is much more concrete, almost corporeal, although he employs approaches which had been developed in seeking to understand the abstract and spiritual dimensions of the world. Historical facts and discursive chains of events are the referents he finds in material and strategies of interpretation that had usually been thought to have referents such as ethical and religious truths—abstract concepts rather than historical facts and sequences. How does Rudbeck arrive at this view? One major difference between historical and ethical interpretation, and the sources they use, is that the historical referent is for the most part concrete, whereas the ethical or religious referent is abstract: it is the difference between, for example, an actual event and a Christian virtue, though this, of course, does not apply in the same way to the typological level of exegesis. The sign may be concrete or abstract, but to Rudbeck the referent is also concrete even in myths whose referent, if it existed at all, had usually been regarded as abstract. Rudbeck is not satisfied with determining whether a myth is literally true or false; he also reads historical facts at an allegorical level. As we have seen, by citing Snorri's statement on kennings, Rudbeck wants to show that concrete referents may be extracted as readily from myths as from ordinary metaphors.

As an example of his allegorical interpretation Rudbeck cites a contemporary allegorical statement, which refers to the war between the Netherlands and England: 'Lejonet lärer speela uppå Harpan, men wakte sig at icke strängen springer af och slår uth ögat' (*Atlantica* I 9) [the lion learns to play the harp, but beware that the string does not break and tear his eye out]. In this instance the symbolic meanings are clear: Dutch heraldic arms include a lion, whilst English ones show a harp. This is the kind of allegory whose referents are most concrete, and which forms a discursive sequence of information. It is perspicuous and translatable, and suggests that these are the qualities of every discourse that is to be interpreted. This example does not, of course, have the same status as Rudbeck's material. It had been constructed in Rudbeck's time and lacks the authenticating weight of antiquity. Its signifying level had been constructed only in order to convey the signified by one means or another. It would be possible for virtually anyone to construct such an allegory with greater or lesser degrees of elegance. This is allegory as representation and not as an object of interpretation. The documents that Rudbeck interprets in his research possess a considerably higher authority, and are not regarded as easily and discursively translatable. The putative content of classical and biblical myths is of such remote and elevated origin that mortal man is seldom considered capable of explaining it fully. As with the examples above, Rudbeck is making use of systems of reference that are not usually considered applicable to old myths and other texts of comparable authority.

Most allegorical interpretations of obscure and revered texts search for concepts as referents—abstract or at least vague, and non-discursive. This is not the case in the *Atlantica*. Rudbeck is constantly on the lookout for historical facts and events, and it is this kind of referent which he extracts from myths, as well as from other sources. To an extent Rudbeck's method had a precedent in the tradition of euhemerising heathen mythology—that is, interpreting heathen gods in terms of men or demons. The gods are considered to have once been prominent individuals in history, whose great reputation led people to regard them as deities, who later developed a cult following. Similarly, demons delude heathens into cult and superstition by posing as gods. In this euhemeristic way, myths related to real people. Mostly, the myths have an historical referent attributed to them, simply in order to discredit any claims that they describe actual gods. The euhemerising of myths is a means of displacing and downgrading deities. A secondary intention may be to identify historical facts or reconstruct historical events, but the primary intention is to provide an earthly location for these mythic characters, and thereby remove their divinity. The Old Norse idea of the Æsir coming from Troy, and making their way to Scandinavia, is an example of rather precise euhemerisation intended to offer an historical background in support of particular patriotic assertions. For Snorri, when using this myth, one function of euhemerism was to connect Nordic history to the broader history of the world and, above all, to the history of Christianity; it was chiefly a means of understanding human development and mentality.[9] It is close to the kind of euhemerisation that is central to Rudbeck's *Atlantica*—but in that work it seems more systematically elaborated, with detailed concrete and factual events organised into larger schemes for specific purposes. Rudbeck euhemerises deities specifically to make use of the myth as evidence for historical facts and events. He is not consistent in euhemerising heathen deities, only doing so when an illuminating interpretation can result. Thus, euhemerisation as used by Rudbeck is more concrete and exact than usual, as it finds its place within a larger interpretative scheme. Rudbeck's use of euhemerisation is governed by what he can gain by it. Alongside the advanced empiricism of Rudbeck, this seems to be an important explanation of the strikingly concrete impression which *Atlantica* gives.

Rudbeck does not always euhemerise heathen myths. When discussing the origin of the alphabet, for example, he exhibits a symbolic view of nature, and still finds an historical referent. The emblematic character of Rudbeck's arguments has been convincingly demonstrated by Eriksson. When discussing the baroque perception of nature in *Atlantica*, he shows how Rudbeck uses evidential detail from nature in such a manner that the 'perception of nature supports the mythical tradition, and the myth supports the perception of nature' (Eriksson 1984, 105). When Rudbeck argues that the old chieftains had twelve judges in their court, he offers as proof the observation that the gods had chosen to assemble under the ash-tree, because they had noticed that it had six pairs of leaves with one single leaf at the end, just as six judges sat on each side of the chieftain.

---

[9]The function of this myth and the method of euhemerisation is, of course, more complex than this. See Weber 1991, esp. pp. 9–15; on Snorri's idea of source criticism, see Weber 1987, esp. pp. 95–97.

To Rudbeck, the fact that the gods chose the ash-tree because of its symbolic significance, becomes a piece of evidence indicating that the old chieftains really had twelve judges or counsellors.

Eriksson then shows how Rudbeck, in a different context, associates the apples of the Hesperides in antique myth with the apples of Iduna in Snorri's *Edda*. Maintaining that the Goths possessed the art of writing earlier than the Greeks, Rudbeck states that the apples should be understood as the runes which were diffused through the world when the Goths left Scandinavia, but which were later brought back to the Nordic countries by Minerva, representing learning, in the shape of a swallow. Eriksson quotes Rudbeck on the significance of the barn swallow:

> Sedan af alla Foglar i heela werden, är ingen som sielfkräfwiandes bygger sitt boo in uti Menniskiornas huus der hon slipper in, och fönstren stå öppne, mera än denna Swalan, som hafwer dhen långa saxen, och röda äpplet under halsen, och så mycket hafwer att sqwatra och språka. Ty dhe andra byggia uthom Huusen, under Taaken, hwarföre afmålas här igenom att Wiisdom, Förstånd, och bookliga konster böra boo hoos Menniskiorna. Den röda fläcken hon under Halsen hafwer, betyder det gyllende Äpplet, hwar igenom förstås, att fast de Boklige Konster bäst förwaras genom Bokstäfwerna innom dhen odödelige Draken, på den hårda oförwanskeliga Stenen, så är dock det fåfängt, emedan han intet tala kan, der icke Tungan genom Strupans tilhielp som Målet giör, alla ens Dygder för verlden utropar. (*Atlantica* I 544–5; Eriksson 1984, 106.)

> [Of all birds in the whole world, there is none that voluntarily builds its nest inside people's houses, entering through open windows, except this swallow, with its long tail-feathers and the red apple on its throat, and with its constant twittering and chattering. The others live outdoors, under the roofs; and thus is depicted how wisdom, reason and literature shall live with man. The red spot on the swallow's throat denotes the golden apple, which means that even though literature is best preserved in letters within the immortal dragon, on the hard and immutable stone [i.e. rune carvings], this is fruitless, since it cannot speak if the tongue does not proclaim all virtues to the world by means of the throat which makes speech.]

Eriksson links this argument to baroque symbolism and points out that 'sometimes signs are signs for signs at several stages, as here: the spot on the throat of the swallow → apple → rune → sound (→ meaning of the sound in its context)', and he concludes that in Rudbeck's opinion the symbols that are to be found in nature have had their symbolic significance attributed to them by man: it is not part of their inherent nature. Eriksson suggests that Rudbeck's claim that the red spot on the swallow's throat denotes the golden apple actually means that this is what the myth maker believed it to denote. Thus, according to Eriksson, Rudbeck thinks that those who made the myth attributed a symbolic value to nature, and interprets this symbolic world by viewing it in the same manner as the ancients did. Rudbeck does not indicate that he is relating what he considers to be the thought of someone else, however: as Eriksson explains, 'he writes, "The red spot on the swallow's throat denotes the golden apple", when what he means is, "The red spot which she has on her throat was interpreted as meaning the golden apple by those who made the saga"'.[10]

Regarding the leaves of the ash-tree, Rudbeck has undoubtedly and explicitly stated that the gods chose it because of the symbolic value that they recognised in the leaves. But Rudbeck's explanation of the apple and the rune is not that the maker of the myth regarded the spot on the swallow in this way. Rudbeck speaks of it as a fact—that the spot *means* the apple, the rune. Could it be that he actually believes that the spot on the swallow *means* the apple, the rune, when he says so? Rudbeck's treatment of the myth clearly merits closer attention.

Earlier, Rudbeck had maintained that runes were in use in the North, and that a 'Merkursman' brought them to the Greeks, where they became the Greek alphabet. Rudbeck sees this historical person and this historical event depicted both in the Greek myth, and in the *Edda*. The apples are the runes, that is, the art of writing; they are in the custody of Iduna/ Minerva in the North. In the Greek myth, the apples are guarded by a dragon, which Rudbeck compares to the rune-stone dragon figures on which the runes are carved. In the Greek myth Hercules took the apples, but later gave them to Minerva, who restored them to where they belonged—just as in Snorri's *Edda* Loki caused Iduna and the apples first to be stolen but later returned to the Hesperides in Scandinavia. Iduna returned in the form of a swallow, Rudbeck explains (*Atlantica* I 218– 219, 542–543). To Rudbeck, this was an enigma in need of an explanation if the historical background was to be understood. He thinks that the myth had previously been misunderstood, for example by Apollodorus, who relates it in Greek tradition. Rudbeck derives four principal points

---

[10] 'Vi behöver förvisso inte tveka om att Rudbeck är väl medveten om att de symboler han finner i naturen har tilldelats sitt symbolvärde inte av naturen själv utan av människor [...]. Rudbeck tolkar en av människor skapad symbolvärld genom att sätta sig in i människors tankesätt. Men hans språkbruk är att vanligen inte redovisa detta tankeled. Han skriver: "Den röda fläcken hon under halsen haver betyder det gyllene äpplet", när han menar: "Den röda fläcken hon under halsen haver tyddes av dem som gjorde sagan som det gyllende äpplet"'. (Eriksson 1984, 106)

from the Greek myth: 1) the apples were in the North; 2) there were
three of them; 3) Iduna/Minerva was to keep them in safe custody; 4) she
was turned into a swallow.[11] This, Rudbeck argues, can all be correctly
understood if two additional clues are considered: 1) the gods (in the
Norse myth) gained life and youth by eating the apples; 2) the apple is
on the swallow's throat (*Atlantica* I 542–543). The apples thus give
eternal life, which is easily comprehensible in literary terms, via the
familiar notion that deeds and virtues must be commemorated and
preserved in literature if they are to be remembered. It is the function of
writing to ensure their preservation—not least writing in the form of
rune-stone carvings. Thus far, this is a symbolic interpretation in which
myth is interpreted as a veiled truth, offering access to historical events.
The other clue to which Rudbeck draws attention, however, does not
belong to myth but to nature. The spot on the swallow's throat is
identified by Rudbeck with the apple/runes/letters; it is an important part
of his argument. It confirms the connection between Minerva (the
swallow) and the art of writing. It also gives a picture of how 'wisdom,
reason and literature belong with the humans', and conveys the idea that
literature should not only be written down but also spoken, as in the
quotation above. Thus, the answer to the enigma of the historical fact is
to be found not only in myth, but also in nature.

The reason, then, why this had not previously been understood is that
the clues were neither available nor correctly combined. The second clue,
as mentioned above, is that the apple is on the throat of the swallow ('Att
Äpplet sitter under Swalans hals'). This is not a notion deriving from
earlier interpreters of the myth, since Rudbeck says that they knew
nothing of it. It is expressed as a fact, and there is nothing to suggest that
Rudbeck regards this as a symbolic value attributed to nature by the myth
maker. It would thus be of no value as a clue unless Rudbeck means that
because he knows that the myth-maker had such an understanding, he
also knows that the same myth-maker would be likely to construct a
myth in accordance with it. Whilst this is possible, it seems to run
contrary to the actual wording in Rudbeck—not only does he say that the
spot *means* the apple/rune, but he even speaks of it as the apple located
on the throat of the swallow (*Atlantica* I 543). In addition, there is no
reason why Rudbeck should not himself think of this meaning as being
inherent in nature—a meaning that is to be found, not placed, there.
Eriksson shows the similarity between the discussion of the swallow and
an emblem, and explains that emblem books could conflict with natural

---

[11]Rudbeck would have found Minerva turning into a swallow in only one
source: Agatarchides (*Atlantica* I 544).

science. The reason why symbolic meanings conflict with empirically verifiable qualities, must be that the symbolic meanings are regarded as factual; true in one sense or another (Dieckmann 1977, 102–115; Harms 1970, 532–534). The meaning of the emblem is mostly seen as *found* in nature, not placed there (Schöne 1964, 25–29; Jöns 1966, 25–42). It seems unnecessary therefore to change or add to Rudbeck's discussion of this point. The clue to the enigma of the alphabet is probably inherent in nature, according to Rudbeck. In any case, in *Atlantica* both signs and referents may be phenomena of reality. The sign of the spot on the swallow's throat does not refer to the historical event of the transfer of the alphabet, but it signifies factual qualities of language which refer to the historical events. The nature of the swallow is a fact that corresponds to the historical fact of the runes, and in this way the antique and the Norse myths are connected. This, I suggest, is a good example of Rudbeck's habit of extracting concrete meaning from myths that would ordinarily not be considered to embody any historical truth. It also provides an example of how Rudbeck uses a strikingly specific sign for his interpretation, thus contributing to the strong impression of concreteness that runs through *Atlantica*.

RUDBECK'S PROJECT

The interpretations that Rudbeck offers are extraordinary in a number of respects. His results are more far-reaching than had previously been achieved; his language is strikingly concrete; and his illustrations are readily comprehensible and down-to-earth. However, the structure of the *Atlantica* is obscure and confusing, and even though its main purpose is obvious, the function of the different parts is not always clear.

How are we to understand this—what more can we learn about Rudbeck's own idea of his project? He gives some clues in his preface. As we have seen, he speaks of his work as 'something old new, or new old', and comparing it to a chain, he asks the reader to be prepared to read *Atlantica* numerous times:

> Här förebringar iag honom något Gammalt nytt, eller Nytt gammalt; bediandes honom der han intet hafwer tijd, att detta werket en gång igenomläsa, han och intet blad der af läser, och der han intet hafwer tijd det tijo gånger igenomläsa, intet häller läser en gång särdeles, der han om det sina goda tankar sanningen til styrkio gifwa wil, hwilket mig mycket kiärkommet wara skall. Ty hela werket är som en keed, på hwilken om en länk är förgiomd, så binder hon intet, fast hon aldrig så stark wore. (*Atlantica* I 6)

[Here I offer him something old new, or new old; asking him [the reader] that if he does not have time to read the work through, he should not read a single page; and if he does not have time to read it through ten times, he should not read it once, if he wishes to appreciate it properly and support truth, which I would greatly appreciate. The whole work is like a chain, and if one link should be forgotten, then it will tie nothing, no matter how strong it is.]

The image of the chain suggests an organic perception of the work. Of course Rudbeck has such a notion, but perhaps not in the way that one would expect. If the links represent every meaning and interpretation of a myth, a word or a name, put together into a chain of evidence, then that chain does not seem to be fully stretched throughout Rudbeck's work—especially not in the later volumes. The message of the image is that *Atlantica* must be read several times if the whole extent of the chain is to be understood. This message seems justifiable enough. The composition of *Atlantica* renders the work more or less impenetrable, and readers are unlikely to dedicate too great a part of their lives to reading it over and over again. The obscure structure of the work has the effect of confirming suspicions already generated by the work's fantastic claims. If the four volumes of the *Atlantica* were more clearly structured, Rudbeck might have been more favourably judged. The first volume is still relatively accessible despite a number of digressions. Could it be that Rudbeck simply made no attempt to render the succeeding volumes as clear?

It is tempting to consider the complexity of the work's structure as a reflection of Rudbeck's broader agenda—a pedagogical introduction to the way of viewing the world that he argues for. We might recall Rudbeck's statement, that when searching for the truth in nature, one can never reach 'the first point', the nucleus behind the phenomena of nature.[12] It is towards this truth, of course, that Rudbeck seeks to progress when drawing aside the veils of myth, but he hardly expects to reach all the way back to the origin. Instead, he tells us, the reader has to assemble the available facts, combine them with others and try to structure his or her paradigm from those resources. What could better illustrate this proposition than the very form of the work that articulates it? Rudbeck's *Atlantica* should be read like the book of nature. The myths are revealed, but there are always strata remaining which have to be analysed in order to reveal the deepest meanings of the material. The

---

[12]We recall the hermetic thought that logic, the abstract knowledge based on reason, does not reach the nucleus of nature; only the intuition of the wise does that (Lindroth 1975, 146).

most important links in the chain have been laid out in the first volume; in the succeeding volumes amendments and supplementary arguments are presented without being closely related to their starting-point. This is how nature is constructed: different systems and spheres are connected in various unknown ways, and every time a new one is contrasted to the starting-point, new dimensions of reality emerge. Rudbeck naturally knows the importance of presentation, but it seems that the disposition of material in *Atlantica* is ultimately governed by his overriding intellectual prospectus rather than by normal considerations of explicatory clarity— the manner of the book is part of its meaning. The first volume of *Atlantica* is relatively lucid and offers a fairly complete discourse, while the remaining volumes give the impression of illustrating their own message of the nature of interpretation.

If this view of Rudbeck seems plausible, the question remains as to how those single items and pieces of evidence which he assembles are to be considered. He has interpreted texts which are supposedly true—in one respect or another—but has he interpreted them completely? That hardly seems possible. Whoever examines Rudbeck's work in a different light should be able to find more truths concealed there—again, the context or the point of view from which one views the material dictates what is found. Furthermore, one cannot be too sure about the validity of the sources. If they are false, then Rudbeck is mistaken in accepting them: 'tala de intet sannt, så lärer jag intet heller giörat. Ty jag hafwer intet lefwat wed Trojæ tiid, ey heller för' (*Atlantica* I 560) [If they do not speak the truth, then I will hardly do so either; because I have lived neither in the time of Troy nor in the period before it]. Mistakes and misunderstandings must exist, since one can never be wholly familiar with all circumstances, and thus can never make a complete and unquestionable evaluation of all enigmas. At best, one can hope to achieve results that come close to the truth. In the light of this notion of the uncertainty of facts, Rudbeck invokes the reader's indulgence and help: 'der han några fel finner i mitt wärck, som antingen i hastighet eller eljest äro förfallne, att han antingen sielf dem ändrar, eller der jag om dhem blifwer påmint, gierna ändra skal; ty att utan fel wara, eller intet kiennas wid dem, är en stor swaghet hos en menniskia' (*Atlantica* I 562) [If he (the reader) finds any errors in my work resulting from haste or otherwise, will he either correct them himself or draw my attention to them and I shall happily correct them, because to be—or to pretend to be—without error is a major flaw in an individual]. This modest disclaimer is of course a traditional humility topos and, taken as such, should probably be regarded as relating to concrete facts of less importance. As to the overall results and propositions, as well as the single interpretations of *Atlantica*, the general idea that the work should

be interpreted in the same way as those old works which it itself
interprets, seems to be stated in the beginning of the second volume: 'Här
uthaff seer man, huru en skal både lära förstå de gamblas gåtor, så och
huru när man will sielff något sinnrijkt skrifwa, får bruka lijknelser och
gåtor' (*Atlantica* II 41) [From this it will be apparent how one can learn
to understand the enigmas of the ancients, and how similes and enigmas
can be used when one wishes to write something ingenious].

Rudbeck's original intention was to write just a single volume. He
once claimed that the later volumes should be regarded as background
material (Lindroth 1975, 286). This partly explains why the first volume
seems relatively well structured, despite lengthy and uncommented upon
quotations and meandering digressions; whereas the material of the other
volumes spins dizzily out of control. The bulk of quotations and the
digressions are of course parts of the argument, but to a great extent they
are left for the reader to negotiate with and interpret, mostly without the
assistance of concluding arguments except of the most general kind.
Rudbeck's material is left to speak for itself; the author offers it for the
reader to arrange and place within a constantly changing perception of
the world.

INDUCTION AND/OR DEDUCTION

Against the background of Rudbeck's ideas about the interpretation of
myths, texts, nature and the world, the reader may hear an admonition to
interpret *Atlantica* in the same manner as the work itself interprets its
sources. The form of *Atlantica* is more expressive and pregnant than
translatable didactic allegory; above all, it is more in harmony with
reality itself. *Atlantica* should be read with the same method that it
explains and employs. It exemplifies itself. In legitimising this method
Rudbeck has engaged the support of one of the foremost Gothic literary
texts, yet still his results do not seem wholly convincing. His *Atlantica*,
in the complexity of its construction, represents a colourful but dead end
in Gothicist antiquarian research.

But the question remains: at exactly what point does Rudbeck's
position become implausible? We have seen how he changes the
conditions for interpreting the world by imposing Snorri's statement
about the nature of poetry on nature itself, and on history. It is a common
opinion that poets convey wisdom and knowledge about the world.
Rudbeck sees the implications: the world can be interpreted with the help
of Old Norse poetics. But is this, combined with an exaggerated
consistency, enough to account for Rudbeck's results? We will never
achieve a full explanation, but the problem can also be treated on another

level than has been done here.

The 'modern' aspects of Rudbeck's work—especially his close relation to Bacon's empirical method—have already been discussed in the light of the practical interpretation of Rudbeck. The theoretical justifications have been treated, but not the underlying conditions. The empirical idea is inductive: facts are collected and put together in order to structure a model of nature or of historical development. One starts from the beginning and works up towards a paradigm. The exegetic and ethical interpretation which we have found to have exercised an influence on Rudbeck's work begins at the other end. It starts from a fixed paradigm and searches for confirmatory evidence. God's creation or the higher spheres of ethical truth are the frames of reference against which the exegete or moral philosopher judges every historical event and every document, whatever its authority. Rudbeck may be modern in several respects, but the paradigm he embraces is quite close to this. His opinion is clear, and his interpretation finalistic: he structures his discourse in accordance with his idea of history. This discourse is empirically inductive, with facts forming the paradigm, but at the same time the paradigm is already shaped and the empirical material is only allowed to develop within certain deductive frames. The scientist Rudbeck wants to approach his subject, the world, empirically, but he nevertheless knows in advance what he is searching for. Induction and deduction are in conflict. The deductive tendency is quite strong in *Atlantica*, and may even lead one's thoughts to the two important deductive paradigms of Rudbeck's time—Cartesianism and Christianity. The deductive paradigm of Cartesianism is, of course, a result of philosophical reason, and does not enjoy the natural authority of the Church. Rudbeck played a part in the introduction of Cartesianism at the University of Uppsala, and whether or not it derives from Cartesianism or from the perception of Christianity, there is a deductive aspect in *Atlantica*. In the end, the question may be whether Rudbeck's paradigm should be considered as belief or knowledge. Perhaps questions such as that, along with questions as to whether Rudbeck believed in his truths or only in his arguments, are now too anachronistic to be asked.

BIBLIOGRAPHY

PRIMARY SOURCES

Aristotle, *The 'Art' of Rhetoric*. Trans. John Henry Freese. London, 1947.

Aristotle, *The Poetics. 'Longinus' On the Sublime. Demetrius On Style*. Trans. W. Hamilton Fyfe. London, New York, 1927.

Edda Islandorum. Völuspá. Hávamál. P.H. Resen's Editions of 1665. Facsimile, with introduction by Anthony Faulkes. Reykjavík, 1977.

Gothrici & Rolfi Westrogothiæ Regum Historia Lingua antiqua Gothica conscripta; Quam e M.s. vetustissimo edidit, & versione notisque illustravit Olaus Verelius. Upsaliæ, 1664.

Heims Kringla, Eller Snorre Sturlusons Nordländska Konunga sagor. Sive Historiæ Regum Septentrionalium â Snorrone Sturlonide, Ante secula quinque, patrio sermone antiquo Conscriptæ, Quas ex manuscriptis Codicibus edidit, Versione gemina, notisque brevioribus, Indici Poëtico vel Rerum, sparsim insertis, Illustravit Johann. Peringskiöld. 2 vols. Stockholmiæ, 1697 (trans. Guðmundur Ólafsson).

Herrauds och Bosa saga med en ny uttolkning iämpte gambla götskan förfärdigat af Olav Verelio. Upsaliæ, 1666.

Hervarar Saga På Gammal Götska Med Olai Verelii Uttolkning Och Notis. Upsaliæ, 1672.

Norlandz Chrönika och Beskriffning: Hwarutinnan förmähles The äldste historier om Swea och Götha Rijken, sampt Norrie, och een-deels om Danmarck, och om theres Wilkår och Tilstånd. Sammanfattad och ihopa dragen aff åthskilliga trowärdiga Bööker, Skriffter och Handlingar. Wijsingzborg, 1670 (Snorri's *Heimskringla,* trans. Jonas Rugman).

Olaus Rudbecks Atlantica, svenska originaltexten. På uppdrag av Lärdoms-historiska Samfundet utgiven av Axel Nelson, 1–5 (Lychnos-Bibliotek 2:1–5). Uppsala and Stockholm, 1937–50.

Snorre Sturlessøns Norske Kongers Chronica. Udsat paa Danske, aff H. Peder Claussøn. Kiøbenhafn, 1633.

Wormius, Olaus. Preface to *Snorre Sturlessøns Norske Kongers Chronica,* 1633.

SECONDARY SOURCES

Agrell, Jan. 1955. *Studier i den äldre språkjämförelsens allmänna och svenska historia fram till 1827.* Uppsala universitets årsskrift 1955, 13. Uppsala and Wiesbaden.

Dieckmann, Liselotte. 1970. *Hieroglyphics. The History of a Literary Symbol.* St. Louis, Missouri.

Eriksson, Gunnar. 1981. 'Olof Rudbeck och Atlantican', *Kungl. Vitterhets Historie och Antikvitets Akademiens Årsbok 1981,* 151–59. Stockholm.

———. 1984. 'Gestalter i svensk lärdomshistoria 1. Olof Rudbeck d.ä.', *Lychnos* 1984, 77–119.

Friberg, Axel. 1945. *Den svenske Herkules. Studier i Stiernhielms diktning.* Stockholm.

Harms, Wolfgang. 1970. 'Wörter, Sachen und emblematische "Res"', in Dietrich Hofmann, ed., *Orbis Sensualium Pictus des Comenius'*, *Gedenkschrift für William Foerste*, pp. 531–542. Köln and Wien.

Johannesson, Kurt. 1968. *I polstjärnans tecken. Studier i svensk barock.* Uppsala.

Jöns, Dietrich Walter. 1966. Das 'Sinnen-Bild'. *Studien zur allegorischen Bildlichkeit bei Andreas Gryphius.* Stuttgart.

Lemmi, Charles W. 1933. *The Classic Deities in Bacon. A Study in Mythological Symbolism.* Baltimore.

Lindroth, Sten. 1975. *Svensk lärdomshistoria II. Stormaktstiden.* Stockholm.

Meissner, Rudolf. 1921. *Die Kenningar der Skalden. Ein Beitrag zur skaldischen Poetik.* Bonn and Leipzig.

Nordström, Johan. 1924. *Samlade skrifter av Georg Stiernhielm II:I. Filosofiska fragment. Inledning.* Stockholm.

———. 1934. 'De yverbornes ö', *De yverbornes ö. Sextonhundratalsstudier.* Stockholm. First printed in *Rudbecksstudier*, 1930. Uppsala.

Olsson, Bernt. 1974. *Den svenska skaldekonstens fader och andra Stiernhielms-studier.* Lund.

Schöne, Albrecht. 1964. *Emblematik und Drama im Zeitalter des Barock.* München.

Swartling, Birger. 1909. *Georg Stiernhielm, hans lif och verkssamhet.* Uppsala.

Weber, Gerd Wolfgang. 1987. '"Intellegere historiam". Typological perspectives of Nordic prehistory', *Tradition og historieskrivning*, 95–141. Aarhus.

———. 1991. 'Euhemerismus', *Reallexikon der Germanischen Altertumskunde* 8. Berlin and New York.

2

The Reception of Old Norse Literature in Late Eighteenth-Century Norway

JAN RAGNAR HAGLAND

Scholarly interest in the reception of Old Norse literature by later literary traditions has paid particular attention to Snorri Sturluson and his *Edda*—its importance as a 'poetological' work (Clunies Ross 1987), and the range of post-medieval responses which it generated. This present essay relates to a larger current project which is attempting to establish an overview of the reception of Snorri's *Edda* both in Scandinavia and elsewhere in Europe. The intention of this paper is to examine the corpus of late eighteenth-century Norwegian literature in order to see whether or not the nature of Norwegian responses to Snorri's *Edda* corresponds to the reception which the work enjoyed elsewhere in Scandinavia and Europe at that time.

This is not the place to comment in detail on eighteenth- and nine-teenth-century Norwegian political history; but it is important to appreciate that terms such as 'late eighteenth-century Norwegian literature' can be rather problematic, when we recall that in the period under discussion Norway formed part of the kingdom of Denmark, both politically and, as far as the written language is concerned, linguistically. There is, however, a long-standing tradition in Norwegian literary history of referring to eighteenth-century Dano-Norwegian writing as Norwegian, with an individual author's place of birth seen as the determining factor. Such Dano-Norwegian literature is generally regarded as a kind of preface to the literature written after 1814, the year in which Norway gained its own constitution, and thus became politically separate from Denmark. It is this post-1814 Norwegian literature which may be regarded as fully 'national'.

The idea of seeking to define a separate Norwegian literary tradition as early as the late eighteenth century need not be attributed to any crude nationalistic approach to literary history. An awareness of Norwegian identity was observed and commented upon by contemporary eighteenth-century observers such as the Danish historian P.F. Suhm, who clearly distinguishes between Norwegians and Danes; in a eulogy over the freedom of the press in Denmark–Norway in 1771, he remarks that 'the Norwegians feel more strongly than do the Danes that they are a people' [Norske føle meere at de ere et Folk end de Danske]. The most striking evidence for such an awareness of Norwegian identity in late eighteenth-century literature is the existence of a literary circle known as Det Norske Selskab [the Norwegian Society], organised by a group of young Norwegian *literati* in Copenhagen after 1772. This society included most of the relatively small group of literary enthusiasts who in one way or another could be regarded at the time as Norwegian. Det Norske Selskab may be—and has been—thought of as a kind of institutionalised preface to the nineteenth-century literary tradition of the politically semi-independent Norway.

How, then, did eighteenth-century Norwegian literature, however imprecisely defined, receive and make use of Old Norse literature in general, and Snorri Sturluson's work in particular? In what ways did the Norwegian response correspond to or deviate from contemporary literary trends and tendencies inside and outside Scandinavia? In addressing these questions, we need perhaps to begin by clarifying the distinction between the aesthetic reception of Nordic myth and literature, and its reception in an historical and nationalistic context.

In aesthetic terms, the response to Old Norse myth and literature observable in late eighteenth-century European writing has frequently been seen as one aspect of a more general quest for literary 'sublimity', and, thus, as part of a pre-romantic reaction against French classicism. The idea of the sublime in eighteenth-century literary theory has been thoroughly discussed elsewhere (see, for instance, Omberg 1976, 67-85) under the two main headings—'Supernatural Sublime' and 'Sanguinary Sublime'. But was there any discernible reaction against classicism in Norway—did the Norwegians turn with any enthusiasm towards the sublime?

Contradictory evidence highlights the problem. On the one hand, we note that the dominant literary circle of the period, Det Norske Selskab, was quite strongly opposed to the kinds of literary tendencies represented by Ewald in Denmark and Klopstock in Germany. Rather than welcoming the Norse Muse, the young Norwegians scholars in Det Norske Selskab wished rather to pay tribute to the Muse's classical cousin: 'Vos exemplaria Græca' would be their motto (see, for example, Heggelund 1974, 574).[1] On the other hand, however, there is the evidence of Anton

---

[1]Their openly expressed adherence to the literary tastes of neo-classicism not only inspired their own parodies of new literary trends, but also led to a search for similar material from abroad. Particularly interesting in this context is an article by Claus Fasting reviewing a group of satirical pieces on 'Die neue Deutschheit nuniger Zeitverstreichungen' (Johan Christian Dietrich, Göttingen), in *Kritisk Tilskuer over indenlandsk og udenlandsk Literatur* (1777), Nos 31 and

Blanck's survey of the Nordic Renaissance in eighteenth-century literature (1911, Chapter 5); this shows that Norwegian literature in the second half of the century does display a measure of interest in and enthusiasm for the glorious Northern past. We should note, too, the significant number of editions of Snorri's work available to eighteenth-century readers (Lundgreen-Nielsen 1979).

If, then, we are looking for evidence of a *Norwegian* reception of Old Norse literary tradition in the period up to *c.* 1820, we cannot rely on information about its aesthetic reception. We need instead to examine our alternative reception category: that which is concerned with expressions of Norwegian patriotism or emerging nationalism. Questions of literature and nationalism in Norway have been and still are much discussed (Lunden 1992; Fjeldstad 1992), though they are beyond the scope of this present paper. But some of the literary evidence cited by such scholars is useful—notably the ways in which eighteenth-century writers claimed that Norway and Norwegians were entitled to an independent political status. Old Norse subject matter may not have been widely used (Lunden 1992, Chapter 5.1), but it does seem reasonable to claim that the work of the historian Gerhard Schøning from 1769 onwards[2] helped to stimulate the kind of nationalistic tone which can be observed in belletristic work of the time. Schøning's depiction of the glorious past was to a large extent based on Snorri—the *Edda* as well as *Heimskringla*—and on other sagas, notably *fornaldarsögur*.

The major Norwegian literary exponent of the patriotic pathos generated by Schøning's work was without doubt Johan Nordahl Brun (1745–1816), with significant contributions from writers such as Christen Pram and Hans Jacob Wille. The work of Odin Henrik Wolf and perhaps Enevold Falsen also deserves mention, given that we are seeking to mark the extent of and follow the direction of Snorri's footprints in late

32. These satires include a parody of what Fasting refers to as the literary use of 'det nordiske Asamaal'; he takes them to be 'et Beviis at Smagen endnu ikke er ganske ødelagt i Tyskland, da de selv indsee deres Fordervelse og de uhyre Misfostre som den nye Smag frembringe [...]' [evidence that taste has not yet been completely destroyed in Germany, as they themselves can see their turpitude and the great monstrosities caused by the new taste[...]].

[2]Beginning with *Afhandling om de Norske og endeel Nordiske Folks Oprindelse* and *Norges Historie* I (Sorøe, 1771).

eighteenth-century Norwegian literature.[3] Dealing first with Brun, we note that he had been Schøning's student at the Cathedral School in Trondheim: 'He revived, oh Norway! your heroes long since passed away' [Han oplivede, o Norge, dine forlængst hensovne Helte] was Brun's comment on his former headmaster (Bull [1945], vii). This may be true in more senses than one. The Trondheim school where Schøning served as headmaster until 1765 seems actively to have encouraged its students to take an interest in their Norse past. So it is that we learn from the official programme for a school's graduation festivities on 19 December 1769 that each of the seven graduating students was to offer a short address, in Danish or Latin, on Old Norse mythology. In 1771 Nordahl Brun himself, then the secretary of the Royal Academy of Arts and Sciences, tried to stimulate and focus the poetic energies and talents of his compatriots by offering a prize of 20 'Species Ducater' for the best poem about King Haraldr Harðráði (Bull [1945], vii). Regrettably, but also perhaps significantly, there are no traces in the Society's archives of any responses to this generous initiative.

Brun himself made use of King Haraldr as one of the protagonists in *Einer Tambeskielver* (1772), a play generally regarded as his major work. It is significant that Brun's literary interests, as revealed by his choice of subject matter, were directed towards the *Heimskringla* rather than the *Edda*, even though both works were by this time available in Danish translation.[4] This play is certainly a major factor in securing a presence for Snorri in eighteenth-century Norwegian literature. Its much commented upon tone of nationalistic pathos is 'conveyed in an understated manner by means of Alexandrine verse' (slightly to rephrase Bull [1945], vi). Apart from occasional breaches of unity of place, the play accords

[3]Wolf's contribution (Wolf 1790) to the reception of Norse poetry was the subject of comment by a contemporary reviewer: 'Hvorfor det skal hedde "gjort efter gammel Maade", sees ikke; thi man skriver endnu ikke paa gammel Maade, naar man sætter Karm for Kareth, og Leding for Felttog; især naar man tillige taler om Te Deum, om Cupido og Pegasus, og lade, kuriøs nok, Helikons Bierg flyde' [It is not clear why it should be referred to as 'made in the old way', as 'the old way' is not followed just by substituting Karm for Kareth, Leding for Felttog, and certainly not by referring to Te Deum along with Cupid and Pegasus; nor by allowing Mount Helicon to float]. Enevold Falsen's contribution to the reception of the prose *Edda* was marginal. His *Festen i Valhall*, composed on the occasion of the King's birthday (29 January 1796) reveals a shallow knowledge of Norse antiquity put to conventional use (Blanck 1911, 232f.).

[4]Worm 1633 and Resen 1665.

well with the formal requirements of neo-classical tragedy. In his book *Drömmen om sagatiden* Jöran Mjöberg (1967, 32) argues that neo-classicism in art and literature seems to obstruct 'a more Nordic grasp of the depiction of the past' [ett mera nordiskt grepp på skildringen av forntiden]; it is as if expressions of 'the sublime' are amongst the elements with which, in Mjöberg's view, classicism cannot cope. *Einer Tambeskielver* illustrates the point perfectly. It is difficult to find sublime moments, whether supernatural or sanguinary, in Brun's neo-classical settings. It seems likely, rather, that by setting his Old Norse subject matter in a neo-classical framework, Brun is seeking to establish a dignified and civilised past for the people of Norway. This is very much the same ideology as that to which Bjørnstjerne Bjørnson was to give expression a century or so later in 1861 (Bull 1937, 478)—the importance of establishing that sense of pride in ancestry which every people striving for nationhood needs to experience. The pre-romantic Brun seems to have regarded the Norse past as insufficiently distant in time to be conceived of as exotic and wild; and thus to offer no stimulus for the creation of 'sublime' aesthetic effects through images of blood and assorted spectral horrors.

There is no reason, however, to maintain that a patriotic or nationalistic programme needed to associate itself with any particular literary form or style. Such sentiments could and did find expression in a variety of ways. A useful contrast to Brun's play may be found in Christen Pram's verse sequence *Stærkodder* (1785), a 'rhymed chronicle' [en Rimkrønike] as the dramatist himself calls it. In the context of the present discussion, Pram (1756–1821) is a particularly interesting figure. Born in Gudbrandsdalen (Lesja) in Norway, he moved with his parents to Denmark at the age of eight. In Norwegian literary histories, Pram is invariably referred to as a Norwegian poet and author. He certainly had links with Det Norske Selskab, but did not perhaps share in full the neo-classical ideals of its members—though his first literary activities were devoted to translating from Greek and Latin. The sequence of fifteen lengthy dactylic poems which make up *Stærkodder* should certainly be read as a political allegory—the poet himself says so; an allegory, it should be added, in which Norwegian patriotism is well to the fore. Pram's treatment of his Old Norse sources is very free; his knowledge of Norse antiquity (Blanck 1911, 225) must to a great extent have been based on Suhm's treatise on Odin (1771), supplemented by Resen's *Edda*, by Saxo, and—in all probability—by Jonas Ramus, whose *Nori regnum h.e. Norvegia antiqua et ethnica* (1689) had been translated into Danish early in the eighteenth century (Borck 1711), with Chapter Four dealing in particular with Stærkodder. Ramus's work, though infrequently referred to, certainly deserves its place in any survey of Snorri's presence in the eighteenth-century intellectual life of Denmark–Norway.

Pram's use of Old Norse subject matter has been seen (as, for example, in Blanck 1911, 225) as merely a decorative overlay to a rather terse and rationalistic political allegory modelled closely on Wieland's work, notably his *Oberon*. Blanck particularly objects to Pram's apparent ignorance of Norse myths and Norse literature, and, just as damaging, to his lack of respect for both. In the present context, however, Pram's allegorical or antiquarian interests need not concern us. My point is that a poetical work of this kind, in spite of its heroic pathos, and its pronounced rationalistic and political intentions, does to a degree employ the 'sanguinary sublime' as a means of voicing its concerns arrestingly. A single brief example can serve to make the point. On his quest for the contents of Mimir's well, Stærkodder has to come to the rescue of Halvor, King of the Norwegian mountains. Pram describes the incident thus:

> Ei noget kan standse hans Løb til hans Ven
> Som strider, som overmandes, han farer
> Som styrtende Strøm giennem Vanernes Skarer.
> Enhver, som forsøger at standse ham, faar
> Af skirnerske Sværd strax dræbende Saar.
> Bestyrtet man aabner ham Løbet, og viger
> Og snart han til Halvor, udbrædende Skræk
> Han kommer; han finder den nordiske Kriger
> Kun væbnet med Spaden, men kiæmpende kiæk
> Og huggende vældig, skiønt eene han staaer
> Rundt om af anfaldende Vaner omgivet,
> Bedækket med Blod af de mægtige Saar,
> Han modtog og gav, og aleene oplivet
> Ved tanken om Norge, sin Pige, sin Ven.
> Han slaar som en Mand, skiønt mod tusinde Mænd.
>
> (*Stærkodder*, pp. 233f.)

> [Nothing can stop his race towards his friend
> who is fighting, overpowered; he runs
> like a rushing stream through the hoard of Vanes.
> Everyone who seeks to stop him receives
> from his Skirnirian sword at once a deadly wound.
> Horrified the crowd retreats, letting him run
> and soon, to Halvor, creating horror
> he comes; he finds the Norse warrior
> armed only with a spade, but fighting bravely,
> and striking vigorously, though standing alone,
> by the attacking Vanes on all sides surrounded,
> covered with blood from the severe wounds
> which he took and gave, and animated solely

by the thought of Norway, his girl, and his friend.
He fights like a man, although against a thousand men.]

Pram and his poem may indeed illustrate the kind of the difficulties involved in trying to identify a characteristically Norwegian response to Old Norse material (see also Lundgreen-Nielsen 1971). But they do represent a significant contribution to the early Norwegian reception of Snorri and the *Edda* and related material. Indeed, there is reason to believe that Pram's *Stærkodder* is one of the 'Skrifter' to whom Hans Jacob Wille refers in the preface to his *Udtog af den nordiske Mythologie* (1787) [Excerpt from Norse Mythology]. One of the reasons which Wille identifies for his eagerness to publish an introduction to Norse mythology is a desire to develop public understanding of works which contain or refer to this kind of subject matter.[5]

Wille's work, quite different in kind to the publications of Brun and Pram, has been largely neglected; it nevertheless deserves particular attention in this essay. Even though listed in comprehensive bibliographies such as that by Ehrencron-Müller (1932), Wille's *Udtog* has been almost completely ignored in historiographical work on Norse mythology and literature. In terms of its scholarly reliability there may, of course, be good reasons for such neglect; but in terms of reception of the Old Norse literature in Norway, Wille is an important writer, and the *Udtog* is a significant text.

Hans Jacob Wille (born 1756) grew up in Seljord, Telemark, where his Danish-born father Hans Amundssen Wille was a vicar. Hans Jacob became a student at the University of Copenhagen in August 1775; he took his degree in theology in January 1779; he then returned home to serve as a curate in his father's parish. In 1786 he became curate to Professor Hans Strøm, a well-known figure as vicar of Eiker. Later that same year, it was Strøm who arranged for his curate to travel around the county of Telemark, collecting Old Norse charters and other source material for antiquarian studies. There is evidence that by this time Hans Jacob had acquired some knowledge of the Old Norse language, an ability which enabled him to make use of charters as sources for his own historical investigations (Hagland 1974, 1975b). One significant result of this work was an historico-topographical treatise on Seljord, published in Copenhagen in 1786 (Wille 1786). Well received at the time, the treatise

---

[5]'Sættes (derved) i Stand til at forstaae de Skrifter, hvori saadant indløber'. We should also note that a 'Wille, J. (Correspondent)' is listed as one of the subscribers to the first edition of *Stærkodder*. In all probability this refers to Hans Jacob Wille.

was even singled out by the Topographical Society in Christiania as a model to be emulated by other writers preparing such works (Hagland 1975a, 3). By 1787, then, Hans Jacob Wille had the makings at least of an Old Norse scholar and was certainly someone experienced in writing for the general public. He was eventually appointed vicar of Grytten in Romsdal (1788–92), then of Vaar Frue in Trondheim (1792–1798), and finally became Dean of Trondheim in 1798; it was a position he occupied until his death in 1808. Whilst in Trondheim, he served for eleven years as Honorary Secretary to the Royal Norwegian Academy of Arts and Sciences (1793–1804).

His *Udtog* has just two chapters. In the first he provides a description—mainly based on *Völuspá*—of how the old religion accounted for the creation of the world. There follows a description of the most important deities, with the main emphasis, naturally enough, on Odin—details of his many different names and deeds, and also of his sons and wives (as Wille puts it). The second chapter is devoted to those gods and goddesses believed by Wille to be next in importance to Odin in the hierarchy of the Norse gods—with Freyr and Niord the first of them. We also learn about characters known only from the *fornaldarsögur* corpus, amongst them King Guthmund of 'Glæsiwoll', Norna-Gest, Herraud and Bose. The chapter is rounded off by a *Völuspá*-derived account of the end of the world; the *Udtog* as a whole is thus framed by those Norse myths which tell of the creation and destruction of the world.

In the brief introduction to his 1787 work Wille appears to be quite explicit about his sources; in fact he fails to identify several of them. The main acknowledged source is the 'Edda Resenii', that is Petrus Johannis Resenius's *Edda Islandorum* published in 1665 (Resen 1665). This edition of Snorri's *Edda* includes texts of *Hávamál* and *Völuspá*, whence Wille's knowledge of the creation myths no doubt derives. From Snorri's *Edda* itself, both *Gylfaginning* and *Skáldskaparmál* are used by Wille— the former in his account of Balder's death in Chapter One, the latter as a source for the many names attributed to Odin.

In addition to the 'Edda Resenii', Wille refers to 'Snorri' and 'Saxo' and to P.F. Suhm's treatise on Odin (1771), the latter work providing Wille, as he rather disarmingly admits, with more information than any of his other sources, as 'it is compiled from so many mythological sagas and tales' ['da den er samlet af saa mange mythologiske Sagar og Fortælninger'; Preface, p. A4]. The 'Snorri' and 'Saxo' texts referred to by Wille are probably Peder Clausøn's Danish translation of *Heimskringla* (Worm edition, 1633), and the 1644 edition of *Saxonis Grammatici Historia Danica* (Stephanius edition, 1644); no other editions of these two works appear in the printed catalogue for the auction of Wille's library in September 1811 (Wille [n.d.]). For *Heimskringla*, he may also have had access to the first three volumes (1777–1783) of the Arna-magnæan edition. There is some evidence to suggest that some of the *fornaldarsögur* material—*Hervarar saga* and *Herrauds och Bosa saga*—may derive directly from editions by Verelius (1672, or 1785, and 1666 respectively), even though only one of these editions appears in the 1811 sale catalogue. There is reason to believe that Wille had been familiar with some of Paul-Henri Mallet's work on Northern history; the catalogue includes the Danish translation of Mallet's History of Denmark (Mallet 1756b), but there is no evidence of Wille's having known or made use of Mallet's influential treatise on Norse mythology and poetry (Mallet 1756a).

The main point is that Wille's Introduction to the old myths, as his *Udtog* may appropriately be called, represents important evidence for the reception of Snorri's *Edda* and may well have stimulated further interest in the mythological and aesthetic aspects of Snorri's work in pre-romantic Norway–Denmark. By the time of the publication of the *Udtog* in 1787, interest in Old Norse mythology had been specifically encouraged in Peter Fredrik Suhm's voluminous treatise on Odin to which Wille (as we have noted) refers. Suhm had intended his own work to be part of a larger historical project *Om de nordiske Folks ældste Oprindelse* [On the Origin of the Nordic People] (Suhm 1770; see also Paludan-Müller 1883–1884, 162ff). The reception by contemporary critics of Suhm's treatise on Odin had been by no means universally positive. The compilation was accused of being dull, and capable of attracting the interest only of 'those who, in the future, might want to provide us with a rational system of our ancestors' mythology' [dem, der engang ville skaffe os et raisonneret System over vore Forfædres Mythologie; *Kritiske Journal* 46–47, 1772, 368].

The nature of Suhm's compilation and its reception might have been one factor influencing Wille's efforts in the same field. Small wonder that he sounds defensive when seeking in his introduction to excuse any deficiencies in his work; he is aware that it might be accused of rashness and impetuosity [Autor-Syge]. He admits that the reason for his being prepared to take the risk and publish the work is that he had been encouraged to do so by 'Conferanseraad Erichsen', that is Jon Erichsen, who had earlier helped Suhm to understand a number of Old Norse passages (*Laerde Eft.* 28, 11 July 1771, 444). His encouragement of Wille, may suggest that Erichsen shared the general disappointment with Suhm's treatise, and welcomed a further opportunity to promote the study of the old religion.

From Wille's viewpoint, Erichsen's encouragement may not have been his only motivation. He may well have felt that publication of his book might help to secure for himself the permanent position in the Church which he had yet to achieve by 1787. This consideration may account for the rather ponderous claims made in the book's introduction as to the potential value of the assembled mythological knowledge in helping readers better to appreciate the virtues of Christianity as a rational faith.[6]

There are, though, additional remarks in Wille's introduction which do seem to indicate a genuine eagerness to be involved in popular education, through the kind of project in which he was engaged—and thus an eagerness to contribute to a wider reception of Old Norse mythology. Learning to understand Old Norse mythology would enable the reader to understand the kind of literature ('de Skrifter') in which such material occurs. This may well imply that Wille regarded it as a worthwhile task to provide the reading public with the means through which they could understand the kinds of literary trends which he himself had identified in contemporary literature such as Pram's *Stærkodder*. At the very least he could offer such readers a more systematic presentation of knowledge about the old religion than was currently available; this, as we have noted, had been called for by critics of Suhm's book. Even the myths themselves, as presented by Snorri in his *Edda*, were by no means easily accessible at this time. Resen's *Edda* would have been a daunting work for the non-specialist to use, and it was not until 1808 that a translation for a general readership appeared (Nyerup and Rask 1808).

Judged, then, by the standards of what had previously been available, Wille's contribution to the mediation of knowledge about Nordic mythology may be looked upon as a significant step forward along the path of pedagogical adjustment to the needs of the interested non-specialist. Wille himself, in his introduction to the *Udtog*, claims that Jon Erichsen planned to recommend to the Royal Commission on Education that the book be promoted for use in schools; Erichsen was himself a member of the Commission, which had been established in 1785. In the event, the work of this Commission had little impact (Holm 1909, 539f).

---

[6]'At kiende vore Forfædres Gude-Lære, saaledes som den var i disse Lande, for Christendommes Indførsel, synes at være nyttigt og fornøieligt; thi derved indsee vi vore Forfædres Vildfarelse, og vi takke Forsynet for en fornuftigere Religion' [Knowledge of our forefathers' mythology, as it used to be in these countries before the introduction of Christianity, seems to be as useful as it is amusing, because knowledge of this kind informs us of our forefathers' misapprehensions and leads us to thank Divine Providence for a more rational religion]. The effort seems to have paid off on this occasion. Shortly after the book was published, Wille went to Copenhagen to seek a position, and was appointed vicar of Grytten in Romsdal soon afterwards.

There is no indication that Erichsen's alleged plans for Wille's book were ever implemented, and Wille's claims on this matter cannot be confirmed. Equally, though, they cannot be disproved; and, in any case, even supposing that such plans had been largely a figment of his imagination, the idea itself reflects the educational impulse behind his enterprise— there is no clear evidence that his project had any other objectives driving it. It is certainly possible to view Wille's brief introduction to Norse mythology as a kind of forerunner to the more earnest efforts to create a poetic language based on Old Norse myths represented by the work of the Swede Per Henrik Ling some thirty years later (Ling 1819).

The extent, however, of Wille's contribution to the wider reception of Old Norse myth and of Snorri's *Edda* is more difficult to assess. We know next to nothing about the book's distribution. It may be that its inclination towards popular education was somewhat premature in Norway and in Denmark during the late 1780s. Its critical reception, in so far as it had one at all, seems to have been marked by condescending indifference. Grundtvig was one of the very few, if not the only one, to pay any attention to Wille's work on mythology. In the preface to his 1808 edition of *Nordens Mytologi*, the Danish scholar identifies a number of reasons for making available reliable sources of knowledge about the Norse gods (Grundtvig 1808, xiv). The principal reason for the growing interest in Norse mythology during the first decade of the nineteenth century was, Grundtvig maintains, the works of Adam Oehlenschläger: 'when Oehlenschläger's harp resounded, a genuine longing to know more about the gods of the North emerged in the hearts of the more advanced people'[Da Oehlenschlägers Harpe klang [frembrød] i de mere Ud-vikledes Barm en inderlig Længsel efter at kende Nordens Guder; Grundtvig 1808, xiv]. Indeed, he maintains that, up to a point, 'no access to the *Edda* existed other than the *Edda* itself, because Suhm had done nothing but collect, and Wille, Bastholm and Møinichen had tried in vain to teach to others what they did not know themselves' [Virkelig var der ingen Vei til Edda uden Edda selv, thi Suhm havde blot samlet, Ville (sic), Bastholm og Møinichen havde forgæves søgt at lære Andre, hvad de selv ei vidste: Bastholm 1802, Møinichen 1800]. This remark seems to have sealed the fate of Wille's contribution to the understanding of Norse mythology. We hear virtually nothing of it thereafter.

Through Wille and Pram we may note that the late eighteenth-century *Norwegian* reception of Old Norse myth and literature in general, and of Snorri Sturluson's work in particular, reflects (to some degree) trends in literature which are more clearly pronounced elsewhere in Scandinavia and Europe. Norwegian interest in Snorri, from the time of Johan Nordahl Brun, paid less heed to poetry and more to history; accordingly Norwegian interest in Snorri tended to be centred on *Heimskringla* rather than the *Edda*. It shared nothing of the fondness for ideas about the wild and exotic Norse past, about that pursuit of the sublime which so characterised the reception of Old Norse writings in eighteenth-century England, Germany and Denmark. Such notions could play no part in a project whose principal aim was the construction of a national identity which was to be so important a part of Norwegian literature in the years thereafter.

BIBLIOGRAPHY

Bastholm, Chr. 1802. *Hist.-philos. Undersøgelser over de ældsteFolkeslægters religiøse og philosophiske Meninger.* København.

Blanck, Anton. 1911. *Den nordiska renässanen i sjuttonhundratalets litteratur. En undersökning av den 'gotiska' poesiens allmänna och inhemska förutsättningar.* Stockholm.

Borck, Anders Jenssøn. 1711. *Det Gamle Hedenske Norge. Oversat i Vort ædele Danske Tungemaal af det Latinske Sprog ved [AJB] Uværdig Slots-Præst ved Aggers Huus Slot.* København.

Brun, Johan Nordahl. 1772. *Einer Tambeskielver. Et Sørgspil i fem Optog.* København.

Bull, Francis. 1937. *Norges litteraturhistorie. Fjerde bind. Fra Februar-revolusjonen til Verdenskrigen.* Oslo.

————. [1945]. Innledning [til] Johan Nordahl Brun, *Einer Tambeskielver,* pp. v–xxv. [Oslo].

Ehrencron-Müller. H. 1932. *Forfatterlexicon omfattende Danmark, Norge og Island indtil 1814.* Vol. 9. København.

Fjeldstad, Anton. 1992. 'Nasjonsomgrepet nok ein gong', *Syn og Segn* 1, 82–89.

Grundtvig, N.F.S. 1808. *Nordens Mytologi eller Udsigt over Eddalæren for dannede der ei selv ere Mytologer.* København.

Hagland, Jan Ragnar. 1974. 'Norske diplom som kjeldemateriale på 1700–talet', *Maal og Minne,* 66–72.

————. 1975a. *Hans Jacob Wille. Norsk Ordbog.* Trondheim-Oslo-Bergen-Tromsø.

————. 1975b. 'Hans Jacob Willes bruk av diplom som kjeldemateriale i Sillejords Beskrivelse', *Heimen* 16, 645–651.

Heggelund, Kjell. 1974. 'Unionstiden med Danmark', in Beyer, Edv., ed., *Norges litteraturhistorie* 1, pp. 343–623. Oslo.

Holm, Edvard. 1909. *Danmark og Norges Historie (1720–1814).* Vol. 6:2. København.

Kritiske Journal = Kiøbenhavnske Kongl. privil. Adressecontoirs Kritiske Journal.

Ling, Per Henrik. 1819. *Eddornas SinnesbildsLära för Olärde framställd*. Stockholm.

Lunden, Kåre. 1992. *Norsk grålysing. Norsk nasjonalisme 1770–1814 på allmenn bakgrunn*. Oslo.

Lundgreen-Nielsen, Flemming. 1971. 'Christen Prams "Stærkodder"', *Edda* 71, 321–330.

———. 1979. (mimeo) *Den nordiske renæssance: det tekstlige baggrund*.

Lærde Eft. = *Kiøbenhavnske Efterretninger om lærde Sager*.

Mallet, Paul-Henri. 1756a. *Monumens de la mythologie et de la poesie des Celtes et particulierement des anciens Scandinaves*. København.

———. 1756b. *Inledning udi Danmarks Riges Historie*. København.

Mjöberg, Jöran. 1967. *Drömmen om sagatiden 1*. Stockholm.

Møinichen, Jac. Bærent. 1800. *Nordiske Folks Overtroe, Guder, Fabler og Helte i Bogstav-Orden*. København.

Nyerup, Rasmus and Rasmus Rask. 1808. *Edda, eller Skandinavernes hedenske Gudelære*. København.

Omberg, Margaret. 1976. *Scandinavian Themes in English Poetry, 1760-1800*. Acta Universitatis Upsaliensis. Studia Anglistica Upsaliensia 29. Uppsala.

Paludan-Müller, C. 1883–1884. 'Dansk Historiografi i det 18de Aarhundrede', *Historisk Tidskrift* 4, 1–188.

Pram, Christen. 1785. *Stærkodder. Et Digt i femten Sange*. København.

Resen, P.H. 1665. *Edda Islandorum*. Hafniæ. (Repr., ed. Anthony Faulkes, Reykjavík, 1977).

Ross, Margaret Clunies. 1987. *Skaldskaparmál. Snorri Sturluson's ars poetica and medieval theories of language*. Odense.

Stephanus Stephanius, ed. 1644. *Saxonis Grammatici Historiæ Danicæ, Libri XVI*. Hafniæ.

Suhm, P.F. 1770. *Om de Nordiske Folks ældste Oprindelse*. København.

———. 1771. *Om Odin og den hedniske Gudelære og Gudstienste udi Norden*. København.

[———]. 1772. *Til mine Landsmænd og Medborgere de Danske, Norske og Holstenere*. København.

Verelius, Olaus, ed. 1666. *Herrauds och Bosa saga*. Uppsala.

———, ed. 1672. *Hervarar saga*. Uppsala.

Wille, H.J. 1786. *Beskrivelse over Sillejords Præstegield i Øvre Tellemarken i Norge*. København.

———. 1787. *Udtog af den nordiske Mythologie, eller Othins Gude-Lære*. København.

[Wille, H.J.]. n.d. *Fortegnelse over sal. Stiftprost Willes Bøger, som auktioneres i Frue Willes Gaard i Trondhiem først i September Maaned 1811*. Trondheim.

Wolf, Odin Henrik. 1790. *Odins Miød, eller aller underdanigst Ledings Sang efter gammel Maade paa Indtogsfesten i Kiøbenhavn, Dagen den 14de Septbr. 1790.* København.

Worm, Ole, ed. 1633. *Snorre Sturlesøns Norske Kongers Chronica. Udsat paa danske, aff Peder Claussön.* København.

3

Grundtvig's Norse Mythological Imagery —An Experiment that Failed

FLEMMING LUNDGREEN-NIELSEN

A legend in his own lifetime, N.F.S. Grundtvig (1783–1872) in his capacity as theologian, preacher, man of letters, poet, philosopher, philologist, historian, teacher, member of parliament, journalist, and writer of hymns, contributed with unrivalled vigour to so many aspects of nineteenth-century Danish intellectual life. His advocacy in favour of establishing folk high schools led to perhaps his most enduring achievement; though his ambition to create a central national academic institution on the site of the old Academy of Sorø was never realised, his theories about popular education still inform the work of the Danish folk high school system today. Grundtvig's national ballads and metrical hymns continue to dominate the *Folk High School Songbook* (first published in 1894; seventeenth printing 1989) as well as the Authorised Danish hymn books (in the 1899 and 1953 versions): his texts are in daily use.

In one enterprise, however, Grundtvig was rather less successful—his attempt to turn ancient Norse mythology into an accessible store of modern national imagery. The notion bore fruit in his own life—his momentous programme for Danish secular education was launched via a weighty volume on Norse mythology; yet the overall idea never achieved popular acceptance.

This present essay seeks to investigate how Grundvig went about his work, and to suggest some reasons why his efforts were ultimately ill-starred. The focus of the paper is on Grundtvig himself rather than the work of those who came after him; and the discussion will, for the most part, be based on a range of previously unpublished manuscript material rather than on more familiar printed works. The central theme is viewed from Grundtvig's own standpoint: his understanding of the Norse myths, and his confident and cheerful linking of mythology and legendary history will be discussed without constant reference to the very different conclusions reached by scholars working more than a century later.

REVIVAL OF NORSE MYTHOLOGY

By the end of the eighteenth century European literature had begun to search with growing enthusiasm and urgency for a new mythology voiced in new imagery fit for a new century. Some romantic writers turned to an idealised vision of ancient Greece; others sought out the wisdom of the Indian subcontinent. Some were attracted by the excitements of contemporary science at a time when natural phenomena such as light, electricity, magnetism and vibration were eagerly studied; others sought to replace legendary explorers like Jason, Aeneas and Ulysses with their modern equivalents—men like Captain James Cook.

If such trends and tendencies were too international, and perhaps too sophisticated to impact significantly on Danish intellectual life, there was no problem in presenting rediscovered ancient Norse mythology as a relatively new and potentially fruitful source of poetic imagery with a patriotic flavour.

Danish historical legends with the capacity for creating or bolstering national self-confidence and identity had in former times enjoyed a measure of scholarly attention. In the late twelfth century, the archbishops Absalon and Anders Sunesøn commissioned Saxo Grammaticus to write a Latin chronicle of Denmark—the *Gesta Danorum*. Later, in the years after the long quarrel between Danish and Swedish historians about the origin and age of the Scandinavian kingdoms had begun in the mid-sixteenth century, the Danish royal house had done much to promote interest in Denmark's heroic past, through enterprises such as Anders Sørensen Vedel's Danish translation of Saxo (1575), and by supporting a long line of officially appointed historians whose job it was to ensure the continuation (in Latin) of Saxo's chronicle.

The ancient religion of Denmark was another matter, however. No good Christian could be seen to delve too deeply into such rude and barbaric tales. Even Saxo in his first nine books time and again depicts the pagan gods as untrustworthy swindlers. A serious interest in native religion can be traced back only as far as learned circles in the seventeenth century. In 1633 Ole Worm supported the printing of Peder Clausøn Friis's century old translation of Snorri's *Heimskringla*, and in the period 1630–1650 published his own Latin writings on the runic alphabet and on Danish runic monuments. The Sorø Academy professor Stephan Stephanius published a fine two-volume critical edition of Saxo. Peder Hansen Resen, a Danish historian, in turn published an edition of Snorri's *Edda*, and editions of *Völuspá* and *Hávamál*, complete with translations. 1689 saw the appearance of Thomas Bartholin's comprehensive and influential 720 page Latin account of the contempt of death exhibited so widely by ancient pagan Danes. The texts of the numerous Icelandic quotations, drawn from some twenty-one Eddic poems, had been supervised by none other than Árni Magnússon. Bartholin died the next year, only 31 years old; his massive and important work has sadly never been made available in any modern language translation.

After the scorn and condescension shown by historians of the Danish Enlightenment towards the Norse past, the atmosphere of European intellectual life gradually changed. In historical research the absolute standards of, for example, Christianity or Graeco-Roman antiquity were confronted with a strongly developing sense of relativism. The French philosopher Montesquieu in his book *On the Spirit of the Laws* (1748) traced all manifestations of freedom in Europe back to Scandinavian roots. Not long after Montesquieu's book, Paul-Henri Mallet, the Swiss-born professor of literature at the Royal Academy of Fine Arts in Copenhagen, published a French translation of Snorri's *Edda* in 1756, thereby affording readers across Europe access to the single most important literary source of Scandinavian paganism.

Poets soon responded to this stimulus. H.W. v. Gerstenberg, a Dane writing in German, included a modernised version of the Ragnarök stanzas from *Völuspá* in his sentimental *Poem of a Scald* (1766), whilst F.G. Klopstock wrote *Hermann's Battle* (1769), a play which stressed the themes of courage and indifference to death among the Germanic tribes. Klopstock paved the way for the Dane Johannes Ewald, who added an element of newly fashionable sentimentalism and sensibility to his two Saxo dramatisations, the prose tragedy *Rolf Krage* (1770), and the musical play *The Death of Balder* (1775). This latter play was staged in 1779—a lavish production with costumes designed by the distinguished painter Professor N.A. Abildgaard. Although the style still savoured of neo-classicism, no effort was spared to lend the correct historical appearance to the production. So it was that Norse mythology began gradually to enjoy a more tolerant and even warm reception.

Learned discussions on pagan culture took place in the academic world. The Icelander Jón Ólafsson submitted a prize essay to the Royal Danish Academy of Sciences and Letters, published in 1786 under the title *On the Art of Poetry in Ancient Scandinavia, its Principal Rules, Metres, Style and Ways of Recital*. After a detailed review of Icelandic kennings, Jón adds that these complex figures can only be appreciated by people with some knowledge of their literary and intellectual background in pagan antiquity.

In February 1800 the University of Copenhagen set a related prize-essay topic: 'Would it be fruitful for poetry in Scandinavia, if ancient Norse Mythology were to be introduced and commonly accepted by our poets as an alternative to Greek mythology?' Three men entered the competition. L.S. Platou, subsequently (from 1813) a professor of history at the new university of Kristiania (Oslo) in Norway, won the first prize for an essay in which he emphasised the desirable (in his view) aesthetic qualities of clarity and harmony reflected in the Greek gods, as opposed to the rude and gigantic beauty of their Nordic counterparts. Adam Oehlenschläger, the herald of Scandinavian romanticism, but in 1800 still a law student, won the first (*sic!*) second prize through his vigorous support of the proposition in the prize-essay title, writing from the viewpoint of the creative artist. He was encouraged by his realisation that Norse mythology, unlike the equivalent classical myths, had not been written and painted to death, and emphasised that Norse myths seemed capable of clothing abstract concepts in a pleasing and beautiful material form. The theologian Jens Møller was awarded the second second prize also for an affirmative response to the title, in his case based on the entertainment value of such new subject-matter.

All these papers were published in 1801 in K.L. Rahbek's monthly *The Minerva*, with the editor clearly in no doubt that his subscribers would find the topic and the debate interesting. Grundtvig had just matriculated at the University of Copenhagen, at the age of 17, on 7 November 1800 and did not himself participate in the essay competition. A few years later, however, it was to be his privilege to establish a new understanding and seek out new uses for these Norse myths.

GRUNDTVIG'S ASA INTOXICATION: A SYNTHETIC VIEW

Several times during Grundtvig's long life he reflected on his relationship to Norse mythology. These reflections, for all their differences of emphasis, come to the same broad conclusions, which are still considered valid by scholars.

His first steps, taken between 1800 and 1804, were determined by what he refers to as 'blind instinct'. Attracted to the Old Norse language without knowing why, he commenced (in the summer of 1804) his study of the Icelandic sagas in the original language. His only lexicographical aid was a word-list which he himself, for want of an Icelandic-Danish vocabulary, had assembled from a scholarly Icelandic-Latin ecclesiastical history book which he had found in his father's library. This period of reading and study represents the philological foundation for what was to follow.

In the years after 1814, Grundtvig himself was to refer disparagingly to the next phase in the development of his Norse literary interests—he calls it 'the Asa [Æsir][1] intoxication'. Lasting from 1805 to 1810, the period saw the publication of Grundtvig's detailed survey of Eddic wisdom, based on his firm conviction that within the myths there were deeper myths encoded.

Grundtvig is the first Danish scholar to offer a synthetic view of this material. He several times presents his vision of the process of events from the creation of the world, through Ragnarök, and on to the re-creation of the earth—most poetically in the periodical article *On the Doctrines of Asa Mythology* (1807), written in only three weeks, without access to manuscripts, but drawing on the first (1787) volume of the Arnamagnæan *(Elder) Edda*, on Resen's 1665 editions of Snorri's *Edda*, *Hávamál* and *Völuspá*, and also on B.C. Sandvig's unfinished Danish translation of the *Elder Edda* (1783–1785).

According to one of Grundtvig's unpublished manuscripts of the time, his interpretations are first of all products of 'a bright glance and an idea engendered by the *Edda* itself'. The 'bright glance' refers to Romantic intuition, whilst the main 'idea' of the *Edda* is identical to the plot of *Völuspá*, the only comprehensive Eddic poem. In another unpublished fragment, *On the Written Monuments of Ancient Scandinavia and in Particular on the Poetic Edda*, Grundtvig declares himself to be 'divided between consideration of the whole and research into details'. The constant and fruitful interaction between imagination and philology prevents Grundtvig from being side-tracked into the abstract speculative constructions of the German natural philosophers. He nominates ancient pagan Scandinavia as 'the home of my spirit, from where I borrow all those images through which I reflect on and express the invisible'— clearly an existentialist approach.

In May or June 1808, when Grundtvig has settled down in Copenhagen near the manuscript collection and the public libraries, he produces another rejected fragment, *On the Sources of Norse Mythology*; in it he writes, 'The question is not whether our forefathers worshipped gods bearing this or that name, for that is in itself of little significance; but rather whether, through the gods they worshipped, they strove to understand life, its origin and purpose'. By November 1808, teaching history at a grammar school, we find him telling his pupils, 'The ideal of life amongst a particular people can always be discerned with great certainty from its mythology.' Here the possibilities for making the old myths speak to a modern age are very clear.

---

[1]Throughout this essay, Eddic names are cited in the spellings used by Grundtvig. The first instance of a name whose Grundtvigian spelling could mislead a reader is accompanied by its Icelandic spelling in square brackets.

Grundtvig's major work of this period is *Norse Mythology* (1808). The book represents a perceptible advance in methods of linguistic scholarship and coherent interpretation. Grundtvig discusses the age of the written sources, distinguishing old from young by means of gleams from his 'bright glance', and the light of the *Edda* itself in *Völuspá*. It is important that Grundtvig, unlike the historian P.F. Suhm in his 1771 handbook *On Odin and on Pagan Mythology*, tries to date the sources instead of just combining them; yet it is characteristic that, if pressed, he allows his feelings a higher priority than cold philological facts. The very enthusiasm of his response to a myth was a measure of its authenticity; lack of spontaneous emotion indicates a late or false source. Acting on this criterion Grundtvig at one point boldly dates *Völuspá* to the fifth century—thereby placing it alongside the Golden Horns of Gallehus: modern scholars date *Völuspá* to *c*. 1000.

Moreover, Grundtvig believes that Norse mythology was the work of a great poet—a wise old sage who, faced with the turmoil and incomprehensible evils of the world, tried to explain all events in terms of some positive process of progression. Since the glass statue of mythology created by this unknown scald had petrified over the course of time, Grundtvig undertakes to try to restore its transparency—the metaphor refers to the Eddic poem *Hyndluljóð*.

One of Grundtvig's central ideas is that there is an absolute ruler, the Allfather, superior to the Asa gods, who makes use of three goddesses of fate, the Norns, as his agents in the unfolding drama of the world. Here Grundtvig ascribes a pre-Christian monotheistic belief to the pagan Scandinavians that can easily be harmonised with his own Christian faith.

While praising the poems of the *Elder Edda*, Grundtvig handles Snorri's prose *Edda* with great suspicion and disdain, regarding it as a late and random collection of scattered and incoherent myths, many of them fitting badly or not at all into the main story line of *Völuspá*. Even Snorri's masterfully narrated story of Thor's journey to Utgard-Loke [Útgarðaloki] is dismissed as insignificant, because the power of the Asa and the wit of the trolls are never directly confronted. Strangely enough, Grundtvig is unable to resist quoting some paragraphs from Snorri's disreputable (as it was then considered) Prologue. The passage in question naively describes the World as one huge living creature, with its manifestations of life comparable to those of birds and animals. Though no reasons are given for the presence of the quotations, it must presumably be attributed to the force of Grundtvig's emotional reaction.

In one respect Grundtvig unknowingly anticipates later use of the myths detached from their strictly historical context. He found such an attitude already present in the textual sources, namely the fables, treated in the third part of his 1808 *Norse Mythology*. To Grundtvig fables were conditioned by space and time (nature and history), and served to supplement proper mythology by pointing to traces and reflections of a higher existence in earthly materialistic forms. Hence fables could be termed the allegorical language of mythology. But since Norse mythology 'did not originate in reflections upon the impressions of phenomena, but welled up from unreflected considerations of *Life* and *Time*', the fables in Scandinavia lacked concrete facts to refer to. They were left in a state of confusion and subjectivity, so that 'no fetter prevented the poet, the thinker and the observer from moving around at his discretion in the wide open field'. However at this early stage Grundtvig does not yet take an active interest in the possibilities inherent in such free treatment of the stories.

In January and February 1810 Grundtvig announces a plan for a translation of the *Elder Edda*, but the obscurity of the specimen stanzas printed in a newspaper drew such sharp criticism from the (subsequently celebrated) philologist Rasmus Rask that the project was shelved. Around Christmas of the same year, in the wake of a severe crisis of religious faith—and a fit of insanity, Grundtvig entered a period of Biblical fundamentalism which lasted until 1815. During these years he saw little or no merit in pursuing the Norse myths and legends.

NORSE MYTHOLOGY AFTER ALL: A RETRIEVAL

The Biblical fundamentalist ice began to break during 1815. Among paragraphs of harsh self-criticism, Grundtvig confesses in an April 1815 letter to a Norwegian friend that he still retains a fondness for the Norse myths. That same summer, in a passing moment of reflection in *Small Poems,* his retrospective collection of occasional poetry, Grundtvig anticipates a new edition of his 1808 handbook. Then on St Stephen's day 1815, from the pulpit of the church of Frederiksberg (a town not far from Copenhagen), Grundtvig declares that in future he does not wish to be a guest preacher in the churches of the Danish capital, as long as the king will not grant him his own parish in the city. At the same moment, in the popular middle-class newspaper *Latest Pictures of Copenhagen,* he expresses regret that sympathetic readers and critics have been bewildered by his aggressively direct Christian proselytising in both verse and prose, and have accused him of fanaticism, intolerance, hypocrisy, conceit and madness. He concludes by promising a return to a more oblique form of expression—in other words to Romantic symbolism.

Much the same attitude can be identified in a large translation project on which he was working at the time. It had been launched in 1812 with his promise to translate first the poems in Snorri's *Heimskringla,* and then the entire prose text. In January 1815, in an 'intoxication of Danishness', he added Saxo's *Gesta Danorum* to the agenda, before in September of the same year accepting a commission to reproduce the (then) newly published Anglo-Saxon poem *Beowulf* in Danish verse.

Instead of 'Oversættelse' [translation] Grundtvig prefers the term 'Fordanskning' [literally: making Danish], implying an intuitively sympathetic poetic re-creation, achieved by a radical recasting of idioms when shifting from one language to the other, and where appropriate by disregarding the demands of strict verbal accuracy.

This new position meant that Grundtvig could again allow himself to engage with Norse mythology, now interpreting the myths more freely, more arbitrarily, and more subjectively. Accordingly, in a Copenhagen literary feud in the last three months of 1818, Grundtvig makes periodic use of imagery taken from Norse myth. In one manuscript he defines Norse mythology as 'the natural mirror of my soul, the poetical side of me, the focal point at which all the rays that were to ignite me had to converge; accordingly, the centre for my spiritual efforts, my treasure chest as well as my arsenal'. This private statement seems to be as accurate as any ever published by Grundtvig.

There remained, however, a problem for a Christian (and a theologian at that) who sought to devote time and energy to the serious study of paganism. In his article *A Few Words on Antiquarian and Archaeological Research*, published in his one-man periodical *The Danne-Virke* (III, 1817), he argues that it is permissible to study pagan myths, as long as some higher, that is Christian, goal lies behind the work. He blames himself for not having linked Norse mythology with universal history in his 1808 study; he now wishes to improve and extend that work. In the 1818 manuscript referred to above, Grundtvig argues that if the Asa mythology could come to mean as much to Scandinavians as the Old Testament did and does to Christians, he would have access to a wealth of images which he could use in songs 'to his heart's content without insulting Christianity'.

Rather surprisingly, Grundtvig's translations did in fact appear at the scheduled times, the Saxo and Snorri chronicles (each three volumes) in 1818–1823, and *Beowulf* in 1820. Norse antiquity, as Grundtvig viewed it in these books, spells out a specific attitude to life, reflecting a national mind. His introduction to the 1818 Saxo translation discusses the historical value of Saxo's versions of the myths: 'a thorough reflection on the facts of human existence most certainly proves that such legends never arise, are never revered and preserved by a people, unless that people has the heart to perform those deeds which the legends report; on the other hand, such a heart can never be found without also finding deeds to match, according to the circumstances and opportunities afforded by different eras'. Saxo understandably demonstrates a Danish identity, but Grundtvig's work on Snorri and *Beowulf* makes him increasingly aware of the universal qualities of Norse myths. An 1823 newspaper postscript to his Saxo-Snorri work concludes that Scandinavia possesses both 'a mythology that in Universal History comprises and demonstrates the heroic life of all humankind, and an ancient history which mythically unfolds this life in Nordic heroic deeds'.

In the eyes of the public over the following fifteen years, Grundtvig is no longer a mythologist; yet his unpublished manuscripts from the period 1821–1825 tell a different story. One such, *On the Value of Mythology* (1821–1823), eloquently argues the case for the universality of myths:

> [they can give] an impression of the historical struggle of mankind that takes place in all periods, pointing to a victory after which evil is destroyed, and to a melting down in which everything noble is purified. The heroes are like grains of gold transported by rivers, they are sifted in the stream and have only to be fused together, while the gods are like precious ore in the rocks, still containing impure elements, until it melts in the fire of the giant Surtur.

This process, claims *Völuspá*, reaches its climax in the battle at Ragnarök, labelled by Grundtvig 'a profound yet erroneous notion of the great change and transfiguration much better known to Christians from other sources'. Yet, even to a modern Christian Ragnarök is a crucial event, serving to establish Norse mythology in the countries where it originated and representing 'a welcome, definite and in a way indispensable symbolism, or form of essential historical poetry; it may not restore history to life, but as a presentiment it contributes to the resurrection of history and as a prefiguration serves to symbolise this resurrection'.

In two *c.* 1823 sketches, *On the Ancient Norse Legends* and *On the Ancient Legends in Saxo*, Grundtvig challenges the hitherto blind eighteenth-century scholarly preference for Icelandic sources. Initially discussing Professor P.E. Müller's newly published paper *Critical Examination of the Legendary Past of Denmark and Norway* (1823), he hails the author's reappraisal of Saxo's handling of mythical material—the first since that of Stephan Stephanius in the 1640s. Grundtvig reminds the reader that Saxo was living and writing in the late 1100s, a period from which hardly any Icelandic manuscript survives. It is thus absurd automatically to consider all Icelandic sources as of unrivalled value, whilst dismissing Saxo's versions as mere gossip. Grundtvig hopes that some form of holy alliance might emerge between the Icelandic and Danish traditions in defending Norse myths from the fierce attacks of German scholars.

At this time Grundtvig seems to have been preparing a second augmented edition of his 1808 mythology. There are extant copies of a draft preface in the form of an impressive sixteen-page survey of the last two centuries of Norse mythological research, apparently dating from 1822-1823. It is Grundtvig's principal thesis that the interest in Norse mythology around 1800 in no way represents a continuation of previous scholarly trends. Neither Suhm's dreary volume nor Sandvig's far too literal translations could win the support of the reading public; the reintroduction of the Norse gods was desperately in need of the kind of rich poetic support which had long been enjoyed by Greek and Roman culture. Unfortunately ancient Icelandic fiction could not serve the purpose; it was not old enough to be regarded as classical, and could only be to Norse myths as Neo-Latin verse was to the myths of Greece and Rome. Moreover, the learned professors in Denmark were incapable of creating anything new. A poet was needed—and duly appeared, as Adam Oehlenschläger's prize essay and early poetry demonstrated how Norse mythology could be revitalised. He certainly inspired Grundtvig, but Oehlenschläger deviated too much from the sources, creating his own mythology out of the genuinely old one. As an antidote Grundtvig published his *Norse Mythology* (1808), (too) long out of print. Grundtvig argues that in spite of Professor Finn Magnussen's admirable translation of the *Elder Edda* (1821–1823), there is still room for a reprint of his own old handbook, not only because national mythology still represents an indispensable aid to the understanding of Scandinavian history, but also because it is a major poetical achievement in its own right. Accordingly Oehlenschläger's brilliant and inventive use of mythical characters should be disregarded along with Magnussen's mundane explanations. For reasons unknown the project was abandoned.

The following year, 1824, sees another and related initiative by Grundtvig as an unpublished manuscript reveals—we read of his *Invitation to Subscribe to the History of Scandinavia*. The aim is to produce a popular history, with Scandinavia defined primarily as Denmark and Norway. During the years which Grundtvig spent translating Saxo, Snorri and *Beowulf*, he had gathered a great deal of superfluous but interesting material which could form the basis for a more informal and lightly-urged historical account of times past in Scandinavia.

In a fragment attached to the *Invitation,* Grundtvig sketches the possible contents of such a book. At the beginning there would be a selection of Norse legends, for their existence as much as their contents represents 'irrefutable evidence as to the sort of ideas that our forefathers had a thousand years ago about the Norse past, and as to what in their eyes was Great, Lovable, Notable and Poetical'.

The plan is then changed. Another manuscript bears the title *Chronicle of Scandinavia for Schools*. In a fragmentary chapter Grundtvig defines ancient Scandinavia according first to language (the Danish Tongue), then according to religion, 'the beliefs, condition, and deeds of Scandinavia, before the introduction of Christianity, for in the Christian period a new life was started, where the pagan citizens either had to endure oppression, or to obey, or to resist: they were no longer allowed openly to rule'. However, Grundtvig finds paganism of great interest, since he believed that you are likely to become a Christian similar in kind to the sort of a pagan that you had previously been: 'That is why even a fully developed Christian people, no longer needing to turn to its early paganism either for reasons of scholarship, or as a reminder of the need for discipline and as a warning against error, neverthelesss wants to take paganism into consideration, just as we someday in Eternity will want to see our earthly existence, vividly remembering everything that then surrounded and influenced us, as images and shadows of the Heavenly and Eternal towards which we were striving'. Accordingly only false and foolish Christianity would seek to ban the study of national antiquity, without which our knowledge of the history of man would be only half complete.

In the next chapter the events in the period up to King Gorm the Old are sketched out. Grundtvig maintains that all mythologies, including Scandinavian, presuppose that, as the Bible teaches, man was created in the image of God, since it is impossible to imagine the invisible creator except in our own image. This imposes a particular duty on any scholar: 'Mythology and history depict the same human life—one depicts its spiritual side, the other its physical side; both sides necessarily complementing each other, relating to each other as spirit to body, as thought to action; therefore it is important to find, not the similarities, but the differences, for you have to differentiate between those elements that the peoples in their ancient legends tried to merge.' After a few more brief chapters on early Danish kings the manuscript ends.

GRUNDTVIG'S MYTHOLOGICAL SILVER WEDDING: AN EMANCIPATION

The three summers of 1829–1831 saw Grundtvig in England, his visit funded by the Danish king, studying neglected Anglo-Saxon manuscripts. He found a British publisher for a comprehensive edition of these texts and in the autumn of 1830 sought to attract subscribers via the prospectus to his projected *Bibliotheca Anglo-Saxonica*. Understandably regarding this unexpected Viking literary raid from Denmark as a insult to themselves, British scholars annexed the idea and the project.

Back in Denmark Grundtvig devoted himself instead to work on a new book about Norse myths, some twenty-five years after his first serious attempt in this direction. He viewed the whole period as a happy marriage culminating in a silver wedding, and the end result was his classic study *Norse Mythology* (1832). Though formally described as a second revised edition of the 1808 book, the volume bears very little similarity to its predecessor.

The work's sub-title reveals the novelty of the publication: *Symbolic language historico-poetically explained and enlightened.*[2] After an introduction of more than 100 pages (distilled from 400 pages of assorted manuscript drafts), the myths are discussed in detail and commended for use in ordinary life 'to revive all our knowledge of human nature and to adorn our life', bringing us closer to a final and absolute understanding of our existence.[3]

Grundtvig calls myths the morning dreams of a people, foreshadowing its later historical life. His desire to place the Norse myths against the context of some universal history causes him to change some of his 1808 views. He had earlier sought to dissociate himself from Snorri's *Edda*—it represented only the court of mythology, not the temple itself; now he praises Snorri's Prologue as 'one of the most ingenious essays ever written on myths [...] the historico-poetical consideration of the natural origin of imagery and paganism that must precede any scholarly mythology and poetics'. The reason for Grundtvig's change of attitude must be that Snorri's work actually shows the birth of natural religion amongst a people who had forgotten the name of the true God. Grundtvig undoubtedly sympathises with those pagan forefathers exactly because they were able to deduce a supreme creator from contemplating the creation—St Paul in a well-known statement had warned that the reverse procedure was unchristian (Romans i 18–25).

Another change since 1808 is that Grundtvig has abandoned the notion that there was once a single old wise author who had created Norse mythology; he instead looks for its origin to the visions of scalds and poets, all of whom represented the mind of the people in its purest form. In 1808 he denigrated Greek myths for their obsession with earthly life; he now juxtaposes Greek and Norse mythology as expressions of, respectively, natural and historical life. And though maintaining the great age of *Völuspá*, Grundtvig lauds Snorri's *Edda* for the originality of its mythology and its poetics—such a book, with all its examples drawn

[2]In Danish the word 'Sindbillede' both means 'symbol' and (literally) 'picture of the mind'.

[3]The Danish word 'Forklaring' denotes 'explanation' as well as 'transfiguration.'

from classical texts in the vernacular, is unheard of elsewhere in the Middle Ages.

Grundtvig does censure Snorri for beginning (in the Prologue and *Gylfaginning*) with material of real richness and depth, but ending by offering the reader merely the 'empty transparent shell' represented by the technical, dictionary-like instructions for future mythological poets. Grundtvig concludes, however, that no-one should doubt the possibility of 'a scholarly union between on one hand beauty and clarity that are the crown of poetry, and on the other hand spirit and life that are the main quality, the heart and soul of poetry'.

The 1832 book was followed in 1844 by the publication of a collection of twenty-five lectures, known as *Bragi's Talks*, which offer a comparative study of Greek and Norse mythology. In both, an important change has occurred in Grundtvig's language. If in 1808 he spoke with pathos or scorn about the sources, he now exhibits a capricious, and even downright jocular style. His 1847 volume, *Greek and Norse Mythology for Young Readers*, commissioned for use in schools, speaks in a quieter voice, yet to much the same effect.

ATTEMPTS TO MOBILISE THE ASA GODS

As the Dano-German language conflict in Schleswig-Holstein sharpened in the 1840s, Grundtvig saw the Norse myths and legends as appropriate weapons in the battle between national identities. Here the Danes had something the Germans could not match!

In a public lecture *On the Historical Circumstances of Scandinavia*, delivered on 20 October 1843 Grundtvig laments the lack of 'an historical handbook on the spirit of Scandinavia, which I could assume to be widely known, could borrow from and could refer to'. Certainly the great speech given by Grundtvig at the national rally on the hill of Skamlingsbanken in North Schleswig on 4 July 1844 assumes considerable background knowledge amongst his listeners, filled as it is with mythical and historical characters and references.

Around New Year 1847–1848 Grundtvig planned to publish a new Danish version of the *Prose Edda* to be called *Snorri's Edda For Everyday Use*. He immediately changed the title to *The Edda Book on Norse Imagery*, only to return eventually to the original title. Two almost identical eight-page outlines of the preface are extant. Grundtvig considers Snorri's book to be a free, independent and great *ars poetica* that 'has really contributed more than anyone can calculate to the potential rebirth of the characteristic imagery of Scandinavia, and in the

event of the success of this rebirth will always contribute incalculably to
the further development and final explanation and transfiguration of this
imagery'. *Gylfaginning* in particular ought to be found and studied in all
homes, and with Rasmus Nyerup's 1808 Danish translation soon sold out,
and never reprinted, Grundtvig takes upon himself the role of a literary
servant in order that this text may be set on its feet again and circulate
throughout the country. He promises to be as accurate as the differences
between the Icelandic and Danish languages will allow, and will avoid
wherever possible that kind of evasive linguistic pedantry which stiffens
the style and impedes the reading of the text. In the event, the project
was never finished: Grundtvig stops at chapter five of *Gylfaginning*, with
only ten pages of translation completed.

An introductory poem on the pagan Germanic names of the days of the
week (from Tuesday to Friday) was intended for this Eddic publication.
Instead it appeared in the first number of Grundtvig's new weekly *The
Dane* on 22 March 1848. He regrets that these names now mean nothing
to his contemporaries, and boldly states his belief that an inspired modern
poet could and should unearth the dead corpses of the Asa gods and
restore them to life.

Grundtvig's own Danish version of *The Old Preface of the Edda*,
printed in the same place on 9 June 1849, accompanied by a three-page
introduction, is probably another remnant of the unfinished Snorri project.
In 1831, in one of the numerous rejected drafts for the Introduction to
Norse Mythology (1832), he had included a lengthy quotation from
Snorri's Prologue, remarking that the Icelander's rendering of the Greek
myth of Chronos had caused him to laugh out loud. In 1849 Grundtvig
restates his overall understanding of Norse religion:

> [it] expresses our forefathers' natural concept of the *Divine*, the
> *Human* and the *Troll-like* or *Monstrous*, as these powers clash and
> fight in the course of time. From this we learn that our ancient *pagan*
> forefathers have *cheered up* and *never despaired*, because they felt
> that the Divine and the Human in principle were of one and the same
> kind, so that these forces in the end clearly had *to join hands* and
> destroy everything Monstrous.

Grundtvig goes on to distinguish between paganism and idolatry. Norse
paganism represents the natural way of thinking and the natural imagery
of the Scandinavians, but the idolatrous worship of Odin, Thor and Frey
and their statues instead of worshipping the one and only invisible God
represents an inane distortion of original paganism, comparable to the
distortion of true Christianity in the Catholic cult of saints and images.
Grundtvig continues:

That is why our Norse forefathers, having become familiar with *Christianity* and the *Bible*, felt that the new religion was indeed opposed to any idolatry, yet could very well be consistent with their own pagan ideas of the powers, the fight and the development of life in the course of time, so that Christianity and paganism just like seriousness and joking (according to the adage) always got on well together in Scandinavia.

Snorri's Prologue, derided by scholars for its historical ignorance, is simply 'a natural, beautiful and clever view of the *human* origin and essence of paganism'.

During the Schleswig–Holstein war of 1848–1850, Grundtvig in *The Dane* fought a dogged battle in prose and verse against the German rebels and intruders and not least against manifestations of the German spirit in Denmark, time and again enlisting the support of the Norse myths. He was forced, however, to admit to a lack of popular response. Discussing old and new social groupings in modern Denmark in an article on 17 February 1849, his conclusion momentarily alludes to legends of King Frode's mill grinding out gold, and of Rolf Krage's sowing gold on the Fyrisvold in Sweden. Clearly aware of the futility of his using such imagery, he sighs:

> Well, on this occasion I will not do as I usually do, and round off a clear account with some obscure sentences, even if in my view these sentences distil perfectly everything relating to the people; I realise that in the eyes of most readers such words would merely throw everything back into the darkness which formerly prevailed. Certainly the reason for such a reaction ought to be eliminated, namely the general lack of familiarity with Danish history and the imagery found there.

As late as 7 December 1850, Grundtvig suggests a reprint of his 1832 book, this time with a list of names, even though he realises that very few readers benefit from reading weighty volumes about the Norse gods, and that they would benefit more from being offered brief surveys of mythological topics in individual numbers of his periodical.

Here the programmatic part of Grundtvig's endeavours ended. In 1861 he issued a lightly revised edition of his dramatic *Scenes from the Descent of Heroic Life in Scandinavia*, originally published 1809–1811. In a new preface he notes sadly that the neo-mythological movement initiated by Oehlenschläger and himself had run into the sand—no-one had followed in their wake. Grundtvig's gloomy view has proved largely correct.

NORSE MYTHOLOGY IN GRUNDTVIG'S OWN PRACTICE

Grundtvig in his youth only interpreted and utilised myths in their proper context. The death of the young national hero Peter Willemoes on 22 March 1808 in a naval engagement against a superior British force inspired Grundtvig to a memorial poem published in a journal two months later. He had met Willemoes the previous autumn, but instead of expressing his personal reactions to the loss, he chooses a very formal and dignified format for his tribute. In a vision he sees Odin dispatch a Valkyrie from Valhalla to the human world to bring back a hero, and after a seat is cleared on the bench of honour between Søren Norby and Peder Skram—two Danish naval celebrities from the sixteenth century —the poet understands that the call concerns Willemoes, and he breaks down in tears. As a modernised version of *Hákonarmál*, the Norse poem on the death of King Hakon Adelstein, Grundtvig's text seems overly contrived and is now known only to literary specialists. In contrast, Grundtvig's classical ballad about Willemoes, called *Come Hither, Little Girls!*, and still heard today, is entirely devoid of mythological references.

A striking instance of Grundtvig's free use of Norse myths can be seen in his 1815 re-creation of the *Þrymskviða*, the Eddic poem which tells of the theft of Thor's hammer. In the opening stanza, Grundtvig reminds the reader of his long silence as a mythologist, claiming (perhaps ironically) that he is returning to this material only to entertain and pass the time. His version of the poem is humorous, twice as long as the original, and bears a political message supposedly relating to the reign of the late fourteenth-century Queen Margaret I, but actually dealing with the Danish cession of Norway to Sweden through the peace treaty at Kiel 1814. In the plot Denmark is the goddess Freya, Norway is Thor, whose hammer represents the union between the two countries, whilst Sweden is the thievish giant Thrym. In this allegory the *Edda* is certainly no longer seen in its own true light. As a further novelty Grundtvig places the poem within a framework of learned annotation, including quotes from a rustic (pseudo-)annotator, a trick perhaps inspired by Holberg's satirical epic *Peder Paars* (1719–1720). This technique allows for a treatment which is simultaneously serious and comic.

Another way of utilising myths can be seen in an 1815–1816 debate with Jens Baggesen on the philosophy of life and poetics, conducted in rhymed epistles and termed *The Valhalla Game*. The point of departure is the myth of Suttung's mead and the birth of poetry, and the combatants become so involved in mythological imagery that they can hardly understand each other; the readers, of course, would understand even less.

A copy of a contemporary handwritten explanation from Grundtvig sent to a bewildered friend demonstrates his new and arbitrary use of Norse myths detached from any original context.

A third use to which myths could be put can be exemplified in the poem *Echo of the Bjarkamál* (*The Sun has Risen*). In an aesthetically perfect form, Grundtvig re-creates the Norse *Bjarkamál* as a morning song, following Snorri in *Heimskringla*, and as opposed to the night scene in Saxo's chronicle. The poem tells of the fall of the king, the loyal struggle of faithful housecarls down to their very last breath, and the revenge of the king; it was published in Grundtvig's periodical *The Danne-Virke* (1817). The manuscript however bears the astonishing title: *Echo of the Bjarkamál in Memory of Martin Luther*. Though the text contains absolutely no Christian references, Grundtvig seems to have felt that it could have a spiritual function—its predominantly heroic mood could perhaps help to energise the drowsy Danish Lutheran church in the tricentennial year of the Reformation.

In subsequent years Grundtvig, especially in a series of memorial poems, takes full advantage of his knowledge of Norse mythology. The prefect of Sorø county, Count Danneskjold, is remembered in 1823 as a Forsete [Forseti] (the son of Balder and a conciliation agent of the Asa gods); Grundtvig's early friend Povel Dons in 1843 as a Skirner [Skírnir] (the unselfish servant of the god Frey); the sculptor Bertel Thorvaldsen in 1844 as a fair elf and a king of the dwarfs (the best artisans in the myths); and Grundtvig's cousin, the philosopher Henrich Steffens in 1845 as a combination of Heimdall (the watchman of the gods) and an Easter angel. In a tribute to Thorvaldsen in 1838 the artist becomes Vaulunder [Völundr] the smith, who retrieved Thor's stolen hammer—in spite of no ancient sources ever combining *Völundarkviða* and *Þrymskviða*. In an unedited poem from 1864 on the cremation of the slain god Balder, Grundtvig in fact offers an answer to the most enigmatic question in all Norse mythology, namely what was it that Odin whispered in the ear of his dead son—naturally, the answer proves to be the Christian greeting 'Come back again!'

Many more instances of Grundtvig's free interpretation of myths could be listed. The guiding principle behind them is given in his 1832 handbook: 'remember that *to us* it matters little or not at all what the creator of the myth once felt, as long as what we see in the myth is worth preserving and *comfortably* fits it'. Such a philosophy must, of course, result in a strong element of subjectivity, as witnessed in several extreme cases from Grundtvig's own work.

It may be sensible enough in 1832 for him to conceive of the well of Mimer [Mímir] as the deep fountain of enthusiasm and the running stream of 'living', that is spoken, words. More strange seems his 1844 reading of the myth about Tyr's right hand lost in the jaws of the Fenris wolf as a coded reference to Cimbrian immigration to the Roman empire and the ensuing absorption of the intruders. In the same myth, even more far-fetched, the rope chaining the wolf, made from the hairs of women's beards, the noise of sneaking cats, the breath of fish and other non-existent elements, is compared to the Franks establishing the river Rhine as the frontier between themselves and the Roman Empire.

In his 1847 book Grundtvig suggests that the relation between the Asa gods and the giants mirrors:

> the academic and philosophical relationship between *history* and *physics* which may be found to be rather conflicting in everyday life, but only becomes irreconcilable, when history abandons its reliance on spiritual values and like a ghost endeavours to scare people to death, or when physics insists on palpable things as the only reality and with heartless conceit strives to disturb the historical realm of spirit in human life, denouncing it as sheer buffoonery and illusion.

In the same work Grundtvig suggests that Thor's fishing expedition to catch the Midgard serpent depicts 'the relationship of the Scandinavians to *the Pope* with his *fisherman's ring*', an interpretation supported by the object of the quarrel, the brewing kettle which Thor wishes to borrow, 'for the issue actually concerns a vessel (a real form) that can hold everything which is genuinely spiritual'. Grundtvig's points are rather better understood from his straightforward explanations than in their mythological disguises. Small wonder that such use of Norse imagery did not catch on!

THE RECEPTION OF GRUNDTVIG'S FREE INTERPRETATIONS

Having wisely obtained the author's approval, Grundtvig's admirer Christian Flor wrote and had printed in 1839 a thorough and sympathetic review of the 1832 handbook in the periodical *Brage and Idun*; it was subsequently issued as a book in its own right in 1865. But though Grundtvig on 21 May 1839 at a meeting of his newly opened discussion club *The Danish Society* promised to put the ancient Asa gods to work at the weekly evening sessions, his intention was never put into practice. His audience of young students and lower middle-class artisans took no interest in Norse mythology. A year later on 17 March 1840, Grundtvig admitted his defeat: his reflections upon Norse myths clearly 'appealed only to a very few'. Of the hundred and more extant texts of introductory talks which Grundtvig gave at sessions of The Danish Society held during 1839–1844 and 1848–1849, only ten are concerned with Norse myths and legends, and some of those are very short and fragmentary.

Grundtvig's mythological ambitions suffered a clear defeat in the public debate about the erection of a monument to commemorate the Danish victory in the Battle of Fredericia on 6 July 1849. A competition had been arranged between two leading sculptors, H.W. Bissen and A. Jerichau. Bissen presented a statue of a brave private soldier, whilst Jerichau offered a statue of Thor. Grundtvig addressed the issue in *The Dane* on 18 May 1850. He favours Thor, for in the case of an anonymous private soldier, what is a father to answer when, in the years ahead, his little son asks about the identity and achievements of such an unreal figure. In principle Grundtvig warns against making 'the transient present a standard for the future'. Moreover, instead of Thor he would rather have chosen the rendition of Uffe the Meek (a legendary prince in Saxo) of which, rumour had it, rough clay models by Bissen existed. The rumours were indeed true, but a ballot among Copenhagen subscribers to the monument resulted in 73 votes for the soldier and only 19 for Thor. Thus was the matter settled, and the statue was unveiled in 1858. It seems strange that Grundtvig, normally so much at ease with richly symbolic meanings, was unable or unwilling to grasp the emblematic significance of the contemporary soldier figure.

Even more miscalculated is Grundtvig's suggestion in the same article that the highly popular marching song *As I Left to Go to War* ought to be replaced as a representative expression of the wartime mood by a modern Norse mythological epic written by a then contemporary living 'scald': 'a beautiful Thor's Drapa, where the fight against Hrungnir the giant has been applied in a clever way to the Battle of Fredericia and to the whole war!' No such epic was ever written, and though both the nineteenth-century Dano-German wars in Schleswig-Holstein produced a good many occasional poems and songs, no contemporary poet effectively mobilised the ancient national gods.

If Grundtvig's efforts to create a national imagery out of Norse mythology petered out in the 1850s, without direct comment from him, he himself could not make do without the myths. He continued to promote them—in speeches at folk high schools, in private conventions and study circles as well as at public rallies. As a poet he employed them to the very day of his death—if not in printed works, then in unpublished manuscripts. It was a never-ending love affair.

Large, carefully preserved manuscripts such as the epic poems *Danish Raven-Spell* (1860), *Hávamál* (1866), and *Rhyming Chronicle of Scandinavia* (1867), are more mythological in title than in content, but during 1864, that fateful and fatal year of war, Grundtvig did actually re-create *The Myths of Scandinavia* in a 128 page version, though this was

not printed until 1930. The loss of the war inspired Grundtvig in 1865 to
work on a book which took the form of a long consolatory letter to the
Danish people. Outlines, drafts and preliminary paragraphs to the tune of
several hundred pages were written and then abandoned at various stages
of completion. It seems to be Grundtvig's general point that Denmark
must wait and weep for the Prussian-occupied province of Schleswig, just
as the goddess Freya (in *Hyndluljóð*) wept tears of gold for her vanished
husband Ottar. If the Danes were to do this, then they, like the widow of
Nain believing in Christ (St Luke vii 11–17), would retrieve their lost
son. Grundtvig seems to have taken little interest in having any of this
material printed. Was it that he himself regarded his use of Norse
imagery in such contexts as outdated?

WHY DID GRUNDTVIG'S EXPERIMENT FAIL?

The development and nature of Grundtvig's view of mythology can be
reconstructed from his manuscripts and printed works. To explain the
failure of his project to popularise it is a more complicated matter. A
tentative series of reasons can be offered.

Firstly, the aesthetic changes which had enveloped Europe since the
middle of the eighteenth century had run their course. It was no longer
fashionable for poets to adhere to any single standardised imagery. Odd
as the expectation of any such adherence may now seem, the fact is that
until around 1800 European culture had long relied on just two or three
networks of generally used and accepted images: the myths, legends,
histories and poetry of classical Greece and Rome; the bestiaries and
other scientific writings of late Roman Antiquity and the Middle Ages;
and the Bible, legendaries and related books of Christianity. That these
familiar stocks of widely acknowledged imagery, accompanied by fixed
ideas about genres, could not and would not make way for some new
common language based on symbols was not yet apparent. Artists of the
nineteenth century sought to convey personal ideas and emotions in
unique forms—it was a process which would be accomplished precisely
by breaking away from collective literary values and tastes. Originality
became the watchword, and during the course of Grundtvig's life it
graduated into an aesthetic norm which through radical individualism
invalidated all norms. In its presupposing a *common* acceptance of a
poetical imagery instituted by external measures, the Copenhagen
University essay prize question of 1800 was already hopelessly mis-
formulated.

In the second place, Grundtvig's characteristic idea of Norse mythology as a symbolic language elucidating Universal History implied 'that

the *events*—fights and great deeds of daring-do—are *the main thing*, whilst the characters are mostly only tools, figures of secondary importance, which is why they cannot be independent, harmonious and distinct in the way that the Greek gods can be; they rather live together in a wondrous manner and are always unstable, so that, according to circumstances, they change their looks and develop qualities which one would never have expected in them' (1847). This is the rationale behind the lack of refinement, polish and clarity in Grundtvig's Norse mythological characters. Their erratic and flickering appearance is intentional. This situation may be advantageous for the interpreter of myths and his successors teaching at the folk high schools, but it certainly reduces their potential popular appeal by eliminating spontaneous recognition. What Neptune with his trident at the top of Adrian de Fries' 1622 water fountain at Frederiksborg Castle represents will be clear to even the meanest uneducated peasant crossing the courtyard, whereas it requires informed reflection to guess the meaning of Freya's golden tears.

In addition, after 1815 Grundtvig for the most part shows a preference for the less-familiar gods—or rather goddesses: Freya, Gersemi (her daughter), Idunna. Among the male characters, instead of using the all-wise Odin and all-powerful Thor, he concentrates rather on reluctant, but honest and (in the end) energetic men such as Prince Hamlet, Folke the warrior, Uffe the Meek, King Skjold as a baby on the sheaf, King Frode the Peaceful and the inactive dead god Balder. Grundtvig's own (lengthy) poetical attempts to illustrate current issues through Norse mythology almost invariably founder—they were read by virtually nobody at the time, and have been read by few people since: *New Year's Morn* (1824), *The Spirit in Scandinavia* and *The Gold of Scandinavia*, both from 1834, and *The Life of Poets in Denmark (A Taste)* from 1851. Those ballads and national songs by Grundtvig which have retained their popularity into the twentieth century include none of the texts loaded with Norse mythological characters and references.

Thirdly, from a scholarly viewpoint, Grundtvig's fifth-century dating for *Völuspá* was shown to be hopelessly wide of the mark by philological research: a late Viking-period date became favoured. The Norwegian Sophus Bugge completed the demolition work during the period 1881-1896, but the kind of early dating favoured by Grundtvig had already been challenged by the critic and theologian Jens Møller as early as 1808. Acceptance of the new dating destroys, or at least considerably weakens, Grundtvig's thesis about pre-Christian monotheism in Scandinavia. Grundtvig himself never abandoned the early dating: in 1832 and again in 1844 he elaborates upon it, claiming *Völuspá* to be the oldest of all Eddic poems, composed by some Norse Homer, presumably among the Anglians in the period after their emigration to England.

Fourthly, interpreting pagan myths in a modern religious (that is Christian) and social context was simply too daring for its time. It was certainly possible to read the myths as disguised history (Suhm) or disguised science (Finn Magnussen); but they could not be accepted as a national Old Testament. Grundtvig's repeated assurances that he did not wish to reinstate the pagan gods and their cult demonstrate eloquently his fear of being misunderstood in a nineteenth-century society much more suffused by conventional Christian attitudes than ours today.

Fifthly, the great 'enemy', Classical mythology, still retained its strong position in the grammar schools and at the university in Copenhagen, and, since nearly all nineteenth-century Danish writers were academics, in literature as well. In daily life the Copenhageners saw the influence of Classical Greece and Rome in the architecture of the capital, not least in the buildings restored after the conflagrations of 1794–1795 and the bombardment of 1807. The Cathedral church of our Lady (1811–1829), the University (1831–1836), the City Hall (1803–1815) and numerous private houses bore the mark of Neo-Classicism. In everyday conversation and writing Greek and Roman myths could be used without difficulty by good Christians, because they represented no threat to Christian belief: they had become objects of aesthetic interest and pleasure. The modern Copenhagen temples of art, Thorvaldsen's Museum (1839–1848) as well as the Glyptotek (1892–1897, expanded 1901–1906), were predominantly devoted to images of Greece and Rome. Moreover, it cannot have helped the afterlife of Norse myths that the cherished sculptor Bertel Thorvaldsen avoided them throughout his life.

Again, unlike the situation in Greece and Rome few if any original pagan artifacts have been found in Scandinavia, and certainly none that would appeal to contemporary taste. Goethe in his 1813 autobiography sees Norse myths as 'nebulous images, nothing but empty sounds'. They were simply not the stuff of which cultured people's dreams were made in the nineteenth century. The sculptor H.E. Freund produced a fine Loke [Loki] statuette (1822) and an ambitious Ragnarök frieze (1823–1841; it was almost entirely lost in the 1884 fire at Christiansborg Castle); and in the 1840s Professor N.L. Høyen at the Royal Academy of Fine Arts commended the artistic use of Norse themes. No obvious masterpieces emerged, however. The best examples of a pictorial re-creation of the Norse pantheon are the large cardboard wall decorations created by J.Th. Lundbye, P.C. Skovgaard and L. Frölich for the Celebration of Scandinavia in Copenhagen on 13 January 1845. The original distemper versions have not survived, but they were recreated by the artists in the same year in a beautiful picture-book (reissued in 1945). None of the ten portraits of gods, however, has found a place in the Danish popular imagination to match that enjoyed by the brave private soldier, the little hornblower, or the huge Isted Lion, a statue from 1862. After 1864 goddesses and Valkyries were replaced by anonymous fair-haired young women as national symbols for either the defeated Denmark or the lost province of Schleswig.

Sixthly, after the defeat of 1864, marked by the non-arrival of the much-needed and expected military support from Swedo-Norwegian forces, the lofty idealism of the Scandinavistic movement vanished for many years to come, dragging the Norse myths down with it.

Lastly, the development of Danish literature in the nineteenth century ran counter to the potential use of Norse myths. In the first decade of the century, the royal or aristocratic heroes of antiquity had been favoured by poets. After the final fall of Napoleon and the decline of Denmark in the wake of the dissolution of his empire, heroism was simply no longer in fashion. By the 1820s a vivid sense of the present, of the simple pleasures of everyday life, and of the common people found its place and voice in literature. Politically oriented newspapers and periodicals emerged, and, as if in anticipation of the democratic structures formally granted in 1848–1849, works of fiction increasingly tended to deal with students, members of the upper middle class and (in the war years) peasants. In this new literary environment, there was no place for Grundtvig's *Echo of the Bjarkamál*, nor for Oehlenschläger's history plays.

Grundtvig's best ally would have been Oehlenschläger; but in stressing the exotic sides of paganism in his *Poems* (1802), *Poetical Works* (1805), and *Norse Poems* (1807), Oehlenschläger was really underlining its decline and fall; and in his last major mythological effort, *The Norse Gods* (1819), he shows the extent to which Norse mythology had been exhausted by his own over-ripe imaginative re-creations, which lacked any of Grundtvig's sense that myths could have universal meanings. To Oehlenschläger the myths were part of the past, rather than of the present; they were certainly not the future.

The development of literary taste in the following decades did little to rescue Norse mythology. The programme of realism known as The Modern Break-through, initiated in 1871 by Georg Brandes, was international in its scope and was hostile to Danish provincialism; it addressed modern society and its problems from the viewpoint of highly individualistic characters, exceptions to rather than representatives of any rule.

SCATTERED ADVANCES

Norse mythology did prosper to some extent in the folk high schools, especially at the institutions of Rødding (Christian Flor, 1845–1846), Askov (Ludvig Schröder, 1866–1908) and Rønshoved (Aage Møller, 1921–1941).

Also, in its political opposition to the Conservative government's constitutional abuses in the years 1876–1901, the peasants' party Venstre (liberal left) adopted some of the Norse symbols. They became weapons in domestic politics, conveying the opinions of a particular party and social class. Viewed artistically, they were weapons of an old-fashioned design, characterised by features usually regarded as romantic. It is this which must help to explain why Norse mythology left so few traces on modern literature.

Twentieth-century writers had to go to elaborate lengths to recycle Norse mythology. Johs. V. Jensen, who won the Nobel Prize for literature in 1944, comments upon the situation after completing his ambitious six volume novel *The Long Journey* (1908–1922; revised version, 2 vols., 1938; English translation, 1922–1924). In this work Jensen sought to delineate the cultural progress of mankind but notes that, due to the influence of Wagnerian opera and the vulgarisation of Norse myths in the folk high schools, it was no longer possible seriously to revive a romantic view of native mythology. In the first volume, *The Glacier* (1908), Jensen renews the myths by describing not Vikings, but Ice-Age people; not Odin, but the one-eyed Dreng (Danish for Boy), who fetches and tames fire; not Thor, but the mighty Hvidbjørn (White Bear), who invents the wheel, the carriage, the sea-going ship and initiates raids against neighbouring tribes.

In 1952 the novelist Martin A. Hansen in his detailed treatment of the abolition of paganism, *Serpent and Bull*, turns the unknown originator of *Völuspá* as well as its protagonist Odin into ancient forerunners of the group of modern Christian existentialists who were published in the Danish post-war periodical *Heretica* (1948–1953): they have all experienced and been victims of a universal breakdown of values. Twenty years later, the left-wing writer Ebbe Kløvedal Reich, first in *Frederik* (1972) his best-selling novel about Grundtvig, and later in his half-socialist, half-Grundtvigian novel *Cattle and Kinsman* (1977), invokes the Norse gods in a campaign to resist the EEC. He developed this strategy in a later series of poetico-historical essays and stories.

Finally the modernist writer and cultural radical Villy Sørensen in his book *Ragnarok* (1982; published in English translation as *The Downfall of the Gods*, 1989) turns all traditional concepts upside down by seeing the giants as a peaceful, but rough-hewn native population of a developing country, being persecuted by Odin the perverted politician and Thor the warmonger. Wisdom has become trickery, strength stupidity. Sørensen's heroes, Loke the peacemaker and Freya the love goddess, are unable to prevent the coming of Ragnarök—and there is no recreation of the world to look forward to afterwards. The book represents an artful demythologising of traditional understandings of Norse mythology, for which Sørensen was to earn a fusillade of protests from folk high school teachers.

IRONIC POSTSCRIPT

One phrase from Grundtvig's mythological writings has achieved widespread currency: 'Freedom for Loke as well as for Thor'. When quoted in speeches or editorials it is usually taken to mean that good and evil ought to have an equal chance in life's great struggle; the phrase thus serves as a catchily proverbious (if not quite proverbial) expression of tolerance and broad-mindedness.

The expression derives in fact from the verse dedication to Grundtvig's 1832 mythology, *Rhymed Epistle to Scandinavian Kinsmen*, where its context reveals that it ought to be understood quite differently from its use by editors and speech-makers. Grundtvig may have been a Manchester liberal who favoured free markets and fair competition, but as a Christian he would never have dreamt of granting a level playing field to Evil, the Devil, or Death.

Loke in the sources is half Asa god, half giant. Admittedly he fathers three monsters (the Midgard Serpent, the Fenris Wolf, and Hel), but at the same time he is Odin's foster-brother. He is tolerated in both camps and tries to take advantage of the fact. One of his principal functions is, by his very presence, to keep the gods on their toes, and constantly to incite them to fight the giants. But the giants themselves, according both to the sources and to Grundtvig, are relentless and single-minded in character and behaviour. They are the permanent opponents of men and gods, representing facets of Evil such as materialistic greed and haughty wilfulness. They are driven by destructive powers comparable to fire, water, pestilence and hunger, and are possessed by the kind of ferocious predatory instinct found in wolves and bears. They represent a sinister union of spiritual aridity and heartlessness.

Though Grundtvig's view of Loke is by no means favourable, he cannot and does not conceive of him in such unvaryingly negative terms. A brief survey of some of Grundtvig's Loke interpretations reveals a

more subtle picture. In a manuscript from 1823, Loke is tentatively
understood as signifying fork-tongued reason and wily worldly knowledge; and also as a personification of conceit forever halting between
gods and the giants, forever ridiculing everything except himself—an
attitude in itself requiring a good deal of spirit.

Grundtvig's 1832 book suggests that by binding Loke, you also bind
your own spiritual hands. In 1844 the same thought emerges: the gods
can never do without Loke—he shares all their great events as '*the soul
of the present moment* or in the present *time*'. The gods 'blindly tied their
own hands taking revenge upon *Loke*', thus entering a second childhood.
Men in effect do the same, when they strive 'to abolish the fickleness of
time and to chain *the present moment* to their own petrified thoughts,
dogmatic systems and institutions, as *Loke* was chained to flat stones.'
Loke is 'the mouthpiece of freedom of speech in the present moment',
demonstrating that you cannot prevent its abuse without also compromis-
ing its normal and proper use.

A victim of absolutist censorship himself during the period 1826–1837,
Grundtvig in his career as a parliamentarian laid great emphasis on print
freedom. In an 1850 campaign for the legal protection of freedom of
speech and printing in Denmark, he refers to the contending parties of
Norse mythology:

> We see that they all, even *Loke* the trickster, were granted *free
> speech*, so that *the words* were as free as *the bird on its wings*, and
> even *the foes* of the gods, *the giants*, could *freely speak* as they
> wanted, unless they, like the giant *Vafthrudnir*, challenged *Odin* to a
> *quiz*, risking their *necks*.

Significantly, Grundtvig (in 1844) casually nominates the philosopher
Henrich Steffens as a Loke, and a little later identifies his faded fellow
poet Jens Baggesen by his 'Loke smile'. All his life Grundtvig held
Steffens in high esteem as a symbol of the intellectual awakening in the
early years of the nineteenth century, whilst he portrayed Baggesen (in
1818) as a man with the eyes of a soaring falcon, able to discern and
innocently to enjoy the spiritual in life's fleeting moments. Both had
earned an unenviable reputation as trouble-makers, but to Grundtvig they
represented a welcome source of irritation, serving to arouse the
slumbering people. Grundtvig intends no harm by these characterisations.
He means what he says; the figure of Loke is always needed.

These quotations should suffice to show that for Grundtvig Loke does
not signify Evil, but rather an amalgam of those qualities possessed by
human beings who find themselves torn between the Divine and the
Daemonic. Teasing wit and intelligence—often termed reason by
Grundtvig—is a sign of spirit, if not yet of faith.

How ironical—and sad—it is that the only surviving phrase from Grundtvig's attempted revival of Norse mythology is invariably used incorrectly. Even in this respect his bold experiement to create a national mythological imagery can be seen all too clearly to have failed.

BIBLIOGRAPHY

MANUSCRIPTS

Manuscripts from the Grundtvig Archive, The Royal Library, Copenhagen, transcribed and translated by the author. Unfortunately, of the relevant printed Grundtvig texts, none is available in English translation; accordingly, citations from these sources have also been translated by the author.

PUBLISHED SOURCES

Lundgreen-Nielsen, Flemming. 1980, 1981. '"Rød og hvid i Billedsalen": Grundtvigs døds- og mindedigte, I–II', in *Grundtvig-Studier* 1980, 23–60; 1981, 47–83.

———. 1982. 'N.F.S. Grundtvigs Auffassung der nordischen Mythen in seiner Forschung und Dichtung', in *Dänische 'Guldalder'-Literatur und Goethezeit*, Text & Kontext, Sonderreihe, Band 14, pp. 160–191. Kopenhagen and München.

Lönnroth, Lars. 1979. *'Frihed for Loke såvel som for Thor'. Den nordiska mythologin som politiskt redskap i grundtvigiansk bonde- och folkhögskole-miljö.* Aalborg.

———. 1988. 'The Academy of Odin: Grundtvig's political instrumentalization of Old Norse mythology', in Gerd Wolfgang Weber, ed., *Idee, Gestalt, Geschichte: Festschrift Klaus von See*, pp. 339–354.

Thyssen, Anders Pontoppidan and Chr. Thodberg, eds. 1983. *N.F.S. Grundtvig: Tradition and Renewal.* Copenhagen.

Toldberg, Helge. 1950. *Grundtvigs symbolverden.* Copenhagen.

Ægidius, Jens Peter. 1985. *Bragesnak. Nordiske myter og mytefortælling i dansk tradition (indtil 1910).* Odense.

———. 1992. *Bragesnak 2. Den mytologiske tradition i dansk folkeoplysning i det tyvende århundrede (1910–1985).* Odense.

4

Vikings, Sagas and Wasa Bread

RÉGIS BOYER

There is no doubt that France was amongst the main European victims of Viking activity in the period from the ninth to the eleventh centuries. Yet we should remember that the unfavourable picture of 'the proud children of the North' to be found in most medieval chronicles, 'histories' and poems is largely the creation of monastic scholars—clerics, monks, abbots; that is, the work of the very people who had been most vulnerable to sudden attack from Scandinavia and thus most hostile to the Viking raiders. As is well known, Viking tactics favoured not so much attacks on armies well able to defend themselves, but rather surprise assaults on undefended locations such as monasteries, abbeys, churches and small towns. It is therefore inevitable that the annals and chronicles written in such institutions are virtually unanimous in depicting these Northern foes, pitiless and cruel as they undoubtedly were, as a wholly evil and irresistible force. So it was that, from the outset, Vikings came to represent the very embodiment of Barbary itself—warriors who were bloodthirsty, unappeasable, and invincible. Without the moderating witness of secular historical sources and records, a more balanced picture of the Vikings and their raids took a long time to emerge (Boyer 1986). It was not until the end of the nineteenth century that more objective and better-informed studies[1] sought to create a more rounded image of the Viking phenomenon in all its forms and features—sagas, runes, mythology, valkyries and the rest. Moreover, even at this late date, the immense popularity in France of Wagner's operatic works ensured that the clear waters of historical truth about Viking life and times were not infrequently muddied!

The myth of the North in France remains to this day a popular and powerful one—it deserves a fuller study than I shall attempt in this essay. The myth has been sustained by the fact that the French have never tried to clarify what *is* the North and what is *not*. We have been content to regard that region as the true home of the mysterious and the otherworldly. We may recall that for the Greeks Hyperborea was the fabulous

[1]As, for instance, today in the works of Lucien Musset.

location for all the possible wonders of the world; and that when Jason set out to look for the Golden Fleece, he headed North—as did Pytheas when searching for Ultima Thule. So, too, in France, at the beginning of the nineteenth century, the claim could be made that 'the North has been a country of marvels for all peoples' (Gråberg di Hemsö 1822). Or, in the words of another traveller a hundred years later, 'we have become used to seeing the Norwegian [he could well have said the Scandinavian] soul through a uniformly thick fog' (Condroyer 1929).

This present essay seeks to trace the development over several centuries in France of the image of the Vikings and of those sagas which tell of their deeds. It is not difficult to summarise the picture of the Vikings which emerges during the lengthy period from the ninth to the eighteenth centuries: 'A furore Normannorum, libera nos Domine' [from the wrath of the Norsemen, deliver us, O Lord]. This was a common prayer in French churches in the Middle Ages. Abbon de Fleury, Benoît, Wace, Guillaume de Jumièges, Ordericus Vitalis, amongst others, are of one voice in their characterisation of the Northern predators—terrifying figures, with huge armies, spreading fire and fear wherever they go. This image was little changed by 1851, when Professor Eichhoff writes: 'Scandinavia, bloody field of Óðinn, suddenly took formidable sway and poured over the rest of Europe its swarms of devastating warriors. Those homeless chieftains, driven over the stormy waves, launched at random by the winds, rushed onwards—like birds of prey or like the wolves whose names they adopted—on defenceless coasts where they exerted their rapaciousness' (Eichhoff 1851, 149). The Vikings were wild ('cruenti', says Abbon), a view echoed in at least one history textbook still in use today in French elementary schools for children aged nine to twelve years old: 'they slaughtered everybody. After their passage, you could walk for hours without seeing the smoke from a chimney, without hearing the barking of a dog.'[2] Dudon de Saint-Quentin (*Chronique de Normandie*) and Denis Piramus (*La Vie Saint Edmund le Rei*) were particularly responsible for the legends associated in nineteenth-century minds with the formidable figure of Robert le Diable, believed by many to have been the first Norman duke. The reputation of Vikings for cruelty, notably their legendary taste for the fresh blood of their recently-slain foes, also found plenty of nineteenth-century scholarly support; whilst, as late as 1835, we find an historian of some repute claiming that the principal form of Viking entertainment involved the seizure of infants from their distraught mothers prior to impaling them 'on the points of spears' (Liquet 1835).

[2]Chaulaunges, F. and S. 1967. Quotation from Guillaume de Jumièges.

When writers turned from the gory narrative detail of Viking depravity to moral or theological analysis, explanations tended to be brief and bleak: the Vikings were 'des paiens maudits' [damned pagans], Satan's faithful servants; they had been visited upon France as a divine punishment for the sins of her countrymen. As with Attila several centuries earlier, the Vikings were 'le fléau de Dieu' [the flail of God], fulfilling remorselessly a divinely-willed punitive mission.

One man and the myths attaching to him came to represent the perfect distillation of a whole complex of ideas, images and feelings associated with the Vikings. Ragnarr loðbrók, who is supposed to have besieged Paris towards the middle of the ninth century, was seen as the embodiment of all the features which medieval writers associated with the term 'Norman'—cowardice, cruelty, theft, murder, rape, pyromania. It hardly needs saying that such images were unsupported by historical evidence. When it comes to representations of the Vikings, we are dealing not with the forensic truths of history but with the mists of mystery and myth. Yet, however unhistorical, these images of Viking murder, rape and pillage have achieved a sturdy life of their own, quite independent of authenticating sources. This stubbornly persistent independent life shows no sign of losing its potency in the late twentieth century, as many a contemporary cartoon confirms.

It was during the eighteenth century, though, that the pugnacious and predatory image of the Viking developed a new and surprising feature. Montesquieu's theories about the relationship of climate to character had become well known:[3] it was the bracing cold of northern Europe which had generated the greater energy exhibited by northern people, whose nerve and sinew, accordingly, far surpassed that to be found amongst the rest of (southern) mankind. Such views, reminiscent of passages in Tacitus's *Germania*—the stigmatisation of the quiescent South by praise of the vigorous North—could have fateful implications, as Europe was to learn towards the middle of the present century. Montesquieu was to find a faithful (not to say dangerous) disciple in Paul-Henri Mallet who, knowledgeable about Denmark, was the first writer to produce a good French translation of the *Poetic Edda* (Mallet 1756), a work which he attributed, with some indifference, to either the Scandinavians or the Celts; and a wide ranging *Introduction à l'histoire de Dannemarc* (1755). Both Mallet's works served to revive interest in medieval ideas about the North and to lend such views a new prestige. Madame de Stael (1810) and other pre-Romantic writers offered sympathetic encouragement to those who sought to 'prove' the superiority of the North in all fields of

---

[3]As expressed in *De l'Esprit des Lois*, XIV 2.

human endeavour, the Viking phenomenon being only one element in a more general theory best summed up in another Latin formula, 'ex Septentrio lux' [out of the North, light]. Such writers found effective support in the work of Jordanes, who, we recall, identifies Scandinavia as the 'vagina nationum', the 'officina gentium' [The source of all (European) nations]. One notes, perhaps with some surprise, that Chateaubriand was amongst those who sought to confirm this opinion in his work *Etudes historiques*. It was not an exclusively French notion, however, with the Swedish scholar Olaus Rudbeck one of many to hold similar views, in the period after Olaus Magnus.

Thus, during the eighteenth century, the figure of the cruel Viking underwent fundamental modification. He developed into an exemplary figure of strength and energy, who, it was believed, had arrived on the scene in the nick of time to perform his crucial historical task—the regeneration of the Occident. This was, moreover, the same period during which the Ossianic poems of the Scot James Macpherson became so immensely popular and fashionable throughout Europe. Ossianic writings were seen to represent a barbarian poetry, albeit somewhat softened by sentiment, which could serve to regenerate contemporary poetry and poets. In these conditions, with Ossianic poems of Celtic origin telling of predatory Vikings and Fenian heroes, it is not difficult to see how the (then common) confusion between Celtic and Germanic-Scandinavian cultures arose. Such confusion notwithstanding, the strange but powerful poetry represented by the Old Norse *Edda* (through Mallet's translation) came to be regarded by many an eighteenth-century French reader as the fruit of Viking genius: in its own way the exemplary verse of an exemplary culture.

Onto this unfamiliar idea of the admirably energetic Viking, the eighteenth century grafted the even more surprising notion of the chivalrous Viking; the idea of the North as the source of medieval European chivalry. Several writers, most of them long forgotten nowadays, sought to trace the introduction of chivalry into Europe back to the Normans, citing as evidence the elaborate rituals of the old Viking *hólmganga*, and the fateful figures of the Norse valkyries. Distinguished historians such as H. Prentout were led to assert that 'it is in Normandy that the chivalrous spirit of the French Middle Ages, indeed of the Middle Ages in general, first blossomed' (Prentout 1911, 191). This proposition accorded well with another of Montesquieu's theories: unlike the languid peoples of the sultry South, the bold 'barbarians' from the icy North could claim to be 'pure'. Thus the wrathful Viking raider was not just the vengeful arm of a righteous God; nor merely an energising power—he was also to be regarded as a purifying social force. As late as 1918, we find the historian J. Revel claiming that, through Viking visitations, 'Scandinavia was, in fact, to bring not devastation but renovation' to the rest of Northern Europe. Rousseau's notion of the noble savage had also, in its time, offered important support for this idea. The North was the seat of virtue—and it was no accident that its vigorous warriors had chosen to attack or invade at precisely the moment when the South was drifting lethargically into vice and Satanism. Mallet had no doubt that the Vikings 'had been sent by Providence', whilst Chateaubriand speaks unhesitatingly of a 'miraculous instinct' that guided the conquerors: 'they fulfilled a mission which they could not explain to themselves'. In 1844 J. Janin, another historian of some repute and reliability, asserts that raids from the North brought 'energy and liberty' in their wake.

So we survey the image of the Viking which had emerged by the end of the eighteenth century: as a warrior he was chivalrous, strong, pure, virtuous, sent by Providence to invigorate the exhausted lands of the Roman Empire. It is in just this way that Mallet depicts Ragnarr loðbrók in his translation of *Krákumál*; he draws particular attention to passages where the snake-pit hero exhibits his most noble traits—love for his wife and children, courage, strength of mind and body. With this treatment of Ragnarr, we are much closer to the spirit of the Arthurian Round Table or to the Amadis des Gaules than to the 'poèmes barbares'.

As we turn to Romanticism's response to the Vikings, a line by Baudelaire marks the transition conveniently: 'Homme libre, toujours tu chériras la mer' [Free man, you always cherish the sea]. Two related images define the new face of the old myth: liberty and the sea, the latter symbolising the potential in human life for adventure, for remarkable discoveries and, not least, for growth and change. It is clear that the Swedish writers Geijer and Tegnér played a major part in developing these fresh aspects of the Viking image—works by both men were translated into French, around 1840, by Xavier Marmier.[4] There are perhaps four features of the French Romantic idea of the Viking on which I would wish to comment: the symbolism of adventure, virtuous violence, the valkyrie, and the (now fraught) notion of the *übermensch*.

First, we should note that the roaming Viking represents not only the fact of actual adventure in the singular, but also the potential for all possible adventures in the plural. The historian Janin again makes the point colourfully: 'These iron men came from Denmark, Sweden, Norway, from all the snows, all the tempests. For ten centuries, they lived by the sword [...]. Like all men born for war, you will find these

----

[4]See, in particular, Tegnér's poem 'Vikingen'. Tegnér's *Frithiofs saga* has enjoyed remarkable popularity in France; see Gravier 1943.

rough warriors on all the expeditions and in all the difficult enterprises'
(Janin 1944, 2). French Romantic writers were devoted to images of the
sea, using it to suggest a cluster of related ideas about Viking adventure
and discovery—partly sentimental, partly heroic, mystical, and historical.
So it was—and is—that the French, for long ignorant of most aspects of
Scandinavian and Viking history, were for ever fascinated by the
possibility that the Norse inhabitants of the Greenland settlement had
gone on to discover North America. I have never been able to understand
why this subject has generated such passion amongst my fellow
countrymen, but the fact is that, during the last two centuries, they have
written far more on this subject than on any other aspect of the Vikings.
French romantic writers certainly exploited this theme—O.J. Richard in
1883, for instance: 'Noble Iceland! Be proud when you think of these
kings, these Vikings who everywhere spread your laws: in Asia and even
in Africa! These tenth-century predecessors of Columbus fixed their
glorious flag as soon as they landed in those places which were later to
be named America.' Even Michelet, for the most part rather cautious
when compelled to speak of the Vikings, nevertheless expresses genuine
admiration for their buccaneering nautical prowess.

The second aspect of Romantic responses to the Viking age relates to
heroic violence. Romantic writers chose to view such aggression in a
sufficiently oblique way to enable them to identify virtuous features
amidst the mayhem: the Vikings hated cowardice, and were thus
compelled occasionally to be cruel. Xavier Marmier is clear—for the
Vikings 'every possible cowardice was repellent [...]. Courage is the
supreme virtue; cowardice the most unforgivable vice.' Thus, a warrior
could not be brave, could not steel himself against cowardice, without
being ferocious. These fearless and fearsome Northmen were 'magnificent
rovers [...] saucy brigands who exchanged the wretchedness of a sterile
soil for the vast empire of the waves [...] they were sea-kings.'[5] In the
heroic level of bravery ascribed to the Vikings, we may identify links
with one of the great Romantic ideals, potent ever since the French
Revolution—*la liberté ou la mort* [liberty or death]. This idea, already
discernible in the works of Montesquieu, becomes a constant source of
fascination for Romantic writers. 'The scald sees death, smiles, darts forth
and dies,' says C.V. d'Arlincourt (1818, 126), clearly echoing the heroic
Krákumál boast 'hlæjandi skal ek deyja' [laughing, I shall die]. d'Arlincourt feels it necessary to explain in a footnote the sensibility underpinning his line—a genuine Viking 'had to die laughing and singing, or else
he would die a coward'. Even Victor Hugo, who generally avoids such

[5]See J.D. Scriptor, *Sous l'oeil d'Odin* (1953).

frenzied visions, has his 'reître' (a kind of Viking) say, 'And we will laugh when we die'. All such imagery is perhaps a manifestation of what we might call the literary temptation of Romanticism, and perhaps of our own time as well: writers simply refused (and refuse) to seek out reality, preferring to write from within the highly charged world of their vividly coloured dreams.

This is even more the case if we turn to French literary images of the Viking woman, a figure noticeably absent during the early stages of the development of the Viking myth. We recall the eighteenth-century claim that the North was the home of chivalry; and it is thus hardly surprising that 'warlike virgins' have attracted the attention of our Romantic authors. Truth to tell, such writers do not always know how best to depict or respond to such a figure: inaccessible virgin, wild warrior, dangerous seer, black magician. Some clear attitudes do emerge, however. There are claims, for instance, that Viking respect for women 'had markedly polished the morals of the pirate warriors' (Bonstetten 1826), whilst all writers view the beauty of Viking women in similar terms—'really beautiful with her golden hair, her azure eyes, her bright whiteness and the purity of her complexion,' says Lagrèze (1890, 211). Léouzon-Leduc adds that she 'possesses still heroical strength and admirable wisdom' (Léouzon-Leduc [n.d.], 19). The Romantic valkyries have arrived on the scene; and they belong at the heart of the myth of the Vikings, as Léouzon-Leduc ([n.d.], 7) confirms: 'You cannot ignore it, the whole of Antiquity bears witness to the fact, every virgin of the North has something celestial about her' [Tu ne peux l'ignorer, l'Antiquité l'atteste, / Toute vierge du Nord eut quelque don céleste]. Yet, though such celestial figures stand at the heart of the myth, the theme is too rich to be developed in this short essay.

The final point in this discussion of the Romantic development of the Viking myth, is, in a sense, the most controversial. In the main, the qualities which had intrigued the Romantic sensibility were the extraordinary vitality and individuality of the Viking—whether civilised or barbarian, whether chivalrous or wild. From here, though, it is but a short and fateful step to the idea of the pure German, the *übermensch*, and to the origin of gruesome deviations from the myth. Most of the features already touched on thus far in this essay have highlighted the idea of the Viking as a superior figure. Under the influence of the nationalistic movements in both Germany and Scandinavia, this idea was to develop still further. It seems appropriate to start with the *berserkr* figure, his divine fury proving a source of fascination to many nineteenth-century writers, particularly those with a vivid imagination: the specialist in magic, for instance, who claimed that a berserkr was able to rush into a pit of fire after having swallowed hot coals (Salverte 1829). There is no doubt that the figure of the berserker lived up to the characteristic Romantic idea and ideal of frenzy; not to mention the Romantic fascination with darkness, the occult and the supernatural. It seems astonishing that one of the most distinguished historians of the period (Ozanam 1847) could believe that in Viking life 'the ideal of virtue was this furious raving'. It is easy to glimpse the potential consequences of such a notion: a belief in the proper predominance of strength over justice and the like. There has existed—and there still exists—a sulphurous prestige attaching to the figure of the fair naked brute; and it has required a good deal of *sang froid* to combat such noxious nonsense.

The nineteenth-century French image of the Viking, then, had epic, romantic and chivalric qualities: to which we should add the virtues of the poet. In the words of G. Dozy in 1847, 'It is the Normans who created epic literature, as well as creating the spirit of chivalry and romantic poetry' (Dozy 1845–1847, 14). The Vikings were to be regarded as important poets. Chateaubriand had already claimed as much; for him Ragnarr loðbrók was 'Lodbrog, warrior, scald and pirate'. Much more recently (Valjac 1954) we find the claim that 'Poetry was introduced in Normandy by the berserkers. Such poets or popular singers were simply scalds'. We note the chain of associations: sacred fire, furore, gift of poetry, poetical enthusiasm. This is a far cry from the lumpen Nordic barbarians of the Middle Ages. The Viking has become *the* poet, called variously 'aède', 'trouvère', 'bard'; in this cultivated literary field, as in earlier windswept martial ones, it was still important that he should excel.

But the cult of excellence has its dangers. Gobineau had already pushed the idea of ancestral excellence to its utmost limits. He was obsessed with his own ancestral links with genuine Normans (not, of course, Vikings). Convinced of Norman superiority over lesser races, he asserted: 'But, Roman, Welsh [...] whoever is not born German has been born to be a servant'.[6] This is not the occasion to dwell on the fearful consequences of such theories in our own century. I simply wish to stress that, from Gobineau down to the present day, and at varying levels of intensity, Norman writers have rarely failed to exalt in their Viking ancestry. So, too, with the modern Frenchman-in-the-street; it is the Wagnerian figure of Siegfried-Sigurðr who has come to embody the folk memory of the tall, fair, blue-eyed, ancient Viking figure—no matter whether he be savage or culture-hero. French people, it seems, are in no doubt that, in the words of the elementary school-book mentioned earlier in this essay, Vikings 'were fearless seamen, afraid of nothing, who kept on singing amidst the rising storms.'

---

[6]In 'Manfrédine', a poem written between 1838 and 1849.

We turn, finally, to the contribution of our own century to the development of the Viking image in the French mind; a century in which, we may claim, science, history and philology have all made striking progress. What are the results of such progress for our own sense of the Viking age? Is the Viking myth now dead? Do we at last know the truth about the Vikings in France? The answer, I fear, is still a negative one, although we now have access to a range of excellent modern scholarly works about Viking culture and literature, works either written in or translated into French. It may be, indeed, that we have no wish to be 'correctly informed': such may be the strength of the myth. It certainly seems clear to me that the Frenchman of 1994, whether educated or not, has decided to retain in his mind at least some of the residual features of the Viking myth which developed from Romanticism; and to them he has sought to add at least one new feature. He accepts that Vikings must excel and be superior in something. In order to accord with the values of the late twentieth century, however, this superiority is now seen to reside in the technical skills of the men of the North—whether juridical, military, commercial or technological. In short, Vikings are good at making ships and swords. In this way Viking civilisation retains its sense of supremacy over other cultures: 'these people were really men,' claims A. Manguin,[7] with the reader left to supply appropriate intonation. Their principal excellence is deemed to be their achievements in marine engineering: the great Viking ships. A Viking ship has always been called a *drakkar* in French, for reasons which I have never been able to explain—does it derive from *dreki*, but, if so, how are we to explain the double *k*, not to mention the plural form, and the medial *a*? Whatever its etymology, *drakkar* is a term so famous in France that most of the inhabitants of Normandy, for instance, carry a *drakkar* sign on their cars. Alternatively, let us take the case of scaldic poetry, an art more or less completely unknown in France (Renauld-Krantz 1964; Boyer 1990). Those few enthusiastic amateurs who have some vague knowledge of such verse now make elaborate claims for its religious or magic or otherwise esoteric nature, thus associating it with contemporary interest in the occult.

But it is the modern material culture which shows the most strikingly persistent influence of the Viking image in contemporary society. A widely read recent novel, *La route des cygnes* (1967) by René Hardy, confronts the reader with a striking display of Norse-looking vocabulary—*papars, lùr, knorr, trold, badhstòfa, feund, vardloktur, bärsärk,*

---

[7]Quoted in Chaulanges, F. and S. 1967.

thinglög, wergeld, herse, doegr—lexical items indicative of the author's reading, philological enthusiasms, and mildly surreal imagination. Vocabulary offers rich opportunities for ingenuity and invention. Observe, for instance, M. Gilbert's etymology of the term 'Viking': *vik-*, 'bay'; -*ing*, 'child'; *viking*, 'child of the bay'. Personal names are also a fruitful area—*Alask, Thorum, Friger, Melorka, Eniar;* so are mythological ones—*Mupelstrem, Heimsdale, Duna* (that is, Íðunn), *Fenhir, Jormugand*.

I have referred to the inclination of the modern French reader not to allow the austere truth to interfere with the colourful myth of the Viking. Indeed we may claim that an important function of the Viking figure is to allow us to examine our own literary imagination. French writers and readers have rarely attempted to speak of the Viking; they have always preferred to speak of themselves through images of the Viking. The Viking belongs to the world of our fancy, and, as we now live in an era of advertising, old and fanciful images can sometimes take on new and commercially profitable roles. There is, for instance, a 'Club Scandinave Viking' specialising in body-building, doubtless a recognition of the levels of physical exertion needed to become a worthy companion for Ragnarr loðbrók. We find a Scandinavian warrior—complete with the sadly unavoidable horned helmet—staring out defiantly from his herring tin label at any prospective purchaser; we find Viking, a good quality Camembert cheese, packaged in a container whose label offers us a scene from the Bayeux tapestry. Such basic fish and dairy products may perhaps be attributed to that elemental aspect of the Viking myth associated with 'les rudes pirates du Nord'. But what are we to make of the shop specialising in baby clothes known as 'Le petit viking'; what of the designer blouse (no ironing required) with the designer label 'Viking'; what of the lamp named and shaped after a horned Viking; and what, finally, of 'Croustik', with the word itself created by adding a Scandinavian-looking -*ik* ending, to *croustillant*, 'a crust'. The product declares itself to be 'the golden loaf of the Vikings', specially toasted, wholemeal bread, made by a special Swedish process.

It is perhaps hard to reconcile these (and many other) products with some of the martial images cited earlier in this essay. The Swedish bread is surely no better than its French equivalent; it seems doubtful whether Camembert cheese would have found favour with real Vikings. It is perhaps possible to link *drakkar* and a famous Guy Laroche perfume ('drakkar noir, eau de toilette') with its associations of virile charm; it may just about make sense for a pair of scissors to be called 'le drakkar'; yet I am at a loss to know why a set of four glasses manufactured in Belgium should be called 'drakkar' (associations of strength, resistance to breakage, perhaps).

I have claimed that the figure of the Viking has been a powerful symbol in France, ancient and modern, and have drawn my illustrations for the most part from medieval chronicles and Eddic poems. Similar research might well have been undertaken in relation to Viking images in the Icelandic sagas (Boyer 1989), save for the fact that Icelandic sagas remained more or less totally unknown in France until the middle of the present century. After 1950, the reputation of the sagas began to grow, as the works themselves became more widely available in translation. It is, of course, still the case that there are few people in France who can speak of sagas having actually read one or more of those works in the original language. Sagas texts remain difficult to read, even for 'l'honnête homme'.

It goes without saying that the folkloric aspect of the North also finds expression in modern French culture: the fire, the ice, the mists and related features. It is quite common to see a 'renard saga', or a 'saga des fourrures'.[8] The epic value of the *Íslendingasögur* also survives in a number of French books and films—we might note P. Bonnecarrère's *La saga des parachutistes* (1971); *Le Monde* (1 August 1986) published an article on 'La saga des banquiers'; and, entirely appropriately in view of the feuding family drama of many a family saga, French newspapers will run stories about well-known families headed 'La saga des Joxe' (*L'Express*, 16 November 1985), or 'La saga meurtrière des Recco' (a family of mafiosi) (*Le Figaro,* 2 June 1986). But it is strange, to put it no more strongly, to read 'la saga du chien', an instructional book on how to train your pet dog, or 'la saga du téléphone' (*Le Monde*, 24 January 1979), an account of difficulties with telephone installations in Egypt. And why 'saga pain plat' (imported Norwegian flatbrød); why 'saga unisexe' (socks); and what links can we identify between Vikings and portable shower fitments?

The answer is that, in late twentieth-century France, the misty North still exercises a powerful imaginative hold. In mystery, and magic, in images both frightening and fascinating, may lie our ultimate refuge from daily disappointments and shortcomings. Perhaps indeed, as a scholar, I am mistaken in my wish to uncover the truth about bewitching concepts like *viking, saga, drakkar*. It may well seem pitiful to claim doggedly that Viking sea-pirates were nothing but tradesmen; that a *drakkar* is nothing but a *knörr*, that sagas have none of the exotic fragrance of *chansons de geste,* that valkyries were neither viragos nor sylphids. And what am I to say about the poetry—born in the North, voiced by Ragnarr loðbrók, represented throughout the sagas, embodied romantically in the

[8]In the advertisement for one of the Parisian Grands Magasins.

drakkar? It would be better for me to admit the mistake of my search for 'reality'; far better for me to speak in the words of Hägar Dunör on his way back to Norway from England: 'Sing hard, boys! Sound, olifants. Soon the drakkars of the valiant Vikings will return to our country, fully loaded with booty "made in England"' (Boyer 1979, 23–25).

BIBLIOGRAPHY

d'Arlincourt, C.V. 1818. *La Caroléide*. Paris.

Bonstetten, Ch.V. de. 1826. *La Scandinavie et les Alpes*. Geneva.

Boyer, Régis. 1979. 'Brève navigation dans les brumes du Nord', in *Le mythe d'Etiemble*, pp. 23–25. Paris.

———. 1986. *Le mythe viking dans les lettres françaises*. Paris.

———. 1989. 'La saga française de la saga islandaise', *Revue de littérature comparée* 2, 249–258.

———. 1990. *La poésie scaldique*. Paris.

Chaulanges, F. and S. 1967. *Images et récits d'histoire de France. Cours élémentaire*. Paris.

Condroyer, E. 1929. *Des fjords aux tulipes*. Paris.

Dozy, G. 1845–1847. *L'influence exercée par les Normands sur l'ancien roman français*. Mémoires de la société des antiquaires du Nord. Lille.

Eichhoff, F.G. 1851. *Essai sur la mythologie du Nord*. Lyon.

Fahlin, H., ed. 1951. *Chronique des ducs de Normandie*. Uppsala.

Gråberg di Hemsö, J. 1822. *La Scandinavie vengée de l'accusation d'avoir produit les peuples barbares*. Lyon.

Gravier, M. 1943. *Tegnér et la France*. Paris

Guizot, M., ed. 1826. *Histoire de la Normandie*. Paris.

Janin, J. 1944. *La Normandie*. Paris.

Lagrèze, G.B. de. 1890. *Les Normands dans les deux mondes*. Paris.

Léouzon-Leduc, L. [n.d.]. *Études sur la Russie et le Nord de l'Europe*. Paris.

Liquet, Théodore. 1835. *Histoire de la Normandie*. Rouen.

Mallet, Paul-Henri. 1755. *Introduction a l'histoire de Dannemarc*. Copenhagen.

———. 1756. *Monumens de la mythologie et de la poesie des Celtes*. Copenhagen.

Ozanam, F. 1847. *Les Germains avant le christianisme*. Paris.

Pluquet, F., ed. 1837. *Le roman de Rou et des ducs de Normandie*. Rouen.

Prentout, H. 1911. *Essai sur les origines et la fondation du duché de Normandie*. Paris.

Renauld-Krantz. 1964. *Anthologie de la poésie nordique ancienne*. Paris

Revel, J. 1918. *Histoire des Normands*. Paris.

Richard, O.J. 1883. *Le roman de l'Islande*. Niort.

Salverte, E. 1829. *Des sciences occultes*. Paris.

Scriptor, J.D. 1953. *Sous l'œil d'Odin*. Levallois-Perret.

de Stael, Madame. 1810. *De l'Allemagne*. Paris.

Valjac, E. 1954. *La grande aventure des vikings*. Paris.

Waquet, H., ed. 1942. *Le siège de Paris par les Normands*. Paris.

Part II:

Iceland

5

Traditionality and Antiquarianism in the Post-Reformation *Lygisaga*

M.J. DRISCOLL

According to the orthodox view of Icelandic literary history the writing of sagas had its 'Golden Age' in the mid-thirteenth century, when *Heimskringla* and the majority of the *Íslendingasögur* are thought to have been produced. The loss of political independence to Norway in 1262–1264—the 'Fall of the Commonwealth' as it is sometimes called—is seen as having ushered in a period of decadence, characterised by an increase in foreign literary influence. This period saw the emergence of the *fornaldarsögur* and, in particular, the *riddarasögur*, at first in the form of translations, mainly from French, and later in the form of native imitations, the majority of which are thought to have been produced in the fourteenth century. These works are cited in most literary histories (though see Glauser 1983; also Schlauch 1934) only in order to draw attention to the deleterious effect which they are supposed to have had on the native saga tradition (Driscoll 1990). By the mid-fifteenth century, received opinion has it, the writing of prose fiction had to all intents and purposes been abandoned in Iceland, until it was revived by the national-romantic novelists of the nineteenth century, in particular Jón Thoroddsen, author of 'the first Icelandic novel', *Piltur og stúlka*, published in 1850.

Even though he cannot be said to have been its author, one of the major champions of this view was Sigurður Nordal.[1] In the introductory essay to his anthology *Íslenzk lestrarbók 1400–1900* (Nordal 1924), entitled 'Samhengið í íslenzkum bókmentum' [Continuity in Icelandic literature], even as he berated foreign scholars of Old Icelandic literature for being 'alls ófróðir um menningarlíf vort á síðustu fimm öldum' [totally ignorant about our cultural life over the last five centuries] and thinking 'að íslenzkar bókmentir hafi orðið sjálfdauðar um 1400' [that

---

[1]See Nordal 1920, 1924, 1933 and 1953. For recent criticism of Nordal's views see Árni Sigurjónsson 1984, and Örnólfur Thorsson 1990. On the impact of Icelandic nationalism on saga-studies see J.L. Byock 1992, 1993 and in the present volume.

Icelandic literature died about 1400], Nordal is prepared to state categorically that 'Um 1400 kulnar sagnaritunin alveg út' [about 1400 saga-writing died out completely]. The sagas, by which he means essentially only the *Íslendingasögur* and *konungasögur*, continued to exert an influence, but only in so far as they continued to be copied 'með óþreytandi elju' [with inexhaustible diligence] in the fifteenth and sixteenth centuries. In the seventeenth and eighteenth centuries, the period to which Nordal gave the name 'lærdómsöld' [the age of learning], interest in saga literature was chiefly of an antiquarian nature, the inspiration for which came from abroad. The 'samhengi í íslenzkum bókmentum' to which Nordal is so keen to draw attention applies, apparently, only to poetry.

This view, which has to my knowledge never been questioned, ignores, among other things, the fact that there is a very large number of sagas—romances, or *lygisögur*—preserved in paper manuscripts from after the Reformation. While some of these are translations of Danish, German, or, in a few cases, Dutch chapbooks (Seelow 1989), or reworkings of older material (Power 1984), the majority, about 150 individual sagas, are original compositions, some perhaps dating from as late as the late nineteenth or even early twentieth century. Their great popularity is beyond dispute, not a few being preserved in as many as fifty manuscripts, and although conditions were not generally favourable to the publication of this sort of material, some three dozen of these sagas appeared in popular editions from the second half of the nineteenth century and first decades of the twentieth. In general, then, saga-production in Iceland seems to have been every bit as great in, say, the eighteenth century as it had been in the thirteenth, even if the sagas produced appeal somewhat less to twentieth-century taste.

But who produced these sagas, and for whom? The answer to the latter question is simple: they were written, certainly in the vast majority of cases, to be read aloud in the *kvöldvaka*, or 'evening wake', held during the winter months on Icelandic farms, a practice dating from medieval times and surviving until the beginning of the present century (Hermann Pálsson 1962; Magnús Gíslason 1977).

Unfortunately, the answer to the former question is less straightforward, since in most cases the authors of these sagas are unknown. There are, however, a few exceptions. One such is séra Jón Oddsson Hjaltalín (1749–1835), now known, in so far as he is known at all, as a writer of hymns and other religious poetry. To him are attributed ten such romances in the 'Rithöfundatal' [List of authors] of Hallgrímur Jónsson (1780–1836), a work preserved in some half-dozen nineteenth-century manuscripts, but never published. Writing in 1822, Hallgrímur claims (Lbs. ÍB 385 4to, 324) to list Jón's various works 'eptir hans egin mèr sendri skírslu' [according to his own report, sent to me], so there is no reason to doubt the attribution. The sagas, in the order given by Hallgrímur, are:

1. Sagan af Reimari keisara
2. Sagan af Natoni persiska
3. Sagan af Marroni sterka
4. Sagan af Bernóti Borneyjarkappa
5. Sagan af Rígabal konungi
6. Sagan af Sarpidon konungi
7. Sagan af Ketlerus keisaraefni
8. Fimmbræðra saga
9. Sagan af Hinriki heilráða
10. Sagan af Mána fróða.

All of these survive except *Mána saga*. *Marrons saga* appears to have been among the more popular sagas of the nineteenth century, preserved as it is in at least twenty manuscripts. Both *Ketlerus saga* and *Hinriks saga* appeared in popular editions from 1905 and 1908 respectively, whilst another, *Sarpidons saga*, was included in the final volume of Bjarni Vilhjálmsson's six-volume collection *Riddarasögur*, published in 1951. The others remain unpublished.

Altogether there are nearly sixty manuscripts containing texts of Jón's sagas, of which only one is an autograph.[2] It is worth noting that in none of them, nor in any of the printed texts, is Jón credited with the authorship of the sagas, though his hymns and other poems rarely appear without attribution.[3]

Jón's sagas are, for the most part at least, typical *lygisögur*. They are examples of what in German scholarship is called 'Schemaliteratur', in that only a very few of the theoretically unlimited number of narrative possibilities are exploited, that is to say only those sanctioned by the tradition. Their 'schematic' nature is evident on all levels. Their underlying structure is essentially that of traditional tales of masculine seeker-heroes as analysed by Vladimir Propp (1968) and Jan de Vries (1954, 1959), whose methods are immediately applicable to this material. The plots are made longer and more complex than those of traditional fairy- or folk-tales through additional episodes, or 'moves', in which

[2]This is Lbs. 893 8vo, written *c.* 1800; although not recognised as such by Páll Eggert Ólason (1918–1937, II 173), the hand is undoubtedly Jón's.

[3]There is another saga, however, *Hrings saga og Hringvarðar*, which is attributed to Jón in one of its manuscripts (Lbs. 1660 4to); for a variety of reasons this attribution is doubtful.

M.J. Driscoll

elements of the basic structure are repeated. A series of battles early on in the hero's career, for example, introduces into the story secondary characters—normally the hero's sworn-brothers—for whom, in turn, wives must be procured, leading to a series of bridal quests in the second part of the saga.

Into this underlying pattern are slotted type-scenes selected from a fairly limited number. These scenes, like the underlying structure, are traditional, consisting of motifs or motif-complexes deriving in part from native tradition (the *fornaldarsögur*), and in part from continental romance (the translated *riddarasögur*, but also *Karlamagnús saga* and *Þiðreks saga*). The scenes are not borrowed or deployed indiscriminately, but rather form part of the general structural package, with certain type-scenes being used to fill particular slots in the underlying structure.

The so-called 'donor' sequence (Propp 1968, 39–50) provides an excellent case in point. 'Donor' figures are found in all the sagas, frequently in the form of dwarfs or giantesses, who, in response to some service rendered by the hero, help him in some way. Two motifs in particular are used to bring the hero into contact with the donor. The first of these is the lion/dragon motif—derived ultimately from Chrétien's *Yvain*—in which the hero rescues a lion from a dragon and is rewarded by its faithful service.[4] This motif is used in its 'original' form in only one of Jón's sagas, *Ketlerus saga*, where the hero, travelling alone, stops for the night by a large forest. The night passes without incident, but the next morning, as he continues on his way:

> Varð þá fyrir honum þykkur skógur og sem hann hafði gengið um hann um hríð, heyrði hann brak og bresti og óhljóð ógurleg. Gekk hann þá á hljóðið og sá hvar ógurlegur flugdreki var að eiga við ljón. Hann hafði hremt báðum klónum í síður þess, og ætlaði síðan að fljúga upp með það, en það hafði fest klær sínar í tré eitt og hélt sér af öllu afli. Ketlerus hljóp þá til og hjó í sundur sporð drekans. Drekin sló þá öðrum hramminum til hans, en hann hjó hann í sundur. Drekinn æddi þá að honum með gapandi gini og bjóst til að gleypa hann. Ketlerus rak þá sverðið allt að hjöltum í kjaft drekans. Drekinn spjó þá eitri miklu en Ketlerus vék til hliðar og hjó á hrygg drekans svo hann tók í sundur í tvo hluti. Á meðan á þessu stóð lá ljónið í dái. Ketlerus gekk að því og þerraði af því blóðið og bar smyrsli í sárin. Ljónið lifnaði þá við og skreið að fótum hans, og sýndist

---

[4]Motif types B360 ('Animals grateful for rescue from peril of death') and B443 ('Helpful lion'); Folktale type 156A; the delivery from a dragon is type B11.11.6. ('Dragon fight in order to free lion'). On the use of the motif in Old Norse see Schlauch 1965; Harris 1970; and Driscoll 1992, lxxiv–lxxvii.

honum sem tár rinni eftir trýninu. Hann mælti þá við dýrið: 'Þú skalt vera fylgjari minn meðan þú lifir.' Við þessi orð reis ljónið upp og þaðraði upp um hann og sleikti fætur hans. Síðan gaf hann því fæðu og hélt svo af stað. Ljónið fylgdi honum, en var þó mjög dasað og seinfara. Varð hann því oft við að standa og hvíla það. (*Ketlerus saga* 1905, 41)

[There was then before him a thick wood, and when he had walked about in it for a time he heard a great din and dreadful noises. He walked towards the source of the sound and saw a terrible dragon fighting with a lion. The dragon had both of its claws clenched in the side of the lion and was trying to fly off with it, but the lion had fastened its claws into a tree and was holding on with all its might. Ketlerus ran over and hewed off the dragon's tail. The dragon then reached for him with one of its claws, which Ketlerus hewed off. The dragon then came toward him with its great maw open, intending to swallow him, but Ketlerus pushed the sword into the dragon's mouth all the way to the hilt. The dragon then spewed great amounts of poison, but Ketlerus jumped to the side and struck the dragon a blow on the back, cutting it into two pieces. While this was happening the lion lay unconscious. Ketlerus went to it and washed off the blood and put balm on the wounds. The lion then came to and crawled towards his feet, and it seemed to him that tears ran down its muzzle. He then spoke to the animal: 'You shall be my companion while you live.' At these words the lion rose up and fawned on him and licked his feet. Then he gave it food and then they departed. The lion followed him, but was quite dazed and slow-moving, and so he had often to pause and allow it to rest.]

This passage, although somewhat abbreviated in comparison with the scene found in, for example, *Sigurðar saga þögla* (1963, 141–144; 1992, 4–7), contains most of the details present in the lion/dragon episodes in the medieval romances. More frequently, however, the basic motif has undergone a series of transformations in Jón's sagas, resulting in episodes in which the hero rescues a child from a dragon, a dwarf from a giant, a man from a lion, and so on. In most cases the episode is one of the hero's first independent acts, and serves always to bring him into contact with the donor figure.

The other principal means by which the hero and the donor are brought together is through the motif of the marvellous or beautiful animal—normally a deer or hart—glimpsed in the forest and pursued by the hero.[5] Here again, there are several variations on the theme, but the function is usually the same.

The staple of the *lygisögur* is without question the battle scene, as many as a dozen of which can be found in any one saga, normally making up at least half the saga. There are two basic types of battles: the land battle, which derives many of its details from the world of continental romance (through the medium of the translated *riddarasögur*, *Karlamagnús saga*, and *Þiðreks saga*), and the battle at sea, deriving principally from native Scandinavian tradition. When these battles include or end in single combat, this takes the appropriate form, that is either *burtreið* [joust] or *hólmganga* [duel]. In the indigenous medieval *riddarasögur* the land battle was more common, the *fornaldarsögur* exhibiting a corresponding penchant for battles at sea, but the two are pretty evenly distributed in Jón's sagas, reflecting the degree to which the *lygisögur* are an amalgam of the two 'genres'. All the battle scenes, regardless of type or length, follow the same basic pattern (Glauser 1983, 114–115; Bell 1980).

In terms of their surface structure the *lygisögur* exhibit a very heavy incidence of formulaic elements, with the various motifs or type-scenes having their attendant vocabulary and formulae.[6] The battle scenes in particular seem to consist of little more than traditional stock phrases. A glance at any of the indigenous medieval romances—*Vilhjálms saga Sjóðs* (1964) or *Saulus saga ok Nikanors* (1963), for example, both of which are singularly rich in battle descriptions—quickly confirms one's

[5]This motif (type N 774, 'Adventures from pursuing enchanted animal'), well known in folktale and legend, is especially associated with the legend of St Eustachius; see Pschmadt 1911. It was common enough in Old Norse literature, appearing in several of the translated romances and in over a dozen *fornaldarsögur* and *riddarasögur*, as well as in some later folktales; see Lagerholm 1927, 25–26; Einar Ólafur Sveinsson 1929, xxxiii; Reuschel 1933, 111; and Boberg 1966, 204.

[6]Although they may be said to 'yield a predominance of clearly demonstrable formulas' (Lord 1960, 130)—once taken as the definitive test of oral composition—Jón's sagas were clearly not composed orally, but were rather composed in written form for people familiar with literary texts. The mechanism of their reception, however, was oral—or rather aural—in that they were written to be read aloud. As Franz Bäuml has argued recently (1984, 1987), if the formulae described by Parry and Lord serve predominantly as a mnemonic device, they do this as much for the benefit of the listening audience as for the composers, allowing them to understand and receive the text in terms of the tradition.

suspicion that the vocabulary of Jón's battle scenes is indeed highly traditional, with at least two-thirds of the formulaic phrases used in Jón's sagas appearing in these two sagas alone. This comes as no real surprise, of course, but should serve as a useful reminder that the *lygisaga* tradition remained stable—and productive—for some four hundred years after the alleged demise of saga writing.

Jón Hjaltalín, although he never travelled abroad or studied at university, appears to have been remarkably well-read. In 1810 he was visited by Sir George Mackenzie, who noted (1811, 140–142) that he possessed 'a considerable collection of books' and 'spoke Latin exceedingly well'. Mackenzie's party included the young Henry Holland, who observed (1987, 153) that Jón's sitting room was 'furnished with a small library, containing probably about 100 books'. A fairly good idea of the contents of this 'small library' can be gleaned from the inventory of Jón's estate (Þjóðskjalasafn, Snæf. XI 11, Dánarbú 1835–1838), drawn up on 9 January 1836, approximately a fortnight after his death, and the inventory of the estate of his second wife Gróa, who had died the year before. Titles are not specified for about a quarter of the items listed, but nearly fifty individual titles are named in the two inventories, most of which are readily identifiable and testify to the wide-ranging nature of Jón's interests. Another source of information of this type is Jón's autograph manuscripts, which contain references to or translations of works by writers such as Voltaire, Rousseau, Fielding, Holberg, and Cervantes. There are a few instances of direct borrowing from these authors in Jón's sagas, and the influence of the Enlightenment is readily discernible in several of them.

Of especial interest to Jón, and to many like him over the centuries, was the medieval literature of his own country, with which he appears to have been intimately familiar. In his autograph manuscripts he refers to most of the major works of medieval Iceland, and texts of many such works are preserved in his hand. There are a number of places in Jón's sagas where the influence of the older literature is such that it is more reasonable to speak of literary borrowings than manifestations of a living tradition.

In *Rígabals saga*, for example, the hero's father bids farewell to his son with the words 'finnumst aftur á feginsdegi' (Lbs. 2784 4to, p. 360), a reference to *Sólarljóð*, v. 82 (1991, 40, 108–109): 'Hér við skiljumst / og hittast munum / á feginsdegi fira' [Now we part, and will meet (again), on the joy day of men (resurrection day)]. The phrase is also found in *Sverris saga* (1920, 42), but Jón is more likely to have known it from *Sólarljóð* since there is a text of that poem in his hand from *c*.

1800 (Lbs. 1249 8vo).

Such literary allusions are not confined to single phrases, however. There is, for example, a scene in *Hinriks saga* involving a berserk named Járnhaus which is clearly modelled on a scene in *Víga-Glúms saga*:

Nú leið sumarið og veturinn fram að jólum, að eigi bar til tíðinda; en jóladag sjálfan, þá jarl var með hirð sinni seztur undir borð, komu þær fréttir, að Járnhaus berserkur sé kominn, og í því var hrundið upp hurðinni og flanaði þar inn albrynjaður berserkur. Hann gekk að þeim, er yztur sat, og spurði, hvort hann þyrði að teljast jafnsnjall sér, en hinn kvað það fjarri fara. Þannig spyr hann mann af manni, en allir gáfu sömu svör, að eigi væru jafn snjallir honum. Loksins kemur hann fyrir Hinrik og spyr, hvort hann þættist jafnsnjall sér. Hinrik svarar: 'Eg hefi enga snilli til þín séð, því þessi þín aðferð er dára glópska, en engin snilli, og er eg því snjallari, að eg kann mig í hófi að hafa, en þú lætur sem gikkur, eða afglapi.' Járnhaus tók nú að grenja og bíta í skjöldinn. Þá mælti Hinrik: 'Ekki fæla mig þessi læti, því fyr hefi eg heyrt naut orga, hund góla og svín rýna, og kalla eg þig þessara líka að snillinni.' Járnhaus stóðst nú ekki lengur þessar ertingar og vildi bregða sverði, en Hinrik stökk úr sæti og hljóp á berserkinn, þreif hann á lopt, og færði hann niður svo þungt fall, að hann lá í óviti. Hinrik heimtaði þá fjötra, og setti hann í járn. Síðan settist hann í sæti sitt, og settist við drykkju. Að stundu liðinni, raknaði berserkurinn við. Hinrik skipar þá tveimur af sínum mönnum, að taka harða hrísvendi, og fletta síðan Járnhaus klæðum, og afhýða hann með öllu. Þeir gjöra nú svo og hættu ekki fyrr, en öll húð er af hryggnum. Járnhaus bar sig lítt og þoldi ílla húðstrýkinguna. Hinrik mælti þá: 'Nú er mönnum kunnugt, hvað mikil er snilli þín. Skaltu nú hér eftir gjöra annað hvort að leggja af þetta villidýrs æði, og gjörast trúr og hollur þjónustumaður jarls, eða þú skalt líða kvalafullan dauða.' Járnhaus mælti: 'Heldur vil eg þiggja líf og þjóna jarli, en vera hér með háðung drepinn.' Sór hann þá eið að þessu, og tók jarl hann í sína þjónustu, var hann ávallt maður skaplyndur, og vinsæll, og hætti öllum ójöfnuði. Öllum þótti Hinrik vel hafa tekist að gjöra gæfan mann úr grimmum berserki. (*Hinriks saga* 1908, 27–9)

[Now the summer and the winter passed without incident until Christmas; but on Christmas day itself, as the earl and his men sat at table, it was reported that the berserk Járnhaus had come, and at that moment the door was broken down and in rushed a berserk in full armour. He approached the one who sat outermost and asked him whether he dared to consider himself as clever as he, but the other said this was far from the case. He then asked each man in turn the same thing and each gave the same answer, that they were no match for him. Finally he came to Hinrik and asked him if he considered himself his match in cleverness. Hinrik answered: 'I haven't seen in you any cleverness, for this behaviour of yours is plain foolishness, and not cleverness, and I am therefore cleverer in that I know how to behave myself, but you carry on like some clown or fool.' Járnhaus began to howl and bite his shield. Then Hinrik said: 'These wailings don't frighten me, for I have heard bulls bellow, dogs howl, and swine grunt, and I would say that you were their match in cleverness.' Járnhaus could bear this provocation no longer and made to draw his sword, but Hinrik leapt up from his seat and took hold of the berserk, lifting him up into the air and throwing him so hard to the ground that he was knocked unconscious. Hinrik called for fetters, and put him in irons. He then sat down in his seat and began to drink. Shortly thereafter the berserk recovered. Hinrik ordered two of his men to take hard switches, then to strip Járnhaus of his clothes, and then to scourge him thoroughly. This they proceeded to do, and did not stop until all the skin was gone from his back. Járnhaus could hardly stand it, and bore the whipping badly. Hinrik then said: 'Now all have seen how great your cleverness is; you must now either cease this savage behaviour and become a staunch and loyal servant of the earl, or suffer a painful death.' Járnhaus said: 'I would rather accept life and serve the earl than be killed here in disgrace.' He then swore an oath to this effect, and the earl took him into his service. He was [thereafter] always even-tempered and popular, and ceased all wrongful behaviour. Everyone thought Hinrik had done well to make a gentle man out of a grim berserk.]

The scene in *Víga-Glúms saga*, takes place 'at vetrnóttum' [at the beginning of winter], rather than 'jóladag sjálfan' [Christmas Day itself], but is otherwise virtually identical:

Ok er menn váru komnir undir borð, þá var sagt, at sá maðr var kominn at bœnum með tólfta mann, er Björn hét ok kallaðr járnhauss. Hann var berserkr mikill ok var því vanr at koma til mannboða fjölmennra ok leitaði þar orða við menn, ef nokkurr vildi þat mæla, er hann mætti á þiggja, ok skoraði á menn til hólmgöngu. [...] En Björn gekk í skálann inn ok leitaði orðheilla við menn ok spurði á inn œðra bekk inn ýzta mann, hvárt hann væri jafnsnjallr honum, en [hann] kvað fjarri þat fara. Síðan spurði hann hvern at öðrum, þar til at hann kom fyrir öndvegit. (1956, 17–18)

[And when everyone had sat down at table it was announced that the man named Björn and called járnhauss had come to the farm with eleven other men. He was a great berserk whose practice it was to come to large feasts and exchange words with people so that someone would say something at which he could take offence, and then challenge them to meet him in single-combat. [...] Björn came into the hall and looked for someone to speak to, asking the outermost man on the higher bench whether he was as clever as he was, but he said that was far from the case. He then asked each man in turn until he came to the high seat.]

There is then a brief exchange between Björn and Vigfúss which has no parallel in *Hinriks saga*, but when Björn reaches Glúmr, still thought by everyone present to be a fool, and asks him 'ef hann væri jafnsnjallr honum', Glúmr's answer is not unlike Hinrik's:

> En Glúmr kvað hann ekki þurfa at eiga við sik ok kvazk eigi vita um snilli hans,—'ok vil ek af því engu við þik jafnask, at út á Íslandi myndi sá maðr kallaðr fól, er þann veg léti sem þú lætr.' (1956, 18–19)

> [But Glúmr said that there was no need for him to bother with him, and said that he knew nothing about his cleverness, 'but I shouldn't like to be equated with you in anything, because in Iceland the man who behaved the way you do would be called a fool'.]

Glúmr then leaps to his feet and, beating the berserk with a firebrand, drives him from the house. Although Glúmr does not kill Björn then and there, his death is reported the next day. In *Hinriks saga*, on the other hand, the saga of Jón's most touched by the spirit of the Enlightenment, the severe punishment meted out to Járnhaus is seen to be justifiable in view of its positive social consequences.

A general indebtedness to *Ynglinga saga* and to a number of other texts in which pagan practices are described is discernible in the section in *Fimmbrœðra saga* dealing with King Eysteinn of Sweden, who is described as 'blótmaður mikill' (*Ynglinga saga* 1941, 47); otherwise there are few verbal parallels, with the various phrases used, such as 'að fella blótspón', and 'að blóta til sigurs', being found in a variety of texts. There is, however, a direct reference to *Ynglinga saga* in the first chapter of the *Fimmbrœðra saga*, where paganism, called 'Óðinsdyrkun' [the worship of Óðinn], is described in the following terms:

> þeím [*sc.* trúarbrögðum] filgdi slíkur kraftur, sigursæld, árgjæzka, og farsæld; því þó Óðinn eígnaði sér mikinn mátt, held eg hann hafi þó bæði vitað og játað an<n>an æðri enn sig, og eý gét eg sjeð hann hafi boðið að tigna sig eda dírka sem Guð; það var að vísu satt, að þegar hann sendi menn sína til orustu, eður í aðrar hættu ferdir, lagdi hann hendur í höfuð þeím og gaf þeím Bjanak það er árnaði farar heílla, og höfdu þeír trú á því, að þá mundi ferdin vel takast. (Lbs. 3810 8vo, 3–4)

> [This religion was accompanied by such power, luck in battle, good seasons, and happiness, because although Óðinn took great power for himself, I think he both recognised and acknowledged another one higher than himself, and I cannot see that he decreed that he should be honoured or worshipped like God. It is admittedly true that when he sent his men into battle or on other dangerous missions he laid his

hands upon their heads and gave them blessing, which brought them good fortune, and they believed that their mission would then go well.]

The reference to 'bjan(n)ak' is taken directly from *Ynglinga saga*, where in the second chapter it is said:

Þat var háttr hans [*sc.* Óðins], ef hann sendi menn sína til orrostu eða aðrar sendifarar, at hann lagði áðr hendr í hofuð þeim og gaf þeim bjannak. Trúðu þeir, at þá myndi vel farask. (1941, 11)

[It was Óðinn's custom that before he sent his men into battle or on another mission he would lay his hands on their heads and give them blessing. They believed that things would then go well.].

Following this is a description of how Óðinn 'gaf og enn firir heít umm sælu fulla vist á Gimli, og sagdi að þar mundu diggar dróttir biggja, og umm aldir indis daga njóta, og að gott yrdi þá að vera á himni' [promised them a joyful residence in Gimli, and said that there the faithful would dwell, enjoying delightful days forever, and that then it would be good to be in heaven]. This is a somewhat corrupt reference to *Völuspá*, v. 64 (1962, 15):

Sal sér hon standa,   sóló fegra,
gulli þacþan,   á Gimlé;
þar scolo dyggvar   dróttir byggia
oc um aldrdaga   ynðis nióta.

[She sees a hall, fairer than the sun,
roofed with gold, at Gimli;
there shall the faithfull dwell,
and have joy for all eternity.]

Jón's familiarity with *Völuspá* is evidenced also by the existence of a text of the poem, complete with Latin translation, in Lbs. 1249 8vo, a miscellany written in his hand, dating from about 1800.

In *Natons saga*, where Flórída, daughter of Dagviður, King of Tartaría, describes to her serving-maids a dream which she has had:

Úti þóktist eg stödd og gékk eg skamt frá borginni. Varð þá fyrir mér dalverpi nokkurt og sátu þar þrjár konur. Þær spunnu garn. Eg þóktist ganga til þeirra og spyrja hverjar þær væru. Þá svaraði ein þeirra: 'Við erum nornir þær sem spynnum forlaga þráð manna og heitum Skuld, Urða og Verðandi.' Eg þóktist spyrja: 'Hvaða forlög spynni þið mér?' 'Þau,' sagði hún, 'að þú skalt aungann þann til egta fá er fæddur er í konungs höll eður maktar manna herbergi, heldur einhvern þann er borinn er í bónda kofa.' Varð eg af þessu mjög hrigg og í því vöktuð þér mig. Kémur mér fyrir lítið að vera konungsdóttir ef eg skal þýðast bændur eður búkarla um ævi mína. (Lbs. 2784 4to, pp. 309–10).

[I dreamt that I was outside, and walked a short way from the castle.
I came to a small dale, in which there sat three women. They were
spinning yarn. I dreamt that I walked toward them and asked them
who they were. One of them said to me: 'We are the Norns [weird
sisters] who spin men's thread of fate; we are called Skuld, Urða, and
Verðandi.' I asked: 'What fate do you spin for me?' 'That fate,' she
said, 'that you shall marry no-one born in a castle or a rich man's
house, but rather one who was born in a farmer's cottage.' This
saddened me greatly, at which point you woke me. It is of little
benefit to me that I am a princess if I have to be wedded to a farmer
or cowherd all my life.]

She need not have worried, of course, since the man born not in a
castle but in a cottage is none other than the hero Naton, whom she does
indeed eventually marry; but the three witches who have provided her
with this information derive clearly from Norse mythology. They are
mentioned in Snorri's *Edda* (1982, 18), but the most probable source is,
again, *Völuspá*, v. 20 (1962, 5):

Þaðan koma meyiar, margs vitandi,
þriár, ór þeim sæ, er und þolli stendr;
Urð héto eina, aðra Verðandi,
—scáro á scíði—, Sculd ina þriðio;
þær lög lögðo, þær líf kuro
alda bornom, ørlög seggia.

[Thence come the maidens, much-knowing,
three from that spring that stands under the tree;
one is named Urðr, Verðandi the other
—cutting on wood—Skuld the third.
They decided fates, and ordained the ages
of the sons of men.]

It would be a mistake, however, to think of Jón sitting with the open
text of *Völuspá* in front of him as he wrote. Many of the borrowings
have an almost accidental quality about them. There is another scene in
Fimmbrœðra saga which appears to be a literary borrowing, but from
more than one source. In Persia, the relatively minor character Desilíus,
attempting to flee the wrath of Arkimagus, is given shelter by an old man
and his wife:

Nú liðu svo 4r dagar, að eý bar neítt til tíðinda, enn sem kom hinn 5ti
Dagur mælti bóndi: Nú er mér grunur á að hér muni koma leítar
menn í dag, hefi eg þá eý önnur ráð enn legg<j>a yfir þig skikkju
Kéllíngar minnar, og skaltu sitja og spinna garn á rokk, enn hún skal
fara út á skóg og felast þar, meðann leítar menn eru hér.—Desilíus
bað hann ráða; Eptir það fer Kéllíng frá húsumm enn Kall að
soðníngu í Eldhúsi, og ber mikið sorp á eldinn. Des(ilíus) settist við
rokk, og spinnur í ákafa, líður nú eý laung stund, áður 10 menn ríða

að húsumm, þeír berja á dir, enn Bóndi geíngur út, heílsa þeír
honumm, og spirja: hvort eý hafi neírn flótta maður þar komið; bóndi
kvað það fjarri vera, þá mæltu þeír: það sagdi þó Biskup vor, að
þessa leíð mundi hann haldið hafa, og viljumm vér rannsaka Bæ þinn;
Bóndi hvað það heímilt, geíngu þeír þá inn og leítuðu, enn sáu
eíngann mann nema konu bónda, sat hún og spann á rokk sinn, og var
óhír við sendi menn, og kvað þeím óskilt að gjöra þar hark í húsumm
sínumm, og bað þá dragast burt sem skjótast, valdi hún þeím hörd
ord, og var bist í svari (Lbs. 3810 8vo, 17–18).

[Now four days passed without incident, but on the fifth day the
farmer said: 'I suspect that a search party will come today. The only
plan I can think of is that you put on my wife's cloak and sit here
spinning yarn on the distaff, and she can go out and hide herself in
the forest while the search party is here.' Desilíus said that he would
leave it to him to decide. After that the old woman went out of the
house and the old man started cooking, and put a large quantity of
sweepings on the fire. Desilíus sat at the distaff, spinning diligently.
It is not long before ten men ride up to the house. They knock on the
door and the farmer goes out. They greet him and ask if any fugitive
has come that way. He says that this is far from the case. They said:
'Our bishop told us that he went this way, and we would like to
search your house.' The farmer told them they could. They went
inside and searched but could find no-one other than the farmer's
wife, who sat spinning at her distaff, and was unfriendly to the
messengers, saying that they had no right to make such a commotion
in her house, and telling them to push off at once. She used strong
words with them, and answered angrily.]

There are clear verbal parallels in this scene with a least three old
Icelandic texts, the most obvious being *Fóstbrǽðra saga*, where Gríma
explains her plan for concealing Þormóður:

Gamli skal festa upp ketil ok sjóða sel; þú skalt bera sorp á eldinn ok
lát verða mikinn reyk í húsinum. Ek mun sitja í durum ok spinna garn
ok taka við komöndum. (1943, 245–6)

[Gamli will hang up the kettle and boil seal-meat; you'll put
sweepings on the fire and make a great deal of smoke in the house.
I'll sit in the door-way and spin yarn, and deal with anyone who
comes.]

The phrase 'að bera sorp á eldinn/eldana' [to put sweepings on the fire]
occurs, so far as I am aware, in only one other place in the whole of Old
Icelandic literature—in *Kjalnesinga saga* (1959, 14–15), where there is
a similar scene in which a smoke-filled room is used to hide a fugitive.
The combination of this phrase with the detail of spinning yarn on a
distaff suggests that *Fóstbrǽðra saga* was the source, however, although
there appears, in this instance, also to be a connection with *Eyrbyggja*

saga (1935, 51), where there is a similar scene in which an old woman, Katla, hiding her son Oddr, 'spann garn af rokki'. Another well-known scene of this type is found in *Gísla saga Súrssonar* (1943, 86–8), where Gísli is protected by the farmer Refr á Haugi and his wife Álfdís, who, the saga tells us, 'var inn mesti kvenskratti' [was a complete shrew]. Gísli is hidden in the bed, with Álfdís lying on top of him. Refr has told her to be 'sem versta viðskiptis ok sem œrasta,—"ok spari nú ekki af, [...] ok at mæla þat allt illt, er þér kemr í hug, bæði í blóti ok skattyrðum [...]"' [on her worst behaviour, and most furious, 'and don't hold back, [...] and say all the evil things that come into your head, oaths and foul language']. When Börkr's men arrive, Refr says he has not seen Gísli. They then ask him if he has any objection to their searching his house. He replies that he has not, and they go in:

> Ok er Álfdís heyrði hark þeira, þá spyrr hon, hvat gauragangi þar væri eða hverir glóparnir starfaði á mönnum um nætr. Refr bað hana hafa sik at hófi. En hon lætr þó eigi vant margra fíflyrða; veitir hon þeim mikla ágauð, svá at þeir máttu minni til reka. (1943, 87–8)

> [And when Álfdís heard the commotion she asked what hooliganism this was, and who the idiots were who disturbed people at night. Refr told her to behave herself, but she didn't let up with her foul language, cursing them in a way they wouldn't soon forget.]

Desilíus's behaviour in *Fimmbræðra saga* is presumably to be traced to this scene in *Gísla saga*, as suggested by the use of the word 'hark' [commotion]. It is hard to believe that Jón knowingly combined motifs and phrases from so many different sources; a much more reasonable explanation is that as instinctively familiar with Old Icelandic literature as he obviously was, Jón has simply used the phrases that most readily suggested themselves to him when composing a scene of this type.

Jón's sagas are, I have argued, part of a unbroken narrative tradition lasting for perhaps a thousand years, from pre-literary times to the post-romantics, a tradition characterised throughout by an openness toward outside influences, a willingness to incorporate 'foreign' material—although traditions tend, by their nature, to be conservative. The highly schematic nature of the material in terms of structure and style ensured continuity in one way. Jón's sagas reveal that in the post-Reformation period one of the areas to which the *lygisaga* author could turn for material was the literature of the Icelandic Middle Ages, thereby establishing an artistic continuity in prose of precisely the kind identified by Sigurður Nordal in verse.

BIBLIOGRAPHY

Árni Sigurjónsson. 1984. 'Nokkur orð um hugmyndafræði Sigurðar Nordal fyrir 1945', *Tímarit Máls og menningar* 45, 49–63.

Bäuml, Franz H. 1984. 'Medieval Texts and the Two Theories of Oral-Formulaic Composition: A Proposal for a Third Theory', *New Literary History* 16, 31–49.

————. 'The Theory of Oral-Formulaic Composition and the Written Medieval Text', in J.M. Foley, ed., *Comparative Research on Oral Traditions: A Memorial for Milman Parry*, pp. 29–45. Columbus, Ohio.

Bell, L. Michael. 1980. 'Fighting words in *Egils saga*: Lexical pattern as standard-bearer', *Arkiv för nordisk filologi* 95, 89–112.

Boberg, Inger M. 1966. *Motif-Index of Early Icelandic Literature*. Copenhagen.

Byock, Jesse L. 1992. 'History and the sagas: the effect of nationalism', in Gísli Pálsson, ed., *From Sagas to Society: Comparative Approaches to Early Iceland*, pp. 43–59. Enfield Lock.

————. 1993. 'Þjóðernishyggja nútímans og Íslendingasögurnar', *Tímarit Máls og menningar* 54, 36–50.

Driscoll, Matthew James. 1990. 'Þögnin mikla: hugleiðingar um riddarasögur og stöðu þeirra í íslenskum bókmenntum', *Skáldskaparmál* 1, 157–168.

————, ed. 1992. *Sigurðar saga þögla: The Shorter Redaction*. Reykjavík.

Edda. 1982. Snorri Sturluson, *Edda: Prologue and* Gylfaginning (ed. Anthony Faulkes). Oxford.

Einar Ól. Sveinsson. 1929. *Verzeichnis isländischer Märchenvarianten, mit einer einleitenden Untersuchung*. Helsinki.

Eyrbyggja saga. 1935. Einar Ól. Sveinsson and Matthías Þórðarson, eds, Íslenzk fornrit 4. Reykjavík.

Fóstbrœðra saga. 1943. Björn K. Þórólfsson and Guðni Jónsson, eds, *Vestfirðinga sögur*. Íslenzk fornrit 6. Reykjavík.

Gesta Danorum. 1931–1957. J. Olrik and H. Ræder, eds. Copenhagen.

Gísla saga Súrssonar. 1943. Björn K. Þórólfsson and Guðni Jónsson, eds, *Vestfirðinga sögur*, Íslenzk fornrit 6. Reykjavík.

Glauser, Jürg. 1983. *Isländische Märchensagas: Studien zur Prosaliteratur im spätmittelalterlichen Island*. Basel.

Harris, Richard L. 1970. 'The Lion-Knight Legend in Iceland and the Valþjófsstaðir Door', *Viator* 1, 125–145.

Hermann Pálsson. 1962. *Sagnaskemmtun Íslendinga*. Reykjavík.

Holland, Henry. 1987. Andrew Wawn, ed., *The Iceland Journal of Henry Holland 1810*. London.

Kjalnesinga saga. 1959. Jóhannes Halldórsson, ed., Íslenzk fornrit 14. Reykjavík.

Lbs. = Landsbókasafn Íslands

Lagerholm, Åke. 1927. *Drei Lygisogur*. Halle.

Lord, Albert Bates. 1960. *The Singer of Tales*. Cambridge, Mass.

Mackenzie, Sir George. 1811. *Travels in the Island of Iceland during the Summer of the Year MDCCCX*. Edinburgh.

Magnús Gíslason. 1977. *Kvällsvaka: En isländsk kulturtradition belyst genom studier i bondebefolkningens vardagsliv och miljö under senare hälften av 1800-talet och början av 1900-talet*. Uppsala.

Nordal, Sigurður. 1920. *Snorri Sturluson*. Reykjavík.

————. 1924. *Íslenzk lestrarbók 1400–1900*. Reykjavík.

————. ed. 1933. *Egils saga Skalla-Grímssonar*. Íslenzk fornrit 2. Reykjavík.

————. 1953. 'Sagalitteraturen', *Litteraturhistorie: Norge og Island*, Nordisk kultur VIII B, 180–273. Copenhagen.

Páll Eggert Ólason. 1918–1937. *Skrá um handritasöfn Landsbókasafnsins*. Reykjavík.

Power, Rosemary. 1984. 'Saxo in Iceland', *Gripla* 6, 241–258.

Propp, Vladimir. 1968. Louis A. Wagner, ed., *Morphology of the Folktale*. Second ed. Austin, Texas.

Pschmadt, Carl. 1911. *Die Sage von der verfolgten Hinde: Ihre Heimat und Wandring, Bedeutung und Ertwicklung mit besonderer Berücksichtigung ihrer Verwendung in der Literatur des Mittelalters*. Greifswald.

Reuschel, Helga. 1933. *Untersuchungen über Stoff und Stil der Fornaldarsaga*. Bühl-Baden.

Saulus saga ok Nikanors. 1963. Agnete Loth, ed., *Late Medieval Icelandic Romances* II, 1–91. Copenhagen.

Schlauch, Margaret. 1934. *Romance in Iceland*. London.

————. 1965. 'Arthurian material in some late Icelandic sagas', *Bulletin Bibliographique de la Société Internationale Arthurienne* 17, 87–91.

Seelow, Hubert. 1989. *Die isländischen Übersetzungen der deutschen Volks-bücher: Handschriftenstudien zur Rezeption und Überlieferung ausländischer unterhaltender Literatur in Island in der Zeit zwischen Reformation und Aufklärung*. Reykjavík.

Sigurðar saga þögla. 1963. Agnete Loth, ed., *Late Medieval Icelandic Romances* II, 93–259. Copenhagen.

Sólarljóð. 1991. Njörður P. Njarðvík, ed. Reykjavík.

Sverris saga. 1920. Gustav Indrebø, ed. Kristiania [Oslo].

Víga-Glúms saga. 1956. Jónas Kristjánsson, ed., *Eyfirðinga sögur*. Íslenzk fornrit 9. Reykjavík.

Vilhjálms saga Sjóðs. 1964. Agnete Loth, ed., *Late Medieval Icelandic Romances* 4, 1–136. Copenhagen.

Völuspá. 1983. G. Neckel, ed., *Edda: Die Lieder des Codex Regius nebst verwandten Denkmälern*. Heidelberg.

Vries, Jan de. 1954. *Betrachtungen zum Märchen, besonders in seinem Verhältnis zu Heldensage und Mythos.* Helsinki.

———. 1959. *Heldenlied en heldensage.* Utrecht.

Ynglinga saga. 1941. Bjarni Aðalbjarnarson, ed., *Heimskringla.* Íslenzk fornrit 26. Reykjavík.

Örnólfur Thorsson. 1990. '"Leitin að landinu fagra": Hugleiðing um rannsóknir á íslenskum fornbókmenntum', *Skáldskaparmál* 1, 28–53.

6

The End of the Saga: Text, Tradition and Transmission in Nineteenth- and Early Twentieth-Century Iceland

JÜRG GLAUSER

This essay deals with the final phase of the manuscript transmission of Icelandic saga literature at the turn of the century. For a variety of reasons this topic has never been properly examined or discussed; neither philologists nor paleographers nor literary historians seem to have regarded the study of late paper-manuscript copies of well-known sagas as a worthwhile enterprise in its own right. This short paper seeks merely to draw attention to some central aspects of a much broader subject area. I shall try to outline the transmission of the traditional Icelandic narrative genres in hand-written and printed forms during the nineteenth and early twentieth centuries, and I shall conclude by identifying some of the reasons which led to the decline of this centuries-old tradition.[1]

STARTING POINT: *FJÓRAR RIDDARASÖGUR* (1852), *FELSENBORGARSÖGUR* (1854)

In the autumn of 1852 the Prentsmiðja Íslands in Reykjavík issued a small and modest looking octavo booklet of 120 pages (7½ sheets), at thirty-two 'skildingar' a copy. The volume contained four texts: 1. *Sagan af Þórgrími og köppum hans*, 2. *Sagan af Sálusi og Níkanor*, 3. *Ævintýri af Ajax keisarasyni*, 4. *Sagan af Valdimar kóngi*. This *Fjórar Riddarasögur* anthology was the first in a long line of popular Icelandic saga

---

[1]Among recent publications on the late manuscript transmission of Icelandic saga literature are Frosti F. Jóhannsson, ed., 1989 (esp. Vésteinn Ólason, pp. 161–227); H. Seelow 1989a, 1989b; M. Overgaard 1979, 1991; M.J. Driscoll in the present volume; Glauser 1994 and forthcoming; Finnbogi Guðmundsson 1965, 1982; Grímur M. Helgason 1972, 1978, 1986; Jón Helgason 1958.

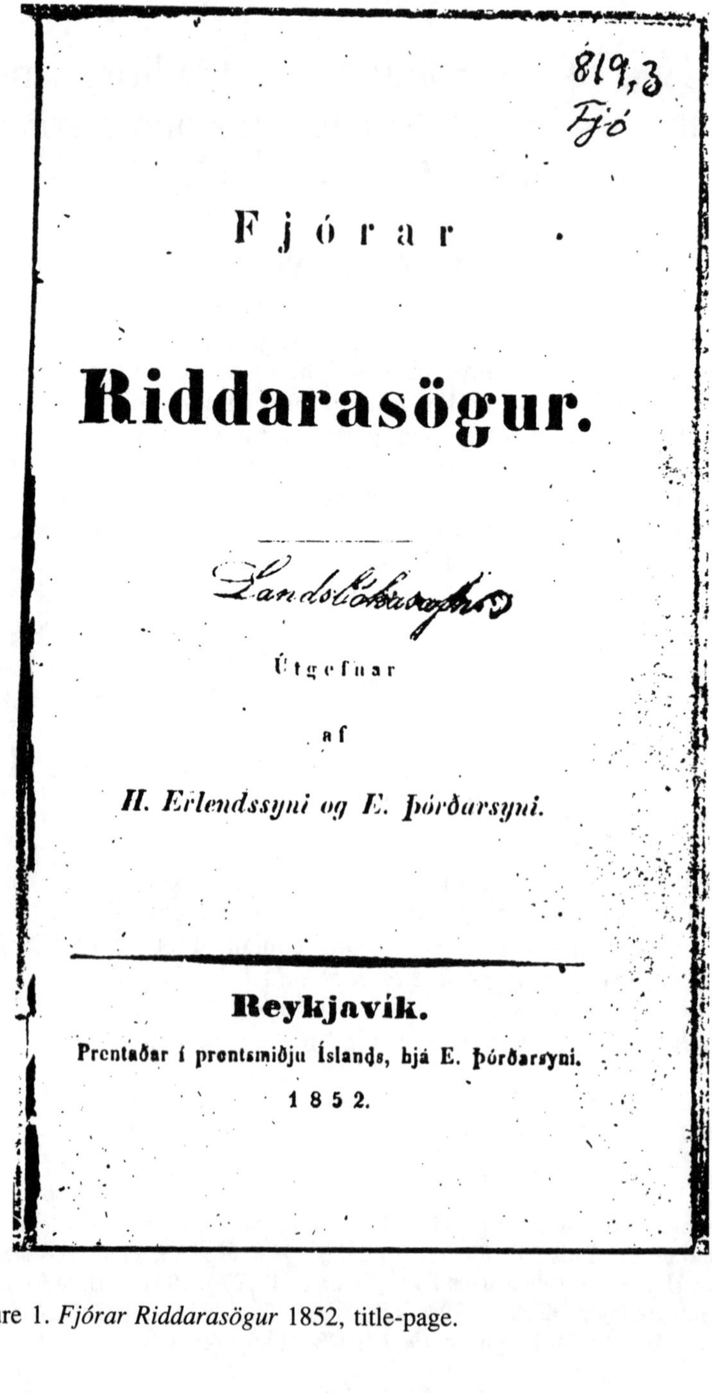

819,3
Fjó

F j ó r a r

Riddarasögur.

Landsbókasafns

Útgefnar

af

H. Erlendssyni og E. Þórðarsyni.

Reykjavík.

Prentaðar í prentsmiðju Íslands, hjá E. Þórðarsyni.

1 8 5 2.

Figure 1. *Fjórar Riddarasögur* 1852, title-page.

editions (Figure 1).[2] The edition was not well received, however. In the journal *Þjóðólfur* 92 (29 September 1852), the romantic poet and novelist Benedikt Sveinbjarnarson Gröndal (1826–1907)—one of the leading literary figures in the tiny Icelandic parnassus—published a scathing review of this first saga edition by Einar Þórðarson which was entirely representative of its time. It is worthwhile to examine in some detail the attitudes struck in this review and in the ensuing rejoinder, since the arguments rehearsed there contain elements of a discourse which was by no means confined to this isolated Icelandic instance. It was rather part of much larger and more systematic process of sociocultural bifurcation which had begun to exercise its influence in most parts of Europe in the post-Enlightenment years:

> [...] En vegna þess, að tíminn, sem öllu vill eyða, og á öllu vinnur, breytir hlutnum meir eða minna í hinum frammrennanda straumi alda og ára, og hlutirnir koma opt fyrir sjónir eptir langan aldur slitnir og eyddir, og eins og annarlegir fyrir þá, sem nú eru uppi: vegna þessa þurfa þeir líka nákvæmari skoðun og vandlegri meðferð, ef þeir á rjettan hátt eiga að sýna oss liðna tíð. Það munu allir skilja, að jeg meina til fornleifa og fornrita, og það er einkum tvennt, sem vakir fyrir sjerhverjum þeim vönduðum manni, er vill halda þeim á lopt, nl. (1) helgi þeirra, svo að þeir sjáist óbreyttir og óbjagaðir, með ummerkjum tíðarinnar, og þó svo fullkomlegir, sem auðið er, og (2) sú nytsemi, sem menn hafa af þeim til að sjá liðinn tíma, sem leiðir af hinu fyrra, og er því óaðgreinanlega sameinað. Þetta hefur nú verið reynt og gjört af hinum ágætustu mönnum, bæði þeim, sem hafa unnið fyrir Fornfræðafjelagið, og þeim, sem hafa tekið þátt í 'Fornfræðafjelagi Norðurlanda'. Til þess að sýna oss gömul rit á prenti í óbjagaðri mynd, og eins og þau hafa fundist, hafa þeir farið rjettan veg, með því, að láta prenta þau nákvæmlega eptir handrit-unum, og skýra frá mismunandi orðum (Variantes loci), og frá því, hvenær þau muni vera rituð, hvaðan þau sjeu o.s.frv.
>
> Einusinni var sú gullöld—eða forgyllta öld—hjá oss hjer á sjálfu voru landi Íslandi, að það átti að fara að gefa út fornsögur vorar hjer í landinu sjálfu, og eptir þær hríðir, sem prentsmiðjan fjekk, fæddist hin svo nefnda 'Viðeyjar Njála'. Hana þekkja allir. Nú eptir að herra E. Þórðarson er orðinn 'valdamaður' í prentstofunni, þá er eðlilegt, að hann vill verka landinu til sæmdar, svo sem opinber embættispersóna, og nú vekur hann upp aptur nýja gullöld (eða forgyllta öld) og fornan hetjumóð, og gefur út—raunar í sameiningu við herra skómakara H.

---

[2]Title and full bibliographical information as printed: *Fjórar Riddarasögur*. Útgefnar af H. Erlendssyni og E. Þórðarsyni. Prentaðar í prentsmiðju Íslands, hjá E. Þórðarsyni. 1852.

Erlendsson—því skómakari er hann—Fjórar Riddarasögur.
Jeg veit raunar, að herra E. Þórðarson er prentari, og herra H.
Erlendsson er skómakari, en jeg þekki ekki þessa menn sem forn-
fræðinga, og það veit jeg, að hingað til hefur enginn, nema fornfræðingar, lagt hendur að því, að gefa út fornsögur—nema um
Viðeyjar njálu. Jeg get því ekki tekið það fyrir annað, en ósvifið
dramb, sem stendur í formálanum, að sögurnar sjeu prentaðar eptir
því 'fullkomnasta, elzta og bezta handriti', sem þeir gátu fengið, því
þessi orð voga engir að leggja sjer í munn, nema þeir sjeu málfræðingar eða fornfræðingar, eða að öðrum kosti ósannindamenn.

Það er líka sjerhverjum manni ljóst, sem nokkuð þekkir hversu á
stendur, að þetta fyrirtæki er einungis stofnað í gróða skyni,—og
sögurnar kvað vera gefnar út 'til að skemmta alþýðu'. Það er ágætt
fyrirtæki, en það er hjer stofnað með því, að hafa þjóð vora að háði.
Er það ekki að hafa þjóðina að háði, þegar tveir taka ráð sín saman,
til þess að hafa fje út fyrir bók, sem gefin er út öll bjöguð, heimildar-
laus og vitlaus? Þegar því er logið upp í opin eyrun á alþýðu, að
menn hafi 'virt sögurnar sjálfar', sem sumar voru aldrei til, og eru svo
ósvífnir að vona, að þetta fyrirtæki muni verða virt? Því hvaða
fyrirtæki er þetta? Það er svona: annar les margar fornsögur, og
spinnur síðan upp sjálfur eitthvert bannsett bull, sem er öldungis út úr
og á móti anda tímans og þjóðarinnar, en hinn prentar bullið, og
bullarinn stendur upp í axlir.

Jeg skal nú skýra betur þessi þrjú orð, sem eru það, að jeg kalla
sögurnar: bjagaðar, heimildarlausar og vitlausar. [...] 3. Að jeg kalla
þær vitlausar, þarf engrar skýringar, því það flýtur af hinu undan-
ganganda, bæði af Nr. 1 og 2, og líka af því, sem jeg annars hefi áður
sagt, að þær ekki neitt eiga við anda þjóðarinnar. Því hversu á það að
eiga við nokkra þjóð og nokkurn tíma, sem er vitleysa? Að minnsta
kosti er það auðsjeð á sumum sögunum, að útgefendurnir eru skáld.
Jeg veit, að mönnum muni þykja leiðinlegt, að heyra upptalningu á
smekkleysum, dönskuslettum, rammvitlausri landalýsingu og öðru
þess konar; en ef nokkurn langar til að sjá þetta, þa lesi hann 'fjórar
Riddarasögur', og enginn skyldi trúa, að þetta sje gefið út 1852!
(Gröndal 1852)[3]

[Because time which creates and destroys everything, changes things
to a greater or lesser extent in its ever-rolling stream, and things are
brought to light which have lain lost or damaged for years, and seem
strange to people alive today: accordingly such things require more
accurate examination and more careful treatment if they are properly
to reveal former times to us. It must be understood that I am referring
to antiquities and old texts, and there are two things in particular
which every careful scholar who wishes to exhibit them should be

---

[3]See also his *Ritsafn* III 15–18, 512.

aware of: (i) their sanctity, so that they may be seen unchanged and uncontaminated, complete with the marks of age on them, and are thus in as perfect condition as is possible and (ii) their usefulness in helping men to catch a glimpse of past ages. This point follows directly on from the first and is therefore indivisibly linked to it. That has been proved by those admirable scholars who have worked for the Antiquarian Society, and those who have played a part in the Old Northern Text Society. In order to show to us old texts in unaltered form, in the condition in which they were found, they have done the right thing in having them printed exactly as in the manuscripts, and in explaining variant readings, and when the manuscripts were written, and their provenance etc.

Once there was the golden age—or the gilded age—with us here in our land of Iceland, so that our ancient sagas ought to be published here; and after such period of time as the printer could find, was born the so-called Viðeyjar *Brennu-Njáls saga.* Everyone knows that volume. Now that Mr. E. Þorðarson has become 'boss' of the printing-house, it is only natural that he should wish to work for the honour of his country as some kind of official office holder, and now he is to create a new golden age (or gilded age) and ancient heroic meed, and publishes—in fact in co-operation with the shoemaker Mr H. Erlendsson (for a cobbler he is)—*Fjórar Riddarasögur.*

I know for a fact that Mr. E. Þorðarson is a printer and that Mr H. Erlendsson is a shoemaker, but I do not know these men to be antiquarian scholars, and I do know that until now no-one other than antiquarian scholars has undertaken to edit old sagas, except the Viðeyjar *Njáls saga.* I cannot therefore regard their assertion, printed in the preface, that the sagas are printed 'from the most complete, oldest and best manuscript' which they could get, as anything other than the most offensive, for no-one would dare to say these words unless he were a philologist, a palæologist or a liar.

It is also clear to everyone who knows anything about it, that this undertaking was designed purely for profit,—and the sagas are said to have been published 'for the entertainment of the common man'. That is a worthy undertaking, but it is here designed to ridicule our nation. Does it not ridicule the nation when two men team up to make money from a book which is published all distorted, without sources, and incorrect; when the people are openly lied to and told that 'these sagas have been respected', stories some of which never existed; and when [these men] are so brazen as to hope that their undertaking will be respected? For what sort of undertaking is this? It is thus: one of them reads many old sagas, and then himself invents some damnable rubbish, which is completely out of touch with the spirit of the time and the nation, and the other one prints this rubbish, and the stuff stands shoulder-high.

I shall explain further what I mean by the three words 'distorted,

without sources and incorrect'[...]. 3. That I call them distorted
hardly needs any explanation, because it follows on directly from
what has previously been said about both (1) and (2), and also from
the other point which I have made already, that they do not suit in
any way the spirit of the people. Therefore how ought it to suit any
people or any period which is stupid? At least it is quite evident from
some sagas that the publishers are poets. I know that people would be
bored by lists of vulgarities, Danicisms, totally warped geographical
descriptions, and the like; but should anyone desire to see that sort of
thing, then let him read *Fjórar Riddarasögur*, and no-one would
believe that such a thing could be published in 1852!

How does Gröndal approach his subject in these paragraphs? Hardly
surprisingly, he adopts the viewpoint of an elitist, educated member of
the bourgeoisie and attacks the *Fjórar Riddarasögur* edition because of
its non-scholarly format. In Gröndal's opinion (see his first section), the
norm for any editorial work on Old Norse saga-literature had been
established by the famous publications of the Fornfræðafélag. Gröndal
contrasts these fine editions with more recent publications such as the ill-
famed Viðey edition of *Brennu-Njáls saga* (1844) or the newly edited
Riddarasögur: volumes which were produced—and this alone is seen as
sufficient reason to discredit the editions in question—by a printer and a
shoemaker respectively. The very willingness of such people to undertake
this sort of work is regarded as little short of 'ósvifið dramb' [pure
arrogance], since scholarly work on the literature of the Icelandic Golden
Age ought to be the sole prerogative of specialists, the 'málfræðingar eða
fornfræðingar' [philologists and palæologists]. In the next section Gröndal
further castigates the two editors because of their evident intention to
profit financially from the sale of these booklets ('einungis stofnað í
gróða skyni') and because of the editors' apparent concern that the books
should entertain the public ('til að skemmta alþýðu'). It is of course no
coincidence that the four narratives printed in the *Riddarasögur* volume
are taken from the sub-genres of legendary sagas (*fornaldarsögur*) and
late fictitious sagas (*lygisögur, Märchensagas*), and not from the group
of more prestigious family sagas (*Íslendingasögur*). Gröndal's dismissal
of such texts as 'bannsett bull' [pure rubbish] reflects a condescending
and ignorant disregard of popular, post-classical genres all too characteristic of many nineteenth-century philologists (Driscoll 1990). Gröndal
criticises among other things the 'bjagaðar', 'heimildarlausar', 'vitlausar'
[distorted, unsupported by sources, incorrect] form of the sagas. It is this
last reproach which is of particular interest here. In Gröndal's view the
Fjórar Riddarasögur are utterly incompatible with the 'anda tímans og
þjóðarinnar' [spirit of the time and the nation], and the book teems with
individual instances of 'smekkleysum' [tastelessness], a key concept in

all enlightened discussion.

The response of the two editors Einar Þórðarson and Hannes Erlendsson to Gröndal's strictures appeared on the last day of 1852. So characteristic is it of other prevailing attitudes that it also deserves to be quoted in full:

Mál er komið, að svara nokkrum orðum uppá útásetníngu *ónefnda mannsins* í 4. árg. Þjóðólfs [...] út á þær *'Fjórar Riddarasögur'*.

Útásetníngar þessar skulum við ekki rekja orð fyrir orð, því þær verðskulda það ekki, fyrst að mergurinn í þeim er þetta: að ekki geti nein sú ritgjörð eða saga verið annað en bull eða vitleysa, sem prentari og skómakari gefa út. Ekki skulum við svo fegra sögur þessar, að ekki kunni mega finna margt þeim betra og uppbyggilegra, en þó meinum við, að þær séu og geti verið eins meinlaus dægrastytting fyrir alþýðu, eins og sumt það, sem snillingarnir úngu eru að banga saman og bjóða fram; vera kann, að t.a.m. 'Kvöldvakan í Sveit', og 'Bónorðsförin' hafi haft eitthvað fram yfir Riddarasögurnar, en það er ófundið enn ágætið í þeim og snildin, og enginn mun finna meiri skemtan af þessum bæklingum en af Riddarasögunum. 'Örvaroddsdrápa' kann að vera fögur skáldmæli,—og eptir vonum af þeim manni er hana orti—, en það eru þá einúngis vísindamennirnir og skáldin, en ekki fáfróður almúgi, sem finnur það. Þetta meinum við að séu nú einhverjir helztu frumritaðir bæklingar, sem komið hafa út á seinni árum, til að skemta alþýðu; því ekki teljum við 'Ungsmannsgamanið', sem að er handa börnum, eða 'Æfintýrin' sem eru söfnuð eptir munnmælum, og ekki útleggíngarbrotið af 'Þúsund og einni nótt'. Við hefðum ekki gefið út Riddarasögurnar hefðu lærðu snillingarnir úngu bæði sigldir og ósigldir, sem að eru gagn og sómi þessa fáfróða og fátæka lands, boðið fram eitthvað sem var betra til að skemta almúganum; en við höldum að við séum saklausir af að hafa smánað landa okkar, eða 'haft þjóð vora að háði' með útgáfu þessara saga, sem svo víða eru til skrifaðar, og hafa verið lesnar til dægrastyttingar, á meðan ekki kemur út annað fróðlegra eða snjallara frá þessara tíma snillingum, en ritlingarnir sem við nefndum. [...] 2, að hann nefni okkur nokkurn þann, sem semur eða útleggur bækur til prentunar, sem ekki gjörir það meðfram til þess að fá uppúr þeim kostnaðinn og fyrirhöfnina—þá skulum við fyrirverða okkur fyrir að hafa ætlazt til að bera upp kostnaðinn fyrir útgáfuna á sögunum; hann mun annars eiga bágt með að sanna, að þetta fyrirtæki hafi fremur verið stofnað í gróða skyni, heldur enn útgáfa hverrar annarar bókar sem er látin gánga á prent, einkum þeirra bæklinga, sem þessir—á meðal útlendra alræmdu—'soltnu höfundar' hlaupa í að semja, til þess að afla sjer málúngi matar í þann svipinn. En við höfum ekki svipt aðfinníngamanninn neinu tækifæri til að vinna sjer inn málsverð þó við ljetum prenta sögurnar; en vel getur okkur skilizt, að hann sje þurftugur, því opt fer það saman, fullur munnur með hroka og gikksháttur, eins og aðfinningin um sögurnar ber vitni um, og tómur magi, og svo á hinn bóginn sjálfslof og ónytjúngsskapur. En hvað sem þessu líður, þá ætlum við okkur ekki að mannskemma okkur á því, að svara fúlyrðum aðfinningamannsins frekar en nú er gjört, í þessum línum; en bindum enda á þær með því, að benda honum til þess sem skáldið sagði forðum, 'Opt má af máli þekkja manninn, hver helzt hann er', o.s.frv. Útg. 4. Riddaras.[4]

[The time has now come to respond in a few words to the criticism of the *unnamed person* in the fourth volume of *Þjóðólfur* [...] to *Fjórar Riddarasögur*. We shall not repeat these criticisms word for word, because they are not worthy of it, since the point of them is that no essay or story published by a printer and a cobbler can be anything other than rubbish and nonsense. We shall not attempt to gild these stories, to say that nothing could be found better than them or more edifying, but we do believe that they are and can be a harmless diversion for common people, as much as some of what the bright young things [snillíngarnir úngu] are churning out; it may well be that, for example, 'Kvöldvakan í sveit' and 'Bónorðsförin' were a cut above the 'Riddarasögur', but their value and genius has yet to be discovered, and no-one could derive more pleasure from these booklets than from the 'Riddarasögur'. 'Örvaroddsdrápa' may well be a fine piece of poetry—not surprisingly in view of its author [sc. Gröndal]—but it is only academics and poets, and not the unenlightened public, who can appreciate it. We reckon these to be the main original works published in recent years for common people [...]. We should never have published the 'Riddararsögur' if the learned bright young things, both here and in Copenhagen, the pride of this poor benighted country, had produced anything better for the entertainment of common folk; we think that we are innocent of the charge of having belittled our countrymen, or having 'ridiculed the nation' by publishing these sagas, which are now so widely found in manuscripts and have been read for pleasure, while nothing more enlightening or clever appears from the bright young things than the booklets we mentioned. [...] 2, that he should name us anyone who has written or translated books for publication who has not also done so in order to make up some of the expense and bother—then shall we reproach ourselves for intending to recover the cost of publishing these sagas; but he will find it difficult to prove that this undertaking was intended for profit to a greater extent than the publication of any other book that is printed, in particular the books which these—notorious abroad—'starving authors' churn out in order to earn themselves a few crusts. But we have not deprived the critic of any opportunity to earn himself a meal through the publication of these sagas; although

---

[4]The editors' rejoinder in *Þjóðólfur* 4, 101, 31 December 1852, 27; see also Gröndal, *Ritsafn* III 512–513. *Örvaroddsdrápa* (1851) is a poem by Gröndal.

we can well understand that he is needy, because a mouth full of arrogance and mockery such as the criticism of the sagas bears witness to and an empty stomach often go together, and so by the same token do self-aggrandisement and ineptitude. But regardless, we have no intention of demeaning ourselves by answering the critic's invective more than we have already done in these lines; but we end by reminding him of the words of the poet: 'Oft by his speech may a man be known, who he really is', etc. [Hallgrímur Pétursson, *Passiusálmar* xi 15] The editors of *Fjórar Riddarasögur*.]

The essence of this rejoinder is an elegant rhetorical strategy: the editors concede that the sagas in question are merely 'meinlaus dægrastytting fyrir alþýðu' [a harmless entertainment for the people], but for 'fáfróður almúgi' [the uneducated common man] they are at least as amusing as the writings of the 'lærðu snillingarnir ungu' [learned young geniuses] in which only 'vísindamennirnir og skáldin' [scholars and poets] can find pleasure. Young poets have produced nothing which could 'skemmta almúganum' [amuse the common people] in the way that the old chivalric sagas can. The second part of the rejoinder addresses the accusation of profit-making. Here one is reminded of the arguments which were deployed a hundred years earlier by the Danish bookseller Fridrich Christian Pelt; in an answer to the learned Ludvig Holberg, Pelt wrote that he was not willing to starve as 'a martyr to good taste'.[5] This rejoinder illustrates very clearly the commercialisation of popular culture described by the English scholar Peter Burke. This commercialisation took place in Western Europe in the period 1650-1800 and reached Iceland by the middle of the nineteenth century. Benedikt Gröndal struck the final blow by writing a parody verdict in a fictional lawsuit:

> Dómur í sökinni 1/1852.--Hið vísindalega gegn útgefendum Fjögra riddarasaga [sic].
> Ár 1852, hinn 31. dag desembermánaðar, var hinn vísindalegi réttur settur og haldinn á hans aðsetursstað í Reykjavík, hvar þá var fyrirtekið ofanskrifað mál, sem þannig er undir komið, að í nóvembermánuði læddust tveir ókunnugir brókfuglar inn í flokk vorra lærðu samverkamanna, og uppvöktu með smekklausum og vitlausum

---

[5]'Fortale', *Den Tyrkiske Robinson eller Prinds Eberards af Westphalen Eleomores og Zulimas Kierligheds= og Levnets=Beskrivelse [...]* (3rd edition, Copenhagen 1750), pp. 2v–3r: 'Det hedder, at vi formedelst slette Bøgers Oplag fordærve den almindelige Smag. Men uden Tvivl er Livet meer værdt, end en god Smag. Synd at forlange, at vi skulde være saadanne Martyrer af god Smag, at vi derover gave Næringen op, og giorde Bekostning paa Skrifter, som ingen, uden et lidet Tal af skiønsomme, læste. De Lærde skulde tale i en anden Tone, dersom de vare i vores Sted. Just det, der bevæger dem til at sætte sig imod den herskende Smag, bevæger os til at følge den.'

afkvæmum sínum þann skarkala, að friðurinn truflaðist í voru lærða ríki. Þeir gáfu út þá bók, sem heitir 'Fjórar riddarasögur', og skírskotast um lýsingu hennar til Þjóðólfs, 4. ár, bls. 367-368, hvar af sést, að bókin er ekki í húsum hafandi. Og þegar rétturinn í góðri meiningu vildi beita sínum föðurlega aga, og taka frá þjóðinni þetta heimskulega leikfang, þá risu brókfuglar þessir upp með ópi og emjan og illum látum, og höfðu þann munnsöfnuð í frammi, sem börnum er ósæmilegur við foreldra sína og sér meiri menn. En þó að sjálfsagt væri, að slíkt ætti hegningu skilið, þar eð þessir menn eru fullkomnir delinquentar fyrir vísindanna og menntagyðjanna dómstóli, þá virtist réttinum samt, að ekki bæri að kveða upp dóm yfir delinquentunum, fyrri en læknar hefðu sagt upp álit sitt um heilsuástand þeirra. [...]

Eftir hinum þannig framkomnu upplýsingum virtist réttinum sem ekki gæti orðið kveðinn upp dauðadómur yfir delinquentunum, jafnvel þó að siður væri að drepa hvern þann, sem tróð sér inn í hin elevsinsku mysteria, og þó að þeir þannig hafi troðið sér inn í vorn vísindalega flokk, er heldur hefur skeð af heimsku en illvilja. En réttinum fannst, að ofannefndir lækna og sálarfræðinga vitnisburðir hlytu að takast til greina, því heilbrigður maður og heilvita mundi aldrei hafa ráðizt í slíka óhæfu og ofuryrði, og enda ekki keypt neinn til að hjálpa sér. Ennfremur ályktaði rétturinn, að þar eð hann er í fyrstu tilsettur og stofnaður af menntagyðjunum á Parnassus og Apollo Musagetes, og honum ber því að vernda þeirra ríki og lönd, þá skyldi dómur ganga yfir delinquentana fyrir það, að þeir með bulli sínu hafa komið trufli á vorn vísindalega frið, eins og uglur, sem koma í dúfnahóp. Ritstjóri Þjóðólfs þar á móti var, þó hann hefði gengið í delinquentanna flokk, frítekinn frá að mæta líkamlega og andlega fyrir réttinum, bæði sökum þess, að hann er einfættur, svo rétturinn áleit, að hann ekki væri fær um að hoppa þangað, og líka sökum þess, að hann að líkindum hefur gert sig brotlegan af þeirri sérplægni, sem leiðir af hungri, þar eð blað hans og álit er á mjög völtum fæti, svo hann getur eigi tekizt til greina.

Í tilliti til alls ens ofannefnda var því *dæmt rétt að vera:*

Delinquentarnir í þessari sök, útgefandur Fjögra riddarasaga, eiga að staðfestast og magnast í sínum andlega ruglingi, en varast þó að hafa fullan munninn með hroka og andann með gikkshátt. Sömuleiðis eiga þeir upp frá þessu að forðast öll fúlyrði og illan munnsöfnuð við þá, sem vilja uppala þá með sínum föðurlega aga og draga þá upp úr heimskunnar leirpytti. Enn fremur skulu þeir marséra burt af lærdómsins vígvelli.[6]

---

[6]Benedikt Sveinbjarnarson Gröndal, 'Dómur í sökinni 1/1852. Hið vísindalega gegn útgefendum Fjögra riddarasaga', Lbs. 179 fol.; see also Gröndal, *Ritsafn* III 18–20, 513.

[Verdict in the case 1.1852.—Scholarship vs the editors of *Fjórar Riddarasögur*.

On the 31st day of the month of December in the year 1852 the scholarly court was convened and held at its address in Reykjavík, where the above-cited case was considered, a case which began in November when two unknown upstarts crept into our learned assembly and with their tasteless and imbecilic products caused such a commotion that the peace was disturbed in our learned kingdom. They published a book called *Fjórar Riddarasögur*, for a description of which see *Þjóðólfur*, vol. iv, pp. 367–368, from which it can be seen that the book is not fit to be in any house. And when the court wished with good intention to exercise its paternal authority and remove from the people this idiotic plaything, these upstarts rose up with a great hue and cry, and spoke in a manner inappropriate for children to adopt with their parents or their betters. And although it is clear that such is punishable, since these men stand completely culpable before the court of scholarship and the muses of learning, yet it seems to the court that it is better not to pass judgement on the accused before a doctor has given his opinion as to the state of their health. [...]

In the light of this evidence it seems to the court that the sentence of death cannot be passed on the accused, even though it was customary to kill anyone who tried to force his way into the Eleusinian Mysteries, and although they have forced their way in the same manner into our scholarly assembly, this has been the result of ignorance rather than malice. The court felt that the medical and psychological evidence cited above must be taken as valid, since a person of sound body and mind would never have ventured into such incompetence and impertinence, and moreover would never have bought the help of anyone else. Moreover, it is the verdict of the court that since it was established and founded by the muses on Parnassus and Apollo Musagetes, and since it is required to protect their kingdoms and countries, the accused should be condemned for disturbing our scholarly peace with their nonsense, like owls among a flock of doves. The editor of *Þjóðólfur*, on the other hand, despite the fact that he had joined the ranks of the accused, was not required to appear physically and spiritually before the court, both on the grounds that he is one-legged, so the court felt that he would not be capable of hopping there, and also because he was in all likelihood guilty of that self-centredness that comes from hunger, since his newspaper and opinion is on an uncertain footing, so that he cannot be held to account.

In view of all the above it was therefore *deemed fitting and proper:*

The accused in this case, the editors of *Fjórar Riddarasögur*, should persist and increase in their spiritual confusion, but should be careful not to have their mouths full of arrogance and their spirits full

of mockery. Similarly they should from now on avoid all invective
and vicious comments against those who hope through their paternal
authority to edify them and drag them out of the mud-pit of ignorance. Moreover, they should march off the battlefield of learning.]

In this piece, preserved in a single manuscript and not printed during
Gröndal's lifetime, the refusal to acknowledge that the two lowly editors
had any right to engage in literary and educational activities is even more
blatant than in the original review. Gröndal arrogates to himself the right
to exercise judgement in the name of science ('Hið vísindalega gegn
útgefendum') and to exclude the editors from the battlefield of learning
('marséra burt af lærdómsins vígvelli'). Gröndal's attempt at denigrating
a popular-literary project resulted in ultimate failure; but his attempt
convincingly illustrates Pierre Bourdieu's theories about the socially
disintegrative, and stratificatory role of education in early modern and
modern Europe (Bourdieu 1979).

Two years after the publication of *Fjórar Riddarasögur* an Icelandic
translation of Johann Gottfried Schnabel's *Insel Felsenburg* appeared
under the title of *Felsenborgarsögur*.[7] Discussion of this work followed
a course similar to the debate over the *Fjórar Riddarasögur* volume. In
a first review in *Þjóðólfur*, the anonymous reviewer criticises amongst
other things the fact that the contents of the book had become old-
fashioned long before this new translation was first made available to an
Icelandic readership:

> Vér skulum að eins líta yfir bókaútgáfurnar þau 16 ár sem síðan eru
> liðin, og bera þær saman við bókaútgáfurnar 16 árin þar næst á
> undan, og vér munum finna mikla og verulega breytíngu á þessu til
> batnaðar. Vér höfum síðan fengið á prenti marga fróðlega gagnlega
> og uppbyggilega bók og smákver þó þar innan um hafi slæðzt
> einstöku smekkleysu og bábylju-bæklíngar eins og 'Riddarasögurnar'
> og 'Barndómssaga Krists', 'Versasafnið' (ný útgáfa 1854), einstöku
> rímur (af 'Þórði Hreðu', og af 'Bernótusi Borneyjarkappa'), og
> einkum *'Felsinborgar-sögurnar'* sem nú er verið að prenta á
> Akureyri.
> Þessar marklausu og smekklausu lygasögur þóktu hafandi til
> dægrar styttíngar fyrir svo sem rúmum mannsaldri hér frá meðal hins

---

[7]Full printed title and bibliographical information: *Felsenborgarsögur, eður
æfisögur ýmsra sjófarenda, einkum Alberts Júlíusar, sem var saxneskur að ætt.
Ritaðar á þjóðversku af sonarsyni bróðursonar hans, Eberharð Júlíusi, en nú
snúið af danskri tungu á íslenzka. 1. partur. Kostnaðarm.*: Grímur bókb. Laxdal,
Akureyri 1854. Prentaðar í prentsmiðju norður- og austurumdæmisins, af H.
Helgasyni.

fáfróðasta almúga í Þýzkalandi og Danmörku,—líkt og 'sagan af Litla Albertus'—ámeðan allur almenníngur var svo ófróður um hin fjarlægari lönd, þjóðir þær sem þau byggja, og um ýmsa þá krapta náttúrunnar sem menn bera nú skyn á. Um þetta leyti mátti bjóða fáfróðum almúga allskonar lokleysu um slíkt, áþekkt og sögur þessar innihalda, en engum hefir komið til hugar neinstaðar, að bjóða nýja útgáfu af slíku. Almúginn hér á landi er sagður, og víst með sanni, betur að sér en flest önnur alþýða; þó er nú verið að bjóða henni þær bækur, sem fáfróðum almúga í öðrum löndum þókti lokleysa fyrir 80 árum liðnum! Þetta er víst vottar um allt annað, en að smekkur og sómatilfinníng hinna upplýstari manna, sem eiga að heita, og sem gángast fyrir útgáfum slíkra bóka, sé jafmikil og jafnrík eins og fróðleiksfýsn og greind sjálfrar alþýðunnar hér á landi.[8]

[Let us look briefly at book publication over the sixteen years that have elapsed since [the publication of Tómas Sæmundsson's article 'Bókmentirnar íslendsku' in *Fjölnir* 5 (1839)], and compare it to publications in the sixteen years before that, and we find a significant change for the better. We have now got many instructive, useful, and edifying books and pamphlets, although in among them there have occasionally crept booklets of tastelessness and drivel such as the *Riddarasögur, Barndómssaga Krists, Versasafnið* (new ed. 1854), as well as the occasional *rímur* ('af Þórði Hreðu' and 'af Bernótusi Borneyjarkappa'), and in particular the *Felsenborgarsögur*, which are now being published in Akureyri.

These meaningless and tasteless fictions were thought suitable entertainment for the benighted folk of Germany and Denmark of a generation or so ago—like the 'Saga of Little Albert'—while they were ignorant of foreign lands and their inhabitants and the various forces of nature that we now understand. At that time it was possible to offer the ignorant populace all kinds of rubbish such as these stories contain, but no one anywhere would have thought of offering a new version of this sort of stuff. The common people in this country are thought, with some justice, to be more knowledgeable than most common people elsewhere; but now they are being offered books which the ignorant public thought were rubbish eighty years ago! This clearly demonstrates something other than that the taste and self-respect of the ostensibly enlightened persons responsible for the publication of such books are equal to the desire for knowledge and intelligence of the common people in this country.]

In the reviewer's opinion the translation belongs to that category of books which had circulated among the least educated people in foreign countries

---

[8] Anonymous review of the *Felsenborgarsögur* in *Þjóðólfur* 7, 4/5, 2 December 1854, 13–14.

a generation and more ago. Now it was to be sold to Icelanders who were
significantly better educated than these foreign readers. The review ends
with an appeal to the 'smekkur' [taste] and 'sómatilfinning' [sense of
honour] of 'hinna upplýstra manna' [enlightened people].

A second and longer review also dismisses the volume as tasteless and
even dangerous. The *Felsenborgarsögur* is here described as the worst
and most worthless book ever printed in Iceland, with criticism directed
at its outward appearance, and the uncultivated language with its many
pornographic expressions. Such a book—translated, moreover, by
clergymen—could not but corrupt the hearts of the young and encourage
them in the use of indecent language. The task of a printing press should
not be conceived in terms of a cow standing available for milking, but
should rather promote public enlightenment and education. Such worthy
ideals seemed unlikely to be fulfilled in this instance, however, with all
but two of the men associated with the printing press in Akureyri being
'ómenntaðir' [uneducated]. As regards style and implicit values, the
Fjórar Riddarasögur and *Felsenborgarsögur* editions are treated
identically in the reviews:

> [...] En þó keyrði fram úr, þegar nýja prentsmiðjan á Akureyri hleypti
> 'Felsenborgarsögunum' af stokkunum, því það má fullyrða, að
> fánýtari og verri bók hafi aldrei komið út á Íslandi. Þá eru 'Andra-
> rímur' og 'Gústavssaga' kóngbornar í samanburði við þessa fánýtu
> lygasögu. En þá allur frágángurinn á bókinni? Hér kastar tólfunum;
> málið er óvandað, stirt og ljótt, og þartil hrúgað saman klámyrðum og
> allskonar óþverra, og það kveður svo rammt að þessu, að útleggjarinn
> hefir orðið að búa til ýms ný orð, til þess að geta sagt lesendum
> sínum skiljanlega til vegar innan um öll þessi foræði allsnaktra lasta
> og ódyggða, sem hér er yfir að fara, t.d. í sögunni af 'Lemelie', og
> margvíða annarstaðar. Það liggur í augum uppi, að slík bók hljóti að
> spilla hjörtum hinna ýngri, og deyfa tilfinníngu þeirra fyrir velsæmi
> og fegurð. Það getur ekki hjá því farið, að þau festi í minni og taki
> sér síðan í munn klámyrði þau og fúkyrði, sem bók þessi er svo
> auðug af; og sé það því satt, að 'geistlegir' menn hafi með fram átt
> þátt í útleggíngu bókarinnar, þá eiga þeir hinir sömu síður en ekki
> þakkir skilið fyrir þenna starfa sinn; hefðu þeir gjört laglegt ágrip af
> bókinni og sleppt úr því, sem ljótt er í henni og hneikslanlegt, þá
> hefði verið allt öðru máli að gegna. En að láta hana svona út í
> almenníng—með þessari viðbjóðslegu lýsíngu lasta og ódyggða í
> hinni viðurstyggilegustu nekt þeirra—því verður aldrei bót mæld, ekki
> fremur en þó mennirnir tæki sjálfir upp á því, að gánga alsnaktir á
> mannamótum;—og að prentsmiðjan skuli ljá sig til að leggja höndur
> að prentun slíkrar bókar, getur ekki annað en spillt fyrir henni í
> augum allra þeirra, sem láta sig það nokkru skipta, hvort þessi stofnan
> heldur uppi sóma sínum og gegnir ætlunarverki sínu eins og vera ber,

og af henni er heimtandi. Forstöðumenn prentsmiðju þessarar varðar
það meir en þeir líklega ætla, að stofnun þessi láta ekki vanbrúka sig
svo herfilega. Hún á ekki að vera nein féþúfa fyrir þá, eða eins og
annar maður hefir að orði kveðið, að skoðast eins og mjólkurgripur
hlutaðeiganda, heldur er henni ætlað að efla almenna upplýsíngu og
menntun. En því er miður, að þetta er enn þá ekki komið fram, og
kemur það að öllum líkindum ekki, á meðan stofnunin er undir
förstöðu þeirra manna, sem sjálfir eru ómenntaðir (—að 2 undan-
skildum) og, sem slíkir, ekki hafa vit á að meta, hver að sé tilgángur
og ætlunarverk hennar, og sjálfir ekkert geta látið henni í té af eigin
ramleik, og ekki litið á annað en það, sem næst liggur við [...][9]

[But things went too far when the new press in Akureyri launched
Felsenborgarsögur, for it may be stated that never has a more useless
or worse book been published in Iceland. *Andrarímur* and *Gústavs-
saga* are as royalty compared to this sloppy piece of fiction. The
production of the book is beyond the pale: the language is sloppy,
stilted, and grotesque, there are heaps of obscenities and all kinds of
filth. It even goes so far that the translator has had to create various
new words in order to lead his readers sensibly through the quagmire
of naked sins and vices which must be crossed here, for example in
the story of 'Lemelie' and in many other places. It is obvious that
such a book is bound to corrupt the hearts of the young and diminish
their feeling for what is proper and beautiful. There is no escaping
their remembering and later employing the obscenities and vulgarities
with which this book abounds. And if it is true that members of the
clergy have had a part in the translation of this book, then they have
no thanks due to them for their labours. Had they made a reasonable
summary of the book, omitting the ugly and scandalous parts of it,
that would have been a different matter, but presenting this to the
public—with these disgusting descriptions of sins and vices—can
never be excused, no more than if the men themselves had decided
to appear stark naked in public, and that the press should have
allowed itself to be part of the production of such a book can only
diminish it in the eyes of all those who care about whether this
establishment is able to maintain its dignity and fulfil its intended
function as it should and as is expected. It is a matter of greater
importance to the directors of the press than they appear to realise
that this establishment should not be misused so terribly. It should not
be a source of income for them nor, as another person has expressed
it, pored over as if it were some dairy cow belonging to them; rather
is its purpose to promote common knowledge and education. But,

[9]Anonymous review of the *Felsenborgarsögur* in *Þjóðólfur* 26, 20 June
1855, 102–103; 27/28, 6 July 1855, 109.

alas, that has not yet happened, and is unlikely to do so whilst the establishment is under the control of men who are themselves uneducated (with two exceptions), and, as such, neither have the intelligence to appreciate its intended purpose, nor are themselves able to provide it with a new focus through their own endeavours, incapable as they are of seeing past the end of their own noses]

MANUSCRIPT AND PRINT TRANSMISSION

The correspondences between these two polemics which appeared almost simultaneously are remarkable, but of course not coincidental. The discussion of education, taste, popular enlightenment, and professionalism matches closely the central elements in Jónas Hallgrímsson's *rímur* review from 1837.[10] This celebrated article appeared at a turning point in the history of Icelandic culture. During the middle decades of the nineteenth century, an important development took place in the transmission of traditional narrative literature—*rímur* and *sögur*; the quasi-medieval tradition of manuscript circulation gave way to the modern printed book.[11] Up to about 1850 it is possible to distinguish between a popular tradition, marked by manuscript diffusion (Glauser 1994), and a quite separate learned print tradition; thereafter, in the wake of Einar Þórðarson's pioneering 1852 edition, the earlier, hand-written form of text distribution is replaced by an increasing number of popular

---

[10]Jónas starts his review with his now famous attack on this traditional and very popular genre: 'Eins og rímur (á Íslandi) eru kveðnar, og hafa verið kveðnar allt að þessu, þá eru þær flestallar þjóðinni til mínkunar—það er ekkji til neíns að leína því—og þar á ofan koma þær töluverðu illu til leíðar; eíða og spilla tilfinníngunni á því, sem fagurt er og skáldlegt og sómir sjer vel í góðum kveðskap, og taka sjer til þjónustu "gáfur" og krapta margra manna, er hefðu gjetað gjert eítthvað þarfara—orkt eítthvað skárra, eða þá að minnsta kosti prjónað meínlausann duggra-sokk, meðan þeír voru að "gullinkamba" og "fimbulfamba" til ævarandi spotts og athláturs um alla veröldina.' (p. 18) [As *rímur* (in Iceland) are recited, and have been recited through the ages, they are, most of them, to the nation's discredit—there is no point in denying it—in addition to which they do quite a lot of harm; they destroy and corrupt the feeling for what is beautiful and poetic and befitting good poetry, and take into their service the intelligence and energy of many who could have done something more useful—composed something better, or at least knitted a harmless sock, while they were 'bumpty-dumptying' and 'rumpty-tumptying' to the eternal sport and amusement of the entire world]; see also Rumbke 1981.

[11]For questions of terminology and methodology see Darnton 1982.

and inexpensive editions during the 1870s and 1880s. With regard to the reviews of *Fjórar Riddarasögur* and *Felsenborgarsögur*, it is worth mentioning that it was only after printed editions had begun to appear more widely that public discussion started about works previously circulated in manuscript. Circulating manuscripts never enjoyed the broadly-based public attention that was accorded to the printed editions. It was this new mass publication format that made possible any modern debate about the aesthetics of literature.

Previous literary debate had been restricted to rehearsing all too familiar eighteenth-century attitudes;[12] the 1746 prohibitions relating to saga reading and *rímur* singing were repeated;[13] the recitation of old tales during the *kvöldvökur* was rejected in favour of Bible reading; a sharp distinction was drawn between respectable (and historical) *Íslendingasögur* and disreputable legendary and chivalric sagas which were rejected because of their fictional (and often fantastic) elements.[14] Confronted by the power of middle-class literary institutions such as printing presses, publishing houses, and literary journals, the 'medieval' practice of distributing saga manuscripts came to an end towards the end of the nineteenth century. It is interesting to observe, however, that these popular printed saga editions adopted important features from the manuscript tradition. These books were still intended to be read aloud and their main form of distribution remained the *kvöldvaka* entertainment, with its largely peasant audience—non-bourgeois, non-urban, non-learned,

[12]See, for example, *Leikafæla* (1757) by Þorsteinn Pétursson (1710–1785): manuscripts AM 936 4to and Lbs. JS 113 8vo.

[13]'From this interesting apartment, I proceeded to a large room adjoining, which is properly the bed-room of the servants. The beds were clean and neatly arranged, and, what is but too little attended to in Iceland, the place was well aired. It gave me peculiar pleasure to be informed, that this apartment also formed the domestic chapel. Here, the whole family, which consists of twenty members, assembles every evening, when a psalm is sung, and, after a chapter of the Bible has been read, an appropriate prayer is presented by the head of the family. Besides this exercise, the Secretary [Brieme] spends an hour or two, in the long winter evenings, in reading to the family, while at work; and, what cannot be sufficiently commended, he has substituted the reading of the historical books of Scripture for that of the Sagas, which was formerly in universal use, and is still kept up by most of the peasants.' (Henderson 1818, I 87)

[14]See, for example, Jón Ingjaldsson (1799/1800–1876), *Andlig Áminningar-Hugvekja*: Lbs. ÍB 720 8vo (1847).

non-specialised readers and listeners.[15] Functionally, saga manuscripts and popular saga editions from the second half of the nineteenth century had their closest parallels in stories which were printed elsewhere as chapbooks, *Volksbücher, Groschenhefte, historier, folkebøger, skillings-tryk*. In line with the cheap French editions of popular stories from the eighteenth century, anthropologists would here speak of an Icelandic *Bibliothèque bleue*. In the following section, some features of these newly available and popular volumes will be illustrated.

Manuscripts

Title-pages. I shall begin this section by examining some saga manuscript title-pages from the late nineteenth century. They indicate something of the variety of content and function represented by these manuscripts.

There is, for example, the rather simple form of a title-page as represented by Lbs. 2956 8vo, a manuscript of 598 pages, written between 1858 and 1864: 'SAGNA. / B.O.K. / SKRIFUD / AF. / I.I.S. / 1858–64'. An index ('Innihald Bókarinnar') lists the titles of the eleven stories at the end of the volume (Figures 2 and 3). A late (1905) copy of *Huldar saga*, Lbs. 3026 4to, 444 pages, has the laconic title 'Sögu / Bók', but a supplementary title-page offers an additional source reference: 'Sagann / af / HULD DROTTNÍNGU / hinni / MÍKLU. /—/ og / ýmsum er við þá Søgu Koma / og er sú sama er Sturla Løgmaður sagði / á skipi Magnúsar Konúngs Lagabætis / 1263.' The manuscript is dated on the last page: 'Endað að skrifa 9 Desember 1905. / af H.B. Jónssyni'. Other manuscripts like Lbs. 3022 4to identify the work's genre on the title-page: 'GAMLAR / RIDDARASÖGR. / Skrifaðar / af / Þorsteini Guðbrandssyni / á / Kaldrananesi. / 1876'. This particular collection contains seven chivalric and fictitious sagas.

Several hand-written title-pages make clear that the manuscripts were used within a certain functional framework of cultural activity.[16] For instance, the title page of Lbs. ÍB 161 8vo, written in 1853, gives an

---

[15]See, for example, the remark of Benedikt Ásgrímsson in the preface to his edition of *Sagan af Júnífer konungi* (Reykjavík 1901), p. [2]: 'Eg vona, af því að sagan er skemmtileg, að menn geti stytt sér eina kveldstund með því að lesa hana.' [I hope that because the story is enjoyable men can while away an evening reading it].

[16]On the variety of written and oral forms of transmission, see Schenda 1993.

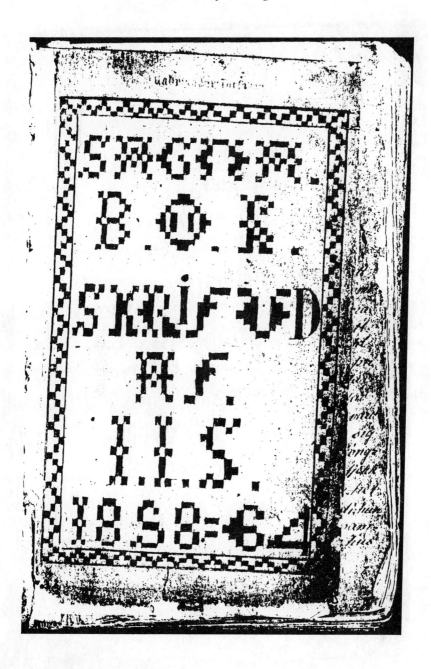

Figure 2. Lbs. 2956 8vo, title-page.

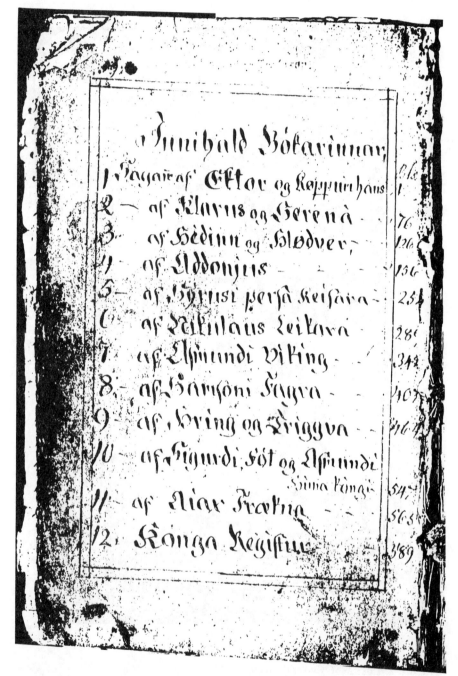

Figure 3. Lbs. 2956 8vo, index.

Icelandic version of the *utile-dulce* topos: 'Eirn Lítill / Samtín / íngur / Til Dægra stittíngar og Fródleiks'. Another similar manuscript Lbs. ÍB 160 8vo, written in 1847–1848, asserts the recreational rather than the didactic function of literature, and underlines its value for the traveller: 'Ein Lítil / Kvøldva / ka / Til skémtunar og Dægra stitt- / íngar'; 'því / Skemten*n* maður er vagn á veg' (Figure 4). The contents of this collection consist of a mixture of *rímur, sögur, gátur, kvæði, ævintýri*. The book closes with a traditional scribal formula: 'endar so / þettað litla æfentíri Bókina / verði hun øllum til á nægju / um eina qvöld stund. / Fines / 2.9.48', thus evoking the image of the *kvöldvaka*, that specifically Icelandic institution of the evening wake which took place during the winter and served primarily as an occasion for the production of woollen articles, but which also served as a source of entertainment for the farm inhabitants (Hermann Pálsson 1962, Magnús Gíslason 1977). In a copy of *Vilhjálms saga sjóðs* from the early nineteenth century, Lbs. 3127 4to, a reference to this form of literary communication, involving a writer, a reciter and a group of listeners, can be found in the formula at the end of the text (Glauser 1983, 78-100; 1985): 'Nw er saga þe*sse* kom / en á enda, hafe þeir stora þock sem hlíða / min*n*e sa er las hin*n* aungva er skrifade'.

The process of copying. Several manuscripts offer precise information as to their sources. Thus the title-page of Lbs. 674 4to, about 1820–30, reads: 'Ein Frodleg / Søgu Book / In*n*i haldandi / Nockrar Merkilegar Fraa / Sagnir af kongum og magtar / Møn*n*um Fornaldar nu ad / Nyu uppskrifadar eftir hund / rad aara gömlu exscripto; / fra Vatnsfyrdi / ad Forlægi og Uppakostnadi, virdulegs'. Such comments are, however, more often to be found at the end of a text, as for example in Lbs. 791 8vo, p. 60: 'og endar so / Sagan af Agnari Hróars Syni / endað að skrifa þan / 16 Dezember 1888 / af Vilhjalmi Einarssini / Skrifað eftir hand riti / Jóns Jónssonar bónda á / Simbakoti 1888'.[17] Certain information offers further insights into the process of copying; as a rule, copies were written during the winter, as in the case of Lbs. 3023 4to: 'Endað að Skrifa Dag 9 Februari 1882 / af / Arna Sveinbjarnarsini / á Oddsstöðum'. This manuscript has the following title-page identifying date and place: 'Nockrir / Smá=þættir / af / markverdum / Islendingum / skrifadir / af / M: Thorarensen / Weturinn 1823 / i / Kaupmannahöfn' (Figure 5).

From the evidence of other dates it is apparent that it could take as

---

[17]Grímur M. Helgason 1986 discusses the texts produced by Jón Jónsson of Simbakot (1834–1912).

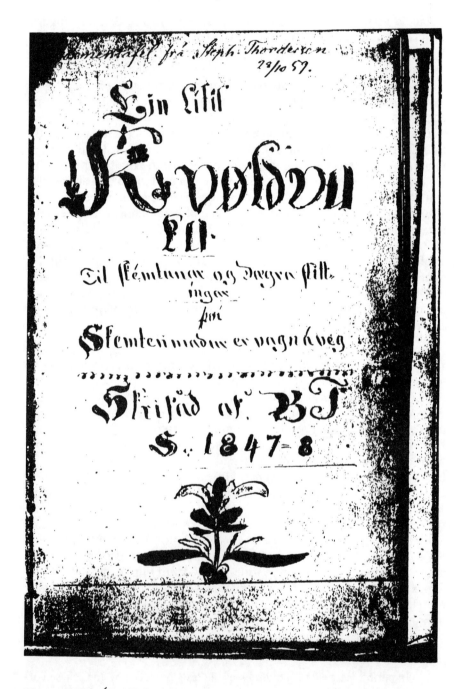

Figure 4. Lbs. ÍB 160 8vo, title-page.

much as a whole year to complete the copying of a 450 page quarto manuscript (Lbs. 1618 4to); that the aforementioned Vilhjálmur Einarsson of Dvergasteinn (Lbs. 791 8vo) finished *Agnars saga* on December 16; he then needed another two days to copy out 'dálítil saga af Adam' (thirty-six pages), and a further month and six days to copy out 'Sagan af Remundi og Melusinu' (thirty-four pages) which he duly finished on 24 January 1889.

Occasionally there are insights into personal tragedies, as in the case of Lbs. 3629 4to in which Helgi Sigurðsson commemorates his late son Helgi (1847–70) by means of a short biography included at the end of *Ajax saga* (1876). The younger Helgi had copied out the two texts in the manuscript at the age of sixteen whilst he was working in the fishing industry; he subsequently died aged only twenty-three. That someone so young should be engaged in the writing of manuscripts is in line with information from other writers' biographies; it seems that young people often acquired their writing abilities through the copying of sagas, thereby also laying the foundations for later, more extensive text collections.

The end of the manuscript tradition. The final stage of the active manuscript tradition was reached when texts were simply copied out into

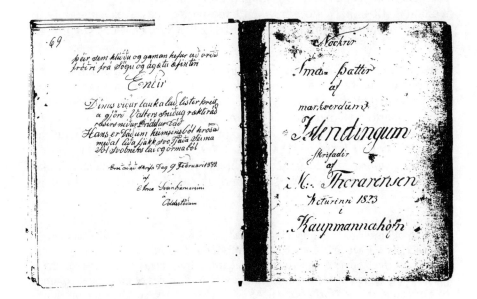

Figure 5. Lbs. 3023 4to, title-page and f. 69.

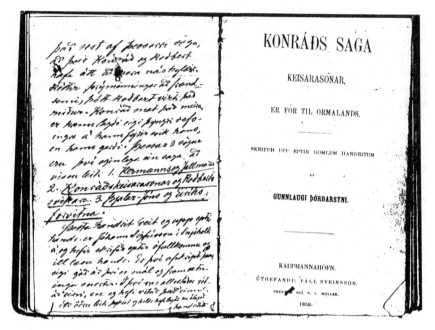

Figure 6. Lbs. 2497 8vo.

exercise-books and were no longer used for traditional purposes of recitation (Lbs. 3027 4to), or when hand-written passages serve only to complete fragmentary printed texts (Lbs. 2497 8vo, *c.* 1902) (Figure 6).

Magnús Jónsson of Tjaldanes. The climax of the manuscript tradition and the conclusion of the centuries-old process of collection and transmission is represented by the work of Magnús Jónsson of Tjaldanes (1835–1922): twenty quarto volumes of *Fornmannasögur Norðurlanda* (Lbs. 1491–1510 4to), 800 pages in each volume (a total of 16,000 pages), with the volumes written between 1883 and 1909.[18] This project represents a kind of a *summa* of Icelandic saga literature in the late nineteenth and early twentieth centuries. As is shown by the example in the illustrations,

[18]In addition to this imposing collection (Lbs. 1491–1510 4to), numerous manuscripts by Magnús Jónsson of Tjaldanes are to be found in the National Library of Iceland and in private collections. It is clear that some of these manuscripts represent second or at times even third copies of individual volumes of *Fornmannasögur Norðurlanda*. As M.J. Driscoll (personal communication) has suggested, it is not impossible that Magnús copied parts or the whole of the vast 16,000 page collection two or three times.

Magnús copies his texts very carefully. He paginates the volumes neatly, uses running titles and establishes a consistent page content of twenty-two lines. He even goes so far as to mimic the appearance of critical editions by paginating the prefaces with Roman ciphers (Figure 7).

Unlike most other writers, Magnús comments on his sources, on his searches for manuscripts, and on his earlier work on this same massive project. He does this by means of 'formálar' [prefaces], thus seeking to imitate printed scholarly editions. In these introductions which very often contain extremely useful information about the late sagas, Magnús addresses such questions as the ownership of his source-manuscripts (frequently it was Guðbrandur Sturlaugsson), and the treatment and reconstruction of texts, as in the case of *Völsunga saga*, in volume twelve of the *Fornmannasögur Norðurlanda* (Lbs. 1502 4to, iii), where he resorts to a printed edition in order to supplement an inadequate source, thereby highlighting the parallel transmission of manuscripts and printed editions. These comments make it clear that it was not Magnús's primary intention to copy sagas which were well known and widely available. His aim was rather to collect and preserve rare and inaccessible narratives. The activity of text collection was to him of greater importance than making use of these *Fornaldarsögur Norðurlanda* texts in *kvöldvaka* recitations. An overall pattern of manuscript transmission has thus been illustrated: the process began during the thirteenth and fourteenth centuries; suffered interruption in the sixteenth century; enjoyed a revival in the seventeenth century (Springborg 1969, 1977; Jakob Benediktsson 1981); and ended with the work of a writer and compiler who assembled his collection of texts in accordance with his antiquarian, historical and (perhaps to some extent) his commercial interests.

Transmission statistics. A tentative and very preliminary attempt at determining statistically the extent of Icelandic manuscript transmission on the basis of available catalogues reveals that in public libraries there are about 550 manuscripts from the nineteenth and early twentieth centuries, with most of them containing several sagas. In comparison, there are about five hundred nineteenth-century *rímur*-cycles, preserved in more than one thousand *rímur* manuscripts; and about one hundred and thirty popular editions of *rímur* were printed between 1800 and 1920.

Editions

It is instructive to compare these (tentative) figures with the number of known saga editions. The following list contains the popular (that is non-

III.

Formáli.

1. Völsunga – saga Sigurðar Fáfnisbana. Sögu þessa skrifaði eh únglíngr er ek var í Ögri eina var vertíð, sextán ára gamall eptir sögubók er Sigurðr Þorsteinsson í Bæ- jum á Snæfjallaströnd átti, þat var almikil bók með gamalli skript, er eh þá átti erritt með að lesa, eh sjálf sagt Gefi eh þá skrifað mörg orð eh setningar rangtega, er eh síðan Gefi lagfært eptir þeirri prentuðu sem er í Forn- aldar sögum norðurlanda, því eh man þat at sögunum ber almikit á milli. Eh yfir þat at eh þá tök ekki betr eptir þessari sögu- bók sem eun Gefa nevit að mörgu merkileg, því at eh Gefi ekki séd Gamla síðan eða til Gennar spurt, en þat var nær því þrjátíggi árum síðan að eh þár at spyrjast fyrir Guar Gám væri niðurkomin, eh Sigurðr þá danðr fyrir nokkurum árum, enda varð eptir spurn mín til enkis; margar þley vi sögr váru á bók þessari, en eh man ekki vel at segja þrá

scholarly) editions from the period 1804–1916. It includes neither scholarly editions published abroad nor the *Íslendinga sögur* of Valdimar Ásmundarson and Sigurður Kristjánsson.

Ajax saga frækna	Reykjavík	1852
Ambales saga	Reykjavík	1886
	Reykjavík	1911
Ármanns saga	Akureyri	1858
Ásmundar saga víkings	Reykjavík	1866
Atla saga Ótryggssonar	Seyisfjörður	1886
Blómsturvalla saga	Reykjavík	1892
Breta sögur	Reykjavík	1914
Clarus saga	Reykjavík	1884
Droplaugarsona saga	Reykjavík	1878
Egils saga	Akureyri	1856
Erex saga	Reykjavík	1886
Eyrbyggja saga	Akureyri	1882
Fastus saga	Gimli	1892
Finnboga saga	Akureyri	1860
Flóamanna saga	Reykjavík	1884
Gull-Þóris saga	Reykjavík	1878
Gunnars saga Keldugnúpsfífls	Copenhagen	1859
Gunnlaugs saga	Reykjavík	1880
Göngu-Hrólfs saga	Leirárgarðar	1804
	Reykjavík	1884
Hálfdánar saga Barkarsonar	Reykjavík	1889
Hávarðar saga	Ísafjörður	1889
Héðins saga	Reykjavík	1878
Heimskringla	Leirárgarðar	1804
Hellismanna saga	Ísafjörður	1889
	Winnipeg	1889
Hinriks saga	Bessastaðir	1908
Holta Þóris saga	Reykjavík	1876
Hrana saga hrings	Copenhagen	1874
Hrings saga	Reykjavík	1909
Hróbjarts saga	Reykjavík	1900
Huldar saga	Reykjavík	1909
	Akureyri	1911
Júnífers saga	Reykjavík	1901
Kára saga	Reykjavík	1886
Ketlerus saga	Reykjavík	1905
Knúts saga	Akureyri	1911
Konráðs saga	Copenhagen	1859

Króka-Refs saga	Copenhagen	1890
	Selkirk	1900
Laxdæla saga	Akureyri	1867
Mágus saga	Copenhagen	1858
	Reykjavík	1916
Margrétar saga	Reykjavík	1907
Marsilíus saga	Reykjavík	1885
Marteins saga	Reykjavík	1880
Mírmanns saga	Reykjavík	1884
Nikulás saga	Winnipeg	1889
	Reykjavík	1912
Njáls saga	Viðey	1844
Ólafs saga helga	Reykjavík	1893
Ólafs saga Tryggvasonar	Reykjavík	1893
Páls saga, Hungurvaka	Winnipeg	1889
Parmes saga	Reykjavík	1884
	Gimli	1910
Postula sögur	Viðey	1836
Sálus saga	Reykjavík	1852
Samsons saga	Reykjavík	1905
Sex søgu-þættir	Reykjavík	1855
Sigurgarðs saga frækna	Reykjavík	1884
Sigurðar saga þögla	Reykjavík	1883
Skáld-Helga saga	Reykjavík	1897
Starkaðar saga	Winnipeg	1911
Trójumanna saga	Reykjavík	1913
Valdimars saga	Reykjavík	1852
Vatnsdæla saga	Akureyri	1858
Vígkæns saga	Reykjavík	1886
Vilhjálms saga sjóðs	Reykjavík	1911
Villifers saga	Reykjavík	1885
Vilmundar saga	Reykjavík	1878
Yngvars saga víðförla	Reykjavík	1886
Þjalar-Jóns saga	Reykjavík	1857
	Reykjavík	1907
Þórgríms saga	Reykjavík	1852
	Eyrarbakki	1911
Þóris þáttr hasts	Copenhagen	1874

In all, seventy-seven editions appeared between 1804 and 1916, only four of them from the first half of the century. In the 1880s alone twenty-three editions were issued.

The places of publication were Reykjavík (forty-seven instances),

Akureyri (eight), Canada (seven), Copenhagen (six), Viðey, Leirárgarðar, Ísafjörður (two each), Seyðisfjörður, Bessastaðir, Eyrarbakki (one each).[19] The generic distribution deserves particular attention. Hardly any kings' sagas, religious sagas, pseudo-historical sagas or chivalric sagas were published in popular editions. Only two legendary sagas appeared in separate editions, in all likelihood because of the existence of C.C. Rafn's edition of *Fornaldarsögur Norðurlanda* (Rafn 1829–32). Thus it was the forty-seven late-medieval and post-Reformation original romances which represented the majority of the sagas listed. Only fourteen family sagas appeared in these inexpensive editions, until Valdimar Ásmundarson and Sigurður Kristjánsson began publishing their popular *Íslendinga sögur* series at the end of the century.[20]

It is very difficult to determine the purchasers and thus the primary users of these editions. In their prefaces and postscripts, the editors usually address their readers as 'alþýða' and 'almúgi' [the general public], and the printed sagas claim to be designed for the 'kvöldvaka í sveit' [rural evening wake]. The subscriber list printed in the third volume of Rafn's *Fornaldarsögur Norðurlanda* states that of the one hundred and fifty subscribers to this expensive, three-volume work almost exactly one third were peasants and farm-hands (forty-two instances of 'bóndi', ten of 'vinnumaður' and 'vinnupiltur'). The second largest group (some 20%) consists of clergymen (thirty-two instances of 'síra'), whilst the remaining subscribers tended to be higher civil servants, physicians, craftsmen and the like. In the case of the small, cheap editions from the end of the century, no lists of subscribers are extant, but the percentage of peasants and farm-hands was doubtless rather higher.[21]

---

[19]This chronological distribution of printed material with its marked peak after the middle of the century has clear parallels with the distribution of Swedish and Danish chapbooks; most of these popular Scandinavian editions were issued during the third quarter of the nineteenth century (Glauser 1993).

[20]*Íslendinga sögur* 1–38 (Reykjavík, 1891–1902). Various editions of *Riddarasögur* and religious sagas appeared in the first part of the century, but such series would have been too expensive for an Icelandic reading public. See also the short comments by Halldór Hermannsson 1966, 4–5. Finnur Jónsson 1918, ch. 10, 'Oldskriftselskabet. Udgivelsen til den nyeste tid,' pp. 41–55, deals only with the scholarly editions. See also Kalinke 1982.

[21]See here the illuminating remarks by Þorleifur Jónsson 1892, v: 'Hœnsa-Þóris saga hefir aðeins einusinni áðr útkomið fyrir almennings sjónir, og var það að þakka "Fornfrœðafélagi Norðrlanda", er Karl Kristján Rafn kom á fót á öndverðri þessari öld. Hún er prentuð samanvið fleiri (5 aðrar) sögur í dýrri bók:

In this context it is interesting to see how printed transmission perpetuated central features of the manuscripts. Time and again these small books state that the sagas are intended to be read aloud during the *kvöldvaka*: 'Mér fannst þess vert að sagan væri gefin út til skemtunar söguþjóðinni' [It seemed to me worthwhile to publish this saga for the entertainment of the saga-nation.] (Þorleifur Jónsson 1886, iv). It is in the prefaces and postscripts of these editions that the historicity of the sagas is discussed: 'Af framanskrifuðu er búið að færa næg rök fyrir áreiðan-legheitum Hellismannasögu eptir Landnámu og eru fáar sögur henni meir samdóma; en svo eru fleiri sögur sem vitna til Hellismannasögu' [From what was written above there should be sufficient evidence for the trustworthiness of *Hellismannasaga* according to *Landnamabók*, and there are few sagas with which it agrees more completely, but there are also other sagas which refer to *Hellismannasaga*].[22] Again, sources for the editions are recorded: 'Sögu þessa af Skáld-Helga, sem nú er í fyrsta skipti prentuð, hefir hreppstjóri Magnús Jónsson í Tjaldanesi skrifað upp eptir mjög gamalli bók, skrifaðri með fallegri settleturs skript, mikið bundinni, en þó vel læsilegri; á þessari bók voru margar fleiri sögur og kvæði [...] hann mun vera einn af sögufróðustu mönnum, er nú lifa á landi hér. S.E.' [This text of *Skáld Helga saga*, which is here printed for the first time was copied from a very old manuscript by Magnús Jónsson, *hreppstjóri*, of Tjaldanes, written in beautiful gothic script, heavily abbreviated but quite readable. There were many other sagas and poems in this manuscript [...]; he is one of the most knowledgeable people now

Íslendingasögur, annað bindi; Kh. 1847, gr. 8to, er Jón sál. Sigurðsson bjó undir prentun. Einsog við er að búast, er þessi útgáfa sögunnar eftir Jón sál. einkar vönduð og af allri snild gør að öllum frágangi. En dýrleiki bókar þessarar mun hafa valdið því, að fáir hafa getað keypt hana hér á landi.' [*Hœnsa-Þóris saga* has only once before been published, thanks to the 'Fornfræðifélag Norðurlanda', which was founded by Carl Christian Rask in the early part of this century. It was printed along with several (five other) sagas in an expensive volume: *Íslendingasögur*, vol. ii (Copenhagen, 1847), 8to, edited by the late Jón Sigurðsson. As is to be expected, Jón's edition is extremely well done and masterfully produced in every way. But the expense of this volume has prohibited many from buying it here in Iceland]. Þorleifur Jónsson was a very industrious and energetic editor of small saga-books; his comments show that the major scholarly editions of saga-texts, mostly edited in Copenhagen or Christiania, rarely reached the majority of the Icelandic reading public.

[22]Title and full bibliographical information as printed: *Hellismanna saga*. Kostnaðarmenn: Prentfjelag Heimskringlu Winnipeg. Heimskringlu prentstofa, 1889. Formáli (Eptir Gunnar Gíslason), p. vii.

living in this country. S.E.].[23] Typical of the printing industry at this time are comments to the effect that additional volumes would follow, if the present one were to be well received: 'Verði þessari sögu vel tekið af löndum mínum, hef jeg í hyggju, að gefa út með tímanum fleiri þessa kyns sögur, eptir þeim handritum, sem bezt verða fengin. Reykjavík í marzm. 1857. Egill Jónsson.' [Should this saga be well received by my compatriots I have in mind to bring out in the course of time more sagas of this kind, based on the best manuscripts available. Reykjavík, March 1857. Egill Jónsson][24] (Figure 8).

Unlike the chapbooks printed in Denmark, Sweden or Germany, Icelandic saga-editions were never illustrated. Nonetheless the parallels as regards function, subject matter, production, distribution, and outward appearance between Central and Northern European stories such as *Helena Antonia af Konstantinopel* (Figure 9) and the late Icelandic saga-editions are striking. In both cases, narratives which had been transmitted over several centuries with few textual changes were now printed in massive numbers. Their explicit mode of presentation was that of story recitation (often including a double scene: Lönnroth 1978, 1979) in front of the fire-place as in the Swedish chapbook,[25] or during the activities of the Icelandic *kvöldvaka*.

ICELANDIC LITERARY INSTITUTIONS DURING THE NINE-TEENTH CENTURY

The examples which have been discussed so far show that Icelandic popular literature from the late nineteenth and early twentieth centuries was persistently marked by traditional and ultimately anachronistic socio-

[23]Title and full bibliographical information as printed: *Sagan af Skáld-Helga*. Kostnaðarmaður: Sigfús Eymundsson. Reykjavík. Prentsmiðja Dagskrár. 1897. Eptirmáli, p. 42. A note on the cover of *Samson fríði og Kvintalin kvennaþjófur*. *Riddarasaga*, Reikjavík [*sic*] 1905, reads: 'Eftir handriti J. Jónssonar á Dufþaksholti.'

[24]Title and full bibliographical information as printed: *Sagan af Þjalar-Jóni*, gefin út af Gunnlaugi Þórðarsyni, kostuð af Egli Jónssyni. Reykjavík. Í Prentsmiðju Íslands. E. Þórðarson. 1857, p. 4.

[25]See for example: *Helena Antonia af Konstantinopel*, Folk-Sagor 16, Kalmar 1854, title page: 'Ack huru roligt,/Wid brasan förtroligt/Att höra talas om jettar och troll/Om winterqwällen,/Då trollen på hällen/Dansa sin ringdans i stjernklar natt.'

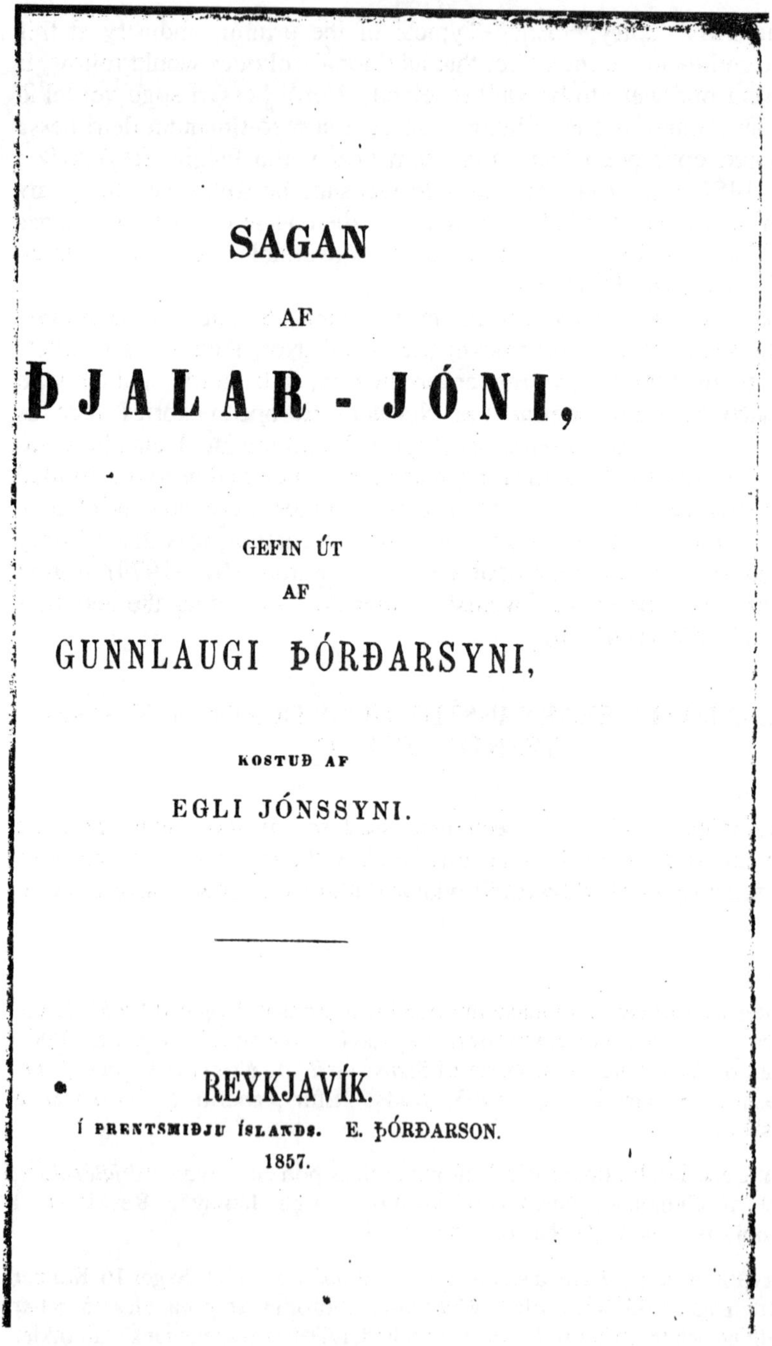

SAGAN

AF

ÞJALAR - JÓNI,

GEFIN ÚT

AF

GUNNLAUGI ÞÓRÐARSYNI,

KOSTUÐ AF

EGLI JÓNSSYNI.

REYKJAVÍK.

Í PRENTSMIÐJU ÍSLANDS.   E. ÞÓRÐARSON.

1857.

Figure 8. *Sagan af Þjalar-Jóni* 1857.

En förunderlig och mycket behaglig

Historia

om

Den Sköna och Tålmodiga

Helena Antonia

Af Constantinopel.

Hwaruti man kan beskåda Lyckans obeständighet.

Stockholm, W. Löfwing, Södermalmstorg, N:o 4.

71

Figure 9. *Historia om Den Sköna och Tålmodiga Helena Antonia Af Konstantinopel*, Swedish Chapbook, Stockholm 1847.

cultural practices. Influenced by foreign, middle-class culture, modern literary institutions developed in Iceland around the middle of the last century. These institutions took the form of the printing-press, literary journals and publishing houses. Besides these modern forms of distribution there was a second, older transmission route by which traditional narrative genres could circulate in manuscript form up to the First World War.

Reflecting on this anachronistic cultural behaviour of the Icelanders it is interesting to recall the findings of French and American scholars who postulate that high degrees of literacy linked to the availability of the print media lead without exception and more or less automatically to significant social changes (Davies 1975, Eisenstein 1968). The evidence from Iceland points in exactly the opposite direction. It reveals a society dominated by a strong sense of cultural continuity; literacy was widespread though not of course universal.[26] These high literacy levels and the actual reading practices in Iceland, which were partly reflected in the manuscript tradition of saga literature, played little part in the modernisation of Icelandic agrarian society. Literacy was to only a very limited degree an agent of social and political progress. The traditional orientation of the popular narratives was too powerful.

A quotation from Halldór Laxness's novel *Sjálfstætt fólk*, published in 1934–1935, may serve to summarise and illustrate the transition from the older, quasi-medieval recitation and reading culture to more modern forms of the European entertainment industry during the first decades of this century:

> [...] En þetta var ekki alt. Það er einsog mig minni að ég hafi lofað þér Örvaroddssögu einhverntíma í vetur, sagði faðir hennar, og þau fóru til bóksalans.
>
> Bóksalinn var aldurhniginn maður [...]. Þráttfyrir það fékk hann orð fyrir að fylgjast alveg ótrúlega vel með tímanum. Bókaverzlun hans var í litlu skoti uppá lofti í gömlu brotnu húsi, sem var falið á bakvið önnur hús. Leiðin lá uppeftir myrkum brakstiga, sem ætlaði eingan enda að taka. [...]
>
> Fást hér bækur? spurði Bjartur.
>
> Bækur og bækur, svaraði bóksalinn,—það kemur an uppá.
>
> Ja það er nú bara vegna hennar Sólu minnar, sagði Bjartur. Hún er farin að reka nefið í skruddur, þetta grey, svo ég mun hafa lofað henni einhverntíma í vetur að gefa henni Örvaroddssögu. Ég borga útí hönd.

---

[26]See the studies by Loftur Guttormsson on literacy in early modern Iceland; for example his 'Læsi' in Frosti F. Jóhannsson 1989, pp. 117–144.

Biddu guð um vitið, maður, sagði bóksalinn. Það eru yfir þrjátíu ár síðan ég lét síðasta stykkið af Örvaroddssögu. Þjóðin stendur á altöðru menníngarstigi nú á dögum. Afturámóti hef ég hér söguna um gullnámur Salómons konúngs, þar sem getið er um hetjuna Umslópógas, sem var að sínu leyti mikill maður, og að mínum dómi eingu síðri en Örvaroddur.

Ekki hef ég mikla trú á því, sagði Bjartur. Ætli það sé ekki einhver andskotans nútíðarheimsádeilan. Og að þessi maður sem þú tilnefndir hafi slagað uppí Örvarodd, sem var fullar tólf álnir danskar á hæð, það þarf einginn að segja mér.

Ja þjóðin er nú einusinni komin á það stig, lagsmaður, að vilja fylgjast með tímanum, og eftir því verðum við að haga okkur, bóksalarnir. Eða álítur þú það ekki, jómfrú litla, að maður verði að haga sér eftír nútímanum? Komdu nú hérna heillin og líttu á nútímabókmentirnar mínar. Þarna er heimsfræg skáldsaga um mann sem var myrtur í vagni, og vísindarit um spillíngu páfadómsins, alt um það hvernig þessar vondu manneskjur í útlandinu, múnkar og nunnur, tældu hvort annað til óskírlífis á miðöldunum. Og hér skal ég sýna þér bók sem er svo til ný, og alveg hæstmóðins nú á dögum, líttu bara á, jómfrú litla, ætli þetta væri ekki eitthvað handa okkur?

[…] En þegar hún leit á titilblað efstu bókarinnar þá stóð hjarta hennar næstum kyrt, svo undrandi varð það. Þetta merkilega efni, sem hún hafði að vísu aldrei heyrt nefnt á nafn þótt hún vissi sitt af hverju, bæði frá jómsvíkingum og búpeníngnum, um það voru þá jafnvel til heilar bækur: Leyndardómur ástarinnar, góð ráð er snerta samband pilts og stúlku.

Samband? hugsaði stúlkan óstyrk af hræðslu einsog hún byggist við að faðir sinn mundi reka henni utanundir,—hvernig er samband milli pilts og stúlku? Hún óskaði og vonaði að faðir hennar kæmi ekki auga á þessa bók. Sjaldan hefur bók vakið forvitni úngrar stúlku svo mjög, og sjaldan hefur úng stúlka verið feimnari við bók […]. En í þessum svifum þurfti faðir hennar auðvitað að koma auga á bókina líka, og náttúrlega varð hann vondur einsog ævinlega útí þessháttar, —þetta er sosum eitthvert fjandans ekkisens ástarþruglið, sem þeir setja saman sunnlíngarnir til að eyðileggja hjartað í kvenfólkinu.

Ja þetta vill nú kvenfólkið hafa fyrir því, sagði bóksalinn, ég er búinn að láta yfir þrjátíu stykki af þessari bók á undanförnum fimm árum, og það er ennþá verið að spyrja eftir henni. Það hjálpa ekki eintóm morð og vísindi. Það verður líka að vera einhver ást í bókmentunum. Lángur var Örvaroddur á sinni tíð, en hver er komin til að mæla leingd ástarinnar?

Það fór einsog við mátti búast, Bjartur lenti í þjarki við bóksalann um anda nútímans og snild fortíðarinnar, en Ásta Sóllilja var alveg utanvið sig […]. Heimsóknin endaði á því að Bjartur keypti söguna af Mjallhvít konúngsdóttur og gaf dóttur sinni.

Hann á ein sjö lausaleiksbörn, einsog líka best sést af því hvað

hann höndlar með, sagði Bjartur, þegar þau voru komin heilu og
höldnu niður þá myrku og brakandi stigu sem leiddu til Leyndardóma
ástarinnar. (Halldór Laxness 1961, I 225–227)

[But that was not all. 'I seem to recollect that I made you a promise
of Orvar-Odds Saga awhile ago,' said her father, so they made their
way to the bookseller's.

The bookseller was an old man [...]. In spite of this he was
reputed to keep remarkably well abreast of the times. His shop was
at the top of a tumbledown old house hidden behind other buildings,
a little room partitioned off from the rest of the garret. The way lay
up a dark, creaking staircase that seemed as if it would never end.
[...]

'Can we get books here?' inquired Bjartur.

'Books and books,' replied the bookseller; 'it all depends.'

'Well, it was just something for our Sola here,' said Bjartur. 'The
little wretch has begun sniffling about between the covers, and it
seems I must have promised her Orvar-Odds Saga at some time or
another. I pay on the nail.'

'Pray God for guidance, man. It's thirty-odd years since I sold the
last copy of Orvar-Odds Saga. The country now stands on an entirely
different cultural footing nowadays. I can recommend the story of
King Solomon's Mines there, all about the hero of Umslopogaas, in
his own way a great man, and in my opinion no whit inferior to
Orvar-Oddur.'

'That's rather more than I'm prepared to believe. Some more of
that damned modern rubbish, I suppose. And no one is going to tell
me that that fellow you mentioned just now could ever have stood up
to Orvar-Oddur, and him fully twelve Danish ells in height.'

'Maybe, but the country happens to have reached a stage in its
development when it wants to keep abreast of the times, and we
booksellers have to take that into account. Surely you, Miss Sola, will
agree that one must adapt oneself to the times? Come here, love, and
take a look at my up-to-date books. Here we have a world-famous
novel about a man who was murdered in a cart, and here is a
scientific account of the depravity of the Papacy, all about how those
bad people abroad, monks and nuns, led immoral lives in the Middle
Ages. And here I can show you a book that's practically new and
absolutely the height of fashion nowadays; just look at it, little miss,
don't you think we'd like to read it?'

[...] And when she looked at the title-page of the topmost volume,
she was struck with such amazement that her heart almost stopped its
beating. That strange, significant business which she had never heard
mentioned by its name, but of which both the animals at home and
her reading of the Jomsviking Ballads had given her an inkling—
whole books had been written about it, then: *The Secrets of Love,
Wholesome Advice Regarding the Union of Man and Woman.*

Union? thought the girl, trembling with fright, as if she thought her father was about to slap her face—how can there be union of a man and a woman? She hoped and prayed that her father would not catch sight of this book. Seldom has a book awakened a young girl's curiosity in such measure, seldom has a young girl been so shy of a book [...]. Her father, of course, must choose this very moment to notice it too, and naturally he lost his temper, as he always did when this subject cropped up. 'This looks like some of the damnable filth brewed by those misbegotten swine in Reykjavik to rot the hearts of the women,' he growled.

'It's what the women want, all the same,' replied the bookseller. 'I've sold thirty copies of it in the last five years and it's still in demand. Murder and science are by no means enough. There has to be a certain amount of love in our literature also. Orvar-Oddur was a long man in his time, but who would care to measure the length of love?

The result was inevitable; Bjartur and the bookseller started wrangling about the spirit of modern literature and the superior skill of the classics, while Asta Sollilja stood looking on in utter bewilderment [...]. The visit ended with Bjartur buying his daughter the story of *Snow White and the Seven Dwarfs*.

'He had seven or eight bastards, as anyone would expect after seeing the sort of stuff he deals in,' said Bjartur when they stood safe and sound at the foot of the dark and creaking stairs that led to the Secrets of Love. [Thompson 1946, 195–7]

At a moment when the books of Rider Haggard were conquering the last of the small trading-posts on the coast, the epoch of Örvar-Oddr and the cheap saga-editions was at an end. Ultimately it was not the attacks of sixteenth- and seventeenth-century theologians directed against the heathen elements in the stories, nor the polemics of the eighteenth-century enlighteners against superstition, nor the aesthetic objections of nineteenth-century romantic writers, which stopped the Icelanders singing the *rímur* and copying and reciting the sagas. With his own characteristic precision and irony Laxness describes the years after the First World War as a period with far-reaching socio-cultural implications for the dissolution of the pre-modern Icelandic culture. Between the quotations from Gröndal (1852) and Laxness (1920–30) lies a period of some seventy to eighty years during which Iceland underwent a gradual transformation from a socially, politically and culturally backward nineteenth-century country, with structures that seemed almost medieval, into a modern Western society. The transition from handwritten manuscript to printed book—in itself, of course, only a minor element in these upheavals—brought about certain changes in cultural behaviour after 1850. But it is only after the replacement of the *kvöldvaka* by modern, middle-class forms of culture during the period 1910–20 that the hand-written and printed narratives from ancient times lost their place irrevocably in Icelandic cultural life.[27] Or, as one of the most prolific writers from the last phase of the saga writing, Guðbrandur Sturlaugsson from Hvítadalur, puts it in 1892:

> Þetta [*Flóres saga konungs og sona hans*] er stórfeingleg Riddara saga enn eigi vil eg ábirgjast sannindi hennar, hún er einsog fleyri þess háttur sögur gérð til gamans og dægrastittingar sem margur hafði áður gaman af á þeim langu vertrarkvöldum en nú er sú skémtun Sögulestursins farin að ganga úr gildi. (Lbs. 1618 4to, 457).

> [This is a fine chivalric romance, but I do not wish to vouch for its truthfulness. Like other such stories it was made for entertainment and diversion, which many find enjoyable in the long winter evenings, although now this kind of saga-reading for pleasure is beginning to lose its validity.]

So it was that the end of the *kvöldvaka* also led to the end of the saga.

ACKNOWLEDGEMENTS

The English translations of nineteeenth-century Icelandic texts in this article are the work of Matthew Driscoll and Andrew Wawn. I am most grateful to them for undertaking this work.

REFERENCES CITED

Bourdieu, Pierre. 1979. *La distinction. Critique sociale du jugement*. Paris.

Burke, Peter. 1978. *Popular Culture in Early Modern Europe*. London.

Darnton, Robert. 1982. 'What is the History of Books?' *Daedalus* 111, 65–83.

Driscoll, M.J. 1990. 'Þögnin mikla. Hugleiðingar um riddarasögur og stöðu þeirra í íslenskum bókmenntum', *Skáldskaparmál. Tímarit um íslenskar bókmenntir fyrri alda* 1, 157–68.

Davies, Natalie Zemon. 1975. 'Printing and the People: Early Modern France', in *Society and Culture in Early Modern France*, pp. 189–226. [Reprinted in Graff 1981].

---

[27]In a recent article (Glauser 1993) I have tried to illustrate comparable developments in the history of Swedish and Danish chapbooks in the nineteenth century.

Eisenstein, Elizabeth L. 1968. 'Some Conjectures about the Impact of Printing on Western Society and Thought: A Preliminary Report', *Journal of Modern History* 40, 7–29. [Reprinted in Graff 1981].

Finnbogi Guðmundsson. 1965. 'Nokkurar sögur [...] í hjáverkum uppskrifaðar', *Landsbókasafn Íslands: Árbók* 22, 146–52.

———. 1982. 'The medieval legacy: its survival and revival in later centuries', in Hans Bekker-Nielsen *et al.*, eds, *The Medieval Legacy: A Symposium*, pp. 71–87. Odense.

Finnur Jónsson. 1918. *Udsigt over den norsk-islandske filologis historie.* Festskrift udgivet af Københavns Universitet i Anledning af Hans Majestæt Kongens Fødselsdag den 26. September 1918. Copenhagen.

Frosti F. Jóhannsson, ed. 1989. *Munnmenntir og bókmenning.* Íslenzk þjóð-menning VI. Reykjavík.

Glauser, Jürg. 1983. *Isländische Märchensagas. Studien zur Prosaliteratur im spätmittelalterlichen Island.* Beiträge zur nordischen Philologie 12. Basel and Frankfurt am Main.

———. 1985. 'Erzähler—Ritter—Zuhörer: Das Beispiel der Riddarasögur. Erzählkommunikation und Hörergemeinschaft im mittelalterlichen Island', in Régis Boyer, ed., *Les Sagas de Chevaliers (Riddarasögur), Actes de la Ve Conférence Internationale sur les Sagas, Toulon, Juillet 1982*, pp. 93–119. Paris.

———. 1990. 'Romances, *rímur*, chapbooks. Problems of popular literature in late medieval and early modern Scandinavia', *Parergon* n.s. 8, 37–52.

———. 1993. 'Eulenspiegels Sünden, Markolfs anderes Gesicht. Ausgrenzungs-und Disziplinierungsprozesse in der skandinavischen Populärliteratur', *Ethnologia Europæa* 23, 27–40.

———. 1994. 'Spätmittelalterliche Vorleseliteratur und frühneuzeitliche Handschriftentradition. Die Veränderungen der Medialität und Textualität der isländischen Märchensagas zwischen dem 14. und 19. Jahrhundert', in Hildegard L.C. Tristram, ed., *Text und Zeittiefe*, ScriptOralia 58, pp. 377–438. Tübingen.

———. Forthcoming. Ausgrenzung und Disziplinierung. *Studien zur volks-sprachlichen Erzählliteratur Skandinaviens in der frühen Neuzeit.* Beiträge zur nordischen Philologie 23. Basel and Frankfurt am Main.

Graff, Harvey J., ed. 1981. *Literacy and Social Development in the West: A Reader.* Cambridge.

Grímur M. Helgason. 1972. 'Handritasafn Einars Guðmundssonar á Reyðarfirði', *Landsbókasafn Íslands: Árbók* 29, 153–161.

———. 1978. '"Af skrifuðum skræðum er allt gott." Þáttur af skiptum Jóns Sigurðssonar og Jóns Borgfirðings', *Landsbókasafn Íslands: Árbók,* nýr flokkur 4, 53–65.

———. 1986. 'Jón Jónsson í Simbakoti og handrit hans', *Landsbókasafn Íslands: Árbók,* nýr flokkur 12, 58–64.

Gröndal, Benedikt Sveinbjarnarson. 1852. Review of *Fjórar Riddarasögur*, *Þjóðólfur* 4/92, 367–368 [29 September].

Halldór Hermannsson. 1966. *Old Icelandic Literature. A Bibliographical Essay.* Islandica 23. Ithaca, NY. [First edition 1933].

Henderson, Ebenezer. 1818. *Iceland; or the Journal of a Residence in that Island, during the Years 1814 and 1815.* Edinburgh.

Hermann Pálsson. 1962. *Sagnaskemmtun Íslendinga.* Reykjavík.

ÍB = Hið íslenzka bókmenntafélag.

Jakob Benediktsson. 1981. 'Den vågnende interesse for sagalitteraturen på Island i 1600–tallet', *Mål og Minne*, 157–170.

Jón Helgason. 1958. *Handritaspjall.* Reykjavík.

Jónas Hallgrímsson. 1837. 'Um rímur af Tistrani og Indíönu, "orktar af Sigurdi Breidfjörd" (prentaðar í Kaupmannahöfn, 1831)', *Fjölnir* 3, 18-29.

Lbs. = Landsbókasafn Íslands

Kalinke, Marianne E. 1982. 'Scribes, Editors and the *riddarasögur*.' *Arkiv för nordisk filologi* 97, 36–51.

JS = Jón Sigurðsson.

Laxness, Halldór Kiljan. 1961. *Sjálfstætt folk.* Third edition. Reykjavík.

Lönnroth, Lars. 1978. *Den dubbla scenen. Muntlig diktning från Eddan till ABBA.* Stockholm.

———. 1979. 'The double scene of Arrow-Odd's drinking contest', in Hans Bekker-Nielsen et al., eds, *Medieval Narrative: A Symposium*, pp. 94–119. Odense.

Magnús Gíslason. 1977. *Kvällsvaka. En isländsk kulturtradition belyst genom studier i bondebefolkningens vardagsliv och miljö under senare hälften av 1800-talet och början av 1900-talet.* Studia Ethnologica Upsaliensia 2. Uppsala.

Overgaard, M. 1979. 'AM 124, 8vo. En islandsk schwank-samling', *Opuscula* 7, Bibliotheca Arnamagnæana 34, pp. 268–317.

———. 1991. 'De islandske oversættelser af De tolv patriarkers Jacobs sønners testamenter og af Josephs og Assenaths historie, med en udgave af Josephs Testamente', *Opuscula 9*, Bibliotheca Arnamagnæana 39, pp. 203–300.

Rafn, C.C. 1829–1832. *Fornaldar Sögur Nordrlanda eptir gömlum handritum utgefnar af C.C. Rafn.* 3 vols. Copenhagen.

Rumbke, Eberhard. 1981. 'Anfänge bürgerlicher Literatur auf Island: Jónas Hallgrímssons *Rímur*-Kritik', in Fritz Paul, ed., *Akten der Vierten Arbeitstagung der Skandinavisten des deutschen Sprachgebiets. 1. bis 5. Oktober 1979 in Bochum*, Wissenschaftliche Reihe 2, pp. 151–165. Hattingen.

Schenda, Rudolf. 1993. *Von Mund zu Ohr. Bausteine zu einer Kulturgeschichte volkstümlichen Erzählens in Europa.* Sammlung Vandenhoeck. Göttingen.

Seelow, Hubert. 1989a. *Die isländischen Übersetzungen der deutschen Volksbücher. Handschriftenstudien zur Rezeption und Überlieferung ausländischer unterhaltender Literatur in Island in der Zeit zwischen Reformation und Aufklärung.* Stofnun Árna Magnússonar á Íslandi, Rit 35. Reykjavík.

——. 1989b. 'Volksbücher im Land der Sagas. Deutsche Volksbücher, dänische Folkebøger und die isländische Literatur nach der Reformation', in Otmar Werner, ed., *Arbeiten zur Skandinavistik. 8 Arbeitstagung der Skandinavisten des Deutschen Sprachgebiets 27.9.–3.10.1987 in Freiburg i. Br.*, 175–189. Texte und Untersuchungen zur Germanistik und Skandinavistik 22. Frankfurt am Main.

Springborg, Peter. 1969. 'Nyt og gammelt fra Snæfjallaströnd. Bidrag til beskrivelse af den litterære aktivitet på Vestfjordene i 1. halvdel af det 17. århundrede', *Afmælisrit Jóns Helgasonar. 30. júní 1969*, pp. 288–327. Reykjavík.

——. 1977. 'Antiqvæ Historiæ Lepores—om renæssancen i den islandske håndskriftproduktion i 1600-tallet', *Gardar* 8, 53–89.

Thompson, J.A., trans. 1946. Halldór Kiljan Laxness, *Independent People: An Epic*. New York and London.

Vésteinn Ólason. 1989. 'Bóksögur', in Frosti F. Jóhannsson 1989, pp. 161–227.

Þorleifur Jónsson, ed. 1886. *Atla saga Ótryggssonar*. Seyðisfjörður.

——, ed. 1892. *Hænsa-Þóris saga*. Reykjavík.

7

'We who Cherish *Njáls saga*': the Alþingi as Literary Patron

JÓN KARL HELGASON

Of the numerous editions, translations, and adaptations of *Njáls saga* produced in the past two hundred years, few volumes offer as fascinating an insight into the configuration and function of literary patronage as the 1944 Icelandic edition of Magnús Finnbogason. The peculiar context of this publication not only reveals the Icelanders' legendary and archetypical attachment to their sagas; its history also reveals in a particularly striking way how the modern dissemination of even the most ancient literary texts may be motivated and affected by conflicting political and personal interests.

In an illuminating discussion of literary patrons, André Lefevere claims that the concept applies to 'the powers [...] which help or hinder the writing, reading and rewriting of literature' (Lefevere 1984, 227). Patronage, he continues, can be exerted by persons, groups of persons (a political party for instance), a social class, a royal court, publishers or the media; but often it operates by means of specific institutions, such as academies, bureaux of censorship, critical journals and the educational establishment.

In many instances it is not easy to identify the contribution of patrons to individual publications, but in the case of the 1944 Icelandic edition that influence was far from being disguised. On the opening page, readers were informed that the edition had been produced under the aegis of the Alþingi [the Icelandic parliament]. As further confirmation of the state's involvement, we may note firstly that the saga was published by Bókaútgáfa Menningarsjóðs og Þjóðvinafélagsins, which was in part a governmental institution; secondly that it was printed by the state printing firm of Gutenberg.

I

According to Lefevere, patronage consists of three interactive elements—*ideology*, *economics*, and *status*, and in relation to the first of these Vilhjálmur Þ. Gíslason's introduction spells out the purpose of the

1944 edition: 'It is essential now for [Icelandic] nationality and national development that the sagas should be thoroughly read and respected' (*Njáls saga* [hereafter *N.s.*] 1944, xvi).[1] In this context, Vilhjálmur adds that the edition was intended to have better 'qualifications' [skilyrði] for a wide circulation than those editions preceding it. Even though he concludes that the aim of the publication is both to open up the saga's 'wonderlands of life and art' [undralönd lífs og listar] to young readers and to give older readers an opportunity to experience its delights anew, the official ideology of the edition was not so much to gratify individual readers as to underpin and promote a sense of national identity and unity amongst the citizens of the Icelandic state.

Vilhjálmur's stress on the urgent need for the new edition ('It is essential now') probably refers to Iceland's declaration of independence from Denmark in 1944, and to the continued Allied occupation of Iceland, by then in its fourth year. Whilst the Allied military presence was generally regarded by the Icelanders as preferable to the alternative of German invasion, it was nevertheless understandable that the indigenous population should be concerned about 'national development' at a time when the nation was in daily contact with English-speaking troops (Björn Þorsteinsson 1991, 398–419).

Establishing the virtues of *Njáls saga* in ideological and nationalistic terms, Vilhjálmur Gíslason's introduction claims at the outset that the Icelandic family sagas in general were 'among the best and the most valuable resources of Icelandic culture' [meðal mestu og beztu verðmæta íslenzkrar menningar: *N.s.* 1944, v]. In that context, he refers to their subject-matter, narrative technique and vocabulary, and their lasting influence on a variety of readers; scholars and artists as well as the general public. *Njáls saga*, he continues, is the most voluminous, comprehensive, and 'in many ways the richest' [auðugust á margan hátt] of the family sagas. Its many surviving manuscripts, Vilhjálmur later notes, testified to the saga's popularity from the earliest times (*N.s.* xiii).

From Vilhjálmur's argument we may infer that the 1944 publication was intended and expected to maintain the beneficial influence of the sagas in an independent Iceland, and to help to secure the stability of a society which was in many ways at a cross-roads. Irrespective of the particular circumstances of 1944, the nation had made remarkable economic, social, and cultural changes since the turn of the century. In

---

[1]All translations from Icelandic are my own. Lengthy original quotations are cited in the footnotes; shorter ones in parentheses within the main text: 'Það er nú nauðsynjamál þjóðernis og þjóðarþroska, að sögurnar séu vel lesnar og vel virtar.'

1901 80% of Icelanders were living in rural areas, with 70% of the total work-force employed in agriculture. By 1940 only 35% of the inhabitants remained in the countryside; the rest had moved to coastal towns and villages. Most strikingly, in this period, Reykjavík had been transformed from a small town of 6,700 inhabitants (8.5% of the population in 1901) into something approaching a small city of almost 40,000 citizens (31.5% of the population in 1940; *Tölfræðihandbók* 1984, 7–33). In the face of these major changes, it is as if Vilhjálmur Þ. Gíslason sought to represent the publication of *Njáls saga* with the backing of the Alþingi as a source of cultural reassurance and stability. No matter how much the world turned and tumbled, the 1944 edition would help to ensure that the Icelanders could continue to read and respect their native cultural resources.

II

In the discussions and debates which led up to this state-sponsored edition of *Njáls saga*, its supporters in the Alþingi did not draw particular attention to the views which later found expression in Vilhjálmur Gíslason's introduction. In the statement accompanying the original proposal its three principal supporters, Helgi Jónasson, Ingólfur Jónsson and Sveinbjörn Högnason, refer to the saga as 'one of the most wonderful works of art' [eitthvert hið dásamlegasta listaverk] ever to have been written in the Icelandic language, in terms of style, subject-matter, and narrative force (Alþingi 1943–1946, A:803). Nowhere in the rest of their submission, however, is the proposed edition linked to Iceland's declaration of independence, or to any possible threat from Anglo-Saxon cultural influence, or to general social and economic developments. The state edition, its advocates claim, is to be seen more as a response to another proposed edition of *Njáls saga*.

As summarised in their statement, the background to the whole affair was a complex one. In the autumn of 1941 the publisher Ragnar Jónsson had announced his plan to publish an edition of *Laxdæla saga* in modern Icelandic spelling; this at a time when the long-accepted custom had been to print editions of medieval Icelandic texts in the so-called 'standardised ancient spelling' [samræmd stafsetning forn]. Ragnar's proposed edition met with opposition, first expressed in several newspaper articles and eventually resulting in a law (nr. 127, 9 Dec. 1941), which granted to the Icelandic state the copyright for all Icelandic texts written before 1400 (Alþingi 1942, A:56–57). Individuals interested in publishing editions of these works now needed to apply for authorisation to the minister of education. Before this law came into operation, Ragnar and his collaborators—his co-publisher Stefán Ögmundsson and the prospective editor Halldór Kiljan Laxness—had been able to publish their edition of *Laxdæla saga*. However, in August 1942, they confronted and challenged the new law by publishing *Hrafnkels saga* in a modern spelling edition, without obtaining the now necessary permission. As a result they were prosecuted and convicted: each of them was sentenced to either a fine of 1000 krónur or a prison sentence of 45 days. They immediately appealed against the sentence on the grounds that it violated constitutional provisions relating to the freedom of the press (Hæstiréttur 1943, 237–244).

While the case was being heard in the superior court, in the early spring of 1943, the Alþingi had to vote on further proposed legislation which sought to invalidate the 1941 copyright law (Alþingi 1943–1946, C:168–220). Before producing its report, the commission appointed to discuss this proposal sought academic advice; they consulted the professors of Icelandic studies at the University of Iceland. These were Sigurður Nordal, professor of Icelandic literature, Árni Pálsson, professor of Icelandic history, and Björn Guðfinnsson, associate professor of Icelandic linguistics. Together, these scholars wrote a report, claiming that even though it was desirable to protect old texts from potential damage and distortion in new editions, the copyright laws themselves were in many ways imperfect. They also indicated that examination of Laxness's edition of *Laxdæla saga* had revealed serious flaws. The editor had modernised some of its vocabulary, had omitted old words and inserted new ones at various points in the text, and had omitted or reorganised sentences or even whole chapters from his source edition. All these changes, the professors concluded, had distorted the substance and character of the saga (Alþingi 1943–1946, A:719–720). On 2 April, the Alþingi agreed to postpone revisions of the copyright law on the grounds that the government was then in the midst of preparing a comprehensive *corpus juris* addressing questions of artistic and literary copyright in Iceland. But the Alþingi also resolved that the revised law should have the power to prevent publication of 'distorted' [afbakaðar] editions of Iceland's early literature (Alþingi 1943–1946, A:764).

The following week, Ragnar Jónsson and Halldór Laxness announced that they were preparing a new modern-spelling edition of *Njáls saga*, having obtained the required authorisation from the minister of education, Einar Arnórsson. It was in response to this announcement that the three members of the lower house of the Alþingi put together a proposal for the state edition of the saga, submitting it for discussion on 9 April. Drawing on the unfavourable comments which Laxness's edition of *Laxdæla saga* had received from the university professors, the three members argued in their statement that Laxness's *Njáls saga* edition would be similarly and seriously impaired. Hence the need for state involvement:

> We, who cherish *Njáls saga*, want to ensure by this parliamentary proposal that the people [of Iceland] have the chance of owning the saga in an inexpensive, good quality edition, free from the fingerprints of those who want to drag everything into the gutter and who will not spare even our most valuable works of art, such as *Njála*, from that fate. (Alþingi, 1943–1946, A:803)[2]

The agenda of those responsible for the proposal seems clear. They wanted the Alþingi to assume the role of a literary patron and to hinder, rather than to help, the 'reading and rewriting of literature', to borrow André Lefevere's phrase. Their fundamental aim was to prevent (or, as they saw it, to protect) the Icelandic nation from reading Laxness's version of *Njáls saga*.

III

For a fuller understanding of the Alþingi's sensitivity to the publication of unauthorised saga editions, it is helpful to examine the second of the three features which Lefevere identifies as constitutive elements in literary patronage—*economics*. In his definition, this element usually involves the writer (whether translator, editor, or whatever) enjoying some form of financial support from the patron; but in the case of *Njáls saga* there are other factors involved. In his 1944 introduction, Vilhjálmur Þ. Gíslason does not make direct reference to the economic aspects of the state edition, but it is interesting to note the kind of imagery in which his references to the sagas are expressed. We read of sagas as 'resources' [verðmæti], and of *Njáls saga* as the 'richest' [auðugust] of these resources. In employing these formulaic metaphors,[3] Vilhjálmur echoes the proponents' statement, in which the saga is referred to as one of the 'most valuable' [dýrmætustu] works of Icelandic art.

This imagery of value or wealth was more fully developed in a speech

---

[2]'Vér, sem Njálu unnum, viljum með þessari þingsályktun sjá svo um, að þjóðinni gefist kostur á að eignast hana í ódýrri og vandaðri útgáfu, þar sem ekki finnist fingraför þeirra manna, sem allt vilja draga niður í sorpið og jafnvel þyrma ekki okkar dýrmætustu listaverkum eins og Njálu frá þeim örlögum.'

[3]In this period, the saga was also referred to as the most splendid pearl of Icelandic literature (Þorkell Jóhannesson 1942, 89).

by one of the bill's three sponsors, Helgi Jónasson:

> We Icelanders have to admit that we are poor and few in number and
> we do not enjoy much material wealth, but we do have one asset, our
> old literature. It must be almost without parallel that a small nation
> such as ours should possess the kind of pearls beyond price which our
> ancient literature represents. (Alþingi 1943–1946, D:191)[4]

For this reason, Helgi continued, it was a delicate matter when any editor
sought to change the language or the subject matter of a saga. He went
on to criticise certain aspects of Laxness's edition of *Laxdæla saga*: not
only had the text of the saga been distorted, but the whole book had been
badly printed on poor quality paper. It was obvious, he concluded, that
the publication of *Laxdæla saga* had been undertaken for profit and not
for the worthier purpose of 'increasing the value' [auka gildi] of Icelandic
literature (Alþingi 1943–1946, D:192).

From Helgi Jónasson's argument, we observe that the cultural 'value'
of the sagas was expected to be at least preserved, if not enriched,
through the scholarly and presentational quality of any new published
edition. Furthermore, if the sagas were to assume the role of national
cultural treasures, that wealth had to be widely and equally distributed.
Laxness's project was seen as violating both of these principles,
comprising both a bad text and a poorly produced edition, with the whole
enterprise driven by the desire to make a profit. Under state sponsorship,
in contrast, individuals could not gain privileged access to Iceland's
precious ancient literary heritage, either as profit-making publishers
(dragging the sagas 'into the gutter'), or as members of that group who
could afford to buy an edition which exhibited the appropriate editorial
and production standards. The nation as a whole would benefit from the
state-sponsored edition; readers would be purchasing a literary 'pearl
beyond price', expertly edited and produced, for the lowest possible price.

The point also needs to be made that by recommending that *Njáls saga*
be published by Menningarsjóður and Þjóðvinafélagið, the Alþingi was
consciously plugging into an established system of subscribers or
members (Alþingi 1943–1946, A:803). The subscription arrangement had
been established by the publishing board of Menningarsjóður in 1940;
members would receive seven books annually in return for a modest
subscription of 10 krónur. This offer proved so popular, that by the end

---

[4]'Það mun nú svo með okkur Íslendinga, að við erum fátækir og fámennir,
og við eigum lítinn veraldarauð, en við eigum einn auð, það eru fornbókmenntir
okkar. Það mun vera nær eins dæmi að svo fámenn þjóð sem við erum eigi slíka
gimsteina sem fornritin eru.'

of the first year the number of subscribers was sufficiently large to allow the company to print twelve thousand copies of each of these seven books—apparently a record in the history of Icelandic publishing (Gils Guðmundsson 1985, 91). For a country of 120,000 citizens, it meant that the publications of Bókaútgáfa Menningarsjóðs og Þjóðvinafélagsins entered a significant proportion of Icelandic homes. Distributed in this way, the state edition of *Njáls saga* would indeed have better 'qualifications' [skilyrði], to recall Vilhjálmur Þ. Gíslason's term, for its circulation than any previous edition.

Despite these advantages, however, individual speakers in the Alþingi found various faults with the whole plan. According to the proposal, the government was called upon to 'encourage' [greiða fyrir] Menningarsjóður and Þjóðvinafélagið to publish a good popular edition of *Njáls saga* (Alþingi 1943–1946, A:803). Questions were soon raised about the government's authority for such interventions in the decisions of the publishing board. Although the board had been appointed by the Alþingi and included several of its members, Bókaútgáfa Menningarsjóðs og Þjóðvinafélagsins was supposedly responsible for its own operations. It certainly ought not to be subject to government interference, argued the minister of education, Einar Arnórsson, who had authorised Laxness's edition of *Njáls saga*. If, however, governmental 'encouragement' merely involved granting Menningarsjóður og Þjóðvinafélagið the required authorisation for publishing the saga, Einar added, that would hardly be a problem (Alþingi 1943–1946, D:193).

As a second concern, Barði Guðmundsson pointed out that Fornritafélagið [Early Icelandic Text Society], which had started to publish scholarly editions of sagas ten years earlier, also had plans to publish a new edition of *Njáls saga* (Alþingi 1943–1946, D:196). Its editions were subsidised by the state and sufficiently well respected for the 1941 copyright law uniquely to exempt the society from having to apply for permission to publish Icelandic works written before 1400 (Alþingi 1942, A:57). In addition to his duties in the Alþingi, Barði Guðmundsson was Iceland's chief national archivist; he said that he could not support the proposed state edition since it would involve Fornritafélagið in a huge financial loss on its own *Njáls saga* edition. Thirdly, Sigfús Sigurhjartarson stressed that a satisfactory popular edition of *Njáls saga* was already in circulation. It could be found in most Icelandic homes and was available in the bookshops for a modest price. In Sigfús's view, this edition already represented just the alternative to Laxness which the parliament sought to establish (Alþingi 1943–1946, D:199).

In his response to these and other criticisms, Helgi Jónasson explained that governmental 'encouragement' certainly included Einar Arnórsson's authorisation of the state edition, but could also extend into other areas.

He noted, for instance, that war-time conditions made supplies of paper difficult to obtain, whilst the printing presses themselves were so busy that it took a long time to have anything published at all. In all these matters the government's support could be helpful. As for Fornritafélagið, Helgi Jónasson said that its president was not opposed to the state edition. It would be a long time before its own proposed edition of *Njáls saga* was published because one particular manuscript, which the editor wanted to consult, was inaccessible in German-occupied Copenhagen. Helgi went on to read a statement signed by ten of the seventeen members of the other chamber of the Alþingi, in which they voiced their support for the proposed edition of Bókaútgáfa Menningarsjóðs og Þjóðvinafélagsins. Additionally, they expressed their willingness to increase the grant which Fornritafélagið received from the state as compensation for any possible loss which the society might suffer from the state edition of *Njáls saga* (Alþingi 1943–1946, D:196–197).

It is clear from this discussion that some very unusual economical conditions were to attend the publication of the state sponsored publication of *Njáls saga*. There seemed not to have been a particular public demand for the edition, and the capacity of the war-time printing industry was in any case severely limited. On the premise that cultural values had priority over market forces, not to mention shortage of raw materials, government involvement was expected to bestow important economic privileges on the new edition. It might also, Helgi Jónasson indirectly acknowledged, prove damaging (with any luck) to the profitability of the proposed Laxness edition (Alþingi 1943–1946, D:215).

IV

In this attempt to analyse the ideology and the economics of the Alþingi's patronage of a saga edition, we have seen that it was expected to operate, to an important degree, in a rather defensive way. The fundamental motive behind the government's support was not so much that Icelanders should buy and read the state edition, but rather that they should not buy or read Laxness's edition. This same pattern of priorities surfaces again when we try to define the *status* of the Alþingi as a literary patron. The point was not primarily that the Alþingi should be sponsoring the publication of sagas; but that Halldór Laxness and his patrons should not be doing so, on the grounds that they lacked sufficient authority.

This does not mean that the advocates of the state edition neglected to assert their right of interference in literary matters. Helgi Jónasson and his followers clearly represented themselves as the elected representatives of the Icelandic voters. Helgi said, for instance, that whilst the Minister of Education, Einar Arnórsson, had not broken any laws in authorising Laxness's edition of *Njáls saga*, he had nevertheless consciously defied the will of parliament and—'I venture to assert' [þori ég að fullyrða]— the will of the great majority of Icelanders. In his conclusion, Helgi claimed that the proposed state edition would represent *Njáls saga* 'as we wish to have it and as the nation wishes to have it' [eins og við viljum hafa hana og eins og þjóðin vill hafa hana: Alþingi 1943–1946, D:192– 193]. The main thrust of Helgi Jónasson's argument was, however, systematically to question Laxness's status as a saga editor. In analysing this strategy, we need to look again at the written submission of the three university professors which dealt both with the 1941 copyright law and Laxness's edition of *Laxdæla saga*. Their comments had been reviewed by parliament only a week before, when the proposal for the invalidation of the copyright law was rejected.

The copyright law stated that the minister of education *could* authorise editions of Icelandic works written before 1400 to follow 'standardised ancient spelling' [samræmdri stafsetningu fornri: Alþingi 1942, A:57]. In their written submission the university professors opposed this attempt to impose such a system of 'standardised' spelling since no such system, they claimed, could ever represent exactly the forms and sounds of the ancient language. Indeed, they argued, the modern spelling sanctioned by law from 1929 (and which Laxness had used in his editions) was in some respects 'closer to the originals' [nær upprunanum] than the system used in the scholarly editions of Fornritafélagið. Secondly, in the context of their criticism of Laxness's edition of *Laxdæla saga*, the university men emphasised that old Icelandic texts had undergone a variety of changes in the thirteenth and fourteenth centuries. Some of these changes had led to improvements in particular texts; younger versions of some sagas were quite properly chosen for publication rather than older ones. The quality of an edition could rest as much on aesthetic merit as on fidelity to some supposed 'original' text. Doubts were expressed as to the qualifications and capacity of the ministry of education to make judgements about which editorial changes to old saga texts would or would not endanger the nation's cultural or linguistic health. They concluded:

> If it is considered necessary to supervise the publication of older works of literature, as many people tend to feel, it seems more natural that such works should be placed in the hands of scholars and writers appointed for that task, whose knowledge and taste can be trusted. (Alþingi 1943–1946, A:720)[5]

---

[5]'Þyki nauðsynlegt að hafa eftirlit með útgáfu eldri rita, svo sem margir munu telja, virðist næst lagi, að það sé í höndum fræðimanna og rithöfunda, sem til þess væru kvaddir og treysta mætti að þekkingu og smekkvísi.'

Supporting the proposal for the state edition, Helgi Jónasson diplomatically avoided direct quotation from these ambiguous paragraphs in the scholars' report. It seems, however, that his approach to the *Njáls saga* case was determined by these very comments. Firstly, he admitted in his introductory speech that the system of spelling in saga editions was a matter of individual taste. Secondly, avoiding any detailed discussion of Laxness's editorial agenda, he argued that Laxness, distinguished writer that he was, simply could not be trusted. Helgi quoted a statement published in an Icelandic newspaper in the early autumn of 1941, in which Laxness had claimed that the only proposed change in his forthcoming edition of *Laxdæla saga* was to modernise the spelling. In view of the fact that Laxness's editorial interventions had been rather more wide-ranging, Helgi argued that Laxness's claims could not be relied on. Citing the negative verdict which the university scholars had reached, he went on to suggest that Laxness's aesthetic taste could not be trusted either. Finally, he referred to the ruling of the lower courts over Laxness's edition of *Hrafnkels saga*, implying that the novelist's character was not beyond reproach. According to the university professors, the editing of old texts should be left to established experts, scholars and writers. Helgi Jónasson's strategy, in short, was to undermine Laxness's authority and to claim that he was bound to 'deform' [skrumskæla] *Njáls saga* (Alþingi 1943–1946, D:191–193)

V

Thus far I have described how the Alþingi sought to regulate the editing and dissemination of early Icelandic literature during the Second World War years. Noting that the lower house passed the proposal for a state edition of *Njáls saga*, I have sought to identify (in the original statement of the three proponents, and also in the speeches of Helgi Jónasson) the rationale behind this proposed publication. This rationale, we have seen, contradicted the thrust of Vilhjálmur Þ. Gíslason's introduction to the published edition. There are, however, additional strands in this complex debate which have not yet been discussed.

First of all, it seems to be of some consequence that the three members of the Alþingi who were officially responsible for the proposal all lived in the district of Rangárvallasýsla, in which a substantial part of *Njáls saga* takes place. Helgi Jónasson, from Stórólfshvoll in Fljótshlíð, and Ingólfur Jónsson, who lived in the small town of Hella, were the two elected representatives of Rangárvallasýsla, while Sveinbjörn Högnason, although representing the neighbouring district of Vestur-Skaftafellssýsla, was a clergyman in Rangárvallasýsla, living at Breiðabólsstaður in Fljótshlíð (Alþingi 1943–1946, C:916).

The links between individual family sagas and inhabitants of certain parts of Iceland are based on the fact that most sagas take place in one particular district of the country. In some cases, as with *Laxdæla saga*, the narrative even derives its title from such a setting. During the 1941 discussions in the Alþingi on the proposed copyright law, which were triggered by Laxness's edition of *Laxdæla saga*, the importance of sagas' local links was clearly revealed by Þorsteinn Þorsteinsson, a *sýslumaður* [judge and revenue officer] of the Dalasýsla district. During the debate, he spoke in support of the copyright proposal:

> The district with which I am involved has been struck by a disaster. Its major saga, *Laxdæla saga*, has been published in a 'modern' spelling edition, without introduction, index or explanatory notes; it is more or less deformed. I have no wish for other districts to be stuck in the same muddy stream and I think it is right to block it at its source. (Alþingi 1942, B:107)[6]

Þorsteinn stressed that the family sagas were 'ancient, classic' [forn, sígild] historical documents. Accordingly, he criticised Laxness for deleting from his *Laxdæla saga* edition detailed information about genealogies and places of residence. He concluded his brief speech by re-emphasising that the history of his district had been 'attacked' [ráðist á], and that he did not wish to see other districts suffer the same sad fate. Although the supporters of the state edition of *Njáls saga* did not present themselves so explicitly as spokesmen for their district, their eager collaboration suggests that they were initially fighting for the interests of their fellow Rangæingar, all residents of the region which is the principal location for *Njáls saga*.

In this context we ought to pay special attention to the arguments of Helgi Jónasson, who shared Þorsteinn Þorsteinsson's basic views on the nature of the sagas as historical documents. Helgi criticised Laxness's very poor (as he regarded it) preface, in which *Laxdæla saga* was characterised as being historically unreliable—a kind of 'fabrication' [*lygisaga*] (Alþingi 1943–1946, D:192). He also stressed that all the genealogies were indispensable for a proper understanding of the feuds in the sagas: 'The men of the past killed other men for family reasons and not for fun' [Fornmenn drápu menn vegna ættartengsla, en ekki að gamni sínu: Alþingi 1943–1946, D:197]. This remark is certainly valid

---

[6]'Það sýslufélag, sem ég er við riðinn, hefur nú orðið fyrir því óláni að fá meginsögu sína, Laxdælu, gefna út með nýmóðins stafsetningu, formála-, registurs- og skýringarlausa og alla meira eða minna skrumskælda, og ég segi fyrir mig, að ég vil ekki óska öðrum héruðum að lenda i sama foraðinu, og tel því rétt að stemma nú þegar á að ósi.'

for many scenes in the sagas, but it also needs to be understood that by
no means all genealogies are important to the plot. For twentieth-century
residents of a district, however, genealogies had an independent validity
as links between living individuals or locations and the ancient saga
narrative.

The genealogy of Gunnar Hámundarson from Hlíðarendi in Fljótshlíð
(Ch. 19), one of the main characters of *Njáls saga*, is entirely representative of Helgi Jónasson's concerns. First, Gunnar's maternal lineage is
outlined, revealing how he is related to Unnur Marðardóttir. Subsequent
events in the saga are determined by Gunnar's service to Unnur and it is
necessary for the reader to understand on what grounds she asks for his
assistance when she has problems of her own. Gunnar's paternal lineage
is then traced; he is the son of Hámundur Gunnarsson. Right at the end
of the narrative this information will prove illuminating when Valgerður
Þorbrandsdóttir, the daughter of Hámundur's sister, becomes involved in
the plot (Ch. 148). The description of the rest of Gunnar's paternal line,
by contrast, serves to explain elements in his character (as presented)
rather than the course of events. Among his relatives are the law-speaker
Hrafn Hængsson, suggesting that powerful intellectual qualities run in the
family, and Ormur the Strong, indicating that correspondingly powerful
physical qualities also run in the family. Finally, one branch of the family
tree leads us to a particular place-name in Rangárvallasýsla: we are told
that the farm Gunnarsholt derived its name from Gunnar's grandfather,
Gunnar Baugsson. Although such knowledge does not in itself illuminate
the narrative significantly, it was important knowledge—a notable
historical fact—for the people of Rangárvallasýsla in the nineteen-forties,
not least for those who lived at Gunnarsholt.

For a more immediate link between person and place we recall that
Helgi Jónasson lived at Stórólfshvoll. According to the saga, Stórólfur
Hængsson was the great-grandfather of Gunnar Hámundarson, being the
brother of the law-speaker Hrafn Hængsson and the father of Ormur the
Strong. Undoubtedly and unsurprisingly, Helgi Jónasson was not at all
keen to have that topo-genealogical connection between himself and the
mighty Gunnar of Hlíðarendi removed from *Njáls saga* in Laxness's
edition. Indeed, Helgi's performance in parliament suggests that the
twentieth-century chieftain from Stórólfshvoll had inherited some of the
qualities of advocacy which characterised Stórólfur's brother, Hrafn
Hængsson the law-speaker.

VI

Having suggested that the proposal for the state edition of *Njáls saga*
initially served the atavistic interests of a specific geographical area and

its inhabitants, I feel obliged, finally, to underline the fact that opposition to the proposal in the Alþingi ran as much along political as geographical lines. The twelve 'no' voters in the lower house of the Alþingi included all the seven representatives of the Socialist coalition of Sameiningar-flokkur alþýðu, Sósíalistaflokkur (SAS) (Alþingi 1943–1946, D:196, 220–222). Similarly, of the seven members of the upper house not to sign the statement in support of the proposal were the three representatives of SAS; one of them was Kristinn E. Andrésson, the man who had asked for the invalidation of the 1941 copyright law only few days before the Alþingi became preoccupied with *Njáls saga* (Alþingi 1943–1946, D:196)

It is also significant that in the discussion about the state edition, Halldór Laxness's editorial plans were consistently supported and defended by three members of SAS—Einar Olgeirsson, Áki Jakobsson, and Sigfús Sigurhjartarson—all of whom maintained that the proposal for the state edition was part of an elaborate political plot, devised by a member of the upper house of the parliament, Jónas Jónsson. Áki Jakobsson said that the purpose of the state edition was to 'persecute' [ofsækja] Halldór Laxness and also conceivably to denigrate the Socialist coalition (Alþingi 1943–1946, D:202). Einar Olgeirsson suggested that this tendency to limit people's freedom of action was no new phenomenon in Icelandic politics: Jónas Jónsson had, for example, recommended that Laxness's novels should be banned in Iceland on the grounds that they were full of Communist propaganda (Alþingi 1943–1946, D:204). Jónas had also drawn up a proposal, accepted by a majority vote in parliament, which would have prevented people with 'particular political opinions' [sérstakar pólitískar skoðanir], as Einar Olgeirsson expressed it, from being employed by the state or from enjoying state financial support (Alþingi 1943–1946, D:205). Finally, Sigfús Sigurhjartarson recalled that Jónas Jónsson, in an extended crusade against the Socialist party, had persuaded a majority of parliamentary members to support a statement claiming that it was disgraceful that they should have to share the parliamentary floor with SAS representatives (Alþingi 1943–1946, D:212). In the course of their speeches, the representatives of SAS referred to the advocates of the state edition as Jónas Jónsson's 'disciples' [lærisveinar], but two of the three proponents—Helgi Jónasson and Sveinbjörn Högnason—happened to be members of Framsóknar-flokkurinn, the 'progressive' farmers party, in which Jónas Jónsson was a leading figure.[7]

---

[7]The third supporter, Ingólfur Jónsson, represented the conservative party, Sjálfstæðisflokkurinn. He did not speak in favour of the proposal during the debate; in fact, he left the debating chamber before the proposal came to a final vote (Alþingi 1943–1946, D:213, 220).

It is beyond the scope of this present paper to trace the twists and turns that the debate between the Socialists and their adversaries took in Iceland in the 1930s and 1940s (see Guðjón Friðriksson 1993). It must suffice to stress that ever since the foundation of the Icelandic Communist party in 1930, Jónas Jónsson had been one of the fiercest opponents of this 'dictatorial pest' [pest einræðisins], as he called it (Gils Guðmundsson 1985, 87). Exercising his power as minister of education in the early 1930s, he had, for instance, introduced measures whereby students who advocated Communist doctrines should be excluded from higher education; a few students were indeed expelled from schools as a result. The revival of publishing activities administered by the state's cultural fund, Menningarsjóður, and its cooperation with Þjóðvinafélagið (an independent cultural society) was, similarly, Jónas Jónsson's response to the success of Mál og menning, a literary society originally established in 1937 by a group of Socialists, mostly writers. It was under his leadership, that Bókaútgáfa Menningarsjóðs og Þjóðvinafélagsins adopted the subscription system used by Mál og menning, which by 1939 had already attracted some 5,000 members. One of Jónas Jónsson's declared aims was to balance the Communist propaganda which, he claimed, Mál og menning was distributing throughout Iceland with financial aid from Moscow.

On a number of occasions during this period there were confrontations between Jónas Jónsson and Halldór Laxness. Although not a registered member of SAS, Laxness was an outspoken Socialist, an admirer of Stalin's Soviet Union, one of the founders of Mál og menning, and an active member of its editorial board. For some time, he co-edited the journal *Tímarit Máls og menningar* with Kristinn E. Andrésson, who became a representative of SAS in the Alþingi in 1942. While Jónas Jónsson criticised Halldór Laxness for his political views and for writing 'perverted' anti-national novels that advocated Communism (Jónas Jónsson 1942b), Laxness attacked the publishing agenda of Bókaútgáfa Menningarsjóðs og Þjóðvinafélagsins. He also attacked Jónas personally for his editorial role in some of the books published by Menningarsjóður (Halldór Laxness 1941). Their quarrel also related to changes in the law during 1939 which entrusted to the cultural board of Menntamálaráð [Education Commission] responsibility for distributing the annual state grant to the arts. Previously, the distribution of such funds had been the responsibility of the Alþingi. As Menntamálaráð chairman and the man behind these changes, Jónas Jónsson was accused of wishing to persecute those artists who were not in sympathy with his aesthetic and political views. Before the first distribution of grants by Menntamálaráð, Jónas Jónsson clashed with Professor Sigurður Nordal over this matter; they also used the opportunity to abuse each other personally (Jónas Jónsson 1942a, 1942c). Jónas stated that Halldór Laxness had been one of the radical writers disproportionately favoured in earlier disbursements by the Alþingi. As if to a confirm this judgement, Menntamálaráð reduced Laxness's grant for 1940 from 5,000 to 1,800 krónur. Laxness's reaction was to use the money to establish a fund for the protection of 'the intellectual freedom of Icelandic writers' [andlegt frelsi íslenskra rithöfunda: Gils Guðmundsson 1985, 94].

In January of 1941, Jónas Jónsson wrote a long article, published in his party's newspaper *Tíminn*, discussing the publishing policy of Bókaútgáfa Menningarsjóðs og Þjóðvinafélagsins. He referred to a recent survey indicating that the Icelandic family sagas were not to be found on the bookshelves of the majority of Icelandic homes. His sense was that the average person could not afford to buy the editions of Fornritafélagið, the only saga editions in print at this time. At nine krónur a volume they were too expensive; Jónas proposed that if the price could be lowered to five krónur Menningarsjóður would be happy to co-operate with Fornritafélagið and distribute the sagas through its subscriber network. If such an arrangement could not be established, Jónas concluded, Bóka-útgáfa Menningarsjóðs og Þjóðvinafélagsins would have to address in some other way the urgent need for inexpensive editions of the family sagas (Jónas Jónsson 1941a). Apparently, some negotiations between Fornritafélagið and Menningarsjóður did take place (Alþingi 1942, B:87), but at the time when the debate on the state edition of *Njáls saga* began in 1943, these had resulted merely in the Menningarsjóður decision to begin publication of saga editions in full conformity with the interests of Fornritafélagið (Alþingi 1943–1946, D:196).

In the meantime, however, Ragnar Jónsson's announcement of Laxness's forthcoming edition of *Laxdæla saga* had upset Jónas Jónsson's plan. In a long article appearing in *Tíminn* in October 1941, Jónas condemned the proposed publication enterprise of the 'Communists':

> There is no doubt that if the Icelandic Communists get the opportunity to publish the old literature, they will attempt to offend general taste and national sensibility in whichever way they believe will produce the best result on every occasion. (Jónas Jónsson 1941b)[8]

Jónas emphasised that Fornritafélagið and the Alþingi (through Menningarsjóður) were already employing qualified editors whose task was to increase the circulation of the sagas. 'Communist' intervention was, in his

---

[8]'Það er enginn vafi á, að ef kommúnistarnir íslenzku fá tækifæri til að gefa út fornritin, þá munu þeir freista að misbjóða smekk manna og þjóðernistil-finningu á þann hátt, sem þeir treysta sér til að framkvæma með mestum árangri á hverjum tíma.'

view, unnecessary as well as undesirable; Laxness's edition would represent merely 'a caricature' [skrípamynd] of the works that, along with the Bible and the psalms of Hallgrímur Pétursson, had for centuries formed the foundations of Icelandic culture.

Two weeks after Jónas's article appeared, members of his party introduced the copyright law into the lower house of the Alþingi (the proposal was presented on 4 November, but was not debated until 10 November; Alþingi 1942, B:83). As with the proposal for the state edition of *Njáls saga* in 1943, Jónas was not an official sponsor of the copyright law, but in both these cases his adversaries claimed that they could sense his controlling hand. During the 1943 debate, SAS representative Einar Olgeirsson even maintained that the state edition was not only directed against Laxness, but also specifically designed to harm the proposed *Njáls saga* edition of Fornritafélagið, since another of Jónas Jónsson's *personae non grata*, Professor Sigurður Nordal, was involved in that edition (Alþingi 1943–1946, D:206–207). Whilst the truth of such claims cannot now be tested, they nevertheless provide us with a vivid sense of the highly charged contemporary political atmosphere in which the state edition of *Njáls saga* found itself caught up.

As for Jónas Jónsson's interest in the state edition, it may have been significant that two months prior to the parliamentary debate, the power structure in Menntamálaráð had changed with the appointment of a number of new board members. At the very first meeting of this new board, Jónas Jónsson was replaced as chairman by a delegate of Sjálfstæðisflokkur, Valtýr Stefánsson, who had been very critical of his predecessor. Consequently, Jónas's influence on the board diminished immediately (Gils Guðmundsson 1985, 95). Two of the five other board members were also members of parliament—Kristinn E. Andrésson and Barði Guðmundsson; both of them were opposed to the whole idea of the state edition. It is conceivable that Jónas Jónsson, in the (for him) unfamiliar role of underdog in Menntamálaráð, designed the parliamentary proposal in order to mobilise the publishing outlet of Bókaútgáfa Menningarsjóðs og Þjóðvinafélagsins against all the odds and thus to regain the saga publishing initiative from Laxness. There were even some advantages in this procedure. An edition of *Njáls saga* was bound to have more prestige, and to carry less the aura of a personal or political vendetta, were it to be authorised by the Icelandic parliament—the elected voice of the national will—rather than appearing as an edition authorised by the controversial Jónas Jónsson.

VII

Some months after the Alþingi had sanctioned the proposed state edition of *Njáls saga*, the Icelandic superior court acquitted Halldór Laxness, Ragnar Jónsson and Stefán Ögmundsson in the *Hrafnkels saga* case, on the grounds that the 1941 copyright law did violate constitutional provisions relating to the freedom of the press (Hæstiréttur 1943, 237–239). In this respect, the literary patronage of the Alþingi was defeated. It succeeded, however, in another respect: Bókaútgáfa Menningarsjóðs og Þjóðvinafélagsins published its *Njáls saga* edition in 1944, whilst Laxness's edition did not appear until 1945.

In the light of our preceding discussion, Vilhjálmur Þ. Gíslason's introduction to the state edition can be characterised as extremely diplomatic and prudent. In it, we find a summary of the various views which people, mostly scholars, had expressed about the nature of the Icelandic family sagas in general and about *Njáls saga* in particular. In controversial matters, of which there were many, Vilhjálmur did not take sides, but rather encouraged those readers who might be interested in specific issues to consult primary sources. He also indicated that a more detailed bibliographical review was likely to appear elsewhere, thus drawing attention to the forthcoming Fornritafélagið edition (*N.s.* 1944, xvi).

As far as practical editorial policy was concerned, Vilhjálmur Gíslason's introductory essay incorporated a statement written by the text editor, Magnús Finnbogason, who claimed that *Njáls saga* appeared in the volume in modern spelling, but with word-forms and linguistic features of thirteenth-century Icelandic duly preserved in all major respects. With the verses, however, old spellings had been retained since most of these verses, Magnús explained, were older than the saga's narrative prose (*N.s.* 1944, xv). Magnús did not mention the controversy in the Alþingi over Laxness's proposed edition, but he was clearly following the editorial line set out by the three university professors. In his statement Magnús Finnbogason also made clear that the publishing board of Bókaútgáfa Menningarsjóðs og Þjóðvinafélagsins had appointed a special editorial board for this project, which had cooperated with him on the publication. The board consisted of Vilhjálmur Þ. Gíslason, who was also a board member of Menningarsjóður; Þorkell Jóhannesson, a librarian at the National Library; and Bogi Ólafsson, who had a degree in English and German. Magnús Finnbogason himself, like Vilhjálmur Þ. Gíslason and Þorkell Jóhannesson, had studied Icelandic language and literature at the University of Iceland, and had subsequently taught

Icelandic at Menntaskóli Reykjavíkur. This powerful group ensured that the state edition of *Njáls saga* could not be accused, as Laxness's editions had been, of insufficient scholarly 'authority'. On the other hand, we may sense a continuing tendency to avoid responsibility for this controversial publication: Jónas Jónsson apparently asked his fellow party-members to ask the Alþingi to ask Bókaútgáfa Menningarsjóðs og Þjóðvinafélagsins to publish *Njáls saga*. The publishing-board had then asked a selected group of scholars to prepare the edition and they, in turn, had asked Magnús Finnbogason to become the editor.

In the state edition, *Njáls saga* is neither presented nor rejected as a reliable historical document, but it complies perfectly with the requirements of those who wanted to read it as the history of a particular district. In the middle of the introduction, a pull-out map of Rangárvalla-sýsla and its neighbouring district can be consulted, showing the geographical location of major farms and other sites mentioned in the saga (*N.s.* 1944, viii–ix). Interestingly, the position of Stórólfshvoll, the farm of Helgi Jónasson, is also shown on the map, even though the farm is quite irrelevant to the plot of the saga. Somewhat in keeping with the sense of *Njáls saga* as a national possession, a fold-out map of Iceland and a series of photographs from various saga-sites can also be found in the volume, linking Iceland's overall geography with the saga narrative. Explanatory notes and an index confirm that the saga is indeed more than a simple 'fabrication'.

Our inquiry into the patronage of the 1944 edition of *Njáls saga* has shown a discrepancy between the official ideology, suggested by Vilhjálmur Þ. Gíslason's introduction, and the complex motivations that led to its eventual publication. In his introduction, Vilhjálmur mentions the lively interest exhibited by the author of *Njáls saga* in law and legal procedures (*N.s.* 1944, vii). He is careful not to exhibit any such interest himself. His voice is impersonal and detached, almost as if seeking to conceal those political and personal controversies which had led to the Alþingi playing the improbable role of saga patron.

ACKNOWLEDGEMENTS

In the preparation of this article I have benefited greatly from the financial support of Vísindasjóður Íslands, and a University of Massachusetts Graduate Fellowship grant. I deal more fully with the publication and translation history of *Njáls saga* in my University of Massachusetts doctoral dissertation.

BIBLIOGRAPHY

Alþingi. 1942. *Alþingistíðindi 1941. Fimmtugasta og áttunda löggjafarþing*. Reykjavík.

Alþingi. 1943–1946. *Alþingistíðindi 1942–43. Sextugasta og fyrsta löggjafarþing*. Reykjavík.

Björn Þorsteinsson and Bergsteinn Jónsson. 1991. *Íslands saga til okkar daga*. Reykjavík.

Gils Guðmundsson. 1985. 'Jónas Jónsson og Menningarsjóður', *Andvari*, Nýr flokkur 27, 78–96.

Guðjón Friðriksson. 1993. *Ljonið öskrar. Saga Jónasar Jónssonar frá Hriflu*. Reykjavík.

Halldór Laxness. 1941. 'Útgafa Jónasar Jónssonar á Jónasi Hallgrímssyni', *Tímarit Máls og menningar* 2, 199–202.

Hæstiréttur. 1943. *Hæstaréttardómar 1943*, 14. Reykjavík.

Jónas Jónsson. 1941a. 'Þjóðarútgáfan', *Tíminn*, 23 January.

———. 1941b. 'Innsta virkið', *Tíminn*, 24 October.

———. 1942a. 'Það er Sigurður sem samdi skjalið', *Tíminn*, 26 April.

———. 1942b. 'Ljótleiki eða fegurð?' *Tíminn*, 9 May.

———. 1942c. 'Aldagamlir brennuneistar', *Tíminn*, 10 May.

Lefevere, André. 1984. 'Why Waste Our Time on Rewrites?', in Theo Hermans, ed., *The Manipulation of Literature. Studies in Literary Translation*, pp. 215–43. New York.

Njáls saga. 1944. Ed. Magnús Finnbogason, with a foreword by Vilhjálmur Þ. Gíslason. Reykjavík.

Þorkell Jóhannesson. 1942. '*Njáls saga*', *Skírnir* 116, 86–112.

8

Modern nationalism and the medieval sagas

JESSE L. BYOCK

First of all the Icelandic people themselves must in a more profound manner appropriate their classical literature, so that it can become one of the many factors which develop and strengthen the feeling for the national characteristics.

(Hjalmar Lindroth 1937)

National consciousness is by no means a private affair. In most cases it is determined not only by what the group asserting a national identity thinks of itself but also in response to the views of outsiders. External opinion has been especially important to the Scandinavians, whose largely agrarian societies lay until the late nineteenth century on the fringes of European cultural innovation. Despite the growth of industry and urbanisation beginning in the early nineteenth century, Scandinavia remained stigmatised as a region of cultural backwardness until the early twentieth century. Even Denmark, one of the most advanced of the Scandinavian states, long felt the scorn of critics. Albeit with a jaundiced eye, Friedrich Engels, writing to Karl Marx from Paris in 1846, said of the Danes:

Als unschuldiges Nebenvergnügen hab' ich in der letzten schlechten Zeit außer den Mädeln noch einigen Umgang mit Dänemark und dem übrigen Norden getrieben. Das ist Dir eine Sauerei. Lieber der kleinste Deutsche als der größte Däne! So ein Klima von Moralitäts-, Zunft- und Ständemisere existiert nirgends mehr. Der Däne hält Deutschland für ein Land, wohin man geht, um 'sich Mätressen zu halten und sein Vermögen mit ihnen durchzubringen [...]' (Engels 1963, 71–72)[1]

[In these recent bad days, I have had as innocent entertainment, apart from the girls, further contact with Denmark and the rest of the North. You would find it a beastly place. Better the least German than

---

[1] I thank Professor Christian Søe for helping me find this reference and referring me to Søe 1991.

the greatest Dane! Such a miserable atmosphere of morality, guild-cliquishness, and consciousness of social status exists nowhere else any more. The Dane thinks of Germany as a country one visits in order 'to keep mistresses with whom one can squander one's wealth [...]']

None too enthusiastic about the Danes, Engels also had thoughts on the Icelanders, a people who, like their medieval ancestors, lived in turf houses whose thick, grassy walls melted into the landscape:

> der [Isländer] noch ganz dieselbe Sprache spricht wie die schmierigen Wikinger von Anno 900, Tran säuft, in einer Erdhütte wohnt und in jeder Atmosphäre kaputtgeht, die nicht nach faulen Fischen riecht. Ich bin mehrere Male in Versuchung gewesen, stolz darauf zu werden, daß ich wenigstens kein Däne oder gar Isländer, sondern nur ein Deutscher bin.[2]

> [the Icelander still speaks the very same language as the greasy Vikings of anno 900. He drinks fish-oil, lives in an earthen hut and breaks down when the atmosphere doesn't reek of rotten fish. I was many times tempted to be proud that I am at least no Dane or even an Icelander but only a German.]

If Engels was harsh on the Danes and derided the well-known Icelandic affinity for cod-liver oil, he as a German was not the only one to define his group through recourse to expressions of cultural superiority. Among the Scandinavian peoples themselves, claims for cultural superiority played a significant role in shaping the identity of the different emerging national groups. The Danes, armed with the delights of Copenhagen and the force of the monarchy, tended to look down upon the impoverished Icelanders as backward provincials. The latter, none too sure of their status within the Danish Kingdom, were keen to counter their reputation for rusticity. And here the seeds of a cultural clash were sown.

Nineteenth-century Romanticism had a special interest in both the

---

[2] The Swedes and Norwegians also enter into Engels' observations (Engels 1963, 71–72): 'der Schwede verachtet wieder den Dänen als 'verdeutscht' und ausgeartet, schwatzhaft und verweichlicht—der Norweger sieht auf den verfranzösierten Schweden und seinen Adel herab und freut sich, daß bei ihm in Norge noch grade dieselbe stupide Bauernwirtschaft herrscht wie zur Zeit des edlen Kanut, und dafür wird er wieder vom Isländer en canaille behandelt' [the Swede despises the Dane as 'Germanised', and degenerate, garrulous, and effeminate—the Norwegian looks with condescension at the Frenchified Swede and his aristocracy and is glad that in Norway the same stupid peasant-economy still dominates as in the time of noble Canute. He holds the Icelander even more *en canaille*.]

medieval world and primitive, untainted rural culture. Through the nineteenth century and into the early twentieth the Danes fell more and more under the nostalgic spell, tending to look upon the Icelanders through increasingly romantic and patronising eyes. In Iceland, however, as Gunnar Karlsson has pointed out, primitive country life was, well into the twentieth century, too close and constant a reality to have ever attracted many advocates (Gunnar Karlsson 1985, 452). A basic fact—and one older than nineteenth-century Romanticism itself—is that those who most admire primitive rural life are almost certainly those who have never been bound to such circumstances. The sobering effects of subsistence agriculture and the attendant desire to participate in contemporaneous European cultural life deeply affected Iceland's emerging twentieth-century urban intellectuals.

As I discuss in this article,[3] a dominant group among these intellectuals found in the *Íslendingasögur* a solution to the long-troubling issue of an Icelandic self-image. They reinterpreted the medieval texts in a manner which gave their new state historical evidence of a long record of high culture. The sagas, which had previously been understood to be the remnants of a flourishing folk-tradition of oral narration, were now elevated to the position of a written genre, the product of an extraordinary, late-medieval period of cultured literary creation. By changing the perception of the sagas, Icelandic nationalists advanced the relative cultural standing of their country among the Scandinavian states. This reinterpretation, however, if so important for an earlier generation, has left an unfortunate legacy. The Icelandic nationalists, in denying the sagas their roots in the oral compositional skills of a yeomanry, tied the origins of this form of insular prose story telling far too closely to classical and medieval traditions of literature and learning.

If the sagas became a literature in the service of twentieth-century national aspirations, how did this come about? The answer is that the sagas had already been seized upon from the very beginning of the Icelandic nationalistic movement in the nineteenth century as clear evidence of the country's identity. The presence of an expansive corpus of texts such as the sagas was a significant factor in distinguishing the Icelanders, separating them from other non-independent Nordic groups within Scandinavia who had no comparable evidence of cultural history. These groups—if we leave aside the ethnically distinct minorities such as

---

[3]This article originally appeared in shorter form in the *Yearbook of Comparative and General Literature* 38–39 (1990–1991), 62–74. A revised Icelandic version, 'Þjóðernishyggja nútímans og Íslendingasögurnar', was published in *Tímarit Máls og menningar* 54/1 (1993), 36–50.

the Saami (Laplanders) and the Greenlanders[4]—include the Faroese, who did not have a significant nationalist movement before the turn of the twentieth century, and the former Danish-speaking population of Skåne. The latter, although a part of the Swedish kingdom for only a few centuries, never seriously sought independence.

From the beginning of the nationalistic movement, the sagas provided the island population with a historical past as well as a measure of self respect. Iceland's Nobel laureate Halldór Laxness offers insight into the Icelanders' view of themselves and the influence of the sagas at the time of Engels' letter. At the opening to his 1960 novel *Paradísarheimt* [Paradise Reclaimed], we find this introspective statement:

> Á öndverðum dögum Kristjáns Vilhjálmssonar sem þriðji síðastur útlendra konúnga hefur farið með völd hér uppá landið [...] voru íslendíngar kallaðir fátækust þjóð í Norðurálfu. Svo höfðu og verið feður þeirra, afar og lángfeðgar, alt aftur á daga fornmanna: en þeir trúðu því að langt aftur í öldum hefði verið gullöld hér á Íslandi: þá voru íslendíngar ekki bændur og fiskimenn einsog nú, heldur konúngbornar hetjur og skáld sem áttu vopn gull og skip. (Halldór Laxness 1960, 7)

> [In the early days of Christian Williamsson [the Danish King Christian IX, 1863–1906], who was the third last foreign king to wield power here in Iceland [...] Icelanders were said to be the poorest people in Europe, just as their fathers and grandfathers and great-grandfathers had been, all the way back to the earliest settlers; but they were convinced that long centuries ago there had been a Golden Age in Iceland, when Icelanders had not been mere farmers and fishermen as they were now, but royal born heroes and poets who owned weapons, gold, and ships.] (Halldór Laxness, trans. Magnús Magnússon 1962, 7)

If Laxness treats such yearning with a characteristic touch of good-natured irony, others took the matter more seriously. Particularly in the 1920s and 1930s, positions with nationalistic overtones had become more strident than they were just a few decades earlier. At this time, the leading Icelandic literary scholar and later diplomat, Sigurður Nordal, took up the cause of having the sagas recognised as the work of well-educated medieval men of letters. For Nordal these narratives were far more than folk traditions. Rather the sagas were a critical element of national self-consciousness, cultural artifacts upon which vital comparisons of the relative worth of a people could be based. The underlying

---

[4]Both these groups were later to experience a strong growth in ethnic and nationalistic sentiment.

issue of status can be perceived throughout Nordal's writings, as for example in the opening statement to his essay, 'Samhengi í Íslenzkum bókmentum' [Continuity in Icelandic Literature]:

> Engin germönsk þjóð, og reyndar engin þjóð í Norðurálfu, á bók-mentir frá miðöldum, er að frumleik og snildarbrag komist í jafnkvisti við bókmentir Íslendinga frá fimm fyrstu öldunum eftir að land byggðist. (Nordal 1924, ix)

> [No Germanic people, in fact no nation in Northern Europe, has a medieval literature which in originality and brilliance can be compared with the literature of the Icelanders from the first five centuries after the settlement period.]

This essay appeared as the introduction and principal commentary to *Íslenzk lestrarbók*, an anthology of Icelandic literature that was used in most Icelandic middle schools for decades. Such essays and their claims had a vast influence upon the people of the emerging Icelandic state. They also had a decisive influence upon the modern interpretation of the sagas and remain in many circles canonical presumptions for saga studies. The rub is that such views continue to inhibit one of the most exciting new areas of saga research—the comparative analysis of saga and society.

Considering the effect of nationalism[5] upon the current tradition of family saga research leads to a concern extending beyond Iceland: the manner in which a dogmatically embedded belief system rooted in political expediency can stunt criticism in a whole field of study. Those who followed in the footsteps of the Icelandic nationalists, tracing the origin of the prose sagas to the epics and romances of continental Europe, have seen the importance of their position diminish as the need for nationalistic interpretation has faded. In its wake, we are beginning to see a more balanced body of criticism; one that treats the medieval texts in light of the island society that created and used them, rather than as the inherited possessions of a modern society in need of redefinition. Awareness of the indigenous aspects of the sagas, including the demands of the audience, are crucial to analysis of these texts as Preben Meulengracht Sørensen notes:

> Baggrunden kan søges i det sociale fællesskab på det islandske gårdbrug, hvor fortællingen må være blevet dyrket aften efter aften

---

[5]Some of the most perceptive writings on the background to Icelandic nationalism are Gunnar Karlsson 1980, 77–89; 1987, 130–145. See also Óskar Halldórsson 1978, 317–324, who early on commented on the Icelandic school's cultural politics (*menningarpólítik*); Árni Sigurjónsson 1984, 49–63, carries the inquiry further.

gennem århundrederne. Her opstod ikke særmiljøer som i klostre og
bispesæder eller ved Hákon Hákonarsons hird i det 13. årh. Den
islandske sagatradition blev aldrig isoleret fra den almindelige
befolkning. Alle var med i tilhørerskaren, bønder og tyende, kvinder
og mænd, lærde og analfabeter. (Sørensen 1977, 123)

[The background [for unity in Icelandic narrative tradition] can be
sought in the social community of the Icelandic farm where the story
may have been cultivated evening after evening for centuries. Here no
special milieu sprang up as in cloisters and episcopal residences, or
at the court of [the Norwegian king] Hákon Hákonarson in the
thirteenth century. Icelandic saga tradition never became isolated from
the common population. All were present in the listening audience,
farmers and farmhands, women and men, learned people and
illiterates.]

Icelandic nationalistic feelings ran high in the decades immediately
preceding and following the attainment of full statehood in 1944.
Beginning in the early decades of the century, Iceland underwent a phase
of therapeutic redefinition which was largely the work of the country's
new urban intellectuals. This experience allowed the emerging nation to
cast off centuries of dependence upon the Danes and to take control of
its own cultural past. Such a readjustment was unusual for Northern
Europe in the period before World War II, and, perhaps because of this
unusualness, the readjustment has not been perceived as part of a larger
pattern. Similar developments were, however, seen in Central and Eastern
Europe before the War and have been witnessed repeatedly in the post-
colonial world; they are a process by which new states cast off a cultural
history that justified foreign dominance (Chatterjee 1986).

In decolonialising their history, new states tend to follow a certain
pattern. They construct perceptions of their past which are the obverse of
those previously imposed upon them by the more 'cultured' colonial
powers (Ferro 1984). Intuitively, the intellectuals and the academic
leaders of developing metropolitan Reykjavík understood the call for
change. Their island community was forced to consider its relationship
with European culture without the Danes acting as intermediaries.
Iceland, detaching itself from Denmark, had to find its own place in
Europe's cultural landscape. As an extensive body of literature with
stories about most of the major fjord and valley regions of the country,
the family sagas offered the potential for redefinition. In part this is
because the sagas do not easily fit standard categorisations. Neither
folktales nor epics, they are also thoroughly different from chronicles or
romances. Rather, the sagas are a prose narration, the form of which is
intimately linked to the decentralised island society of settled pastoralists
that created them (Byock 1988). The stories tell of quarrels erupting into

violence, and of feuds being mediated through arbitration and through legal methods of dispute resolution on both regional and national levels.

Filled with intricate detail, the family sagas are a register of the basic values of medieval Iceland's conservative rural society. In particular, the stories centre on personal crises, and, unlike other contemporaneous medieval literatures, they offer a clear view of the 'little' people of history. Through the Icelandic narratives we enter into the mentality of the culture and perceive the conditions of life on the farms. We learn of chieftains, large and small farmers, and women. We see people on the margins of society, such as farmhands and crofters, and we come to know a parent's love or dislike for his or her children. Together the sagas portray the operation of normative codes and illuminate the choices faced by individuals to a degree unmatched by any body of medieval charters or cartularies.

Here, then, is a splendid body of texts for the study of literature and society (Sørensen 1977; Byock 1982). The stumbling block is that a long-standing theoretical exclusion of the sagas from social and historical analysis remains partially in force. These exclusionary views were raised by the group of scholars now known as the 'Icelandic school'. This urban group rose to prominence in the first half of the twentieth century and championed 'bookprose', the belief that the saga was a late written invention rather than the product of an oral tradition. The intellectual roots of the Icelandic school can be traced to the ideas of the nineteenth-century German scholar Konrad Maurer. The concepts were then significantly reformulated by Björn M. Ólsen, who in 1911 became the first professor of Icelandic language and literature at the new University of Iceland. The guiding force, however, behind the bookprosists was Sigurður Nordal.[6] In 1921, Nordal succeeded Björn M. Ólsen as professor, and under his guidance the movement achieved full international momentum in the 1960s and 1970s.

Nordal was a forceful leader with firm beliefs, and his views about the sagas were strongly reinforced by the writings of his students and fellow Icelandic scholars such as Einar Ólafur Sveinsson and Jón Jóhannesson.[7]

---

[6]*Tímarit Máls og menningar* 45/1 (1984) contains a series of wide-ranging articles about Sigurður Nordal by Gunnar Karlsson, Páll Skúlason, Páll Valsson, Steinunn Eyjólfsdóttir and Vésteinn Ólason: see bibliography below.

[7]Different aspects of the Icelandic school's bookprose concept, as well as views on the long debate in the first half of the twentieth century between bookprosists and freeprosists, believers in the oral origins of the sagas, have been reviewed by Andersson 1964; Marco Scovazzi 1960. See also Hallberg 1962,

Influenced by Nordal's views, these scholars wrote the critical introductions to the Íslenzk fornrit saga editions. The first volume of this new series, *Egils saga Skalla-Grímssonar* (1933), was edited by Nordal and publication of this standardised series continues today. From a philological point of view these editions are indisputably a crucial contribution to the study of the sagas, providing critics with excellent, standardised, and trustworthy texts. From the viewpoint of the study of literature and society, however, we can be more circumspect about the Íslenzk fornrit investigations. The major social or historical aspect within the often long introductions is the search for the anonymous authors of the medieval texts, a subjective enterprise that builds from one supposition to the next, creating a hierarchy of great authors and serving to establish a canon of texts.

This hierarchy and canon remain intact today. If we are to chart a successful new direction in the study of early Iceland and its texts, then we need to come to grips with the theories of the Icelandic school, especially with their prohibitions. Of particular importance is an understanding of the bookprosist injunction against using the sagas as historical source material. Injunction is a strong term, but it is an accurate measure of the degree and the effect of the bookprosists' 'hands off' message to anyone with social/historical interests. In 1957 Sigurður Nordal delivered a paper, 'The Historical Element in the Icelandic Family Saga' in Glasgow while he was ambassador to Denmark. In this memorable address, Nordal, surely with irony, but perhaps also with a touch of sarcasm, treats the related issues of historical validity and the role of historians in the study of saga literature:

> A modern historian will for several reasons tend to brush these sagas aside as historical records. He is generally suspicious of a long oral tradition, and the narrative will rather give him the impression of the art of a novelist than of the scrupulous dullness of a chronicler. Into the bargain, these sagas deal principally with private lives and affairs which do not belong to history in its proper sense, not even to the history of Iceland. The historian cuts the knot, and the last point alone would be sufficient to exempt him from further trouble. It is none of his business to study these sagas as literature, their origin, material, and making. (Nordal 1957, 14)

But what does Nordal mean by history? Certainly he does not think of history in a modern sociological sense. His statement is almost a classical

49–69; Holtsmark 1959; Byock 1982, 7–10; 1985. Two collections of older articles pertinent to the debate are Bætke 1974; Mundal 1977. See also Mundal 1975, Mitchell 1991, 1–6.

formulation of institutional history, that is, history seen as a chronology of facts. In this older concept of history, human endeavour is understood through the actions of prominent individuals, the progress of governmental institutions, and the status of political structures. Conceived in this way, history ignores the private life of the majority of people. Instead, institutional history seizes on major events, follows the logic of chronology, and concentrates on the decisions and acts of the few who wield power. It is thus not surprising that history conceived in this way finds only a few facts of value in saga narratives and discards the rest of the text as fiction. In doing so, it ignores the lives of a major portion of the population; it skips over the realistic details of daily life so abundant in the sagas and so descriptive of the needs, the desires, and the emotions of ordinary people.

But this distinction between fact and fiction, the one upon which the bookprosists placed so much weight—wasn't it always a bit too simple? In other words, why would the bookprosists accept the argument that the sagas with their accounts of private lives and affairs 'do not belong to history in its proper sense, not even to the history of Iceland'? Surely, by 1957 Nordal's statement against historical interpretation of the sagas and his narrow focus on the veracity of historical events were more than a little conservative. In the late 1940s the effects of the approach of social history and the discipline of anthropology were widely felt. Much work in fields other than Icelandic studies had already analysed the past in a way more enlightened than a history limited to the facts listed in a dry chronicle. Among scholars who led the way in this work were well-known historians, anthropologists, and sociologists such as Max Weber, Karl Polanyi, Talcott Parsons, R.H. Tawney, Arnold Toynbee, Marc Bloch, and Lucien LeFebvre, to name a few.

Is there another, more fundamental reason for the injunctions of the Icelandic school than just its blanket commitment to literary interpretation? Again, the answer is nationalism. Although the subject is a big one that goes well beyond the parameters of this article, we can nevertheless focus here on a crucial element: consideration of the political climate at a time when the bookprosists' position was being formulated. It was in an atmosphere of urbanisation and emerging nationhood that the Icelandic school put forward its distinction between history and literature. For its followers, determination of the origin of the sagas was more than simply an obscure academic question.

The late nineteenth and the first half of the twentieth century in Iceland were marked by intense agitation for independence from Denmark. The island had not been independent since the end of the Free State in 1262–1264; it was first ruled by the Norwegians and then, after 1380, by the Danes. The Danes have had a bad press in Iceland, not least because their rule was intimately connected in the minds of nineteenth- and twentieth-century Icelanders with one of the worst periods in Icelandic history, the last two decades of the eighteenth century. This was also a period of dynastic, political, and economic instability in Denmark, and in part the often callous Danish treatment of Iceland in these decades can be attributed to the turmoil and declining economy that Denmark experienced in the era preceding the French revolution and continuing through the Napoleonic wars. In Iceland in the 1780s volcanic eruptions deposited ash over a wide area, which in turn caused the death of livestock; this calamity, plus a period of unusually cold weather, led to a famine in which one-fifth of the population perished. By 1800 the total population of Iceland, a land mass equal to two-thirds the size of England and Scotland together, was only 47,000. Adding to the troubles of this period were the policies of the oppressive Danish trade monopoly. Established in 1602, it had by the mid-eighteenth century become so unresponsive to Iceland's needs that during the famine year of 1784 the island was required to export food.[8]

It was in the years following this troubled period that the sagas began to play an expanded role in shaping an Icelandic national/political consciousness. Icelanders had earlier derived ethnic pride and cultural identity from the old stories, but in the decades following the French Revolution, the medieval texts assumed a new political meaning. As the nineteenth century advanced, the sagas provided documentation for a political self-awareness, that combined cultural, governmental, and economic goals. Iceland's poverty, hardship, and decline continued well into the nineteenth century and stood in sharp contrast to the prosperous life pictured in the old texts. The sagas, which were read in manuscript, were becoming available in inexpensive editions in the nineteenth century, published by Sigurður Kristjánsson. As Laxness notes, they portrayed the past as a life of noble independence replete with feasts, trading ships, and fine gifts—a time when upstanding Icelanders met with and received respect from the royalty of ancient Scandinavia and the British Isles. Comparison with the past was a common pastime among nineteenth-century Icelanders. Underlying the sense of national decline and impoverishment was the knowledge that only in the 1870s did the island's population finally surpass the 70,000 mark believed to have been

---

[8]Despite such actions, the Danish monopoly may not have been as repressive (especially when one considers the other choices available) as the nineteenth- and twentieth-century nationalists assumed it to be. Nevertheless, to some extent trade policies instituted in Copenhagen continued to hinder Iceland's economic development until well into the nineteenth century: Gísli Gunnarsson 1987.

the total in the period of Iceland's medieval independence. In Icelandic eyes, the reality of conditions under Danish suzerainty contrasted sharply with the *Gullöld Íslendinga* [Golden Age of the Icelanders], as the early period of the medieval Free State came to be called.[9]

Despite their problems, the Icelanders did have a number of advantages. They managed over the centuries to hold onto their language, culture, and literacy. These elements were put to good use in the mid-nineteenth century, when the political situation began to change. In 1845 the Althing, which had been disbanded in 1800, was re-established in Reykjavík as an advisory body. At the same time revolutionary stirrings in Denmark aided the Icelandic cause. In 1848 the king renounced absolutism, although for a while there was no diminution of royal authority in Iceland. New ideas, however, were taking hold among Icelandic intellectuals, particularly among those who lived in Copenhagen. A prominent force in the Icelandic awakening was the influence of the German philosophers Johann Gottfried Herder and Wilhelm von Humboldt (Gunnar Karlsson 1980, 81). In particular, Herder's views encouraged the nationalistic searchings of Icelandic students and intellectuals in Copenhagen in the 1830s, giving the Icelanders a theoretical explanation of why life had been better during Iceland's medieval independence. According to Herder, a nation controlled by foreigners, with foreign institutions imposed upon it, was bound to stagnate. Progress for a nation was based upon the freedom to develop its national spirit without hindrance. If Iceland was poor, it was because it was not free. As the sagas, with their prosperous farmers and chieftains, showed, the quality of life was markedly different when Iceland was independent.

Although such concepts helped to stir nationalism among Icelandic intellectuals, they also revealed a philosophical split that was to divide Icelanders for the next hundred years and which ended with the victorious ascendancy of the bookprosists in the 1930s. The division between the two groups, the traditionalists and the futurists, centred on different conceptions of the new Iceland. For the traditionalists, especially the early nineteenth-century group called the *fjölnismenn*, the new Iceland was to resemble the medieval past. It was conceived in a national romantic light that idealised Iceland's past freedom and medieval culture as witnessed by the sagas. For the futurists, the model was a new urban culture, with refined middle-class tastes and values. This division deepened in the debate over reestablishment of the Althing in the 1840s

---

[9]*Gullöld Íslendinga* was the name of a popular history from the first decade of the twentieth century: Jón Aðils Jónsson 1906.

(Aðalgeir Kristjánsson 1993). The traditionalists, such as Jónas Hall-grímsson and Þorleifur Repp (Wawn 1991), argued not only for reestablishing the Althing at Þingvellir but also for investing it with many of the Althing's traditional features. The other group, led by Jón Sigurðsson, argued for Reykjavík as the seat of government. Jón and his colleagues looked to the future, foreseeing a modern parliament in an urban-centred society. The futurists won, but as they took control of the movement for independence, their vision for Iceland had to compete with that of the Danes.

The Danish view was that Iceland, as an underdeveloped country, was in need of continued guidance. If sometimes arrogant and often conde-scending, the Danes, even in the early nineteenth century, behaved rather well. At least no Icelanders were ever executed during their independence struggle. Despite the sometimes shrill rhetoric of Icelandic speeches, the long Icelandic struggle for self-determination was an exercise in decorum. If not really a bad lot, the Danes were stubborn and very persistent. Seeing themselves not as colonial masters but as helpful big brothers, they tended to look down their noses at the Icelanders, whom they patronised with quaint respect for their rustic, yeoman virtues.

However generous the Danes became—and they had become generous by the late nineteenth century when Iceland's upkeep cost the Danish treasury more than it earned from the island—they won few friends. On the contrary, the Icelandic independence movement became more determined as the nineteenth century wore on. Led first by Jón Sigurðs-son, Iceland's nationalists were constantly dissatisfied and remained uncompromising in their desire for a free Iceland, whereas the Danes were convinced of the wisdom of finding an accommodation. The independence struggle [*sjálfstæðisbaráttan*, as it came to be called] was not fought in a vacuum, for Denmark was simultaneously undergoing the change from a central to a constitutional monarchy. Thus the Danish position on Iceland's quest for independence often depended upon whether the liberals or the conservatives were in power.

Denmark's disastrous war with Prussia in 1864 engendered a highly nationalistic sentiment among Danes during the following years. It is within this context that the Danish parliament in 1871 passed the King's Law on the Status of Iceland. The law defined Iceland as an inseparable part of the Danish realm, although giving the island's people some special national rights. The Icelanders, who had not been consulted, refused formally to accept the Status Law as valid, yet operated under its provisions. A crucial provision, which the Icelanders condoned, was the receipt of a yearly subsidy from the Danish treasury. In 1874, to celebrate the millennium of Iceland's founding, the Danish king gave the island a new constitution, but this too was unsatisfactory to the Icelandic nationalists. It allowed Denmark to retain significant control through veto power, leaving the Althing weak. A new separate ministry for Iceland was established, but the Danish minister of justice handled Icelandic affairs as a sideline.

The situation remained unsettled until 1901, when a liberal government came to power in Denmark. In 1904 it granted Iceland home rule, under whose terms an Icelandic minister for domestic affairs was to be appointed by the Althing and was to reside in Reykjavík. The Icelandic nationalists, however, were still not satisfied. In 1918 Denmark was in a quandary. With Germany defeated in World War I, the Danes saw an opportunity to retrieve some of the Danish-speaking parts of Schleswig, which had been seized by Germany after the Danish defeat in 1864. In view of their own arguments for self-determination of the Danish-speaking population of Schleswig, the Danes could hardly deny Icelandic aspirations. As a result, Denmark repealed the old Status Law in 1918 and granted Iceland a new status of union with Denmark.

Under the new law, called the Act of Union [*Sambandslögin*] of 1918, the island officially became the Kingdom of Iceland [*Konungsríkið Ísland*] in 1918 (Ólafur Jóhannesson 1960). It was a separate state in a personal union with the king of Denmark. Internally the country became autonomous; externally Copenhagen continued to manage Iceland's affairs. The 1918 law also specified that either country could terminate the agreement after twenty-five years. On paper at least the Icelandic nationalists would seem to have finally achieved their goal, but the matter is not that simple. Like many of the earlier laws, the Act of Union did not settle the matter. It did not satisfy the nationalists' desire for total independence, a desire that became stronger as Iceland underwent a new period of cultural adjustment.

A profound change had come to the once almost entirely rural society toward the end of the nineteenth century, when towns began to grow. In 1880 Iceland had only three townships whose inhabitants together numbered 3,630, and that was only 5 percent of the population. Urbanisation had progressed rapidly by 1920, when seven townships with 29,000 inhabitants accounted for 31 per cent of the population.[10] Yet despite urban growth, the island remained largely rural, inhabited by farmers and fishermen. Reykjavík, the country's administrative and commercial centre, grew in population from approximately 6,000 in 1900 to 30,000 in 1930.

[10]Focusing on literary development, Halldór Guðmundsson 1987 ably analyses the cultural forces at work in Reykjavík during the first decades of the twentieth century. See Jóhannes Nordal and Valdimar Kristinsson 1967 for statistics.

The Icelanders were proud of the new university there, founded in 1911. The new urban intellectuals strove not only for national self-determination but also for liberation from the centuries-old stereotype of Icelanders as coarse farmers.[11] The Danes strengthened the Icelanders' desire for liberation from the stereotype by patronising them as too impoverished, culturally and economically, to manage a fully independent state.

In this climate, nationalism spilled over into analyses of the national treasure, the family sagas. The problem facing Icelandic intellectuals was how to lift the sagas from their status as traditions of unlettered storytellers and elevate them to the front rank of world literature. In his famous monograph *Hrafnkatla*, written in 1940 and translated into English in 1958, Nordal leaves little doubt about his views:

> Því virðist það eðligast og jafnvel einsætt, að Hrafnkatla sé *verk eins höfundar*, sem ætlaði sér alls ekki að segja sanna sögu, heldur að semja skáldrit,—manns, sem í senn var gæddur ríku ímyndunarafli, mannþekkingu og skáldlegri djörfung og var lyft til flugs af einhverri voldugustu bókmenntahreifingu, sem sögur fara af. (Nordal 1940, 68)

> [It seems quite natural, and even obvious, to believe that *Hrafnkatla* was *the work of a single author*[12] whose purpose was not to narrate a true story but to compose a work of fiction; a man who, endowed with a powerful imagination, literary virtuosity, and a knowledge of men, was sustained by one of the most powerful literary movements in recorded history.]

As part of his analysis of *Hrafnkels saga*, Nordal defines its narrative art as 'the technique of a branch of fiction which is rarer than either the novel or the short story' (Nordal 1958, 55). The first bookprosists, especially Björn M. Ólsen, left a good deal of room for the oral saga but, by the time of Sigurður Nordal, the positions had hardened. Crucial to the bookprosist argument was the assertion that the sagas could not be oral because they were not historical, that is, factually accurate.

Not only literary scholars among the bookprosists but also historians were stirred by Nordal's claims. Jón Jóhannesson, Iceland's rising

---

[11]Jónas Hallgrímsson's 'Alþing hið nýja' (1840) had helped to sustain the alternative (and more heroic) stereotype of the farmer and his farm as the pillar of society: 'bóndi er bústólpi / bú er landstólpi' (Jónas Hallgrímsson 1989, I 112, ll. 10–11).

[12]R. George Thomas's English translation of this passage from Nordal 1940 reads, 'It seems quite natural to believe, almost without any demonstration, that *Hrafnkatla* was the work of a single author [...]' (Nordal 1958, 57).

medieval historian, who became Professor of History in 1950, was
Nordal's student and a firm member of the Icelandic school.[13] In his
1950 introduction to the Íslenzk fornrit edition of *Austfirðinga sögur*, Jón
Jóhannesson wrote a critical analysis of *Hrafnkels saga*. This saga,
affectionately called *Hrafnkatla*, was to become the bell-wether of the
new anti-historical view.[14] Referring to Nordal's study of the saga, also
titled *Hrafnkatla*, Jón Jóhannesson wrote:

> Um Hrafnkels sögu hefir meira verið ritað en nokkra aðra sögu af
> Austurlandi [...]. Merkasta ritgerðin, sem birzt hefir um söguna, er
> *Hrafnkatla* eftir Sigurð Nordal. Hann kemst að þeirri niðurstöðu, að
> sagan sé skáldsaga, samin skömmu fyrir 1300 af vitrum manni og
> hámenntuðum. Áður höfðu allir verið þeirrar skoðunar, að sagan væri
> reist á arfsögnum [...]. Niðurstaða Nordals er prýðilega rökstudd, og
> verður eigi betur séð en hún sé örugg og óhrekjanleg í öllum
> meginatriðum. Ritgerð hans byltir því gersamlega hinni gömlu skoðun
> á sögunni, og eigi nóg með það. Hún markar einnig tímamót í sögu
> rannsókna og skilnings á íslenzkum fornsögum yfirleitt. Ef hugsanlegt
> er, að nokkur Íslendinga saga hafi verið skráð óbreytt eða lítt breytt
> af vörum þjóðarinnar, þá er svo um Hrafnkels sögu sökum þess, hve
> hún er fast mótuð og heilstept, og því auðvelt að muna hana og
> endursegja. En ef hún reynist samt sem áður skáldsaga, samin af
> þeim, er fyrstur skráði hana, eins og Nordal hefir rökstutt, þá hlýtur
> að veikjast sú trú, að aðrar sögur, sem lengri eru og torveldara að
> muna, hafi nokkurn tíma verið sagðar í heilu lagi, í þeirri mynd, sem
> þær hafa fengið á bókfellinu. Hér á eftir verður mjög stuðzt við
> ritgerð Nordals [...] (Jón Jóhannesson 1950, xxxix–xl)

> [More has been written about *Hrafnkels saga* than about any other
> saga from the East Fjords [...]. The most notable study which has

---

[13]Other bookprosists, such as Einar Ólafur Sveinsson, also set their stamp
on the history of early Iceland: see Byock 1986.

[14]It is worth noting that much of the bookprosist use of *Hrafnkels saga* in
its argumentation has an element of the 'straw man' about it, since this particular
saga is one of the few tales of Icelandic feud which cannot be taken as an
example of traditional saga narration: Byock 1982, 201–204. Unlike most
Íslendingasögur which use easily discernible traditional elements and follow
distinct social patterns, *Hrafnkels saga* is clearly different, being structured and
composed in the manner of a consciously written story. Why then not drop the
smoke and mirrors and take this specific text for what it obviously is, a novella?
Then we are free to see that, rather than being an example of general saga
writing, this unusual saga may be the exception that by its very difference proves
the rule.

appeared about the saga is *Hrafnkatla* by Sigurður Nordal, in which
he comes to the conclusion that the saga is a novel [*skáldsaga*],
composed shortly before 1300 by a wise and highly-learned man.
Previously, all had been of the view that the saga was based on a
traditional story [...]. Nordal's conclusion is thoroughly well supported, and one cannot but agree that it is secure and irrefutable in all of
its main attributes. His essay completely revolutionises the old view
of this particular saga, but not only this. It marks a turning point in
the history of research and understanding of the Icelandic sagas in
general. If it is conceivable that any family saga could have been
copied down unchanged, or at least little changed, from the lips of the
people, then this is the case with *Hrafnkels saga*, since it is so tightly
formed and flawlessly shaped and so easily remembered and told. If
this saga should be, despite appearances to the contrary, a novel,
composed by the person who first wrote it down, as Nordal has
concluded, then the belief must diminish that other sagas, which are
longer and more difficult to memorise, have at some time been orally
told as whole entities. From here on my analysis will be strongly
supported by Nordal's study...]

From a theoretical viewpoint, Jón Jóhannesson's stance is understandable. He was a firm practitioner of institutional history and was, in his
writings, thoroughly committed to the fact/fiction distinction so fundamental to the bookprosists' position. His two-volume history of Iceland
(Jón Jóhannesson 1956–1958, 1974) remains a standard reference book
for factual information about Iceland's governmental institutions,
chronology, and events. There is in this book, however, almost no
attempt to investigate private lives. In tracing the genealogy of institutions, Jón Jóhannesson generally ignores the sociological bent of modern
history. He neither analyses how medieval Iceland functioned as a
cohesive body politic nor considers fundamental aspects, such as how
power was acquired and maintained in a society in which warfare was not
an integral factor.

But was Jón Jóhannesson aware of the limitations thrust upon him by
adherence to the theories of his teachers? The answer, at least in his
unguarded moments, seems to be, yes, he was aware of problems. In
1986 Jónas Kristjánsson recounted the following anecdote:

Um miðjan fimmta áratug þessarar aldar var Jón Jóhannesson
sögudósent (síðar prófessor) önnum kafinn að kenna mér og öðrum
stúdentum réttarsögu Alþingis hins forna. Hann studdist við bók
Einars Arnórssonar, en lét okkur strika vandlega út allar tilvitnanir
Einars til Íslendingasagna, með þeirri röksemd að sögurnar væru
ótraustar heimildir. Og 1956 birti Jón Jóhannesson sjálfur sögu
íslenskrar fornaldar, *Íslendingasögu I*, stórfrumlegt verk þar sem beitt
er nýrri sagnfræðilegri heimildarýni. Hann gengur svo langt að hann

nefnir næstum enga atburði sem frá er sagt í Íslendingasögum fremur en þeir hefðu aldrei gerst. Þó var Jón fjarri því að vera einstrengings-legur í skoðunum. Ég spurði lærimeistara minn skömmu eftir að sagan kom út hvort hann héldi þá að Íslendingasögurnar væru eintómt skrök og skáldskapur. Nei, alls ekki, svaraði Jón, en ég veit bara ekki hvað ég á að gera við þær.

Og þannig er ástandið enn í dag. Íslenskir sagnfræðingar láta eins og Íslendingasögur séu ekki til. (Jónas Kristjánsson 1987, 240)

[In the mid-1940s, when Jón Jóhannesson, Professor of History at the University of Iceland, was busily teaching me and Hermann Pálsson the legal history of the Alþingi, he made us carefully cross out all of Einar Arnórsson's[15] references to the sagas on the grounds that they were untrustworthy sources. And in 1956 Jón Jóhannesson published his own work on Iceland's early history [Jón Jóhannesson 1974], in which he followed the same course and mentioned almost none of the events recounted in the *Íslendinga sögur*, just as if they had never taken place. Yet, Jón Jóhannesson was far from being extreme in his views. Shortly after his *History* appeared, I asked my teacher whether he believed that the sagas were pure fiction. 'No, not at all,' he answered, 'I just don't know what to do with them.'

And this is still the situation today. Icelandic historians treat the sagas as if they did not exist.] (Jónas Kristjánsson 1986, 187)

At the time that Nordal and Jón Jóhannesson were writing, most people in Iceland, as well as those in other countries, considered the sagas to be the product of an oral tradition. For the bookprosists, providing the sagas with the new literary lustre was more of an uphill battle than it might seem to us today. This was because the view that sagas were a written creation gained ascendancy chiefly among the growing urban population, an evolving community in search of an identity and sometimes at odds with the countryside. The capital at this time was filled with new ideas as old perceptions fell and horizons were broadened. There was a touch of iconoclasm in the air and, characteristically, large numbers of the new urban population enthusiastically embraced spiritualism and eastern religious concepts, consciously moving away from the traditionally narrower beliefs of their immediate rural forefathers.

The bookprosists carried the new literary transformation of the medieval stories to the extreme, with Nordal declaring in his analysis of *Hrafnkels saga* that '*Hrafnkatla* is one of the most completely developed "short novels" in world literature' (Nordal 1958, 55). In espousing this

---

[15]Einar Arnórsson was an earlier professor at the University. Here Jónas Kristjánsson is refering to Einar Arnórsson 1930, a legal history of the Althing.

view, the bookprosists found themselves at odds with traditional scholars such as Finnur Jónsson, Professor of Icelandic at the University of Copenhagen, and with the conservative Icelandic *bændur*. These modern-day farmers, who habitually read the sagas, believed in the historical accuracy of the texts. Many of them lived on the farmsteads that still carried the names mentioned in the sagas and saw the sagas as local history. Finnur Jónsson, a major academic voice in his day, was prepared to battle head on against the new theory of literary invention. Feelings were running high in 1921 when he wrote, 'sagaernes historiske troværdighed—hvor "stolt" dette end lyder—vil jeg hævde og forsvare, til jeg tvinges til at nedlægge min pen' (Finnur Jónsson 1921, 141) [I will uphold and defend the historical reliability of the sagas, however 'grand' this may sound, until I am forced to lay down my pen]. Although farmers and other Icelandic traditionalists lost their chief academic spokesman in 1928 when Finnur Jónsson retired, they remained doubtful of the new ideas coming from Reykjavík. Halldór Laxness playfully touches on this element of division among Icelanders in *Atómstöðin* [The Atom Station], a 1948 novel which treats the tensions in Icelandic society at that time. His main character, a young woman who was brought to Reykjavík from the countryside to be a maid in a wealthy household, says, 'Mér var kent að trúa aldrei orði sem stendur í blöðum, og aungvu nema því sem stendur í íslendíngasögum' (Laxness 1961, 48) [I was taught never to believe a single word that is written in the newspapers, and nothing except what is found in the sagas].

The bookprosists, and Nordal in particular, were at odds, culturally and politically, with both leftist radicals, such as Laxness, and Icelandic traditionalists.[16] The bookprosists had a ready answer for the farmers and others who treated their sagas as history. In referring to *Hrafnkels saga* and the arguments surrounding the historicity of its text, Nordal wrote:

> Eg er ekki sagnfræðingur, og það skiptir litlu máli fyrir landssöguna, hvort Hrafnkatla er nýtileg heimild eða ekki. (Nordal 1940, 8)

> [I am not a historian and it makes no difference to the history of Iceland whether *Hrafnkatla* is a reliable historical source or not.] (Nordal, 1958, 5)

Almost as a warning to his opponents, Nordal argued against their pursuit of oral traditions and their elevation of the ordinary man to the status of sagaman:

---

[16]The disputes, both cultural and political, erupted into a sometimes bitter series of newspaper articles and pamphlets in the 1920s. See Hallberg 1956, 29–31 and Árni Sigurjónsson 1984, 55–57.

Fyrir þá, sem vilja halda því fram, að hún [*Hrafnkels saga*] sé
mynduð í munnmælum, er ekki nema um tvo kosti að velja: annað-
hvort að gera sig starblinda á listina í sögunni, hina frábæru tækni og
hinn djarfa og djúpsæja skilning efnisins, — eða að gerbreyta öllum
þeim hugmyndum, sem menn hafa um þjóðsagnir og hver takmörk
þeim eru sett, um sálarlíf og sálarfræði alþýðu manna. (Nordal 1940,
67)

[Those who wish to maintain that it [*Hrafnkels saga*] follows the
pattern of oral tradition must choose between these alternatives: either
to turn a blind eye to the art of this saga, its technical skill and
profound understanding, or else to alter completely the current
conceptions about folktales and their limitations, about the concerns
and psychology of ordinary people.] (Nordal 1958, 57)

The bookprosists were able to take such a stand because, as part of a
new urban milieu, they were moving apart culturally from the farmers.
Many of the Icelandic school's members were educated in Copenhagen,
frequently moving back and forth between the Danish capital and
Reykjavík. For them the sagas were not simply validations of national
greatness, but evidence of cultural uniqueness. If they could be shown to
be products of 'one of the most powerful literary movements in recorded
history', then the emerging Icelandic urban culture would no longer be
a poor cousin of the Danes' culture. Rather, Iceland with its sagas would
have reached a state of cultural sophistication centuries in advance of
anything that the Danes achieved before the nineteenth century. The
literary basis of the sagas equipped Iceland with a cultural heritage
worthy of its status as an independent nation.

In turning to their narrative traditions, Icelandic intellectuals were
following a well-established pattern: a similar development had occurred
in several emerging northern European countries in the nineteenth
century. In Germany, for example, through the work of scholars such as
the brothers Grimm, folktales and fairy tales were embraced as a national
heritage that could be appreciated by a literate culture. Similar developments occurred in Finland with the *Kalevala*. In Norway, which gained
its independence from Sweden in 1905, orally collected folktales
provided a sense of national consciousness, and the rediscovery of the
kings' sagas (written by Icelanders) offered a historical past.

In Iceland's case, however, several significant differences separated it
from the pattern of the previous nationalistic experiences in Northern
Europe. First the Icelanders were moving toward full independence in the
twentieth century. Particularly after World War I, the nineteenth-century
national romantic adoration of oral heritage was no longer flourishing.
The bookprosists were influenced by the intellectual currents of their own
day. They wrested the sagas from their base within folk culture and
reinterpreted their origin and nature in a manner compatible with

contemporary literary criticism and their own urban environment. A further difference separating Icelandic experience from previous usages of folk traditions in emerging northern European states is that the Icelanders were not a fragmented people who needed to reconstruct a common historical past. Politically and historically they had always conceived of themselves as an island-wide, homogeneous entity. In addition to the information contained within the sagas, their past was amply documented in extant medieval historical writings such as *Íslendingabók* [The Book of Icelanders] and *Landnámabók* [The Book of Settlements] (Jakob Benediktsson 1968).

In the face of virtually no new political opposition from the Danes after 1918, the drive for full independence became to a large degree a question of creating a new Icelandic self image. No longer did the Icelanders have to fight for legitimacy with an occupying power, and there was a gradual but distinct shift in emphasis within Icelandic writings. Nationalistic arguments were now directed less at convincing the Danes that the country was ready to stand completely alone, than in reassuring the Icelanders themselves. To be sure, there was still considerable, and perhaps in some quarters even growing, anti-Danish feeling. The documents of the period, however, readily display a conflicting sentiment: an underlying sense of unease with the coming actuality of abandoning the security of Denmark. This unease was to some degree countered by self-promotion and exaggeration.

The change after 1918 was a process with emotional and psychological cost. We saw this earlier in the discussion of the farmers and their attachment to the sagas. As part of this process one of Iceland's major political parties, the *Sjálfstæðisflokkur* [the Independence Party—formerly the *Íhaldsflokkur*, the conservative party] was renamed/re-established in 1929, that is, after the external *sjálfstæðisbaráttan* was over. The name of this renewed party played on two meanings: the independence of the state and the independence of the individual. This naming and the title of Laxness's major novel, *Sjálfstætt fólk* [Independent People, 1934–1935], extolling the virtues of the nation and subjecting the nationalistic sentiment to sometimes bitter introspection, are just two among a flood of indications that after 1918 the struggle for independence became a highly personal matter. It was a time of choice and adaptation, as different groups vied to define a new present as well as to create a new past.

In this ambience, the call for a reliant self-image permeates Icelandic writings, going far beyond the essays of the bookprose group. Consider the treatment of literacy found in an essay on the subject of education in the eighteenth century. Written in 1925 by the prominent librarian, Hallgrímur Hallgrímsson, the section on eighteenth-century literacy starts with the subject period, quickly moves to a comparison of Icelanders with other Scandinavian national groups, and finishes with an exhortation to the current leaders of the country:

> En um 1780–90 eru Íslendingar orðnir öllu betur læsir en þessar þjóðir. Þessi mikla framför í lestrarkunnáttu er því merkilegri, sem engir barnaskólar voru til hér á landi. Hún er eingöngu verk prestanna og heimilanna. Þessi mentunarauki Íslendinga á síðari hluta 18. aldarinnar er þrekvirki, sem varla á sinn líka, og sýnir best hvernig þjóðin er. Íslensk alþýða er gáfuð og námfús, og ef þeir, sem eiga að stjórna henni, eru starfi sínu vaxnir, er engin hætta á að Íslendingar muni ekki skipa virðulegt sæti meðal mentaþjóða heimsins. (Hallgrímur Hallgrímsson 1925, 85)

> [Around 1780–90, it is the Icelanders who become the most literate of all the [Scandinavian] peoples. This great advance is even more remarkable as no elementary schools existed here in this country. Such literacy is completely the work of the priests and the individual households. This cultural advancement among the Icelanders in the last part of the eighteenth century is a feat which scarcely has its likeness elsewhere, and which shows best the very nature of the nation. The Icelandic common folk are intelligent and eager to learn, and if those who are to govern these people grow to a stature equal to their task, then there is no danger that Icelanders will fail to occupy an honourable seat among the cultured nations of the world.]

To such yearnings for cultural maturity the Icelandic school provided tangible solutions. They did not create the environment of national redefinition or the desires and hopes that accompanied it, but they were prepared to make the most of the situation. The bookprosists stepped forward as leaders, harnessing the forces of their period to advance their particular interpretations. From their platform as spokesmen of the new University, they offered the prestige of scholarship to the on-going process of state building.

And prestige was needed, since the Icelandic school chose a particularly challenging task. Unlike the charge that is often placed upon academics in emerging nations, the bookprosists did not have to define who the Icelanders were as a people, since both the Icelanders themselves and the world at large already looked upon the island and its inhabitants as distinct. For the bookprosists the matter was one of refining the Icelandic public's already developed conceptions of nationalism and patriotism. We see this in Nordal's newspaper essay, 'Eðlisfar Íslendinga' [The Nature of Icelanders], published in 1926, supporting Guðmundur Finnbogason's nationalistic views. There Nordal calls for 'nýja ættjarðarást á dýpri þekkingu lands og þjóðar, sögu og bókmenta' (Nordal 1926) [a new patriotism built on a deeper understanding of land and people, history and literature]. The task that the Icelandic school set for itself was to repossess what had been taken from the nation. This need arose because Iceland's national literature had long since been claimed by mainland Scandinavians. In particular the Danes, Swedes, and Norwegians had for over a century incorporated the Old Icelandic texts into their own national heritages. In their school books, national histories, and literary studies, they treated Icelandic medieval writings, including the family sagas, as the product of a shared Scandinavian heritage of storytelling and collective history. For the mainland Scandinavians, the Icelandic texts were remnants of Viking traditions that were not created in Iceland but only recorded and preserved there by Norse emigrants.

Iceland's continued rural nature, with a part of its population still living until World War II in turf houses, contributed to the maintenance of the old stereotype. What was more logical than the oral past of northern peoples being preserved amidst the noble farmers of the most backward and isolated part of Scandinavia? Such patronising Scandinavian romanticism, which saw 'the saga island' as a living relic of the Middle Ages, did not fit the cultural self-perception of Reykjavík's intellectuals. And here genre distinctions acquired political interpretations. The Icelanders were prepared to share the king's sagas about Norway and Denmark as the Icelandic contribution to the Pan-Scandinavian past. Eddic and Skaldic poetry, with their mythic and historic subject matter, also could be shared, but the family sagas were, as Nordal wrote in 1931, a different matter:

> Þjóðlegar bókmentir Íslendinga fyrir 1300 greinast í þrjá þáttu, ef frá eru talin lögin. Eru tveir þeirra norræn arfleifð, en einn af alíslenzkum toga spunninn. (Nordal 1924, xiv)

> [The national literature of Icelanders before 1300 is divided into three parts, if one does not count the laws. Two [Eddic and Skaldic verse] are of common Scandinavian heritage, while one [the family sagas] is spun from entirely Icelandic thread.]

In essence, Nordal and many of those who followed his lead underwent an experience common today among western educated scholars from newly independent third-world countries. The members of the Icelandic school were trained in Euro-centric cultural perceptions but remained committed to their native nationalism. Perhaps somewhat unconsciously, the bookprosists set out to harmonise their nationalist goals within the basic reality that for Western society the past of small or distant peoples counts only in respect to how and when it touches upon the mainstream of European development. The sagas, newly reinterpreted in light of standard European concepts of literary development, now took their seat among the artifacts of European high culture.

In many ways the work of the Icelandic school is a process of integrating Icelandic aspirations into a European context, while filtering out the influence of the Danes and the claims of other Scandinavians. In the process social and historical aspects of the literature are denied, a development that explains the prominence of the fact-fiction dichotomy in bookprose writings. Since the effects of bookprose are still very much with us today, the least that can be said is that much remains open to reconsideration.

BIBLIOGRAPHY

Aðalgeir Kristjánsson. 1993. *Endurreisn alþingis og þjóðfundurinn.* Reykjavík.

Andersson, Theodore M. 1964. *The Problem of Icelandic Saga Origins: A Historical Survey.* Yale Germanic Studies 1. New Haven.

Árni Sigurjónsson. 1984. 'Nokkur orð um hugmyndafræði Sigurðar Nordal fyrir 1945', *Tímarit Máls og menningar* 45/1, 49–63.

Byock, Jesse L. 1982. *Feud in the Icelandic Saga.* Berkeley and Los Angeles.

———. 1985. 'Cultural Continuity, the Church, and the Concept of Independent Ages in Medieval Iceland', *Skandinavistik* 15/1, 1–14.

———. 1986. 'The Age of the Sturlungs', in Elisabeth Vestergaard, ed., *Continuity and Change: Political Institutions and Literary Monuments in the Middle Ages*, pp. 27–42. Odense.

———. 1988. *Medieval Iceland: Society, Sagas and Power.* Berkeley and Los Angeles.

Bætke, Walter, ed. 1974. *Die Isländersaga.* Wege der Forschung 151. Darmstadt.

Chatterjee, Partha. 1986. *Nationalist Thought and the Colonial World: A Derivative Discourse.* London.

Einar Arnórsson. 1930. *Réttarsaga Alþingis.* Reykjavík.

Engels, Friedrich. 1963. *Karl Marx Friedrich Engels Werke.* Institut für Marxismus–Leninismus, 27. Berlin.

Ferro, Marc. 1984. *The Use and Abuse of History: or How the Past is Taught.* London.

Finnur Jónsson. 1921. *Norsk–Islandske kultur- og sprogforhold i 9. og 10. årh.* Det Kgl. Danske Videnskabernes Selskab, Historisk-filologiske Meddelelser 3, pt. 2. Copenhagen.

Gísli Gunnarsson. 1987. *Upp er boðið Ísland.* Reykjavík.

Gunnar Karlsson. 1980. 'Icelandic Nationalism and the Inspiration of History' in Rosalind Mitchison, ed., *The Roots of Nationalism: Studies in Northern Europe*, pp. 77–89. Edinburgh.

———. 1984. 'Saga í þágu samtíðar', *Tímarit Máls og menningar* 45/1, 19–27.

————. 1985. 'Spjall um rómantík og þjóðernisstefnu', *Tímarit Máls og menningar* 46/4, 449–457.

————. 1987. 'Folk og nation på Island', *Scandia* 53/1, 130–145.

Hallberg, Peter. 1956. *Skaldens hus: Laxness' diktning från Salka Valka till Gerpla.* Stockholm.

————. 1962. Paul Schach, trans., *The Icelandic Saga.* Lincoln, Nebraska.

Halldór Guðmundsson. 1987. *Loksins, loksins: Vefarinn mikli og upphaf Íslenskra nútímabókmennta.* Reykjavík.

Hallgrímur Hallgrímsson. 1925. *Íslensk alþýðumentun á 18. öld.* Reykjavík.

Holtsmark, Anne. 1959. 'Det nye syn på sagaene', *Nordisk tidskrift för vetenskap, konst och industri* 35, 511–523.

Jakob Benediktsson, ed. 1968. *Íslendingabók og Landnámabók*, Íslenzk fornrit 1. 2 vols. Reykjavík.

Jón Aðils Jónsson. 1906. *Gullöld Íslendinga. Menning og lífshættir feðra vorra á söguöldinni. Alþýðufyrirlestrar með myndum.* Reykjavík.

Jón Jóhannesson, ed. 1950. *Austfirðinga sögur.* Íslenzk fornrit 11. Reykjavík.

————. 1956–1958. I *Íslendinga saga*, Reykjavík; II *Fyrirlestrar og ritgerðir um tímabilið 1262–1550.* Reykjavík.

————. 1974. Haraldur Bessason, trans., *History of the Old Icelandic Commonwealth: Íslendinga saga*, University of Manitoba Icelandic Studies 2. Winnipeg.

Jónas Hallgrímsson. 1989. Haukur Hannesson, Páll Valsson, Sveinn Yngvi Egilsson, eds, *Ritverk Jónasar Hallgrímssonar*, 4 vols. Reykjavík.

Jónas Kristjánsson. 1986. 'The Roots of the Sagas', in Rudolf Simek, Jónas Kristjánsson, and Hans Bekker-Nielsen, eds, *Sagnaskemmtun: Studies in Honour of Hermann Pálsson on his 65th Birthday, 26th May 1986.* Philologica Germanica 8. Vienna.

————. 1987. 'Sannfræði fornsagnanna', *Skírnir* 161, 233–269.

Laxness, Halldór Kiljan. 1934–1935. *Sjálfstætt fólk.* 2 vols. Reykjavík.

————. 1948 (second ed., 1961). *Atómstöðin.* Reykjavík.

————. 1960. *Paradísarheimt.* Reykjavík.

————. 1962. Magnus Magnusson, trans., *Paradise Reclaimed.* New York.

————. 1982. Magnus Magnusson, trans., *The Atom Station.* London.

Lindroth, Hjalmar. 1937. Adolph B. Benson, trans., *Iceland: Land of Contrasts.* Princeton.

Mundal, Else. 1975. 'Til debatten om islendingasogene', *Maal og Minne*, 105–126

————, ed. 1977. *Sagadebatt.* Oslo, Bergen, Tromsø.

Mitchell, Stephen A. 1991. *Heroic Sagas and Ballads.* Ithaca.

Nordal, Jóhannes and Valdimar Kristinsson. 1967. *Iceland 1966: Handbook Published by the Central Bank of Iceland*. Reykjavík.

Nordal, Sigurður. 1924. 'Samhengi í Íslenzkum bókmentum', in *Íslenzk lestrarbók*. Reykjavík.

————. 1926. 'Eðlisfar Íslendinga', *Vísir*, 26 March.

————. 1957. *The Historical Element in the Icelandic Family Sagas*. W.P. Ker Memorial Lecture 15. Glasgow.

————. 1940. *Hrafnkatla*. Studia Islandica 7. Reykjavík.

————. 1958. *Hrafnkels saga Freysgoða: A Study*, trans. R. George Thomas. Cardiff.

Ólafur Jóhannesson. 1960. *Stjörnskipun Íslands*. Reykjavík.

Óskar Halldórsson. 1978. '"Íslenski skólinn" og Hrafnkelssaga', *Tímarit Máls og menningar* 39/3, 317–324.

Páll Skúlason. 1984. 'Heimspekin og Sigurður Nordal', *Tímarit Máls og menningar* 45/1, 29–36.

Páll Valsson. 1984. 'Leit að lífsskilningi: Um Hel eftir Sigurð Nordal', *Tímarit Máls og menningar* 45/1, 64–72.

Scovazzi, Marco. 1960. *La saga di Hrafnkell e il problema delle saghe islandesi*. Arona.

Steinunn Eyjólfsdóttir. 1984. '19 ára í vist hjá Sigurði Nordal', *Tímarit Máls og menningar* 45/1, 37–47.

Søe, Christian. 1991. 'Dänemark und Deutschland, oder: Wer teilt schon gern das Bett mit einem Elefanten?' *Nordeuropa* 1/3, 6–9.

Sørensen, Preben Meulengracht. 1977. *Saga og samfund: En indføring i oldislandsk litteratur*. Copenhagen.

Vésteinn Ólason. 1984. 'Bókmenntarýni Sigurðar Nordals', *Tímarit Máls og menningar* 45/1, 5–18.

Wawn, Andrew. 1991. *The Anglo Man: Þorleifur Repp, Philology and Nineteenth-Century Britain*. Studia Islandica 49. Reykjavík.

Part III:

The English Language Tradition

9

The Image of Norse Poetry and Myth in Seventeenth-Century England

JUDY QUINN and MARGARET CLUNIES ROSS

The conceptual world of Norse mythology was introduced into England in the seventeenth century through the works of English antiquarians in contact with Scandinavian scholars, but its impact beyond a small circle of septentrionalists, as they were known, appears to have been slight during that century. The line of continuity between the early medieval culture of the Germanic peoples in England and their seventeenth-century descendants had been reduced to the barest thread of genealogical convention: Woden's name continued to feature in royal genealogies (Farley 1903, 15–17), probably as a result of chroniclers' reliance on learned speculation rather than a continuing familiarity with the tradition which included him in the first place. The presence of the Germanic pantheon inscribed in the names of the days of the week in English was also the subject of occasional comment from Bede onwards (Jones 1943, 212–213), and provided the basic structure for the first accounts of Saxon gods in the seventeenth century (Verstegan 1628, 68). Right up until the late sixteenth century, however, the sources on Germanic religion available to the English were limited to Latin authors: Tacitus, Jordanes, Procopius, Adam of Bremen and Saxo Grammaticus (Farley 1903, 2; Seaton 1935, 244). The extant early English sources on the pre-Christian past of the Anglo-Saxon people could not have been read, as knowledge of Old English was rare until the latter half of the seventeenth century.[1]

William Camden (1586)[2] was apparently the first to connect material from Anglo-Saxon authors writing in Latin, such as Bede and Æþel-

---

[1] For a masterly discussion of the beginnings of Anglo-Saxon and Norse studies in England, see the (alas) unpublished D. Phil. thesis of Bennett 1938. Chapter 1 surveys the use made of Anglo-Saxon sources by sixteenth century ecclesiastical and legal historians. Bennett 1946–1953 contains a summary of his thesis research as it relates to so-called runic studies.

[2] Camden's *Britannia* was first published in Latin in 1586; it was translated into English by Philemon Holland and enlarged by the author in a 1610 edition.

weard, with descriptions of Scandinavian religious practices in the writings of Adam of Bremen, Dudo of St Quentin, and Ditmar of Merseberg (Seaton 1935, 244). Camden described Woden as 'that false imagined God, and Father of the English Saxons' (1610, 241). His work was extended by Richard Verstegan, in his *A Restitution of Decayed Intelligence in Antiquities concerning the most noble and renowned English Nation*, first published in Antwerp in 1605 and reprinted several times in London from 1628. Verstegan made a clear distinction between the Northern gods and gods of the classical world (1628, 80), under whose identities deities of other cultures were commonly subsumed (cf. Camden 1610, 135 and Herbert 1663, 72 and 209). Verstegan appears to have drawn on the *Historia Gentibus Septentrionalibus* of Olaus Magnus (1555), a work that was not translated into English until 1658.

The first publication of Icelandic textual material in English consisted of translations of the work of Arngrímur Jónsson.[3] His *Crymogæa sive rerum Islandicarum libri tres* (1609) was translated from Latin and excerpted (along with Dithmar Blefken's account of his voyage to Iceland) in *Purchas his Pilgrimage* (1625). Section III of Arngrímur's work, entitled in the English translation 'Of their Politie, and Religion in old times', provides a brief survey of Norse gods presented with reference to better-known Mediterranean deities,[4] though it is clear that the author had to do some juggling of identities to represent properly the character of Óðinn (Purchas 1625, XIII 547):

> This Odinus, as aforesaid, for his notable knowledge in Devillish Magicke; whereby like another Mahomet, hee affected a Divinitie after his death, was reckoned among the number of the Gods: from whom at this day, Wednesday, is called Odens Dagur, the day of Odinus: whereupon peradventure, I shall not unaptly call Odin Mercurie, as Thor Jupiter. Yet the ancients honoured Odin in the place of Mars: and such as were slaine in the warres, they say were sacrificed to Odin.

The lack of comprehensive material about Saxon culture was the starting point for Richard Verstegan's[5] study, *A Restitution of decayed*

---

[3]His *Brevis Commentarius de Islandia* (1593) was reprinted with an English translation in Hakluyt's 1599 *Collections of Early Voyages*.

[4]In a marginal note Purchas makes the connection between Norse and Saxon mythologies: 'Odinus the same that Woden in our Saxon storie' (XIII 547).

[5]Although he was born in London, and sometimes took the name of Rowland or Rowlands, Verstegan was of Flemish parentage and later lived in Antwerp (Bennett 1938, 24).

Intelligence in Antiquities, concerning the most Noble and Renowned English Nation. In his preface he explains:

> The thing that first moued mee to take some paines in this studie was, the verie naturall affection which generally is in all men to here of the worthiness of their Ancestors, which they should indeed be as desirous to imitate, as delighted to vnderstand.

He set out to distinguish the 'Antiquitie of Englishmen' as opposed to the legacy of the 'Brittans', and includes a chapter on 'the antient manner of liuing of our Saxon ancestors' and 'the idolls they adored while they were Pagans'. But with a few exceptions, the attitude of English scholars to Norse mythology in the seventeenth century was harsh, to say the least. In his comparative study of religions, published in Latin in 1663 and translated into English in 1705, Edward, Lord Herbert of Cherbury, described 'Heathen gods, [as] not only meer men, but also some of the most vile'. Even Verstegan (1628, 81) vents his disapprobation of them in a description of the idol Þórr: 'This great reputed God being of more estimation than many of the rest of like sort, though of as little worth as any of the meanest of that rabble'.[6]

Verstegan included in his treatise engravings of various Norse gods, which are thought to have been inspired by illustrations in Olaus Magnus's work. Their quality excited some interest on the Continent in correspondence between the Danish scholars S.J. Stephanius and Ole Worm (Worm 1751, 213–214 and 243). The personal contacts between scholars in England and on the Continent were clearly of critical importance to the transmission of Norse material to England, both through reports in letters and in the trading of books. Although the trade in books and ideas was predominantly one way, from Scandinavia to England, often via Holland, it was an English antiquarian, Sir Henry Spelman, who first proposed the derivation of the word 'rune' from the Old English word denoting a secret or hidden thing. Spelman's suggestion, communicated in a letter to Ole Worm in 1630, was taken up in Worm's influential work of 1636, *Antiquitates Danicae seu Litteratura Runica*.[7] In the second half of the century, during the revival of interest in Anglo-Saxon texts led by a group of English scholars at Oxford (Fairer

---

[6]Note, too, the observation of Aylett Sammes 1676, 435: 'What strange and monstrous Opinions the Saxons conceived of WODEN, may be gathered out of most of their Authors, who seldom mention his Name without some excessive Encomium of his Person'.

[7]See further Seaton 1935, 226–227. Worm in fact sent fifty copies of his book to Spelman's bookseller in 1638 (Bennett 1938, 215).

1986, 807–29; Bennett 1938, 11), close contact was maintained with Scandinavian scholars, and some Scandinavian students, including Ole Worm's grandson Christian Worm, visited Oxford (Seaton 1935, 173–174; Bennett 1938, 24). Christian Worm undertook an edition of Ari Þorgilsson's *Íslendingabók* while he was in Oxford in 1696–1697, but it was not published until 1716.[8] George Hickes, who in 1689 published the first Icelandic grammar in England,[9] had quite extensive connections with Swedish septentrionalists, including Jonas N. Salan and Johan Peringskjöld (Harris 1992, 59–61), as did William Nicolson, the first to teach Old English at Oxford (Bennett 1938, 224–225).

Spelman's contribution to the etymology of the word 'rune' was part of a general fascination, in England and on the Continent, with the nature and antiquity of runic writing and its association with Óðinn. Ole Worm maintained that all early medieval sources in Scandinavia were written in runes, and this notion was quickly accepted in England where the first printed texts of Norse poems were cast in runes following Worm's example (Seaton 1935, 229). The first runic type was imported to England by the Dutch scholar, Franciscus Junius and the fonts were acquired by the University of Oxford in 1677 upon Junius's death. As well as making a valuable contribution to Anglo-Saxon research, Junius was also an important influence on Norse studies, both during his employment and later retirement in England (1621–1642, 1646–1651, 1674–1677)[10] and in his period of residence in Holland (1642–1646, 1651–1674). One of his former students with whom he collaborated,

---

[8]According to Richard Harris's recent edition of George Hickes's correspondence with his collaborators on the *Thesaurus linguarum septentrionalium* (1992, 158–182), Christian Worm's edition must have been printed at least by the end of 1696. Worm brought the septentrionalists some important new Icelandic texts and his expertise was of considerable assistance to Hickes, but he left Oxford hurriedly under something of a cloud in 1697, after only one year of residence (Harris 1992, 53–58).

[9]The *Grammatica Islandica* of Runólfur Jónsson (published in Copenhagen in 1651) was published along with Hickes's own *Institutiones Grammatica Anglo-Saxonicae et Moeso-Gothicae* (1689) and his *Thesaurus* (1703–1705). There is also evidence that both Hickes and William Nicolson had access to another Icelandic grammar. This was the 1683 *Lexicon Islandicum* compiled by Guðmundur Andrésson and published by Peder Resen (Harris 1992, 55 and fn. 6). Junius had a copy of Guðmundur's manuscript, which Nicolson used in his transcript of MSS Bodleian Junius 2 and 3.

[10]For details of Junius's residence in England, see *Dictionary of National Biography*, X 1115–1116; Bennett 1938, 22ff.; Harris 1992, 6–8.

Thomas Marshall, moved to Holland during the Parliamentary interregnum in 1647 and remained there while waiting for the right moment to return to Oxford (Harris 1992, 52–56). He later became Rector of Lincoln College, and it is to this college that Junius retired to work upon Marshall's invitation in 1676. Marshall owned a manuscript copy of the Uppsala version of Snorri Sturluson's *Edda*, which he may have obtained during his time in Holland.[11] Robert Sheringham, who was educated and later taught at Cambridge, was another English septentrionalist who also spent time in Rotterdam in the 1650s. Marshall had sent Sheringham a copy from Holland of the recently published trilingual edition of *Snorra Edda* by Peder Resen (1665).[12]

As knowledge of the language of Icelandic manuscripts was probably slight and confined to a very few people,[13] the most significant publication of the century, as far as English septentrionalists were concerned, was Peder Hansen Resen's editions of Snorri's *Edda* and the two poems *Völuspá* (published as *Philosophia Antiquissima*) and *Hávamál* (*Ethici*

---

[11]It is Bodleian Library MS Marshall 114. According to Einar G. Pétursson, in various oral presentations, this manuscript copy was the work of the Icelander Jón lærði Guðmundsson, which, like another early paper manuscript of Snorri's *Edda*, the Codex Trajectinus, had probably made its way to Holland. Marshall 114 shows little, if any, sign of use; sadly, it seems to have languished in the Bodleian from the seventeenth century until the recent late twentieth-century upsurge of interest in the history of Old Norse studies.

[12]In the preface to his 1670 work, *De Anglorum Gentis Origine Disceptatio*, Sheringham observed 'Usus etiam sum *Edda Islandorum*, vetusto monumento, quam mihi insignis vir, & summus meus amicus Thomas Mareschallus S.T.D. ex Hollandia misit' [For I have made use of the *Edda* of the Icelanders, an ancient record, which the distinguished man and my very good friend Thomas Marshall S.T.D. sent me from Holland]. It is likely that Sheringham was referring here to a copy of Resen's edition of the *Edda* rather than to the Icelandic manuscript Marshall 114.

[13]See Bennett 1938, 221–245, for a discussion of Icelandic learning among Junius and his colleagues. Farley (1903, 214–227) has judged that even up until the nineteenth century, no Englishman apart from George Hickes had a thorough acquaintance with the language, though a small number appear to have understood it to some degree. Our positive assessment of their ability is likely to increase, we suspect, with the publication of many still unpublished seventeenth- and eighteenth-century studies, editions and letters. See, for instance, Hickes's list of his students and their projects in his *Linguarum Veterum Septentrionalium Thesaurus Grammatico-Criticus et Archaeologicus*, 1705, I iv.

Odini) in 1665. Resen offered the world outside Iceland a translation into
Latin, a language the educated classes throughout Europe could understand. Robert Sheringham was the first Englishman to make use of the
new resource in his *De Anglorum Gentis Origine Disceptatio,* published
in 1670. In this work he makes use of a wide range of other sources,
including Pontanus, Ole Worm, Stephanius and Messenius. In the
following decade other Englishmen made use of Resen's work: Daniel
Langhorne in his *Elenchus Antiquitatum Albionensium* (1673), particularly in the Appendix to his work that was published in 1674, and Aylett
Sammes, who published *Britannia Antiqua Illustrata; or the Antiquities
of Ancient Britain* in 1676, a work that is marked by eccentricity,
particularly in the author's overriding aim of demonstrating the Phoeni-
cian origin of the British race. Nevertheless, Sammes's is the first
substantial work in English to treat Northern mythology. Edward
Stillingfleet (1676, 157–160) cited Snorri's *Edda* as evidence for his
theory that all peoples recognise one supreme deity (he quotes the first
exchange of *Gylfaginning* where Alföðr is said to be the oldest of gods).

The subjects of runes and Óðinn's powers were central to both
Sheringham's and Sammes's treatment of Northern mythology. Both
quote the Loddfáfnir stanzas of *Hávamál* (1670, 288ff; 1676, 442ff) and
Sammes ties the use of runes to a Saxon context (1676, 442):

> These Runes our Ancestors set up against the Enemies, others they
> had otherwise prepared, which had the vertue to stop the course of
> Rivers and Tides, to raise and then allay Tempests, to give Winds, to
> cause Rain, to cure Diseases, to charm Agues, Head-ach [...] and
> such like, the invention of all which Delusions (too frequently yet
> used) is attributed to WODEN, who is said, by these Arts, to have
> deprived one Rinda, a young Girl, of all her reason and senses.

Sheringham (1670, 239) describes the Æsir/Vanir war and the figures of
Kvasir and Mímir in his Latin account, and Sammes treats them in
English (1676, 435). Sammes added to these details about Óðinn's
prophetic trances[14] and descriptions of minor deities (1676, 447ff).

Sammes translated his quotations of the *Edda* straight from Sheringham's Latin work, rather than from Resen's edition,[15] and later writers
too appear to have been dependent on Sheringham's work rather than on

---

[14]'When he awaked, he would constantly aver he had been in foraign
Countries, and had exact knowledge of what passed in them'.

[15]Farley 1903, 63 n. 1, has shown that Sheringham's correction of Worm's
runic text and his alteration of the Latin text had been copied by Sammes
without comment.

Continental editions of Norse originals, even when they cite Snorri or his *Edda*.[16] This raises a number of questions about the environment in which antiquarians were working in the latter half of the seventeenth century in England, including those of the availability of books,[17] their familiarity with runic script, and the level of their understanding of the Icelandic language.

Outside this rather small circle of scholars, some idea of the regard in which Norse poetry and myth were held can be gleaned from references made to them during the course of the century in an ongoing debate about poetics, or more precisely, about the relative merits and pedigrees of rhymed as opposed to quantitative and later blank verse. Before medieval Norse texts were available in England, and before there was much knowledge of the character of the Scandinavian poetic tradition, Germanic gods and peoples were frequently associated with rhymed compositions. In this debate,[18] quantitative verse was associated with perfection ('true numbers') and rhyme was judged, within the framework of classical Rhetoric, as appropriate for an occasional ornament but not as a structural principle.[19] Along these lines, the train of thought seems to have passed from *barbarismus* to barbarian to Germanic culture in general.

[16]See again Farley 1903, 64 n. 6 on William Temple's use of Sheringham's text.

[17]Although the editions of Resen were available in England a short time after their publication, they were probably always very scarce and may not have been much used (Farley 1903, 219). The three volumes by Resen appear to have been donated to the Bodleian Library by Peder Worm, son of Ole, in the early 1670s (Seaton 1935, 342–343).

[18]For a survey of the debate in the sixteenth century, see Fraser 1973, 306–311. Thomas Nashe, Sir Philip Sidney and at one time Edmund Spenser were averse to rhyme and subscribed to the theory that it was introduced into Europe by 'Goths and Huns'. In his note on the verse-form of *Paradise Lost* (Darbishire 1952, 3–4), John Milton called rhyme 'the Invention of a barbarous Age, to set off wretched matter and lame Meeter'. He saw himself setting an example 'of ancient liberty recovered to heroic poem from the troublesome and modern bondage of rhyming.'

[19]'[...] that Rhetoricall figure which we tearme *similiter desinentia*, and that being but *figura verbi*, ought (as *Tully* and all other Rhetoritians haue iudicially obseru'd) sparingly be vsd, least it should offend the eare with tedious affectation' (Thomas Campion 1602, 4). On the actual frequency and diversity of rhyme in Classical works, see Guggenheimer 1972.

Perhaps the most exuberant champion of quantitative verse was
Thomas Campion, who, in a pamphlet published in 1602, complained that
the 'facilitie & popularity' of composing in rhyme had created 'as many
poets as hot summer flies' and he called on poets to follow the example
of the Greeks and Romans in 'the strict observation of poeticall numbers,
so abandoning the childish titillation of riming' (1602, 4–5). He set about
proving the superiority of quantitative metres by demonstrating their
appropriateness to the English language in a series of examples inter-
spersed with commentary.[20] His demonstration of 'Licentiate Iambicks'
(1602, 12), for example, begins:

> Goe numbers boldly passe, stay not for ayde
> Of shifting rime, that easie flatterer
> Whose witchcraft can the ruder eares beguile;
> Let your smooth feete enur'd to purer arte
> True measures tread [...]
> You are those loftie numbers that reuiue
> Triumphs of Princes [...]
> He [Apollo] first taught number, and true harmonye,
> Nor is the lawrell his for rime bequeath'd,
> Call him with numerous accents paisd by arte
> He'le turne his glory from the sunny clymes,
> The North-bred wits alone to patronise [...]

Campion's extravagant treatise called forth a more level-headed and
circumspect appraisal of contemporary English poetry by Samuel Daniel
the next year. Daniel defends rhyme by arguing that it was the customary
mode of versifying in many cultures[21] (1603, 6), including among the
Danes and Saxons (1603, 9):

---

[20]Despite its very different orientation, Campion's work is not unlike the Old
Icelandic *Háttatal* in some respects, both works presumably drawing on the
tradition of the *clavis metrica*. Campion dedicates his work to Lord Buckhurst,
Lord High Treasurer of England, and gives the names of metres along with a
description and example.

[21]Daniel (1603, 19) also defends the cultural heritage of the Northern peoples
of Europe, noting that the 'laws and customes' of the 'Gothes, Vandales and
Langobards' had provided the basis for most of the constitutions of Christendom.
The idea of the Northern Germanic nations as the custodians of legally expressed
democracy is a recurring theme in the antiquarianism of the period and was
undoubtedly one of its motivating forces. A similar point is later made by
Temple (1690, 226), who reassesses the legacy of the 'savage Nations',
expressing his doubts that the 'Governments erected by them, and which have
lasted so long in Europe, should have been framed by unthinking Men.'

The Sclauonian and Arabian tongs acquaint a great part of *Asia* and *Affrique* with it, the Muscouite, Polack, Hungarian, German, Italian, French, and Spaniard vse no other harmonie of words. The Irish, Briton, Scot, Dane, Saxon, English, and all the Inhabiters of this Iland, either haue hither brought, or here found the same in vse.

The debate continued throughout the century, but, as the domain of contention shifted to the style of verse appropriate for dramatic works, the rival styles swung around to rhymed versus blank verse. Rhyme was still viewed as originating within Northern 'barbaric' culture,[22] but the history of its use now included such eminent European writers that it was considered suitable for compositions in certain genres, such as heroic plays. While classical precedents could not be claimed for these works, an appeal was made to contemporary practice in Europe:

Neither do the Spanish, French, Italian, or Germans acknowledge at all, or very rarely, any such kind of poesy as blank verse among them [...] all the French, Italian, and Spanish tragedies are generally writ in it [rhyme]; and sure the universal consent of the most civilized parts of the world ought in this, as it doth in other customs, to include the rest. (Dryden 1668 [1962], 83–84)

Whereas quantitative verse had earlier been lauded for the control it exercised over poets, it was now rhyme that was responsible for reining in 'the high-ranging spaniel' of poetic imagination.[23] With access to the editions of P.H. Resen, the *Litteratura Runica* of Ole Worm, S.J. Stephanius's edition and preface to Saxo Grammaticus and other learned Scandinavian works, Robert Sheringham was in a better position than his predecessors to describe the poetic art of the North. Sheringham discusses the value of the *Edda* at length (1670, 259–268, 272–274), and clearly believed it to be very old: *Ab Edda auspicior antiquissimo omnium monumentum* (1670, 234) [I take my beginning from the Edda, most ancient of all records]. Within a long account that appears to be derived in part from chapters 2 to 9 of *Ynglinga saga*, Sheringham describes

---

[22]'But when, by the inundation of the Goths and Vandals into Italy, new languages were brought in, and barbarously mingled with the Latin (of which the Italian, Spanish, French, and ours, made out of them and the Teutonic, are dialects), a new way of poesy was practised' (John Dryden 1668 [1962], 83–84).

[23]'For imagination in a poet is a faculty so wild and lawless that like an high-ranging spaniel it must have clogs tied to it, lest it outrun the judgement.' John Dryden 1664, *To Roger, Earl of Orrery*, prefixed to *The Rival Ladies*. Reprinted in Watson 1962, I 8.

Óðinn's poetic facility (1670, 242):

> Tanta etiam Suada & eloquii dulcedine audientes demulcere poterat,
> ut ipsius dictis nullam non fidem adhiberent. Rhythmis etiam &
> carminibus inter loquendum crebro prolatis miram sermoni gratiam
> conciliabat. Unde & ipse & complices ipsius Schialdri & poetae dicti.

> [Yet he was able to soften his hearers with such great persuasion and
> sweetness of eloquence that they put not a little faith in the sayings
> of the man himself. To the extent that verse and song were repeatedly
> interspersed in what he had to say, he brought a wonderful charm to
> his discourse. Whence both he and his confederates were called
> Schialdri and poets.]

The citation at the beginning of this section (237) is 'Aliam de Wodeno
narrationem ex Chronico Norwegico itidem antiquo desumam cujus
Author ut ait Stephanius, Snorro Sturlæsonius putatur' [In the same way
I choose another story about Woden from the ancient Norwegian
Chronicle, whose author, as Stephanius says, is thought to be Snorri
Sturluson], presumably a reference to Stephanius's 1645 work, *Notæ
Vberiores in Historiam Danicam Saxonis Grammatici,* and possibly to a
translation of *Heimskringla.*[24]

The word *rhythmus* is used on several other occasions in citations of
learned authorities on Norse poetry (writing in Latin), and appears to
simply mean verse.[25] In Resen's trilingual edition of the *Edda,* the word
kveðskapur in Magnús Ólafsson's prologue is rendered in Latin as *res
Rythmica* (Faulkes 1977, I 1r), and translated by Sammes (1676, 431)
into English as 'Rhythmical writing'. In Runólfur Jónsson's Icelandic-
Latin glossary published by Hickes (1689, 114) the term *kveðlingur* is
also translated as *rhythmus.* Perhaps the field of signification of this Latin
word played some part in the popular misconception that traditional

---

[24]*Heimskringla* was published in 1633 in a Danish translation by Hans Peder
Claussøn and (later than Sheringham's treatise) by Johan Peringskjöld in
Icelandic and Latin in 1697. On the circulation of quotations without precise
citation among septentrionalist scholars, see Faulkes 1977, 14ff.

[25]See, for example, Sheringham (1670, 260) 'Ex veterum Rhythmis', and
other instances on pp. 262–263. In medieval Latin, the terms *rithmi* and *rithmici
versus* were used to denote accentual in contrast to quantitative verse (*metra*).
As similarity of the terminal sounds was a common feature of accentual verse,
rithmus came to have the sense of 'rime' (See the *OED* entry for 'rime').
'Metre' is given as one of the senses of 'rhyme' in a 1565 Thesaurus (see *OED*
entry on 'rhyme'), but the predominant meaning of the word in English in
seventeenth-century citations is 'consonance of terminal sounds'.

Norse poetry was rhymed.[26] It is clear from a later quotation in Sheringham (1670, 284–285) that he regarded Stephanius as authoritative on this point:[27]

> Wodenum insuper ad Gothos ex Asia literas Runicas attulisse, Scaldorum patrem, artisque poe/ticae Gothis authorem fuisse, multa suadent, illud perquam maxime, quod sermonem Runicum modosque loquendi Scaldorum veteres *Asamal*, id est, *sermonem Asianum* appellabant [...] Stephanius in Præfatione ad Saxonem Grammaticum. *Linguam Danicam antiquam, cujus in rhithmis usus fuit, veteres appellarunt [...] Asamal*

> [Many things speak in favour of the view that Woden, father of the Scalds, had moreover brought the Runic alphabet from Asia to the Goths, and had been the originator of the poetic art for the Goths, above all the fact that the ancients used to call the Runic speech and ways of speaking of the Scalds *Asamal*, that is, 'Asian speech' [...] Stephanius [writes] in his Preface to Saxo Grammaticus, 'the ancients called the Danish language, the practice of which was in rhyme, *Asamal*']

Rather than opening the way forward to a better understanding of traditional Norse poetry, Sheringham's comprehensive work seems to have been used by later writers very selectively. Indeed, it generally true that the literati of the seventeenth and early eighteenth centuries turned a deaf ear to what the antiquarian septentrionalists could tell them about Old Norse literature and culture, because for the most part it did not accord with their preconceptions of the early Germanic world. Aylett Sammes (1676, 438), invoking Snorri's *Edda* as his authority, strengthens the association between rhyme and the peoples of the North, although the source for his elaboration on poetic form is unclear:

> Woden (saith 'the author of the *Edda*') introduced the way of composing Verses in numbers, and such Rythms as are now used in the Teutonick dialect, differing in this point from all other Languages in the World whatsoever, for that the last words of the Verses answer to one another exactly in sound. And this he did with such pleasing cadences, that mixing them in his common discourse, he wonderfully allured the Hearers, and is reputed the Inventer of Poetry among the

---

[26]In *Ynglinga saga* Snorri says of Óðinn 'mælti hann allt hendingum, svá sem nú er þat kveðit, er skáldskapr heitir', a description that may have lost some definition during translation.

[27]Sammes 1676, 444 also translates this passage, using the English word 'Rithms' for *rhithmus*.

Saxons, and the Founder of that Tribe called Scalders, which, like the
Bardi among the Britains, made it their business to set forth in
Verses, and sing to the People the noble Actions of their Progenitors.

Sammes goes on to quote Tacitus and Saxo Grammaticus on the poetic
customs of the Scandinavians (438–9) and prefaces a quotation of stanza
142 of *Hávamál* with the following observations:

> This change of the use of the Characters, from plainly writing the
> sense of things to form mysterious Incantations, is, by some,
> attributed to WODEN, wherefore they call him in this sense Run-
> hofdi, that is, the Inventer of the Run; But the Runick Character was
> long before this time, if we may believe the Edda, cited by Worm,
> which attributes the invention of it to the Gods, the delivery to one
> Fimbul, and the manner of Ingraving, that is the use of it in Magick,
> to Woden (1676, 441; see also Sheringham 1670, 286–287).

Since on this point both learned antiquaries (writing in English) and
tradition concurred, it is perhaps not surprising that the identification of
Óðinn with rhyme gained hold. In his *Essay on Translated Verse* (1684),
Lord Roscommon allowed himself considerable freedom in the depiction
of Norse deities engaged in rhymed declamation:

> Of many faults Rhyme is (perhaps) the Cause,
> Too strict to Rhyme we slight more useful Laws.
> For That, in Greece or Rome, was never known,
> Till by Barbarian Deluges o'erflown,
> Subdu'd, undone, They did at last Obey,
> And change their own for their Invaders way.
> I grant that from some Mossie, Idol Oak
> In Double Rhymes our Thor and Woden spoke;
> And by Succession of Unlearned Times,
> As Bards began, so Munks rung on the Chimes.
> But now that Phæbus and the Sacred Nine,
> With all their Beams on our blest Islands shine,
> Why should not We their Ancient Rites restore,
> And be, what Rome or Athens were before?

Despite his earlier defence of rhyme in dramatic works, Dryden
prevaricates in later writings, and is much impressed by Roscommon's
argument. Already in his defence of the essay *Of Dramatic Poetry* he had
argued that rhyme was simply the taste of his age.[28] By 1678, he had

---

[28] 'All I can say is this, that it [rhymed composition] seems to have
succeeded verse by the general consent of poets in all modern languages [...]
[which] shews that it attained the end, which was to please. For I confess my
chief endeavours are to delight the age in which I live.' 'A Defence of *An Essay*

written a play without rhyme, *All for Love*, explaining in his preface:

> I have endeavoured in this play to follow the practice of the Ancients, who, as Mr. Rymer[29] has judiciously observed, are and ought to be our masters [...]. In my style I have professed to imitate the divine Shakespeare; which that I may perform more freely, I have disencumbered myself from rhyme. Not that I condemn my former way, but this is more proper to my present purpose. (1678, I 230–231)

The second edition of Roscommon's essay (1685) was prefaced by a verse tribute from Dryden in which he developed Roscommon's argument. According to their version of literary history, the non-rhyming quantitative poetry of Greece and Rome had been superseded by rhymed composition, whose origin was attributed to the Germanic gods. The new fashion was given momentum by the practices of the medieval Church, which used rhyme in hymns and other compositions. Even though Renaissance writers had made rhymed poetry into an art form, it was still inferior to Classical verse, which these English writers thought it their mission to revive:

> Till barb'rous Nations and more barb'rous Times
> Debas'd the Majesty of Verse to Rhimes;
> Those rode at first: a kind of hobbling Prose:
> That limp'd a long, and tinckl'd in the close:
> But Italy reviving from the trance
> Of Vandal, Goth and Monkish ignorance,
> With pauses, cadence, and well vowell'd words,
> And all the Graces a good Ear affords,
> Made Rhyme an Art, and Dante's polished page
> Restor'd a silver, not a golden Age:
> Then Petrarch follow'd, and in him we see,
> What Rhyme improv'd in all its height can be;
> At best a pleasing sound, and fair barbarity.
> The French pursu'd their steps; and Britain, last
> In manly sweetness all the rest surpass'd.

Other poets also deferred to Roscommon's authoritative account of the origin of rhyme in Western poetry, and a decade later the lines describing Óðinn and Þórr under the mossy oak were quoted by Sir Thomas Pope Blount in his substantial treatise on poetry, *De Re Poetica* (1694, 105–

Of Dramatic Poesy', prefixed to *The Indian Emperor* (1668), I 115–116.

[29]True to his name, the playwright Thomas Rymer did use rhyme in his dramatic compositions, but he argued for the restoration of classical precepts in his critical work, *Tragedies of the Last Age Considered* (1678), to which Dryden here refers.

106). It was not until a century later that the confusion of Saxon with Celtic mythology (and the confusion of attributing rhymed verse to Óðinn) was pointed out by Samuel Johnson (1783, 237) in his appraisal of Roscommon's life and works:

> The *Essay* [on Translated Verse], though generally excellent, is not without its faults [...] he has confounded the British and Saxon mythology [...]. The oak, as I think Gildon has observed, belonged to the British druids, and Thor and Woden were Saxon deities. Of the 'double rhymes',[30] which he so liberally supposes, he certainly had no knowledge.

Another writer on poetics, William Temple, demonstrated two rather different attitudes to medieval Scandinavian culture in his two essays 'Of Heroick Vertue' and 'Of Poetry' (1690). In the former, Temple (1690, 232) canvassed the idea that the 'Runick Characters', invented by Óðinn and brought to the North by him, may have been more ancient than writing in Latin.[31] Following his quotation in Latin of two stanzas from 'that song or Epicedium of *Regner Ladbrog* which he composed in the Runick Language about eight hundred years ago', for which he acknowledges his indebtedness to Ole Worm's *Litteratura Runica* of 1636, Temple finds himself unexpectedly impressed (1690, 235–236):

> I am deceived, if in this Sonnet, and a following Ode of *Scallogrim* [...] there be not a vein truly Poetical, and in its kind Pindarick, taking with it the allowance of the different Climats, Fashions, Opinions, and Languages of such distant Countries.

The same poem had also made a slightly different impression on Aylett

---

[30]See *OED* for seventeenth-century citations on the use of the terms 'double' and 'triple rhyme' meaning 'rhyme involving two or three syllables respectively'. Thomas Percy was one of the most vehement late eighteenth-century correctors of the common confusion between Celtic and Germanic myth and literature. It is the main theme of the preface to his *Northern Antiquities* (1770), in which he criticises the Swiss writer Paul-Henri Mallet, whose *L'Histoire de Dannemarc* (1763) he translated and in which he found this misapprehension rife.

[31]'Runes were properly the Name of the antient Gothick Letters or Characters, which were Invented first or Introduced by Odin [...]. But because all the Writings, they had among them for many Ages, were in Verse, it came to be the common Name of all sorts of Poetry among the Goths, and the Writers or Composers of them, were called *Runers* or *Rymers*. They had likewise another name for them or for some sorts of them, which was *Viises* or *Wises*, and because the sages of that Nation, expressed the best of their Thoughts, and what Learning and Prudence they had, in these kind of Writings, they that succeeded best and with most Applause were termed Wise Men' (Temple 1690, 315–316).

Sammes (1676, 436) who depicted Ragnarr 'in as good Verses as Ale could inspire, hugging himself with the hopes of Full-pots in the World to come'.

In his essay 'Of Poetry', however, Temple assumed the received view of European literary history (1690, 312–315), describing 'the cloud of ignorance [...] coming from the north', obscuring learning and replacing the Classical art with rhymed verse: 'as if true Poetry being dead, an Apparition of it walked about.' His history of poetry leads him to propose a novel etymology for the word 'rhyme':

> With these Changes, the antient Poetry was wholly lost in all these Countries, and a new Sort grew up by degrees, which was called by a new Name of Rhymes, with an easy Change of the Gothick Word *Runes*, and not from the Greek, *Rhythmes*, as is vulgarly supposed.

His ingenuity in etymological derivation does not end there, and he goes on to explain the origin of the word 'wise' in 'Viises'.[32] Temple described the poetic form of medieval Scandinavian verse in some detail, apparently acknowledging the principle of alliteration and the ornamentation of kennings (1690, 316):

> Of these Runes, there were in use among the Goths above a Hundred several sorts, some Composed in longer, some in shorter Lines, some equal and some others unequal, with many different Cadencies, Quantities, or Feet, which in the pronouncing, make many different sorts of Original or Natural Tunes. Some were Framed with Allusions of Words, or Consonance of Syllables, or of Letters either in the same Line or in the Dystick, or by alternate Succession and Resemblance, which made a sort of Gingle, that pleased the ruder Ears of that People.

It was not until Hickes's *Thesaurus* of 1703–1705 that a full account of Old Norse poetic form, based on Ole Worm's survey in *Litteratura Runica*, was published in England. In the meanwhile Temple proposed that rhyme developed in Germanic culture because of the great number of monosyllables in the language[33] and quickly supplanted older forms.

---

[32]This idea had earlier been put forward by Olaus Magnus (1555) translated into English in 1658, though it appears to go back to Snorri's *Edda* and the *Third Grammatical Treatise*. See Meulengracht Sørensen 1989 for an analysis of the medieval evidence.

[33]'And because their Language was composed most of Monosyllables, and of so great Numbers, many must end in the same Sound; and another sort of Runes were made, with the Care and Study of ending two Lines, or each other of four Lines, with Words of the same Sound, which being the easiest, requiring less Art, and needing less Spirit (because a certain Chime in the Sounds supplied

Whatever admiration he felt for Ragnarr's *Death-Song* as poetry seems to have been dissipated by his examination of poetic form in the broad context of European literary history, where eddic verse is given the status of unsophisticated, popular poetry[34] (1690, 318):

> The common Vein of the Gothick Runes was what is Termed *Dithyrambick*, and was of a raving or rambling sort of Wit or Invention, loose and flowing, with little Art or Confinement to any certain Measures or Rules [...]. And such as it was, it served the turn, not only to please, but even to Charm the Ignorant and Barbarous Vulgar, where it was in Use.

He goes on to claim that the use of poetry for magical purposes was a late development, resorted to by inferior poets.[35] His examples of this kind of practice 'to make Women kind or easy, and Men hard or invulnerable' are clearly derived from *Hávamál*: 'as one of their most antient Runers affirms of himself and his own Atchievments, by Force of these Magical Arms' (1690, 320).

While the new material on Northern antiquity may not have clarified the nature of traditional Norse poetry, the matter of Germanic mythology was taken up with some enthusiasm by John Dryden, in his play *King Arthur, or, The British Worthy* (1691), which was set to music as a semi-opera by Henry Purcell and designed to be performed in The Queen's Theatre, Dorset Gardens, the largest and most sumptuous in England at the time, especially equipped for spectacular effects. A Christian King Arthur fights to subdue a heathen Saxon King, Oswald of Kent, who, as well as vying for the throne, is also Arthur's rival for the love of Emmeline, the beautiful, blind daughter of the Duke of Cornwall. In Act I, scene 2, in preparation for battle (which is to take place on St George

that Want, and pleased common Ears); this in time grew the most general among all the Gothick Colonies of Europe, and made Rhymes or Runes pass for the modern Poetry, in these parts of the World' (Temple 1690, 316–7). The idea that Germanic languages were predominantly monosyllabic was commonplace in the late seventeenth and early eighteenth centuries. Elizabeth Elstob (1715) inveighs against this misapprehension in the preface to her Old English grammar.

[34]In noting that the Goths admired their poets just as much as poets were admired in 'learned Nations', Temple (1690, 318) explains: 'For among the Blind, he that has one Eye is a Prince.'

[35]'But as the true Flame of Poetry was rare among them [...] those Runers who could not raise Admiration by the spirit of their poetry, endeavoured to do it by another, which was that of Enchantments [...] [they] turned the use of them very much to Incantations and Charms' (1690, 319–320).

of Cappadocia's Day), Oswald and Osmond ('a Saxon Magician, and a
Heathen') engage in pagan rituals, sacrificing to Thor, Freya and Woden
(Summers 1932, 251–253):

> *The Scene represents a place of Heathen worship; The three Saxon*
> *Gods, Woden, Thor, and Freya placed on Pedestals. An Altar.*

Osmond:	'Tis time to hasten our mysterious Rites;
	Because your Army waits you.

> *Oswald making three Bows before the three Images.*

Oswald:	Thor, Freya, Woden, all ye Saxon Powers,
	Hear and revenge my Father Hengist's death.
Osmond:	Father of Gods and Men, great Woden, hear.
	Mount thy hot Courser, drive amidst thy Foes;
	Lift high thy thund'ring Arm, let every blow
	Dash out a mis-believing Briton's Brains.
Oswald:	Father of Gods and Men, great Woden, hear;
	Give Conquest to thy Saxon Race, and me.
Osmond:	Thor, Freya, Woden, hear, and spell your Saxons,
	With Sacred Runick Rhimes, from Death in Battle.
	Edge their bright Swords, and blunt the Britons Darts.
	No more, Great Prince, for see my trusty Fiend,
	Who all the Night has wing'd the dusky Air.

> *Grimbald, a fierce earthy Spirit arises.*

[Grimbald chooses six Saxons to be sacrificed to Mother Earth and Woden, and
intends to divine Oswald's chance of victory from the entrails of the victims.
With the six Saxons dressed in white and ranged in two columns of three facing
each other, the stage is filled with Priests and Singers]

	Woden, first to thee,
	A Milk-white Steed in Battle won,
	We have sacrific'd.
Chorus.	We have sacrific'd.
Verse:	Let our next oblation be,
	To Thor, thy thundring Son,
	Of such another.
Chorus.	We have sacrific'd.
2 Voc.	A third; (of Friezland breed was he,)
	To Woden's Wife, and to Thor's Mother:
	And now we have atton'd all three
	We have sacrific'd.
Chorus.	We have sacrific'd.
Verse:	The White Horse Neigh'd aloud.
	To Woden thanks we render.
	To Woden we have vow'd.

Chorus.   To Woden, our Defender.

[The last four Lines in Chorus.]

Vers.   The Lot is Cast, and Tanfan pleas'd:
Chorus.   Of Mortal Cares you shall be eas'd,
              Brave Souls to be renown'd in Story.
              Honour prizing,
              Death despising,
              Fame acquiring
              By Expiring,
              Dye, and reap the fruit of Glory.
              Brave Souls to be Renown'd in Story.
Vers. 2   I call ye all,
              To Woden's Hall;
              Your temples round
              With Ivy bound,
              In Goblets Crown'd,
              And plenteous Bowls of burnish'd Gold;
              Where you shall Laugh,
              And dance and quaff,
              The Juice, that makes the Britons bold.

The Six Saxons are led off by the Priests, in Order to be Sacrificed.

Oswald: Ambitious Fools we are,
              And yet Ambition is a Godlike Fault:
              Or rather, 'tis no Fault in Souls Born great,
              Who dare extend their Glory by their Deeds.
              Now *Britany* prepare to change thy State,
              And from this Day begin thy Saxon date.

Although there is much in this scene that is clearly fantastic, it shows the early impact of information about Norse mythology on English writers (see also Blackmore 1695, in which Thor lives in Lapland), an influence that was further developed in the eighteenth and nineteenth centuries. As well as depicting Woden as the patron of Hengist, Dryden calls him father of gods and men, who rides a 'hot courser' and has the power to decide a man's death or safety in battle. The Saxon deities are also attributed with the ability to cast spells and use runic rhymes to affect their victims. Dryden's association of Tanfan with the casting of lots probably shows his familiarity with Sheringham's work (1670, 333–

336) or that of Sammes (1676, 450–451), though in his Dedication[36] he cites his sources as Bede, Bochart and others.

More often at the turn of the eighteenth century, however, those devoted to uncovering England's Germanic heritage were the butt of jokes. In his 1699 mock-heroic poem, *The Dispensary*, Samuel Garth lampoons antiquaries fond of septentrionalist works (Canto iv 127–132):

> Abandon'd Authors here a refuge meet,
> And from the World, to Dust and Worms retreat.
> Here Dregs and Sediment of Auctions reign,
> Refuse of Fairs, and Gleanings of *Duck-Lane*.
> And up these *shelves* much *Gothick* Lumber climbs,
> With *Swiss* Philosophy, and *Danish* Rhymes.

And some decades later, Alexander Pope names one Worm in his caricature of antiquarian dullness in *The Dunciad* III 185–190 (ed. Sutherland 1963, 170–172):

> 'But who is he, in closet close y-pent,
> Of sober face, with learned dust besprent?'
> 'Right wel mine eyes arede the myster wight,
> On parchment scraps y-fed, and Wormius hight.
> To future ages may thy dulness last,
> As thou preserv'st the dulness of the past!'

George Hickes had promised 'in the name of the Arctic Muses to all those now ignorant of [Icelandic] literature' that it would prove 'no less ardently enjoyed than that knowledge of the classical humanities which they so much extol' (1703–1705, I iii). It was some time before this promise was to be realized.

BIBLIOGRAPHY

Arngrímur Jónsson. 1593. *Brevis Commentarius de Islandia*. Copenhagen.

———. 1609. *Crymogæa, sive rerum Islandicarum libri tres*. Hamburg.

---

[36]'When I wrote it, seven Years ago, I employ'd some reading about it, to inform myself out of Beda, Bochartus, and other Authors concerning the Rites and Customs of the Heathen Saxons', *Dedication to the Marquiss of Hallifax*. Reprinted in Montague Summers (ed.) 1932, 241–242. The Bochartus reference is to the *Geographica Sacra* I–II of Samuel Bochartus, published in Caen 1646. Summers (1932, 559) argued Dryden's debt to Tacitus, *Annals*, for a number of the details of Germanic ritual in *King Arthur*, including the reference to Tanfan.

Bennett, J.A.W. 1938. *The History of Old English and Old Norse Studies in England from the Time of Francis Junius till the End of the Eighteenth Century.* Oxford University D.Phil. thesis. Bodl. MS. D.Phil. d. 287.

————. 1946-53. 'The Beginnings of Runic Studies in England', *Saga-Book of the Viking Society* 13, 269–283.

Blackmore, Sir Richard. 1695. *Prince Arthur, An Heroick Poem in Ten Books.* London.

Blount, Sir Thomas Pope. 1694. *De Re Poetica: or Remarks upon Poetry with Characters and Censures of the Most Considerable Poets, whether Ancient or Modern [...].* London.

Camden, William. 1586. *Britannia.* London. (Translated into English by Philemon Holland and enlarged by the author in 1610 as *Britain, or A Chorographical Description of the most flourishing Kingdoms of England, Scotland and Ireland).*

Campion, Thomas. 1602. *Observations in the Art of English Poesie. Wherein it is demonstratively prooved, and by example confirmed, that the English toong will receive eight severall kinds of numbers, proper to itself [...].* London.

Claussøn, Hans Peder, trans. 1633. *Snorre Sturleson's Norske Kongers Chronica.* Copenhagen.

Daniel, Samuel. 1603. *A Defence of Ryme: Against a Pamphlet entituled: Observations in the Art of English Poesie. Wherein is demonstratively proved, that Ryme is the fittest harmonie of words that comportes with our Language.* London.

Darbishire, Helen, ed. 1952. *The Poetical Works of John Milton,* Vol. 1, *Paradise Lost.* Oxford.

Dictionary of National Biography. Article on 'Junius, Francis, or Du Jon, François, the younger (1589-1677)', X 1115–1116.

Dryden, John. 1668. 'Of Dramatic Poetry', in Watson 1962.

————. 1691. *King Arthur, or the British Worthy,* in Summers 1932, pp. 231–289.

Elstob, Elizabeth. 1715. *The Rudiments of Grammar for the English-Saxon Tongue. First given in English with an Apology for the Study of Northern Antiquities.* London. (Facsimile reprint Scolar Press, Menston, 1968).

Fairer, D. 1986. 'Anglo-Saxon Studies' in Sutherland, L.S. and L.G. Mitchell, eds, *The Eighteenth Century,* Vol. 5 (pp. 807–829), of T.H. Aston, ed., *The History of the University of Oxford,* Oxford, 1984–.

Farley, F.E. 1903. *Scandinavian Influences in the English Romantic Movement,* Studies and Notes in Philology and Literature, 9. Cambridge, Mass.

Faulkes, Anthony, ed. 1977. *Two Versions of Snorra Edda from the 17th. Century.* 2 vols. Reykjavík.

Frazer, Russell. 1973. *The Dark Ages and the Age of Gold.* Princeton.

Garth, Sir Samuel. 1699. *The Dispensary.* Second edition. London.

Guggenheimer, Eva H. 1972. *Rhyme Effects and Rhyming Figures. A Comparative Study of Sound Repetition in the Classics with Emphasis on Latin Poetry.* The Hague and Paris.

Hakluyt, Richard. 1599. *The Principall Navigations, Voiages, Traffiques and Discoveries of the English Nation, made by sea or over land [...] at any time within the compasse of these 1500 yeeres, &c.* 3 vols. London.

Harris, Richard L. 1992. *A Chorus of Grammars. The Correspondence of George Hickes and his Collaborators on the* Thesaurus linguarum septentrionalium. Publications of the Dictionary of Old English, 4. Toronto.

Herbert, Edward, Lord. 1663. *De Religione Gentilium.* Amsterdam. Translated in 1705 by William Lewis, *The Ancient Religion of the Gentiles, and Causes of their Errors Consider'd etc.* London.

Hickes, George. 1689. *Institutiones grammaticæ Anglo-Saxonicæ et Moesogothicæ.* Oxford. (Scolar Press facsimile, Menston, 1971).

———. 1703–1705. *Linguarum vett. septentrionalium thesaurus grammaticocriticus et archæologicus.* Oxford. (Scolar Press facsimile, Menston, 1970).

Johnson, Samuel. 1783. 'Roscommon', in *The Lives of the Poets.* London. (Page references are to the 1905 edition based on the 1783 4-volume octavo edition).

Jones, C.W., ed. 1943. Bede, *De Temporum Ratione* in *Bedæ Opera De Temporibus.* Ithaca, NY.

Langhorne, Daniel. 1673. *Elenchus Antiquitatum Albionensium, Brittanorum, Scotorum, Danorum, Anglosaxonum [...].* London.

Mallet, Paul-Henri. 1763. *Introduction a L'Histoire de Dannemarc, ou L'on traite de la Religion, des Loix, des Moeurs & des Usages des anciens Danois.* 6 vols. Geneva.

Meulengracht Sørensen, Preben. 1989. 'Moderen forløst af datterens skød', in Andrén, A., ed., *Medeltidens fødelse.* Symposier på Krapperups borg 1. Lund, 263–275.

Olaus Magnus. 1555. *Historia de Omnibus Gothorum Suenumque Regibus.* Rome. Translated (epitome) into English in 1658 as *A Compendious History of the Goths, Swedes and Vandals, and other Northern Nations.* London.

Percy, Thomas. 1770. *Northern Antiquities: or, a Description of the Manners, Customs, Religion and Laws of the Ancient Danes, And other Northern Nations; Including those of Our own Saxon Ancestors [...].* 2 vols. London.

Peringskjöld, Johan. 1697. *Heimskringla [...] sive Historiæ Regum Septentrionalium.* Stockholm.

Purchas, Samuel. 1625. *Purchas his Pilgrimage, or Relations of the World and the Religions, observed in all Ages and Places Discovered.* London. (J. Maclehose, ed., *Purchas his Pilgrimage* I–XX. Glasgow, 1906).

Resen, Peder Hansen, ed. 1665. *Edda Islandorum, an. Chr. MCCXV, Islandice, conscripta per Snorronem Sturlæ Islandiæ.* Copenhagen. (Facsimile ed. by Faulkes 1977, I).

————. 1665. *Ethica Odini, pars Eddæ Sæmundi vocata Haavamaal una cum ejusdem appendice appellato Runa Capitule.* Copenhagen.

————. 1665. *Philosophia antiquissima Norvego-Danica dicta Woluspa, quae est pars Eddæ Sæmundi.* Copenhagen.

Roscommon, Lord. 1684. *Essay on Translated Verse.* London.

Runólfur Jónsson. 1651. *Recentissima antiquissimæ linguæ septentrionalis incunabula; id est, Grammaticæ Islandicæ rudimenta.* Copenhagen.

Sammes, Aylett. 1676. *Britannia Antiqua Illustrata; or The Antiquities of Antient Britain.* London.

Seaton, Ethel. 1935. *Literary Relations of England and Scandinavia in the Seventeenth Century.* Oxford.

Sheringham, Robert. 1670. *De Anglorum Gentis Origine Disceptatio.* Cambridge.

Stephanius, Stephen Hansen. 1645. *Notæ Vberiores in Historiam Danicam Saxonis Grammatici.* Notes and preface to his 1644 edition of Saxo's Latin text. (Facsimile edition of *Notæ* by H.D. Schepelern. Danish Humanist Texts and Studies 2, 1978. Copenhagen).

Stillingfleet, Edward. 1676. *Defence of the Discourse concerning Idolatry.* London.

Summers, M., ed. 1932. *Dryden. The Dramatic Works.* London.

Sutherland, James, ed. 1963. *Alexander Pope, The Dunciad.* Third edition. London and New Haven.

Temple, Sir William. 1690. *Miscellanea, The Second Part.* (Contains the essays 'Of Heroic Virtue' and 'Of Poetry'). London.

Verstegan, Richard. 1605. *A Restitution of Decayed Intelligence concerning the most noble and renowned English Nation.* Antwerp. Also published in London (1628; repr. 1634, 1655).

Watson, George, ed. 1962. *John Dryden, Of Dramatic Poetry and other Critical Essays.* London.

Worm, Christian (ed. from the notes of Árni Magnússon). 1716. *Arae multiscii schedae de Islandia.* Oxford.

Worm, Ole. 1636. *Antiquitates Danicæ; seu Litteratura runica.* Amsterdam.

————. 1751. *Olai Wormii et ad eum [...] Epistolae.* Copenhagen.

10

The Cult of 'Stalwart Frith-thjof' in Victorian Britain

ANDREW WAWN

> Though the mythology of the Edda, and the exploits of the Sagas,
> have been replaced in our nurseries, and our fancy, by the softer
> dreams of our Southern invaders, we may, nevertheless, hail an
> occasional interview with the grim heroes of Valhalla, with feelings
> not altogether alien to their grandeur and their gloom. ([Anon.],
> *Edinburgh Review*, February 1828, 137)

On the evening of 19 March 1894, the Reverend John Sephton read
portions of his new translation of *Friðþjófs saga hins frœkna* to seventy-
nine members of the Liverpool Philosophical and Literary Society. It was
one of the society's best attended meetings during the 1893–1894 winter
season (Sephton 1894, xxix–xxxi): papers on 'Gypsies' (28 members
present), 'Mushroom Beds of South American ants' (50), 'Recent
Socialistic and Labour Legislation in New Zealand' (59), and 'Astro-
photography' (75) had fared rather less well. Indeed only Charles Darwin
attracted more listeners than the Icelandic saga: ninety-five members
attended a paper by the Liverpool surgeon John Newton on 'Recent
Discoveries as to the Origin and Early History of the Human Race'.

Three related questions arise out of Sephton's successful March
meeting in Liverpool's Royal Institution. Why, when others had lectured
on ants, astronomy and anthropology, did he choose to discuss an
Icelandic saga; why did so many Merseyside intellectuals come to listen
to him; and why of all possible Icelandic narratives did Sephton choose
Friðþjófs saga hins frœkna, a work now washed over by the waves of
scholarly neglect. In short, why medieval Iceland, why modern Liverpool,
and (above all) why Friðþjófr?[1] In addressing these questions, this essay

---

[1] In this essay frequent reference will be made to the Icelandic *Friðþjófs saga
hins frœkna* and to translations of Bishop Esaias Tegnér's 1824 *Frithiofs saga*.
Whilst Victorians confused and conflated the two works, not least when spelling
the names of the characters, the present essay discusses both versions of the
story, and seeks wherever possible to use the appropriate Icelandic or Swedish
name forms.

seeks to examine the remarkable cult of 'stalwart Frith-thjof' (Baring Gould 1863, 439) in nineteenth-century Britain; and to set that particular enthusiasm into the broader context of the Victorian discovery of and devotion to the Viking past.

AN AUDIENCE FOR ICELAND

The level of engagement with Northern antiquity reflected in John Sephton's impressively large Liverpool audience was in fact a nationwide phenomenon in Victorian Britain. One has only to examine the correspondence of Eiríkur Magnússon, Sephton's immediate predecessor as translator of *Friðþjófs saga hins frækna,* to sense how greatly the idea of Iceland had come to intrigue and inspire the nation's antiquaries, littérateurs and travellers. Eiríkur had arrived in Britain in 1863, and worked as a librarian in Cambridge for forty years from 1871. It was in that same year that he and William Morris first published their joint translation of *Friðþjófs saga* (Morris and Eiríkur Magnússon 1871, 1875, 1900). Eiríkur's correspondents throughout this period may be taken as a representative cross section of the potential Victorian audience for Icelandic sagas in general, and for *Friðþjófs saga* in particular. The letter writers were the saga readers.

The letters came thick and fast from all over the British Isles. There were invitations for Eiríkur to lecture far and wide,[2] whether in the wilds of Wisbech (with Eiríkur's wife instructed to turn up in national costume: Lbs. 2190a 4to, J.N. Brightman, 19 February 1876), or to the Literary and Philosophical Society of Newcastle upon Tyne (three lectures in a week: Lbs. 2188a 4to, William Lyall, 21 September 1871), or within the hallowed portals of the Royal Institute in London (Lbs. 2187a 4to, 29 June [?1872]). This latter meeting was organised by Queen Victoria's physician, the Iceland explorer Sir Henry Holland, eighty-three years old in 1871, and newly returned from his first visit to Iceland since 1810, when he had been an influential member of Sir George Mackenzie's celebrated expedition (Wawn 1987). Holland himself had been a protégé of his Merseyside neighbour John Thomas Stanley, whose 1789 Iceland expedition had helped to trigger young Henry's lifelong fascination with the lava and lyme-grass of 66° North (Wawn 1981). In turn, it had been Holland who had helped to secure a post for Eiríkur in Cambridge University library from which he eventually retired in 1911. So it is that

[2]Several of Eiríkur's lectures are extant in manuscript: Lbs. 406 fol., Lbs. 1860 4to (5), Lbs. 4555 4to.

these two friendships span a century and more of Icelandic enthusiasms in Britain. In his latter years, Sir Henry may indeed have deserved his reputation as a cavalierly ham-fisted high-society diagnostician, but Queen Victoria and his other well-connected patients kept taking the tablets, and Holland kept speaking up for Iceland at the highest levels of society until the last days of his very long life. As he wrote to Eiríkur shortly before his death, 'I feel myself half an Icelander if there can be such a condition of existence' (Lbs. 2187a 4to, 27 October 1873).

For a whole Icelander such as Eiríkur Magnússon, along with the requests for lectures came other saga-related offers and invitations: would he care to write a book on King Haraldr hárfagri Hálfdanarson in Blackwood's 'Men of Action' series (Lbs. 2186a 4to, Walter Besant, 21 January 1878); or could he attend the première of Hall Caine's play *The Prodigal Son*, at London's Drury Lane Theatre on 2 September 1905 (Lbs. 2186a 4to, 28 August 1905). Hall Caine was a saga-reading Manxman who had visited Iceland, befriended the poet Matthías Jochumsson, and written several novels and plays with strong Icelandic links. *The Prodigal Son,* based on Caine's 1904 novel of the same name, tells of Oscar Stephensson, a young and irresponsible native of Akureyri who returns home having chosen (for some reason) to be educated in Oxford. He soon leaves his wife (the most patient of Icelandic Griseldas) and baby daughter, and runs off to Monte Carlo with Helga, a 'modern' woman. He duly cheats his father-in-law by forging cheques in order to finance Helga's lavish Riviera life-style; he watches in horror as a fellow native of Akureyri shoots himself following exposure as a card cheat; he then watches in despair as his modern woman runs off with an even more modern theatre director. Duly penitent, Oscar makes his way to London, where he becomes world famous as a composer of operas based on Icelandic themes: 'I say Iceland is stark and wild [...] but if someone could set it to music, grim as its glaciers and fierce as its fires, it would take the world by storm' (Caine 1905, 89). At the end of the play Oscar returns to Akureyri just in time to pay off his destitute father-in-law's debts, and to be reconciled with his long-lost daughter who could whistle the tunes from all his operas without realising that they were the work of her father. Limp melodrama it may now seem, but at the time Hall Caine's play was by no means just a provincial side-show: it was premièred in London and at the New Amsterdam Theatre in New York on the same day. By the end of the nineteenth century there were, assuredly, committed Icelandophile audiences to be reached on both sides of the Atlantic.

Moreover, the adaptation of Icelandic sagas for stage and concert hall was no mere figment of Oscar Stephensson's imagination: it was a fact of artistic life in the latter days of Queen Victoria. In 1888, just a year before his death, Guðbrandur Vigfússon was asked to advise on a projected musical based on *Jómsvíkinga saga* (Bodleian MS Eng. Misc. d.131, George Silk, 24 November 1888); Beatrice Barmby's *Gísli Súrsson, A Drama* (1900) was read at the Viking Club in London, produced in Winnipeg, and (via Matthías Jochumsson's translation) used by W.P. Ker as an Icelandic text book at King's College (Lbs. 2808 4to, letters from Mabel Barmby to Matthías Jochumsson); whilst Sir Edward Elgar's now (sadly) neglected oratorio *King Olaf*, based on Longfellow's poem, was premièred in Hanley in 1896 (Wawn 1992b, 214). There was also, as we shall see, a play based on *Friðþjófs saga*.

Inevitably, however, much of Eiríkur's mail from enthusiasts of the North took the form not of invitations to Icelandic plays, but of calls for help with more mundane matters Icelandic—anything from language learning to landscape gardening, from geology to game birds. The Welshman George Powell, with whom Eiríkur collaborated on translations of sagas and folk-tales shortly after his arrival in Britain (Powell and Eiríkur Magnússon 1864, 1866; Wawn 1992, 234–235), requests that ptarmigan be sent from Iceland to William Morris's friend Edward Burne-Jones (Lbs. 2190a 4to, 29 April 1869).[3] Another of Eiríkur's correspondents wonders whether birch trees could be sent from Þingvellir for planting in a friend's garden (Lbs. MS 2186a 4to, Charles Babington, 4 August 1869); could a five-year-old chestnut horse from Iceland be shipped to the Lord Mayor of London's secretary (Lbs. 403 fol.), a request hard to refuse at a time (1875) when Morris had invoked the assistance of the Lord Mayor in establishing a famine relief fund for Iceland; could Eiríkur arrange for a supply of Iceland spar to be sent for the manufacture of spectacles in Britain (Lbs. 2186a 4to, Richard Baker, 18 February 1884); could he supply a list of *Íslendingasögur* horse references for Gilbert Goudie, the Edinburgh scholar, who was writing a book on Shetland ponies (Lbs. 2186b 4to, 28 November 1910); could he help finance a friend's son who was trying to start a bakery in London (Lbs. 2184 4to, John Thorkell Clements, undated); could he arrange for a native speaker to help Henry Sweet with his Danish pronunciation (Lbs. 2189a 4to, 15 July 1872); would he be available to escort the Prince of Wales on a trip to Iceland (Lbs. 2187 4to, Francis Holland, 18 March

---

[3]The love triangle in the Morris household at this time (Jane Morris in love with Dante Gabriel Rossetti) was painfully similar to that in *Kormaks saga*, a work which Morris chose to translate shortly afterwards (Morris and Magnússon 1970, 10–11). Possibly intended for inclusion in the 1875 *Three Northern Love Stories* volume which contained the Morris-Eiríkur Magnússon *Friðþjófs saga* translation, Morris's *Kormaks saga* version remained unprinted until 1970.

1874); could he explain why there is a pig reference in *Víga-Glúms saga* when there are no pigs in Iceland (Lbs. 2187a 4to, J. Harold Herbert, 12 January 1901); and could he prepare a translation of the heroic poem *Bjarkamál* to be performed by a massed choir of (doubtless) horned-helmeted Vikings sitting in long ships on the River Thames in front of thousands of people celebrating the Empire Festival (Lbs. 2188b 4to, Albany Major, 3 May 1910)? How fortunate for Eiríkur that he died before the invention of e-mail.

Throughout his life in England, Eiríkur Magnússon took particular pleasure in teaching Icelandic in person and by post. He translated *Friðþjófs saga hins frækna* for those unable to read it in Old Icelandic, but he spared no effort in developing an Icelandic reading capability amongst interested Victorian scholars. Amongst Eiríkur's earliest pupils was Sir Edmund Head (Lbs. 2187 4to, 20 July 1863), whose translation of *Víga-Glúms saga* was published in 1866.[4] Influential Cambridge figures such as J.R. Lumby (Lbs. 2188a 4to, 25 November 1868) and the local member of parliament J. Beresford Hope (Lbs. 2187 4to, 13 July 1869) sought Eiríkur's assistance in learning to read Icelandic sagas, and subsequently were happy to pull the appropriate strings when Eiríkur applied for a post at the University library. Once settled in Cambridge, Eiríkur instructed small but keen groups of students, three of whom (Israel Gollancz, Bertha Phillpotts, and Henry Sweet) became celebrated scholars of Icelandic; whilst another, George Rowntree from Newcastle upon Tyne, won the Cambridge University poetry prize in 1875 with an earnest and (in all truth) arthritic poem on Iceland.

A single representative trail of Eiríkur Magnússon's influence, and of the Icelandic enthusiasms which he helped to generate in Victorian England, can be followed in the career of the politician and diplomat James Bryce. Eiríkur first assisted the young Irishman on his Icelandic travels in the early 1870s (Bryce 1923, 1–43); he later helped him to work up his 'rusty Icelandic' (Lbs. 2186 4to, undated). Bryce in turn lectured on Icelandic topics throughout Britain (Leeds in 1891, for instance). He proposed at one point to campaign for the award of an Oxford honorary degree to Jón forseti Sigurðsson, before conceding that no-one in Oxford would be in the least interested (Lbs. 2186 4to, 20 May [no year])—he might have stood a better chance promoting the claims of Hall Caine's Oscar Stephensson. Bryce was an energetic member of the Mansion House Fund Committee in 1882, helping to raise cash for what everyone except Guðbrandur Vigfússon (letter to *The Times*, 13 October

---

[4]Head 1866, xvi mentions the help he has received from Guðbrandur Vigfússon and George Webbe Dasent, but strangely does not refer to Eiríkur.

1882) seemed to regard as a disastrous famine in Iceland (Harris 1978–1979; Ellison 1986–1989). As a parliamentarian, Bryce fought long and hard (and in vain) to prevent the passage of an 1896 bill which sought to abolish sheep imports from Iceland. It is small wonder that Eiríkur encouraged Bryce's opposition to this measure: he had after all played a major part in establishing this trade (Lbs. 2186a 4to, James Bridges, 13 October 1876, 3 November 1877), which had been much to the benefit of the Eastern fjords of Iceland, where Eiríkur had family connections. Bryce eventually became a British diplomat in the United States, where we find him on one occasion seated in the Oval office of the White House sharing the delights of Icelandic sagas with a fascinated President Theodore Roosevelt (Fisher 1927, I 144). As his friendship with the well-connected Bryce shows clearly, Eiríkur Magnússon's energy, his dedication as a teacher, his ability to combine a passion for serious philology with an active interest in politics and business, politicians and business men, ensured that neither he nor Iceland wanted for friends in high places in late Victorian Britain. And this was the man who helped William Morris to translate *Friðþjófs saga*.

THE LIVERPOOL CONNECTION

Eiríkur Magnússon's correspondence helps to explain why John Sephton chose to share his own knowledge of and enthusiasm for medieval Iceland with a public audience in nineteenth-century Britain. Victorian levels of curiosity were high. It was the idea of Iceland that many people found so intriguing. Lectures were well attended, and translations of sagas such as *Friðþjófs saga hins frækna* clearly enjoyed an appreciative readership. But with two of its four nineteenth-century English translators (George Stephens and John Sephton) born and bred in Liverpool, and with a third (Eiríkur Magnússon) in frequent postal contact with friends there, the specifically Merseyside associations of *Friðþjófs saga* merit some attention. The question of 'why Liverpool?' needs addressing.

Liverpool was a port with a strong tradition of pre-Victorian Icelandic contacts, as well as a city which played its full part in the main Victorian wave of interest in the North. Pioneering British travellers to Iceland had strong Merseyside and Cestrian connections: John Thomas Stanley lived most of his life at Alderley Edge in Cheshire, enabling him to have close contact with his protégé Henry Holland, born and brought up in nearby Knutsford (Wawn 1981, 1987). It was the Liverpool merchants Horne and Stackhouse who traded with Iceland during the Napoleonic wars, and thus ensured that Icelandic woollens, skins, down, whale oil and dried fish were a familiar sight on the busy quayside at Pier Head; and it was

James Robb, their Reykjavík agent, who settled in Iceland, married an Icelandic woman, and whose family business flourished in the Icelandic capital for several generations: the modern central Reykjavík store 'Liverpool' bears at least token witness to this link (Wawn 1985, 114–115, 130–131). It was to David Gladstone, whose family name lives on in one of the port's most famous docks, that the influential Enlightenment intellectual Magnús Stephensen of Viðey turned for help when seeking an English publisher for his book on eighteenth-century Iceland. The first native Englishman to hold a major British university appointment in Icelandic was John Sephton, born and bred in Liverpool; the appointment was at Liverpool University and partly funded by Alfred Holt, Iceland traveller ([anon] 1881), Liverpudlian shipping magnate, philanthropist, and friend of both Eiríkur Magnússon and the poet Matthías Jochumsson, who himself had strong links with both Liverpool (through Unitarian friends) and the story of Friðþjófr/Frithiof (through his 1864 Icelandic verse translation). Surely the finest paintings of Icelandic scenes by a nineteenth-century artist anywhere in Europe are the hundred and seventy and more watercolours produced from sketches made during his 'Pilgrimage to the saga-steads of Iceland' by W.G. Collingwood, born and bred in Liverpool (Haraldur Hannesson 1990). In another context, there was considerable late Victorian and Edwardian scholarly effort devoted to identifying Bromborough, on the Wirral side of the River Mersey, as the site of the battle of Vinaheiðr in *Egils saga*.

Eiríkur Magnússon had lent support to this theory (Lbs. 2190 4to, Francis Tudsbery, 4 May 1907; also Tudsbery 1907), a fact perhaps not unconnected with his own close ties with Merseyside. One of Eiríkur's first Cambridge pupils, Edward Rae, worked in Liverpool and lived in Birkenhead, where Eiríkur and his wife visited him on several occasions. Rae had travelled to Iceland, where he had acquired some antique Icelandic silver, much to the disapproval of Eiríkur's wife, who was less than impressed by Rae's breezy assertion in one of his frequent letters (Lbs. 2190 4to, 10 June 1872) that he was 'merely inspired with a sacred love of his country and a desire to restore to her bosom objects which had been looted by Mrs Magnússon's ancestors in some warlike descent upon the English coast'. Eiríkur's enthusiasm for the northern counties of his adopted homeland even extended to his colourful suggestion that *Beowulf* was a Northern-English poem which had been taken to Iceland by Auðunn skökull, the only *landnámsöld* settler from England, a grandson of Ragnarr loðbrók, and the grandfather of Grettir Ásmundarson whose saga duly borrows a number of motifs from the Old English epic (Lbs. 1860 4to).

It was perhaps inevitable that the extensive links between Iceland and the greatest port in the British Empire should even find expression in a late Victorian novel, *The Dane's Daughter, an Icelandic Story*, written by Walmer Downe, and dedicated to Lord Dufferin whose *Letters from High Latitudes* became one of Victorian England's most widely read travel books about Iceland. In this flat-footed fable, Bartholemew Brattle-Browne, a dashing but dastardly gigolo from Liverpool travels to Iceland, where he meets and courts Helga, a steadfast young Icelandic maiden. Torn between marriage to her laconic peasant fiancé Kentil, and seduction by the brazen Brattle-Brown, helpless Helga duly follows the English Lothario back to Liverpool, only to discover that the unscrupulous cad is married, and had been interested only in Helga's dowry. The dim-witted but loyal Kentil follows in their wake to Liverpool, seeks out Brattle-Brown at his gentleman's club, and prevails in the ensuing fisticuffs. He and Helga then return to the honest agrarian simplicities of Iceland.

There is, as I have argued elsewhere (Wawn 1992b), a serious point behind all this Liverpudlian, and more generally Northern-English enthusiasm for Iceland. Nineteenth-century Britain did not revolve relentlessly around London; much of the industrial wealth of the country lay in the North, and there were many eager to establish and proud to celebrate links between the ancient presence of Viking settlers in the region and its modern industrial and commercial success. Viking blood—and values—had survived in the veins of Victorian Merseyside. The kind of triumphalism to which George Webbe Dasent gave expression at a national level:

> They [the Vikings] were like England in the nineteenth century: fifty years before all the rest of the world with her manufactories and firms—and twenty years before them in railways. They were foremost in the race of civilisation and progress; well started before all the rest had thought of running. No wonder therefore that both won. (Dasent 1873, I 247)

received an additional regional spin in the North of England. The Victorian descendants of Lake District Viking dalesmen were identified as:

> the sturdy squires and canny statesmen of the North, dwelling in thrift and industry, and sending out their sons to roam the world, and to rise in it by sheer force of worth and wisdom. (Collingwood 1896, 101)

Sturdy local antiquarians and canny amateur philologists, with their dialect and place-name studies, uncovered an array of reassuring cultural continuities (Ferguson 1856; Fergusson Irvine 1893, 297–304). Many Merseyside place-names were seen to bear vivid witness to the presence of the Northmen a thousand years earlier: the present writer was born in

West Kirby [ON *kirkjubær*], brought up in Meols [ON *melr*, 'sand-dune'], and used as a boy to climb the local Grettistak known as Thor's Stone, at the top of Thurstaston [ON *Thorsteins tún*] hill—Viking names every one (Dodgson 1972, IV 280). Victorian archaeologists excavated feverishly in search of Norse antiquities, and reported their finds in the local antiquarian journals, as well as in the District Secretary reports to *Saga-Book,* the scholarly journal of the London-based Viking Club which had been founded in 1892 (Townsend 1992).

Among Viking enthusiasts on Merseyside we find not just the worthy ranks of doctors, teachers and ministers of the church, but also successful business men and entrepreneurs—men like Alfred Holt, who had read widely about and travelled to Iceland, befriended learned Icelanders, and sat on Eiríkur Magnússon's Iceland famine committee in 1882. Here was a successful figure from the world of commerce, eager to discover the Norse antiquities of his neighbourhood, and happy to fund their more professional investigation at the local university which his commercial success was helping to support. Writing to John Sephton in 1886 and talking (positively) about another Liverpudlian scholar, Guðbrandur Vigfússon remarks that '[he] is a fine man and deserving of respect for having literary interests at all in Liverpool, where all the world rotates around bales of Cotton' (Sidney Jones Library, University of Liverpool, Sephton MS 3.33, GV to Sephton, 29 October 1883). It is a gormless remark of the kind which Guðbrandur may often have heard in his place of work: the lofty disdain of old southern land for new northern cash, of gentry for trade, of gentlemen for players. The notion may never have occurred to Guðbrandur that it was precisely because of those bales of cotton and the wealth which they generated within the region that a university college such as Liverpool was thriving and expanding. This wealth in turn created for John Sephton the opportunity to relinquish his headmaster's duties at Liverpool Institute in 1895, and to assume the responsibilities of University Reader in Icelandic, a post which his scholarly publications, most recently his 1894 translation of *Friðþjófs saga,* had helped to secure for him.

So that is 'why Liverpool'. There were people on Merseyside who regarded themselves as every bit as much descendants of the ancient Northmen as any Icelander—or member of the Auden family (see Sveinn Haraldsson's article, above)—could. Moreover, the energetic pursuit of trade with many lands (including Iceland) ensured that there was local wealth and leisure to underpin these antiquarian interests. Liverpool was a city with a spring in its cultural stride. It had a vigorous scholarly tradition, and an array of learned societies at which, as we have noted, research of every sort could be presented—on South American ants as well as North Atlantic sagas. It was thus an entirely appropriate region to father two translators of *Friðþjófs saga*.

THE RECEPTION OF FRIÐÞJÓFR/FRITHIOF

If Eiríkur Magnússon's post-bag helps us to understand 'why Iceland', and if the attitudes and achievements of Merseysiders as diverse as Henry Holland and Alfred Holt, John Thomas Stanley and John Sephton help to explain 'why Liverpool', there remains the third and principal question: 'Why *Friðþjófs saga*?' Any attempt to address this central issue must be prefaced with an outline of the saga story, and also with some indication of the extent of its popularity in Victorian Britain.

The longer of its two Icelandic versions tells of the aged King Beli of Sogn and a noble freeborn man Þorsteinn Víkingsson, lifelong friends who are eventually buried in mounds on opposite sides of the fjord. The royal princess, Ingibjörg, is fostered after Beli's death by a worthy yeoman Hildingr; so too is Friðþjófr after his father's death. The two foster-children fall in love, but Ingibjörg's brothers Hálfdan and Helgi refuse to allow their sister to marry the wealthy but lower-born Friðþjófr. Threatened with invasion by the neighbouring King Hringr, the brothers shamelessly ask the rejected Friðþjófr for assistance. This he understandably withholds. To prevent secret assignations between the lovers, the brothers conceal Ingibjörg in the temple of Baldr, but the young couple nevertheless contrive to meet at this location. King Hringr agrees peace terms with the brothers in return for his taking Ingibjörg in marriage. Learning of Friðþjófr's liaisons with Ingibjörg, the brothers are outraged at this blatant desecration of temple and sister. Accordingly, Friðþjófr is sent on a penitential voyage to the Orkneys to collect tribute money, ostensibly so that the brothers can pay Ingibjörg's dowry to King Hringr—in reality so that they can have him killed. They burn down Friðþjófr's homestead in his absence. Friðþjófr endures a perilous journey, harassed by sea-witches who (at the brothers' command) conjure up storms which are expected to engulf the hero. Friðþjófr and his companions survive, emboldened by a fine sequence of heroic songs, and with the aid of his magic ship Elliði. Arriving in Orkney, Friðþjófr fights berserks, wins fame, and is warmly welcomed; the Orcadian udallers deny any obligation to pay tribute to King Helgi but offer a large free-will sum for Friðþjófr to use as he sees fit. Returning to Norway, Friðþjófr confronts Ingibjörg's brothers in their hall, and strikes the particularly unpleasant Helgi in the face with the money bag. He sees the statue of Baldr being warmed over the fire by Helgi's wife, on whose arm Friðþjófr notices the ring which he had once given as a love-token to Ingibjörg. When Friðþjófr grabs at the ring, the image of Baldr falls into the fire, and the whole temple burns down. Friðþjófr escapes, and embarks on a three-year Viking expedition. He receives a warm welcome from King Hringr whom he visits in disguise. He subsequently rescues Hringr and Ingibjörg from broken ice on an otherwise frozen lake, and then, out hunting, rejects the temptation to kill King Hringr as he sleeps in the wood, his sword at his side. Friðþjófr loyally guards his royal host and casts the weapon away. The aged Hringr finally unmasks his mystery guest and tells him that after his death Friðþjófr may marry Ingibjörg, but must rule Hringr's kingdom responsibly until the dying king's own children reach maturity. This pledge duly honoured, Friðþjófr marries Ingibjörg, returns to Sognefjord, kills Helgi, receives a pledge of loyalty from Hálfdan, and accepts the title of king.

This, in outline, is the story which enjoyed such widespread exposure and esteem in Victorian Britain. Yet, in its original Icelandic form, we may now wonder why it enjoyed any sort of cult status. During most of the twentieth century *Friðþjófs saga hins frœkna* has been an almost wholly neglected work in the English-speaking world; and the current scholarly silence on the saga is well-nigh deafening. In 1921 Henry Goddard Leach could still speak of *Friðþjófs saga* as amongst the Icelandic sagas 'most familiar to us' (Leach 1921, 162), but we can see now—as Leach could not then—that his words reflect more the residual enthusiasm of previous generations than the condition of long-term decline into which the story's fortunes had already entered. The last English translation of the saga known to the present writer is that of Margaret Schlauch in 1928. By 1931, Bertha Phillpotts uses the past tense when speaking of the saga's popularity (Phillpotts 1931, 18), and the choice of tense seems justified if one reads between the lines of W.A. Craigie's cool judgement, dating from just before the First World War: '[*Friðþjófs saga*] is attractively written, but has not the slightest historical value [...] It would be tedious to enumerate and describe all the other sagas of this type' (1913, 95). Stefán Einarsson (1957, 160) finds room for only seven bland lines about the saga in his *History of Icelandic Literature*. Richard Beck's view (1993 XII 101) that *Friðþjófs saga* is 'amongst the finest' medieval prose works of Icelandic tradition represents a rare modern tribute—and that in the form of an unrevised encyclopædia entry of mature vintage, the youthful judgement of a now deceased senior scholar. Now, in the final decade of the twentieth century, the decline in the saga's fortunes could hardly be more complete, notwithstanding enterprising efforts of the inhabitants of Balestrand and Vangsnes in western Norway to awaken the interest of tourists in the local Viking hero: the giant statue of Friðþjófr has dwarfed all visitors to the area since its erection, a gift of the Kaiser, in 1913 (Marschall 1991, 80f.). In Iceland there is no edition (scholarly or popular) of the saga

readily available—the last one was first published in 1944. Indeed, there
has been no edition with full scholarly apparatus in any language since
the efforts of Ludvig Larsen (1893) and Gustav Wenz (1914). Twentieth-
century critical interest in the saga has also been limited (Gould 1921–
1923; Schlauch 1934; Power 1984; Kalinke 1990, 110–129), even in the
current period of sympathetic scholarly revaluation of other *fornaldarsögur* (Tulinius 1992). The circle of neglect was recently completed
when, in an otherwise illuminating study of *fornaldarsögur* transmission
(Mitchell 1991, 29–31), the author contrives a definition of the genre
which ensures that *Friðþjófs saga* is excluded from his discussion, in
spite of the vivid witness which that work could have brought to bear on
the broader processes of post-medieval literary dissemination and
'revitalisation' of ancient Scandinavian narrative material which the book
seeks to trace.

   Such neglect of the story of Friðþjófr would have seemed incomprehensible in Victorian Britain—and in the Victorian United States, for that
matter. For the saga's first English translator, George Stephens, it
represents 'one of the most beautiful [sagas] in the whole Cycle of
Icelandic literature' (Stephens 1839, vi); Samuel Laing (1844, I 17–23)
sees 'this beautiful story' as among the high points of the 'wonderfully
extensive' Old Icelandic corpus of sagas; writing to friends in advance of
the first publication of his translation, William Morris spoke of it as
'lovely' and 'very complete and beautiful' (Kelvin 1984, 126, 132);
Captain H. Spalding, of the 104th Fusiliers (no less) claims that the
Icelandic story is of 'surpassing beauty' (Spalding 1872, [v]); for Olivia
Stone the story is 'one of the finest [...] the world possesses' (Stone
1882, 27); and for W.P. Ker, a powerful and characteristic voice of late-
Victorian enthusiasm for things Icelandic, it is 'one of the best, and one
of the most famous' (Ker 1896, 277) of the romantic sagas of Iceland, to
be distinguished from the later romances, which he dismisses as 'among
the dreariest things ever made by human fancy' (*ibid*, 281). Parts of the
story found their way into a volume of the 'Library of the World's Best
Literature' series in 1897 (Benson 1926, 150); and in introductory
remarks to his translation (from German) for the Chicago-based series
'Life Stories for Young People' in 1907, George Upton renews the claim
that the tale of Friðþjófr is 'one of the most beautiful' of sagas.

   It was well thought of by those who knew it; and it was widely known.
Indeed, a plausible case can be made for the proposition that in nineteenth-century Britain—indeed throughout nineteenth-century Europe—
the story of Friðþjófr/Frithiof, in either its original or one of its refracted
forms, was better known than any other medieval Icelandic narrative
except the poetic Edda. The original *Friðþjófs saga hins frækna*, in one
or other of its two extant versions, certainly enjoys a unique position in

the history of Icelandic saga reception in the English-speaking world. It was the first complete Icelandic saga ever to be published in an English translation (Stephens 1839): earlier than Samuel Laing's *Heimskringla* (1844), and much earlier than George Webbe Dasent's celebrated versions of *Brennu-Njáls saga* (1861) and *Gísla saga Súrssonar* (1866).[5] Moreover, as we have noted, during the nineteenth century the saga appeared in three separate English translations—more than any other Icelandic saga.[6] Public performances by both William Morris (Kelvin 1984, 130) and John Sephton ahead of the publication of their *Friðþjófs saga* translations ensured that saga-reading appetites were appropriately whetted. Subsequently, re-publication, re-packaging and the preparation of breezy summary versions ensured that various forms of the saga story retained their place in the public domain on both sides of the Atlantic. We thus find a version of the saga in Cox and Jones's *Tales of Teutonic Lands* (1872, 210–246); there was the 1877 Chicago reprint by Rasmus Anderson and Jón Bjarnarson of Stephens' 1839 translation, enterprisingly supplemented by a translation of the later and lamer *Þorsteins saga Víkingssonar*, with its breezy tales of Friðþjófr's troll-slaying father.

Behind the high Victorian profile enjoyed by the Icelandic *Friðþjófs saga hins frækna* through printed translation and summary, moreover, there was the silent witness of several paper manuscripts of the saga awaiting discovery and attention in the libraries of Britain. One such (MS BL Add. 4860), brought back by Sir Joseph Banks at the end of his 1772 visit to Iceland and deposited in the British Museum, offered eighteenth-century texts of fourteen *fornaldarsögur* including *Friðþjófs Þorsteinssonar saga* (BL Cat. 1977, 242). It was joined some years later by MS BL Add. 24972, a manuscript which Sabine Baring-Gould had acquired under the most poignant circumstances during his visit to Akureyri in 1862: 'a native reduced to great poverty' sold it to the British traveller with tearful reluctance: 'These sagas [...] are our joy; without them our long winters would be blanks. You may have these books, but, believe me, it is *prava necessitas* alone which forces me to part with them' (Baring-Gould 1863, 225). Baring-Gould, a far more animated and

---

[5] Dasent was translating directly from the Icelandic: Laing from Danish.

[6] Stephens (1839), Sephton (1894), and William Morris and Eiríkur Magnússon (initially published in 1871; reissued as part of their 1875 *Three Northern Love Stories* which was reprinted in London in 1901, and again in 1911 as volume 10 of Morris's *Collected Works*). The *Friðþjófs saga* translation was reprinted separately in Boston, Mass. in 1900. Morris regarded Stephens' translation as 'vile and not always correct' (Kelvin 1984, 126).

romantically committed enthusiast of Icelandic sagas than the austerely enlightened Sir Joseph Banks ever was, lists 'the story of stalwart Frith-thjof' amongst the 'Histories of Ancient Heroes' in the Bibliography to his 1863 travel book (1863, 439), but remains otherwise silent about the worthy son of Þorsteinn. Baring-Gould had eyes only for the saga-steads of Iceland—and Friðþjófr never went to Iceland.

The British-based manuscripts from Iceland did not even have to be texts of *Friðþjófs saga* to be texts, in a sense, about *Friðþjófs saga*. A Friðþjófr-related manuscript in the Advocates' Library in Edinburgh makes the point. Scotland had been fertile ground for Icelandic enthusiasms since the end of the eighteenth century: Grímur Thorkelín's honorary degree in St. Andrews in 1787 (Benedikz 1970); John Thomas Stanley's party of Edinburgh students exploring Iceland in 1789 (Wawn 1981); Sir George Mackenzie's version of *Gunnlaugs saga ormstungu* on the stage of the Theatre Royal, Edinburgh in 1812 (Wawn 1982); Sir Walter Scott's *The Pirate* (1822) (Wawn 1994a forthcoming); and the appointment in 1826 of a learned Icelander, Þorleifur Repp, to the position of Assistant Keeper of Books at the Advocates' Library, where his duties included the cataloguing and supervision of the collection of Icelandic manuscripts recently purchased from Grímur Thorkelín and Finnur Magnússon (Wawn 1991, 60). These manuscripts included texts of two late eighteenth-/early nineteenth-century sagas attributed (by Repp and others) to the Icelandic lawyer and antiquarian Jón Espólín (Müller 1817–1820, II 672–675; Wawn 1994b forthcoming), *Huldar saga* and *Sagaan af Hálfdani gamla og sonum hans*. The latter work (Adv. MS 21. 2. 7) contains a remarkably large number of references to and summaries of events in *Friðþjófs saga*; Espólín clearly knew the saga well enough, and regarded it highly enough to use events in the life of its hero as major chronological reference points in his own latter-day saga writing.

Friðþjófs saga, or at least its hero, found its way before the eyes of the British public in other improbable ways in the years before its first published appearance in an English translation. A case in point is Ove Malling's *Store og Gode Handlinger af Danske, Norske og Holsterne* (1777), which was translated into English by Andreas Feldborg (Nielsen 1986) and published in 1807 as *Great and Good Deeds of Danes, Norwegians and Holsteinians*. It is not clear how widespread or well-disposed a British readership this (or indeed any) book on Danish virtues could hope to enjoy in the year of the spectacular bombardment of Copenhagen by the British navy: Danish support for Napoleon had not played well in the corridors of Whitehall. Nevertheless, those with sufficient generosity of spirit (eleventh of the sixteen virtues illustrated in Malling's work) to wade through the tales of exemplary Scandinavian heroes, ancient and modern, would learn that what Kjartan Ólafsson was to Integrity, Bartholinus to Learning, and the villagers of Hornbech to Humanity, so Friðþjófr was to Firmness, defined as that quality of steady glowing courage whose nature surpasses the fleeting flames of instinctive boldness (Malling 1807, 119).

It is clear, then, that the Icelandic saga of Friðþjófr was known in Victorian England, and that summary accounts of its hero had been available for pre-Victorian readers to reflect on. Yet, even if all the unread manuscripts of the saga had been edited, and each of the three translations poured over, even if British readers had been tireless in their study of works by Malling, or Jón Espólín, or Þormóður Torfason (Torfæus), a devoted believer in the saga's historicity (Pope 1866; Andersson 1964, 8), it is unlikely that any Victorian cult of Friðþjófr would have developed without one crucial additional impulse. That came in the form of successive English translations of Bishop Esaias Tegnér's 1824 Swedish narrative poem based on the Icelandic saga. Whilst Tegnér's paraphrastic version follows the contours of the saga faithfully enough, there is much importation and amplification of incident, leading to an important new ending in which Frithiof the headstrong destroyer of Balder's temple undertakes its complete restoration as an act of spiritual atonement. The temple priest looks forward to the coming of Christ, the 'new Balder' (Stephens 1839, Bk. 24, stanza xxviii); in the meantime, the poem ends with Frithiof and Ingeborg prostrate in front of the pagan god's restored image. Underpinning such individual narrative modifications, much of work is marked by a striking new lyricism, as signalled in lines from Longfellow's 'Tegnér's Drapa', written to mark the Swedish poet's death in 1847:

> The law of force is dead!
> The law of love prevails!
> Thor, the thunderer,
> Shall rule the earth no more,
> No more, with threats,
> Challenge the meek Christ.
>   (Longfellow 1886, III 285)

It was, if the truth be told, largely because of Tegnér that H.L.D. Ward's 1864 British Museum catalogue of Icelandic manuscripts could refer to the Icelandic saga of 'famous Frithiof' (f. 129). Previously 'locked up [...] in its soft yet sonorous dialect' ([anon.] 1828, 137), the story suddenly became widely accessible: in the period 1833–1914 at least fifteen independent (to a greater or lesser extent) English versions of Tegnér's poem were published (Benson 1926, 146–160). Moreover, the work enjoyed an additional life through the publication of summary

versions: in two translations (Henderson 1872; Upton 1907) of Ferdinand
Schmidt's German version of the story; in Emily Cappel's 1882 selection
of saga re-tellings, published in the 'Illustrated Library of Fairy-Tales'
series; in Lady Clara Paget's privately printed *King Bele of the Sogn
District and Jarl Angantyr of the Orkney Islands* (1894); in Zenaide
Ragozin's *Frithiof—Viking of Norway* (1899); in Margaret Watson's 1897
Dublin Review article in Olive Beaupré Miller's 'Bookhouse for
Children' series (Miller 1920); in Helen Adeline Guerber's *Legends of
the Middle Ages* (1896), and *Myths of the Norsemen from the Eddas and
Sagas* (1909), this latter work making use of extracts from three of the
available Tegnér translations (those of Stephens, Longfellow, and
Spalding).

In lending this wholly new glamour to a faded medieval figure, Tegnér
was to Frithiof what Tennyson was to King Arthur—and over much the
same period. Henry Sweet may have regarded Tegnér's poem as 'rubbish'
(Wawn 1990, 7), but few Victorians agreed with him. In nineteenth-
century Britain there was at least as much a cult of Tegnér's Frithiof as
there was of the Icelandic Friðþjófr. The two figures and the very
different literary works which gave them life were cheerfully intermin-
gled by most Victorian readers untroubled by questions of primary
authenticity: their reception theory and practice was blessedly uncompli-
cated.

The Victorian cult of Friðþjófr/Frithiof extended beyond words to
pictures and music. It is to mainland Scandinavia that one has to look for
a richness and diversity of pictorial responses to the story comparable
with the Arthurian paintings of Victorian England (Mjöberg 1967).
Nevertheless, the tradition of illustrated versions of the story established
by George Stephens' Stockholm translations in 1839 was maintained
subsequently in Britain, as with the gently pre-Raphaelite drawings which
enliven the re-tellings by Cappel (1882) and Guerber (1909). In Allen's
1912 version, the pictures were in creditably good colour. As for music,
George Stephens' Tegnér translation offered enough accompanying songs
to fill (if not enliven) many a Victorian musical evening; whilst, years
later, the coronation entertainment for George V at the Drury Lane
Theatre in London featured Frithiof references via a performance of the
German Kaiser's 'Song of Aegir' (Allen 1912, Preface).

The cult of Friðþjófr/Frithiof also extended to travel. Detailed attention
has been drawn in recent years (Wawn 1987, 1992b; Aho 1993) to the
growth in popularity of Iceland as a visiting place for Victorians weary
of Alpine sublimity and Grecian grandeur. From the 1860s, indeed, there
were complaints that it had become impossible to move in Iceland
without running into parties of up-market British tourists: 'a rush of
vulgar Englishmen, alike ignorant of the language and the manners of the

race' ([anon.] 1876, 223). Similar grumbles can now be heard about the lower slopes of the Himalayas. But the British[7] also journeyed to Norway, a number of them clearly aware of the Friðþjófr/Frithiof legends, and on the lookout for material remains or at least spiritual resonances (for example Forester 1853, 395; Anderson 1853, 16, 77); there were even guidebooks to point the way to the sagasteads (Bennett 1882, 92). One such traveller, R.G. Latham, was more than just aware of the story: he first translated Tegnér's poem as *Frithiof, A Norwegian Story* (1838), then he visited Norway, and finally published his account of *Norway and the Norwegians* (1840).[8] British travellers visiting the Sogn district could sometimes encounter breathless local enthusiasm about Friðþjófr/Frithiof:

> My next adventure was a journey from Balholm [Balestrand] to Sogndal over the mountains, with an old fisherman as porter. On the ascent, we had a glorious view of the scene of 'The Frithjof Saga.' My companion was enchanted, and recited the whole saga most dramatically, going up hill all the time! He lost his wind, and eventually I was obliged to carry both knapsacks again.[9]

By the end of the century, indeed, the knapsacks could have been further weighed down by copies of Edna Lyall's popular (eleventh edition 1893) Victorian novel *The Hardy Norseman*;[10] in which Frithiof, the sturdy young Norwegian hero, successfully woos the impressionable daughter of a visiting English merchant by rowing her up and down Sognefjord reciting the events of the ancient saga in generous detail. How much excitement could a Victorian girl take? Blanche Morgan could not resist the tale, and neither could Victorian Britain.

[7]In the case of Sir Charles Anderson, at least, the same British who had also travelled to Iceland: Anderson 1984.

[8]Latham even quotes extensively from his version of Tegnér's poem in his massive handbook *The English Language* (Fifth edition 1862), pp. 183–186.

[9]Most scholars can recall an occasional instance of noting down an interesting quotation, and subsequently being unable to locate its source. The quotation must therefore either be omitted, or, as here, accompanied by an apologetic footnote. It derives from an elusive Victorian travel book about Norway.

[10]I am grateful to Dr Carolyne Larrington for drawing my attention to this non-canonical classic.

WHY FRIÐÞJÓFR/FRITHIOF?

The widespread Victorian fascination with 'stalwart Frith-thjof' is more easily demonstrated than accounted for, however. That the saga was popular is clear; why it was popular is a more complicated question. *Friðþjófs saga hins frækna,* with its resolutely Norwegian (and Orcadian) setting, could never hope to win a place in the honoured canon of sagas narrating heroic events from the settlement period in Iceland; consequently, its characters, events and spirit were never invoked by nineteenth-century Icelanders in connection with their struggle for independence. At least one prominent nineteenth-century Icelander, Guðbrandur Vigfússon, was quite baffled by the phenomenon of the saga's popularity. Asked what he thought of the 1875 Morris/Eiríkur Magnússon *Three Northern Love Stories* volume containing translations of *Friðþjófs saga, Víglundar saga* (heavily influenced by *Friðþjófs saga*) and *Gunnlaugs saga ormstungu,* the curmudgeonly Guðbrandur replied, 'I am sick of love stories,' regarding their 'sentimental moonshine' as an unseemly aspect of Iceland's literary past, and quite unsuitable for importation to Britain (Bredsdorff 1960, 305). Guðbrandur's dismissive judgement, rather different from the sympathetic engagement with the saga which he had exhibited when visiting Sogn in 1854 (Guðbrandur Vigfússon 1990, 51, 53), was no doubt generated in part by Eiríkur Magnússon's involvement with the *Three Northern Love Stories* volume: by 1875 the two distinguished philologists had become bitter opponents on both a personal and professional level.

As its translator, Eiríkur himself was naturally more benevolently inclined towards the saga. Quite apart from his published translation, his library (as catalogued after his death by Bertha Phillpotts: Lbs. 405 fol.) contained English translations of Tegnér's poem by Latham (1838), Spalding (1872), and Hamel (1874), with his copy of the Spalding version heavily annotated and corrected. He was also in possession of a French translation of the Icelandic text, a complimentary copy from the editor Félix Wagner in 1904;[11] and of the first published Icelandic translation of Tegnér's poem, the work of Matthías Jochumsson in

---

[11]Reviewed by W.G. Collingwood in *Saga-Book* 4 (1905), 253–254.

1864.[12] When Messrs Marcus Ward contemplated the publication of yet another Tegnér translation, Eiríkur was invited to write the introduction: 'you are the man to do it' (Lbs. 2189a 4to, Robert Pritchett, undated). Eiríkur was also consulted by Beatrice Clay, an enthusiastic former pupil and subsequently a Chester school-teacher, who had written a play based on the Icelandic saga version: could Eiríkur advise her as to the date of the saga, on appropriate vestments for the pagan priests, on Old Icelandic forms of divination and casting of spells, on whether Norwegian and Icelandic customs were identical, on whether Ingibjörg would look better in blue or scarlet, and on his view of Miss Skeat's alternative ending to the saga, written in order 'to bring the conclusion into accord with modern feeling' (Lbs. 2186b 4to, 27 September 1911)?

Yet, for all his many-faceted engagement with the Friðþjófr and Frithiof works, Eiríkur's explanation for the saga's popularity (in a draft review of Goddard 1871: Lbs. 405 fol.) seems defiantly simplistic. In his view *Friðþjófs saga* was written 'for the evident purpose of a merry evening [...] of making the listeners merely merry'. He speculates that it may be a 'determined chaff on the gods who in this story are kept alive by being baked and greased by women before the fire, which is evidently meant as a burlesque presentation of the old custom in the north for the old decrepit men to have their backs rubbed by the fire in winter' (Lbs. 405 fol.). Eiríkur had little sympathy for readings of this saga (or of any other tale in the Julia Goddard *Wonderful Stories from Northern Lands* collection which he was reviewing) which sought relentlessly to identify some displaced solar myth behind the narrative: as with 'Gods and men all mourn the absence of the bright being without whom life and gladness seem alike to belong' (G.W. Cox, Introduction to Goddard 1871, xiv). Ingibjörg's marriage to Hringr is likened by Cox to Baldr's death, Iðunn's abduction, and Rapunzel's claustration—all are assigned to an infinitely flexible 'absences of the bright' category. Small wonder Eiríkur felt that Cox had been wounded by the 'mistletoe of one-sidedness'.[13]

---

[12]There is a little-known Icelandic version of Tegnér's *Frithiof* which pre-dates that of Matthías Jochumsson. The author is séra Guðmundur Torfason (1798–1879), who had never read a word of Swedish when he began, and enjoyed no help from any dictionary or translation. There are three texts of this version: Lbs. 480 4to, Lbs. 2399 4to, ÍB 10 8vo. The preface to this latter text is dated 12 February 1846. Séra Guðmundur says that the original is rightly regarded as *snylli verk* [a work of genius].

[13]Cox was not alone, however, in his mythic readings. The Norwegian Rudolf Keyser, who was lecturing on *Friðþjófs saga* at Christiania University as early as 1830 (Wiesener 1913, 62), also argued that the story was fundamentally

The question of Friðþjófr's/Frithiof's popularity in Victorian Britain can certainly be addressed more searchingly than either Guðbrandur or Eiríkur managed to do. Some straightforward explanations suggest themselves immediately. Firstly, there was the lingering popularity of Ossian. The Reverend William Strong, first English translator of the Bishop Tegnér version, includes on the title-page of his 1833 volume a quotation from Tegnér which confirms the link. Those who had responded to the misty melancholy of the Ossianic *œuvre*, as millions of readers all over Europe certainly had, would also relish the Frithiof romance:

> If you prefer the significant and profound, what ministers to serious-ness and contemplation; if you delight in the gigantic, but pale forms which float on the mist, and darkly whisper of the world of the spirits, and of the vanity of all things save true honour—then I must refer you to the hoary—to the saga-stored world of the North, where Vala chanted the key tone of creation, whilst the moon shone upon the cliffs, the brook trilled its monotonous lay, and seated on the summit of a gilded birch, the night-bird sang an elegy upon the brief summer—a dirge over expiring nature.

The mist, the moonlight, the night-bird, the spirits, the whispers, the gloom, the pathos: admirers of Keats as well as of Ossian would have been alerted instantly, and Ossian was to remain a constant reference point in commentary notes provided by British translators throughout the nineteenth century. Secondly, the story of Friðþjófr/Frithiof is a bridal-quest medieval romance, and as such was likely to find a receptive readership amongst British antiquaries rediscovering their own native traditions of medieval chivalry and romance. The saga, notably the hero's remarkably patient wait to recover his bride, was seen as a significant text for understanding the origins of medieval chivalry (Muckleston 1862, v). Thirdly, the story of Friðþjófr/Frithiof earned its popularity through its memorable poetic sequence of poems which accompanied the prose narrative of the hero's hazardous voyage to the Orkney Isles. In the words of the Oxonian Icelandophile Frederick Metcalfe, it is a scene 'so vivid and lifelike that our breath bates and our limbs move in unison as we read of his hair-breadth escapes and deeds of daring' (Metcalfe 1880, 287). Nineteenth-century Britain saw itself as the greatest sea-power on earth, and many British readers exhibited a powerful appetite for nautical adventure stories—anything from Captain Marryat to Conrad. Nor was this simply the taste of *Boys' Own* magazine. In his 1877 Oxford prize-

mythic, albeit that the treatment was thoroughly romantic (Keyser 1854, 63f.).

winning essay *The Place of Iceland in the History of European Institu-tions*, C.A. Vansittart Conybeare voices the widespread feeling that 'it is to the seafaring instincts of the [Viking] race that England owes that naval supremacy which has long been her glory, and is still her strength' (Conybeare 1877, 4).[14] Such feelings were clearly still alive half a century later, when the perilous voyage sections of the Morris/Eiríkur Magnússon *Friðþjófs saga* translation were included in a published collection of *Great Sea Stories of All Nations* (Tomlinson 1930, 993–999).

A fourth and related point is that the Friðþjófr/Frithiof story benefited from its local (for British readers) Orcadian links. Two of the Icelandic saga fragments first translated into English were published principally because of their local interest to readers in the British Isles: James Johnstone's 1782 version of the final part of *Hákonar saga gamla Hákonarson* (which tells of the Norwegian king's final and fatal expedition to Scotland), and Grímur Thorkelín's 1788 extract from *Laxdæla saga,* which concentrates on Melkorka's Irish ancestry. There is a draft translation of parts of *Orkneyinga saga* dating from *c.* 1830 (Scottish Registry Office, Heddle MS GD 263/124, unidentified translator 'Mr W.W.'), a decade before the first published saga translations of George Stephens or Samuel Laing. The Orkney and Shetland Isles, still in the early nineteenth century remote destinations for all except travellers to Iceland, had also found their way into the drawing rooms of Victorian Britain through Sir Walter Scott's richly evocative 1822 novel *The Pirate,* whose eery events take place in both locations, and whose characters are frequently cited in Victorian travel books about Norway and Iceland. In fact the post-Victorian reception of Scott's novel resembles all too closely that of *Friðþjófs saga*—there is as yet no really modern edition, and hardly anyone now reads it; but the many Victorian enthusiasts of the novel, whether sympathetic to the romantic Viking vision of Minna Troil, or the sturdy udaller values of her father Magnus, would have followed the progress of Friðþjófr/Frithiof to and through Orkney with particular interest.

Merry evenings at home, a taste for salty sea-stories, the romance of the misty and saga-stored North, Orcadian localism: all these factors may well have helped to win an audience for the story of Friðþjófr/Frithiof in Victorian Britain. Arguably, though, there were other broader intellectual currents playing around its reception. Firstly, there was the question of

[14]Amongst the British authors widely read in nineteenth-century Iceland was Captain Frederick Marryat, many of whose stories (such as *Mr Midshipman Easy*) are of just this type.

language. It was important that the language of the George Stephens' pioneering translation of *Friðþjófs saga hins frækna* was English and not Latin. Latin had served medieval Icelandic literature nobly throughout the period of the European Enlightenment. The dual-language editions of Eddic poems and sagas published in Copenhagen under the auspices of the Arnamagnæan commission had won many new readers and much prestige for these previously little-known works. By 1839 the linguistic theories of Rasmus Rask and the Grimms had begun to be absorbed in Britain (Aarsleff 1983, 162–210) with the result that previously acknowledged hierarchies of language were now unsustainable—Latin and Greek could no longer enjoy an unchallenged rule of the cultural roost. The serious study of Old English and Old Icelandic texts (not least *Friðþjófs saga)* flourished in the new atmosphere. Ideally this and every other saga deserved to be read in its original language, but in the years prior to the publication of the 1874 Cleasby-Vigfússon *Icelandic-English Dictionary*, this was very much a counsel of perfection. People relied on translations, with Latin now to be superseded by English. For George Stephens this was not before time. He regarded Latin as the language of corrupt and despotic Rome (Stephens 1883, 413–414).[15] Written originally in one Northern vernacular, sagas ought always to be translated into another. Stephens' particular problem as *Friðþjófs saga*'s first English translator was to find an appropriate voice for Icelandic narrative prose in a nineteenth-century English language much of whose educated vocabulary and syntax remained heavily Latinate. First in the field, Stephens had no stylistic models to work from, but he did have an ideology, albeit an eccentric one, to refer to.

Stephens believed that there had originally been a single common Scandinavian language, out of which had developed local variants such as middle voice verbs and suffixed definite articles after the arrival of the Vikings in England. That original common language was, he claimed, the language of Old Northern England—the language of the Danelaw and, even, the language of his native Old Northern Merseyside (Stephens

---

[15]There was, it must be said, in George Stephens a strong element of the cantankerous ex-patriot. He had been introduced to Northern literature by his brother Joseph, a hot-headed reforming pastor who established a ministry in Stockholm (Bradley 1898). George Stephens prepared and published his *Friðþjófs saga* translation in the same city. He was to spend most of his adult life as Professor of North European Languages in the University of Copenhagen, a controversial runologist, and fiery disciple of the principles of linguistic purification as applied to the English language. Not for him any alien Grecian 'Prologue': he was assuredly a 'for-mole' (OI *formáli*) man.

1883, 320–322). Throughout his life Stephens strongly resisted claims that English was a fundamentally German language, despising 'den modern trafik at germanisere England og Englænderne' (Stephens 1890, 27). When searching for the origins of early English society, scholars and true Englishmen should look to, learn about, and celebrate the Norse inheritance, and pay less—a lot less—attention to Germany. Moreover, Stephens argues, the much-bruited German mythology was not German at all, but rather a modern German misappropriation of older Scandinavian and English sources (Stephens 1883, 306). So when considering the first appearance of the Icelandic *Friðþjófs saga* in English, we need to be sensitive to the political implications of Stephens' chosen language and style. The opening paragraph reads thus:

> This Saga begins as follows.—King Bele governed Sygna-fylke, in Norway; he had three children; Helge was his first son, Halfdan his second, and his third child was Ingeborg, a daughter. Ingeborg was fair to look upon, and of great understanding, and was reckoned first and best among the royal offspring. There, west of the frith, stretched the strand, and thereupon stood a considerable village called Balder's Hage, where was a Sanctuary and a great Temple, hedged round about with a lofty plank-work. Here were many Gods, but Balder was the most honoured among them all; and so zealous were those heathen men, that they had forbidden any harm being done there to either man or beast, nor could a male have any converse with a woman. At Syrstrand was the dwelling of the King, but on the other side the firth was a village called Framnås, where lived that man hight Thorsten the son of Viking, and his village lay opposite the residence of the King. Thorsten's spouse bore him a son called Frithiof, who was the tallest and strongest of men, and, from his very youth, was versed in all manner of exploits; hereby got he the name Frithiof the Bold, and was so happy in his friends that all men wished him well. (Stephens 1839, 3–4)

We observe the translator's apparently determined attempt at linguistic archaism, reinforced in the original text by a Gothic typeface. Noteworthy features include a fondness for coordinate syntax throughout the opening section, inversions, alliterative clusters, vocabulary of Northern origin, phrasal contractions, and compound nouns. Overall, Stephens's translation is uncertain in its register, with determined austerity subverted by occasional glimpses of regency grandeur. Yet, whilst saga translation searches here for its own stylistic decorum, an ideological subtext is discernible. I believe that Stephens sought to develop a method of translation which had its verbal roots in 'that mighty and noble and thoroly Scandinavian (*Old* Scandinavian) NORTH ENGLISH which is now the birth-tung of England and her colonies' (Stephens 1884, xv), and, by extension, in the Norse culture which he idolised all his life, and whose imprint could still proudly be identified both in the legislative and legal procedures at home, and in the imperial strength and influence which Britain wielded abroad.

If the style of Stephens' saga translation may have had cultural and political implications which flicker around the Gothic print on the page, similar resonances were identified in the story itself. The preface to Oscar Baker's 1841 English version of the Tegnér poem claims: 'It is in these sagas [...] that we have to look for the origin of the political institutions of England'. The institutions which the translator had in mind were trial by jury, representative legislature, freedom of speech, the right to own property, the security of that property, and the ability of the individual to influence public affairs. In making these claims, Baker was already firmly under the influence of the Orcadian scholar Samuel Laing, whose *Journal of a Residence in Norway during the Years 1834, 1835, 1836* is as eloquent a record of Laing's admiration for Norwegian culture as his parallel volume on Sweden (Laing 1838) is a stern indictment of the haughty feudalism of the Swedes. In Laing's Norway *Journal* are to be found in distillate form the political attitudes which were to dominate the hugely influential preface to his 1844 translation of Snorri Sturluson's *Heimskringla*. Twelve years earlier the British government had commissioned an Icelander to write a book on the origins of the jury system in Britain; his name was Þorleifur Repp, and he argued with abundant illustration from Edda, saga, and chronicle that the British system was indeed securely based on Scandinavian models (Wawn 1991, 95–101). Repp himself soon vanished from Britain, and his book was little cited subsequently; but it would be difficult to exaggerate the influence throughout nineteenth-century Britain of Laing's *Heimskringla* preface and its claims about the essentially Norse nature of such British institutions as trial by jury. They are repeated everywhere: in school books, travel accounts, academic treatises, prize essays, poems, and prefaces to translations of *Friðþjófs saga*/*Frithiofs saga*. A single further instance must serve for many. In the opening section of William and Mary Howitt's *The Literature and Romance of North Europe* (1852), there is an unblushing celebration of Britain's imperial prowess—the power and prestige, the political stability, the enterprise, the commerce, the territorial conquests, the diffusion of the language, the ubiquity of the British fleet. None of these triumphs could have happened if the English race really had been of Anglo-Saxon origin. The modern Saxon Germans are seen as a passive and slavish race, with no tradition of representative government or justice (Howitt 1852, 3–4). Never mind searching for the forefathers of England in the pages of Tacitus's over-promoted *Germania*; much better to examine the myths and sagas of Scandinavia.

Several pages of Laing's *Heimskringla* preface are then quoted with ringing approval.

QUEEN VICTORIA'S SAGA

Filtered through Laing's construction of ancient Scandinavia, the Friðþjófr/Frithiof story can be made to sound very democratic, very un-German, very Northern, and for that matter very male (an issue to be addressed later in the essay). None of these characteristics will have commended the saga to the very undemocratic, rather German, and very female Queen Victoria, whose attitude to Northern England is best (if no doubt apocryphally) expressed in her habit of drawing the curtains on the royal train when passing through the region so as not to be distressed by the satanic grime. How, then, did Queen Victoria and the household at Windsor cope with the saga of Friðþjófr/Frithiof?

This is no idle question. The very first of the Victorian translations of Tegnér's Frithiof poem was dedicated to the youthful Princess Alexandrina Victoria, just four years before she was crowned queen. The translator was the Reverend William Strong, King George IV's Chaplain in Ordinary at Windsor. *Frithiof's saga* was thus not just a Victorian story: it was, from its earliest exposure in nineteenth-century Britain, Victoria's story. Its title-page identifies the work as 'a Skandinavian Legend of Royal Love', whilst the preface assures us that Princess Victoria represents 'a living impersonation of the graces and attractions, of the inflexible rectitude and fine sensibility, of the conscious dignity and patriotic devotion, of all the native attributes ascribed by the fiction of the poet to the Royal Maiden of Norway'. Here was just the Scandinavian tale to encourage Victorian matrons, shocked by Sarah Bernhardt's Cleopatra, to cry 'how *very* like the home life of our own dear Queen' (*ODQ* 1980, 5/20). Tegnér's Ingeborg is physically beautiful but demure and sexually unthreatening; she is self-effacingly obedient to her brothers; in her refusal to elope with Frithiof, and in her willingness to marry the affable but wrinkled King Ring, she places familial duty before private love: 'the glorious conquest of the sense of female dignity and patriotic duty, over fervent and deep-rooted affection' (Strong 1833, xiii). In this early Anglican version of the 'male gaze', passive female stoicism is made to seem an active virtue. Throughout Strong's version of Tegnér, the presentation of the two lovers is a great deal more lyrical than in the Icelandic saga, where Ingibjörg in particular seems more moody and taciturn. The courage and camaraderie of Frithiof and his crew during their tumultuous sea-voyage is properly celebrated but, unlike the ending of the Icelandic saga where Friðþjófr kills Helgi before receiving

Hálfdan's submission, Tegnér's hero slays no-one: Helgi dies in an ignominious accident, crushed by a falling idol in a pagan temple in Finland (Stephens 1839, Bk. 24, stanza xxx). Indeed, despite the wit of Tegnér's Frithiof, his mental strength during the storm, and his consummate skill as a poet, it is the Ingeborg/Victoria figure who is the focus of all the hero's actions and most of the reader's thoughts. Strong's edition thus becomes a sonorous tribute to the future head of Britain's beloved royal family.

Yet in Britain in the 1830s Britain's royal family was not especially beloved. By no means everyone shared the royal chaplain's trembling obsequiousness. This was, after all, the age of revolution in Europe; the age of the reform bills in Britain. There were those for whom the monarchy had become a circus, full of foreigners, mostly German. The majesty of monarchy, fast fading in late twentieth-century Britain, has been seen as a creation of the late nineteenth-century royal spin-doctors, nurtured subsequently by an alliance of canny newspaper editors and craven Reithian broadcasters. David Cannadine reminds us of the seediness of royal ceremony in the early nineteenth century (Hobsbawm and Ranger 1983, 118): that at the funeral of Princess Charlotte the pallbearers had been drunk; at the coronation of George IV prize-fighters had to be employed to control the guests; at the funeral of that same unlamented monarch the service was frequently disturbed by the embarrassingly loud voice of the as yet uncrowned King William IV; at the Windsor wedding of Princess Alexandra, the travel arrangements were so chaotic that the Prime Minister had to return to London in a third-class railway coach, accompanied by Disraeli sitting on his wife's knee; whilst at the coronation of Victoria herself, the wrong-sized rings were produced for her finger. Knowledge of this comedy of errors may have been confined to the high-born few: but the *Times* obituary for George IV was available to the lower-born many. It was a merciless indictment: 'most reckless, unceasing and unbounded prodigality [...] tawdry childishness [...] indifference to the feelings of others', and, even worse, 'the late King had many generations of intimates with whom he led a course of life, the character of which rose little higher than that of animal indulgence' (Hibbert 1976, 782–783). From the time of George III onwards monarchy had too often meant madness or mistresses, or both. Victoria's immediate predecessor as monarch, the bluff King William IV, was a more popular figure than George IV (he could hardly have been less popular), but at the time of the young Princess of Kent's accession to the throne in 1837, the monarchy could not assume the unquestioning loyalty and esteem of its subjects. In an age of revolution, there was no guarantee that the monarchy would last the century—or even the decade. Viewed in this light, whilst the Royal Chaplain's version of Tegnér's

Frithiof's saga remains primarily a work of literary obeisance, it is possible also to identify a monitory element in it. Ingeborg represents what any Queen of England ought to be like, with the story as a whole assuming the role of a contemporary Mirror for Princes(ses)—a cautionary tale, as much anxiously prescriptive as securely descriptive.

If for William Strong *Frithiof's saga* was firstly a story about monarchical duty and morality, it was also a story about religious faith. The Icelandic *Friðþjófs saga* offers the potentially disturbing (to Victorian ears) vision that temples of religion were places where courting couples could engage in illicit love-making, and places which could be burnt down without remorse. In the saga Friðþjófr ultimately trusts himself rather than the pagan gods; no Christian god is mentioned. Tegnér's poem will have seemed altogether more congenial to Princess Victoria's chaplain. The God Balder is treated far more respectfully than in the saga. Indeed, the love of Frithiof and Ingeborg is spoken of as an earthly reflection of Balder's love for his wife Nanna in Norse myth; the burning down of Balder's temple is seen as an act of desecration; and Frithiof's final action in the poem is to rebuild the temple as an act of atonement. The poem's paganism is presented as the natural religion of the righteous heathen awaiting fulfilment in Christianity, and commanded respect as such. Victoria's chaplain, one of Tegnér's first literary critics in Britain, interprets the restoration of Balder's temple as 'a victory of the religious principle over youthful arrogance'. George Stephens was amongst those to claim that for Victorian England, any 'religious principle' (even paganism—even Catholicism) was preferable to materialistic nihilism.

This was indeed the view of other mid-century Victorians as, like John Newton in his Liverpool lecture, they tried to accommodate new Darwinian theories on the origin of species. The publication in English translation of J.J.A. Worsaae's *The Primeval Antiquities of Denmark*, a study of stone-age and iron-age Denmark, had played an important part in challenging the idea of literal biblical time, and the notion of original Edenic purity and subsequent degeneration. History should rather be seen as progress: but what sort of progress? For some it was a random evolutionary process governed solely by the laws of physics and chemistry rather than by any divine providence. Skulls grew larger, and brains expanded to fill the space. The Iceland explorers Sir George Mackenzie and Robert Chambers were amongst those who lent their support to such theories (Bowler 1989, 88–89). Progress of this sort could hardly be depicted in terms of a ladder with steps leading up to some single divine purpose; evolution was more like a tree with roots and branches leading everywhere or nowhere, but with no central bough. This was potentially all very disturbing. Where in this model, for instance, could a place be found for divine authority?

There are some striking parallels here with what the new philologists were saying about language. Traditionally, languages had been perceived in terms of a hierarchy, headed by Greek and Latin, and with all the other tongues representing subsequent stages of development and (in the eyes of many) degeneration. In George Webbe Dasent's somewhat tendentious formulation, 'Greek and Latin [had] lorded it over the other languages of the earth [...] twin tyrants [...] with a pedant's rod' (Dasent 1903, xviii). The new philology had demonstrated that all ancient and modern European languages were siblings descended from some more remote Indo-European parent language, whose very existence had been revealed by scholars such as Sir William Jones who had been able to study Sanskrit whilst residing in India serving the needs of an expanding empire. For some the link between ancient philology and modern imperial power was a source of triumphalist confidence: 'The Saxon now rule[s] with uncontrolled sway over that antique land, whence the heritage he so gloriously holds was originally transmitted to him' (Blackwell 1873, 45). The study of Old Icelandic in Britain had certainly benefited from challenges to the enshrined prestige of Graeco-Roman antiquity. Yet, ultimately, in dethroning Greek and Latin, the New Philology was not about to enthrone Anglo-Saxon and Old Icelandic in their place as some alternative cultural and linguistic gold standard. This was a source of disillusion for the zealous supporters of both languages. When the effects of the New Philology, and of Darwin's theories were reflected upon, there was much unease at the erosion of linguistic, moral and spiritual authority which many people attributed to them (Dowling 1986).

It is small wonder, then, that even as early as 1833 a British Royal Chaplain in Ordinary had seized on Tegnér's version of the Frithiof tale as a source of spiritual solace. It is even less surprising that, as the century progressed, many other readers empathised with the poem's lyrical piety: 'its story is that of a fine nature, driven, half-unwittingly into wrong-doing; of his repentance, atonement, and final forgiveness' (Watson 1897, 30). Here was the kind of Old Northern story which the New Philology may have helped to highlight, but which in Bishop Tegnér's version could be reconciled securely with the central importance of the 'religious principle'.

THE VICTORIAN POLITICS OF FRIÐÞJÓFS/FRITHIOFS SAGA

We have seen, then, that within the walls of Windsor castle the story of Frithiof was read as a tale about duty and loyalty; and also as a paean of praise for worthy paganism, highlighting the importance of retaining and revitalising one's religious faith. Outside the royal circle, a range of more robust and less deferential readings emerged. Firstly, the story's treatment of the Friðþjófr/Frithiof figure drew attention to the theme of 'manliness', to employ (with appropriate diffidence) a much-used word in Victorian writings about the North. By it was signified the vigorous, buccaneering spirit which had once helped to create and must now sustain the modern British Empire. That spirit was even associated with the sound of the old Northern language: in Sir George Dasent's view the Viking forefathers of the English 'spoke with a manly mouth', whilst the diphthongs of the decadent, house-bound West Saxons sounded 'mincing' (Dasent 1873 I 14). The problem was, how to instil Viking virtues in Victorian manhood, and one answer lay in the public schools of Britain, such as that in which the Iceland explorer Sabine Baring-Gould taught: cold showers in the morning, Viking stories on Sunday afternoon walks, and bracing floggings in the evening. The first ever Victorian Viking novel, *The Icelander's Sword, or The Sword of Oraefadal*, was the work of Baring-Gould in the years immediately preceding his 1862 journey to Iceland; he published it in twenty short episodes in the magazine of Hurstpierpoint School. On his return from Iceland (with his manuscript of *Friðþjófs saga*), and under pressure from former pupils who were themselves now parents, Baring-Gould was prevailed upon to publish his re-telling (for schoolboys) of *Grettis saga,* complete with pictures marking the stages in Grettir's awkward progress from gilded youth to gallant old age. Tegnér's Frithiof story also appeared in illustrated versions for children. In 1833 the Windsor chaplain may have seen the story as focusing primarily on the Ingeborg/Victoria figure; but for the illustrator of G.C. Allen's 1912 version, it was the glamorous hero who took centre stage. We see him (in colour) in various guises: on a snow-covered hillside brandishing his gleaming Excalibur-lookalike sword; attempting to persuade a demurely Pre-Raphaelite Ingeborg to elope; and fearlessly piloting the magic ship through the devilish storm, with the vessel's dragon head exhibiting considerably more fear than the defiant features of stalwart Frithiof. In the illustration which shows the firing of Balder's temple, the hero is depicted as the soul of stern righteousness towering over Jezebel-like female figures—clearly the artist (T.H. Robinson) understood this scene somewhat differently from William Strong. Far from troubling Victorian readers, Frithiof's sexual patience—not to say reticence—may have proved a positive recommendation.

Outside Windsor, too, as I have already suggested briefly, the Friðþjófr/Frithiof story was read as a challenging account of ancient democratic processes. This theme is worth developing here in greater detail. The tale offers several archetypal images of the process whereby

power ought to pass from older generation to younger. It can certainly be
read as a rite of passage narrative about an individual—a kind of family
drama sequence—but it was also read at a more social level as a story
about legitimising authority within a community. The two brothers offer
a negative model of this process: inheriting their father's royal power by
hereditary succession, they abuse it, and are unable to defend it convincingly against a threat from outside the kingdom. Their authority is
unconvincing because it is, in a sense, immature—the young men demand
or assume by virtue of their inherited titles a deference which they have
yet to earn, and which has not been popularly bestowed. They huddle
regressively on their dead father's mound; they are defenceless against
and capitulate to the elderly King Hringr/Ring, himself an urbane father
figure. The brothers are unable to raise a popular force to fight him,
because their power has no popular mandate. They then seek to employ
the supernatural power of the witches (aficionados of Bruno Bettelheim
might be tempted to designate these as displaced mother figures) to
sustain their authority.

Friðþjófr/Frithiof, by contrast, is of honourable but not royal birth, and
has thus to earn and then to have granted by consent of the community
any authority which he is to exercise. He has to win by nature what
nurture has not provided. When the brothers burn down his home village,
it is as if in the underlying symbolic logic of the story the hero is being
forced to become his own man, to leave home, to quest, to place himself
in jeopardy, and eventually to wait like the most patient of Prince
Charmings until his Sleeping Beauty wakes up. King Hringr's/Ring's
children by Ingibjörg/Ingeborg will rule their kingdom, while Friðþjófr/
Frithiof and his new wife defeat the discredited brothers and establish a
new dynasty based, especially in Tegnér's poem, not on automatic
hereditary succession but on popular consent formally expressed. There
were plenty of opportunities for Friðþjófr/Frithiof to seize power by
stealth. He could have allowed the elderly King Hringr/Ring to drown in
the ice during a sledging accident, but he rescues him; he could have
murdered the old king whilst he lay, sword at his side, sleeping in the
woods during a hunting trip, but Friðþjófr/Frithiof, having drawn the
weapon, throws it away. After the old king's death, he could have
usurped the throne from Hringr's/Ring's children, but instead (like
Beowulf's treatment of Hrothgar's heirs) he guards it selflessly until they
themselves are old enough to exercise the power which is popularly
bestowed on them at a great thing meeting near the end of Tegnér's
poem.

That is the model of constitutional royal power on offer, certainly in
Tegnér's work: an elective monarchy, legitimised by popular vote. Such
a system is commended in the dying King Beli's speech to Halfdan his

son. George Stephens' 1839 accompanying commentary leaves no doubt as to the intensity of his own views on this issue:

> The Kingship of the old North was originally, as it should be—an Elective Presidency; though the history of the Scandinavian kingdoms affords melancholy proof enough, how respect for the 'divine races' (as the families said to be descended from Oden were called) overwhelmed the land with destructive minorities, or imbecile manhood. With the 'hereditary principle', whether monarchic or aristocratic equally cementing Dynasties formed in Kingdoms gained by the sword, came in also 'hereditary degradation'. (Stephens 1839, 228)

The detecable undertow of asperity becomes a flood tide in the lines from Alexander Pope to which the conscientious reader is then directed. First on monarchical authority:

> Who first taught souls enslav'd, and realms undone,
> Th' enormous faith of many made for one;
> That proud exception to all Nature's laws,
> T'invert the world, and counter-work its Cause?
> Force first made Conquest, and that conquest, Law;
> 'Till Superstition taught the tyrant awe,
> Then shar'd the Tyranny, then lent it aid,
> And Gods of Conqu'rors, Slaves of Subjects made:
> (Essay on Man, III 241–248)

Then attention is drawn to Pope's withering scorn at the expense of the hereditary principle:

> Stuck o'er with titles and hung round with strings,
> That thou mays't be by kings, or whores of kings.
> Boast the pure blood of an illustrious race,
> In quiet flow from Lucrece to Lucrece:
> But by your father's worth if your's you rate,
> Count me those only who were good and great.
> Go! if your ancient but ignoble blood
> Has crept thro' scoundrels ever since the flood,
> Go! and pretend your family is young;
> Nor own, your fathers have been fools so long.
> What can ennoble sots, or slaves, or cowards?
> Alas! not all the blood of all the HOWARDS.
> (Essay on Man, IV 205–216)

There can thus be no doubt as to the sharply politicised nature of George Stephens' attachment to the Friðþjófr/Frithiof story.

Belief in power legitimised by popular acclaim; rejection of the hereditary principle with its long lines of in-bred lunatics: these were

positions unlikely to promote the cause of George Stephens' Friðþjófr/
Frithiof volume with the British royal family. The supine obsequiousness
of William Strong's 1833 preface was much more in line with their house
style. King William IV's brief reign had certainly not been marked by
any monarchical inclination to submit meekly to the will of the people,
however expressed: the king dismissed the government three times in
seven years, he twice dissolved parliament ahead of time, and interfered
in the formation of coalition administrations (Gash 1965, 5).

Stephens was not alone amongst Victorian saga translators in his
aversion to such abuses of hereditary power. In an essay on Viking
virtues written immediately before beginning work on his famous
translation of *Njáls saga,* George Webbe Dasent strikes a similarly
uncompromising note:

> We do not, now-a-days stop to inquire if the infant be deformed or
> a cripple. With us the old house will stand as well upon a crooked as
> upon a straight support. But in Iceland, in the tenth century, as in all
> branches of that great family, it was only healthy children that were
> allowed to live. The deformed, as a burden to themselves, their
> friends and to society, were consigned to destruction by exposure to
> the mercy of the elements [...]. In this old age of the world the law
> holds us in her leading-strings, as though we had fallen into a second
> childhood [...] for incapacity that [Viking] age had no mercy. No
> 'tenth transmitter of a foolish face' would have been tolerated merely
> because one of his ancestors, generations back, had been a man of
> merit. (Dasent 1858, 211–212)

The virtues of a vigorous representative democracy were also extolled
by Samuel Laing. In his travels through Norway he had warmed to the
culture of the small farmer (Laing 1844 I 99–100; 1854, 258). It was
indeed on the farm of one such 'bonder' during his winter stay in
Norway that Laing had first read *Heimskringla* in a Danish translation
(Laing 1844 I 202). And what did an Orcadian liberal such as Laing find
so sympathetic in Snorri's great work? The answer appears to be: all
those meetings, all those speeches, all that acrimony, all that artful
persuasion which participatory democracy encourages (Laing 1844, I
114–117). Such a system was infinitely preferable to the 'slavish torpidity
and superstitious lethargy' (*ibid,* 15) of priest-ridden Southern Europe,
with the peoples enslaved precisely because they had no property to
protect, and hence no inclination or reason to assert themselves politically. In Britain Laing mocked the monarchy for its abuses of power and
feckless triviality: life at Holyrood House was dismissed as a 'puppet
show' (Laing 1854, 247). In Norway it had never been possible to build
such castles on the ground—never mind in the air: the rock was too hard,
as if even geology had conspired to frown on feudalism (Laing 1844, I

120). Nor, in the absence of any system of primogeniture, was it possible to accumulate large holdings of land. Accordingly, Laing has much to say about the virtues of the small and independent landholder, the udaller. The accession of any new monarch had to be proposed and agreed by the 'bonder' class at district and national thing meetings. A royal daughter could contemplate marriage to a bonder without hesitation: 'there was no idea of disparagement, or inferiority, in such alliance' (Laing 1844, I 104-105). Indeed, though perhaps more franklin than farmer, Friðþjófr's/ Frithiof's suit for Ingibjörg/Ingeborg needs to be seen in this positive light. Udallers held their land in free: subject to no-one, taxed by no-one, forfeitable to no-one. Much better forty small independent farms run this way, than thirty-nine small farms subject to the arbitrary control of a single overbearing feudal lord, some latter-day Helgi or Hálfdan figure.

Friðþjófr's/Frithiof's Orcadian adventures may also have had a political dimension for Victorian readers. Samuel Laing was an Orcadian who had relished finding the values of his native islands alive in Norway and dead in Sweden. Another Orcadian, Alfred Johnstone, was Secretary of the Viking Club many of whose founding members had strong Orcadian and Shetlandic links (Townsend 1992); he was also the driving force behind the so-called Udal League in the 1880s. According to its Constitution, the League sought 'to promote and encourage a general revival and assertion of the Teutonic or Norse characteristics of the British nation—straightforwardness, and obedience to Constitutional law and government'. Nowhere were these characteristics more richly expressed than in Viking Orkney and Shetland. The Udal League Constitution lists amongst its aims the 'upholding and revival of peasant proprietorship in Orkney and Shetland'; the redress of grievances relating to double taxation and alienation of lands; and, in the event of any move towards devolved government in Britain, the advocacy of islanders' wishes to be allowed to 'form a division by themselves' (all quotations from Lbs. 2186b 4to, Alfred Johnstone to Eiríkur Magnússon, 25 March 1887; see also Thomson 1985). This late Victorian recognition of residual Norse qualities of life in Orkney and Shetland echoes closely the claims made by Þorleifur Repp in his election address to the voters of Árnessýsla in Iceland in 1849: in their struggle for independence from (as Repp saw it) German-influenced Denmark, Icelanders should adopt the Viking-derived constitutional provisions of England as a model. Repp invites comparison between the depopulation and economic stagnation of the Danish Faroes and the bustling entrepreneurial energy and population growth of the British-ruled Orkneys and Shetlands (Wawn 1991, 203–204). Repp's favourite novelist was Sir Walter Scott, and his favourite novel was unsurprisingly *The Pirate*, in which Magnus Troil is a striking literary embodiment of those Viking values which Repp and Alfred Johnstone prized most in the northern Isles of Britain. Another embodiment of those same principles is surely Angantýr, the spirited Orcadian chief who dealt so nobly with Friðþjófr/Frithiof in the saga. It is, accordingly, not difficult to identify the Victorian politics of Orkney in the story of Friðþjófr/Frithiof.

Confronted by the disturbing political implications of such rediscovered udaller radicalism, not every Victorian enthusiast of northern antiquity shared the eagerness for fundamental constitutional change exhibited by Laing, Johnstone and others. Writing in the wake of the 1848 European convulsions, Thomas Forester felt that any attempt to transfer the Norwegian pattern of constitutional monarchy and social equality to Britain would lead to revolution. He favoured instead a judicious process of 'timely and voluntary concessions' such as the elimination of 'exuberance of luxury' amongst the ruling classes (Forester 1850, 457–459). Yet Laing's radicalism was far more influential than Forester's nervous gradualism. It was Laing who set the agenda for the ways in which Icelandic sagas were read during the reign of Queen Victoria. Both *Friðþjófs saga* and Tegnér's poem lie comfortably along the grain of such attitudes.

Along with the promotion of manliness and representative democracy there was a third and final implication of the Friðþjófr/Frithiof story for Victorian readers outside the walls of Windsor. We recall that Darwin and Friðþjófr had proved the 1893-1894 season's most popular lecture topics at the Liverpool Literary and Philosophical Society. As I hinted earlier in this paper, the two subjects have a number of elements in common, not least via periodic references to Darwin in nineteenth-century travel books about Iceland (for example Paijkull 1868, 43, 180–181). Darwin's description of man's ascent, from ape to conquest of savagery to multiplication round the globe, was an image of upward human mobility which must have sounded well in the ears of the upwardly mobile ranks of Victorian society. As an excellent recent biography puts it, what Darwin offered to Britain's *nouveau riche* was 'a romantic pedigree, an epic genealogy. Disregarding the apes, as many did, they found the *Descent [of Man]* a tremendous family saga' (Desmond and Moore 1992, 580). It is a striking image to use about a mid-century period which was enjoying for the first time the real Icelandic family sagas in newly available English translations. *Brennu-Njáls saga*, for instance, available from 1861 in George Webbe Dasent's lavishly produced version, dramatises memorably the ancestry and heroic evolution of great Icelandic families and the Icelandic state. Though it seems almost too convenient to be true, Dasent's nickname amongst his travelling companions in Iceland during their 1861–1862 travels was in fact Darwin ([Clifford] 1865), and it is not hard to see why when we recall Dasent's scornful hostility to the unnatural protection by law of hereditary succession. It was John Ruskin who had posed what for Dasent was the crucial question: '"Who is best man?" [...] the Fates forgive much,—forgive the wildest, fiercest, cruelest experiments—if fairly made for the determination of that' (quoted in Carlyle 1875, 309). Read in this context, the story of Friðþjófr/Frithiof could be seen to encode a powerful set of *arriviste* middle-class values. Ruskin's 'best men' would emerge as clearly in Victorian Liverpool's Cotton Exchange, as on a storm-tossed Viking long ship en route to Orkney. The saga community of Sogn ended up with the best leader, precisely because the succession of King Beli's sons was unsustainable—they were 'best men' through birth alone, and they were compelled to yield to Friðþjófr/Frithiof, a 'best man' in deed. To ambitious Victorian ears, both the Icelandic saga and the Tegnér poem must have seemed thoroughly reassuring texts.

ENVOI

The uncomfortable realities of Iceland and Victorian Britain did not allow such radiant optimism to stand unchallenged, however. Charles Darwin had written about survival of the fittest, whilst bearing the burden of knowing that his children were subject to an hereditary lung disease. The lucky ones survived—but it was hardly a survival of the fittest. They were the (just about) living proof of the bleak human truths behind the bookish abstractions.

W.G. Collingwood, Ruskin's secretary, was another victim of the cruel tensions which could develop between theory and reality. One of the finest pictures (now in the British Museum; reproduced Karlsson 1992, 55)[16] from his 1897 Iceland visit is not a landscape, but an imaginary historical scene at the Alþingi. It is a sunny day at Þingvellir; we see the brightly-coloured tent tops; the place is full of brightly-dressed *alþingis-menn* and their followers debating, plotting, cutting deals and making decisions. It is a picture full of saga-age energy; it is a society being social, a community communing. I count 131 people in the picture, only one of whom is a woman—a young couple stand arm in arm in the foreground, separated from the main throng, more intent on love- than law-making. Above and to the right of Almannagjá, on a rocky outcrop, stand the indistinct figures of what look like three guards: an alert

---

[16]I know of no evidence to support the statements made by Sir David Wilson and Else Roesdahl (Karlsson 1992, 54) that (i) the picture dates from *c.* 1875, and (ii) Collingwood had accompanied William Morris on his 1873 Iceland visit.

community needs external defence as well as internal coherence.

It is hard to imagine a more positive image of the Viking age in Iceland. It looks like the work of a man whose 'pilgrimage to the sagasteads' has been fully rewarded. Collingwood's published account of his 1897 journey certainly suggests this, yet the reality was painfully different. Collingwood left Iceland deeply depressed about all that he had seen. He had set out with such a vivid sense of what ancient Viking values had been, and of what modern Iceland should be like, with Laing and Stephens amongst the writers responsible for creating that image. Not surprisingly, Collingwood had found his confrontation with lethargic and down-trodden Icelandic reality deeply disillusioning. This was degeneration on a grand scale. In Darwinian evolutionary terms, it all fitted the theory perfectly—the descendants of the Vikings had simply adapted to their bleak contemporary environment. But Collingwood did not like the implications of what he had witnessed: if Iceland today, why not Britain tomorrow—that British empire built on Viking values, buttressed by residual Viking blood. His September 1897 letters to Eiríkur Magnússon (Lbs. 2186 4to) show all too painfully the gloom just beneath the surface of Victorian glory. Collingwood had tried to explore Iceland, but Iceland had succeeded in exploring him and his dreams.

Collingwood's visit to Iceland had, thus, in its own way been as disturbing as the Friðþjófr/Frithiof voyage to Orkney. Both journeys had involved their heroes in uncomfortable confrontations with the worrisome margins of life. To travel to Iceland was to travel to the margins of European civilisation; indeed to the margins of creation itself. Wherever else on earth *terra* was *firma*, it was not Iceland. As periodic nineteenth-century volcanic eruptions reminded the tented Northern traveller, the island of Iceland was not securely in being—it was still in the process of becoming. It was much safer to stay at home and satisfy a fascination with the marginal from the leather-bound volumes of a well-stocked library. There is no primitive like an armchair primitive. Such readers could (and did) devour the many tales of outlaws and giants for whom the popular Icelandic imagination had constructed an existence in the pock-marked surface of the Icelandic interior (Powell and Eiríkur Magnússon 1864, 1866); they represented phenomena at the psychological margins of a marginal civilisation. These same readers could follow the fortunes of the eponymous hero in Victor Hugo's folkloristic novel *Han d'Islande* (1823), which in its six nineteenth-century English translations depicts the margins of Norwegian society being terrorised by Hans, a cannibalistic wildman imported from Iceland.

The literary marginal with its murky supernatural forces could be explored safely within the covers of a book, particularly in a saga much of whose murk had been rationalised away—in other *fornaldarsögur* of similar pattern the Friðþjófr/Frithiof journey motif involves a visitation to underworlds far spookier than Orkney (Power 1984). The romance shape of the Friðþjófr/Frithiof story generates successive images of danger (reluctant brothers-in-law, predatory sea-witches, hostile berserks) which are triumphantly overcome through individual prowess and social cohesion. The grim realities of a degenerate saga-isle civilisation which devastated Collingwood will have troubled few of the Victorian followers of Friðþjófr/Frithiof. As the saga ends, the fearsome margins of existence have been confronted and contained, the old has given way to the new with a minimum of disruption, worthy rulers are in legitimate charge, and the long-delayed but star-crossed marriage of the stalwart hero has finally taken place. It is an optimistic and humane vision reminiscent of Shakespearean romance. If the evidence of the story's widespread diffusion is any guide, many Victorian readers of *Friðþjófs saga hins frækna* and its Swedish offshoot responded eagerly to the mood.[17]

BIBLIOGRAPHY

MANUSCRIPTS

Bodleian MS Eng. Misc. d.131. George Silk to Guðbrandur Vigfússon.

Lbs. [Landsbókasafn Íslands] Bréfasafn Stefán Einarsson; letters from William Morris.

Lbs. 405 fol. Eiríkur Magnússon's library holdings, list prepared by Bertha Phillpotts; Eiríkur Magnússon's comments on *Friðþjófs saga hins frækna*.

Lbs. 406 fol. Eiríkur Magnússon lectures.

Lbs. 480 4to. Guðmundur Torfason's translation of Tegnér's *Frithiofs saga*.

Lbs. 1860 4to (5). Eiríkur Magnússon lecture.

Lbs. 2181a 4to. Eiríkur Magnússon letters.

Lbs. 2186–90 4to. Eiríkur Magnússon letters.

Lbs. 2399 4to. Guðmundur Torfason's translation of Tegnér's *Frithiofs saga*.

Lbs. 2808 4to. Letters to Matthías Jochumsson.

Lbs. 4555 4to. Eiríkur Magnússon lecture.

Lbs. ÍB 10 8vo. Guðmundur Torfason's translation of Tegnér's *Frithiofs saga*.

[17]I am grateful to Professor Jan Ragnar Hagland and Dr Terry Gunnell for sharing their first-hand knowledge of the Sogn region with me, and for several valuable references. Dr Gunnell, Dr Fritz Heinemann and Dr Jim Binns have commented helpfully on earlier drafts of this paper.

Lbs. JS 141 fol. Guðmundur Torfason's translation of Tegnér's *Frithiofs saga*.
Scottish Registry Office, Heddle MS GD 263/124.

Sidney Jones Library, University of Liverpool, Sephton MS 3.33.

[Ward, H.L.D.]. 1864. *Numerical List of the Icelandic Manuscripts in the British Museum. November 1864*. (Xerox copy of the manuscript in Stofnun Árna Magnússonar in Reykjavík).

PRINTED SOURCES

Aarsleff, Hans. 1983. *The Study of Language in England 1780–1860*. Revised edition. Minneapolis and London.

Acker, Paul. 1993. 'Norse sagas translated into English: A Supplement', *Scandinavian Studies* 65, 66–102.

Adolphus, Joseph, trans. [*c.* 1890?]. 'The Story of Frithiof'. Mimeograph copy, Bodleian Library, Oxford.

Aho, Gary. 1993. '"Með Ísland á heilanum": Íslandsbækur breskra ferðalanga 1772 til 1897', *Skírnir* 167, 205–258.

[anon.] (Amelia Gillespie Smyth). 1828. 'Frithioff: A Swedish poem, By Esaias Tegner, Bishop of Wexio', *Blackwood's Edinburgh Magazine* 23, 137–161.

[anon.] (George Webbe Dasent). 1876. '[Review of] Richard Burton, *Ultima Thule, or a Summer in Iceland* (London, 1875); "Unpublished Journals of Two Journeys in the Summers of 1861 and 1862"', *Edinburgh Review* 143, 222–250.

[anon.]. 1881. *A Narrative of the Voyage of the Argonauts in 1880; Compiled by the Bard from the most Authentic Records*. [?Liverpool].

Allen, G.C., trans. [1912]. *The Song of Frithiof*. London.

Anderson, Sir Charles. 1853. *An Eight Weeks' Journal in Norway*. London.

———. 1984. Trans. Böðvar Kvaran, *Framandi Land: Dagbókarkorn úr Íslandsferð 1863*. Reykjavík.

Anderson, Rasmus B. and Jón Bjarnarson, trans. 1877. *Viking Tales of the North*. Chicago.

Andersson, T.M. 1964. *The Problem of Icelandic Saga Origins*. New Haven and London.

BL Cat. 1977. *British Library Catalogue of Additions to the Museum 1756–1782*. London.

Baker, Oscar, trans. 1841. *The Saga of Frithiof: A Legend*. London.

Baring-Gould, Sabine. 1858–1864. 'Oraefa-Dal: An Icelandic Tale', *The Hurst Johnian* (Brighton), 1–2.

———. 1863. *Iceland: Its Scenes and Sagas*. London.

———. 1894. *The Icelander's Sword, or the Story of Oraefadal*. London.

Barmby, Beatrice. 1900. *Gísli Súrsson: A Drama; Ballads and Poems of the Old Norse Days and Some Translations*. London.

Beck, Richard. 1971. Entry on '*Frithiof*', *Encyclopedia Americana* XII 101. New York.

Benedikz, B.S. 1970. 'Grímur Thorkelín, the University of St Andrews, and Codex Scardensis', *Scandinavian Studies* 42, 385–393.

Bennett. 1882. *Bennett's Hand-Book for Travellers in Norway*. 22nd edition. Christiania.

Benson, Adolph. 1926. 'A List of the English Translations of the *Frithjofs Saga*', *Germanic Review* 1, 142–167.

Bettelheim, Bruno. 1978. *The Uses of Enchantment: The Meaning and Importance of Fairy Tales*. London.

Blackley, W. Lewery, trans. 1857. *The Frithiof Saga, or Lay of Frithiof*. Dublin. (Reprinted in *Poems by Tegnér*, Scandinavian Classics 2, New York and London, 1915).

Blackwell, I.A., ed. and trans. Paul-Henri Mallet, *Northern Antiquities*. Revised edition. London.

Bowler, Peter J. 1989. *The Invention of Progress: the Victorians and the Past*. Oxford.

B[radley], H[enry]. 1898. 'George Stephens', *Dictionary of National Biography* 54, pp. 173–174. London.

Bryce, James Viscount. 1923. *Memoirs of Travel*. London.

Caine, Hall. 1905. *The Prodigal Son*. London.

Cappel, Emily S. [1882]. *Old Norse Saga*. London.

Carlyle, Thomas. 1875. *The Early Kings of Norway*. London.

Cleasby, Richard and Gudbrand Vigfusson. 1874. *An Icelandic-English Dictionary*. Oxford

[Clifford, Charles]. 1865. *Travels by 'Umbra'*. Edinburgh.

Collingwood, W.G. 1896. *The Bondwoman*. London.

———. 1897. A *Pilgrimage to the Saga-steads*. Ulverston.

Conybeare, C.A. Vansittart. 1877. *The Place of Iceland in the History of European Institutions, being the Lothian Prize Essay 1877*. Oxford and London.

Cox, G.W. and E.H. Jones. 1872. *Tales from the Teutonic Lands*. London.

Craigie, W.A. 1913. *The Icelandic Sagas*. Cambridge.

Dasent, George Webbe. 1858. *The Norsemen in Iceland*. Oxford.

———, trans. 1903. *Popular Tales from the North*. Second edition; first edition 1859. Edinburgh.

———. 1873. *Jest and Earnest: A Collection of Essays and Reviews*. 2 vols. London.

————. 1875. *The Vikings of the Baltic*. 3 vols. London.

Dodgson, John McN. 1972. *The Place-Names of Cheshire*. Part IV. London.

Downe, Walmer. 1902. *The Dane's Daughter, An Icelandic Story*. London.

Dowling, Linda. 1986. *Language and Decadence in the Victorian fin de siècle*. Princeton, New Jersey.

Ebbutt, Maud Isabel. 1910. *Hero Myths of the British Race*. London and New York.

Ellison, Ruth C. 1986–1989. 'The Alleged Famine in Iceland', *Saga-Book* 22, 165–179.

Fahlcrantz, Carl Johan. 1829. *Framnäs och Balestrand. Frithiofs och Ingeborgs hem*. Stockholm.

Falk, Hjalmar. 1890. 'Om Friðþjófs saga', *Arkiv för nordisk filologi* 6, 60–88.

Ferguson, Robert. 1856. *The Northmen in Cumberland and Westmorland*. London and Carlisle.

Fergusson Irvine, W. 1893. 'Place Names in the Hundred of Wirral', *Historical Society of Lancashire and Cheshire: Transactions*, n.s. 7–8, 279–304.

Forester, Thomas. 1850. *Norway in 1848 and 1849*. London.

————. 1853. *Norway and its Scenery*. London.

Fry, Donald K. 1980. *Norse Sagas translated into English*. New York, N.Y.

F[rye], W. E, trans. 1835. *Frithiofs Saga or The Legend of Frithiof*. London.

Gash, Norman. 1965. *Reaction and Reconstruction in English Politics, 1832–52*. Oxford.

Goddard, Julia. 1871. *Wonderful Stories from Northern Lands*. London.

Gould, Chester Nathan. 1921–1923. 'The Friðþjófssaga, an Oriental Tale', *Scandinavian Studies* 7, 219–250.

G[reen], W.C. 1905. Review of Félix Wagner 1904, *Saga-Book* 4, 253–254.

Gudbrand Vigfusson, ed. 1878. *Sturlunga saga*, 2 vols. Oxford.

Guðbrandur Vigfússon. 1990. Ingeborg Donali, trans., *Ein Islending i Noreg: Reiseskildring frå 1854*. Introduction by Hallfreður Örn Eiríksson. Oslo.

Guðni Jónsson and Bjarni Vilhjálmsson, eds. 1943–1944. *Fornaldarsögur Norðurlanda*. 3 vols. Reykjavík.

Guerber, H.A. 1908. *Myths of the Norsemen*. London.

Gustavson, Alrik. 1961. *A History of Swedish Literature*. Minneapolis.

Hamel, Leopold, trans. 1874. *Esaias Tegnér's Frithiof's Saga*. London.

Haraldur Hannesson. 1988. *Fegurð Íslands og Fornir Sögustaðir*. Reykjavík.

Harris, Richard L. 1978–1979. 'William Morris, Eiríkur Magnússon and the Icelandic famine relief', *Saga-Book* 20, 31–41.

Head, Sir Edmund, trans. 1866. *The Story of Viga Glum*. London.

Heckethorne, C.W., trans. 1856. *The Frithjof Saga; A Scandinavian Romance.* London.

Henderson, J., trans. 1872. *The Story of Frithiof.* London and Edinburgh.

Hibbert, Christopher. 1976. *George IV.* London.

Hilen, Andrew. 1947. *Longfellow and Scandinavia: A Study of the Poet's Relationship with the Northern Languages and Literature.* New Haven.

Hobsbawm, Eric and Ranger, Terence, eds. 1983. *The Invention of Tradition.* Cambridge.

Holcomb, T.A.E. and Martha A. Lyon, trans. 1877. *Fridthiofs Saga. A Norse Romance.* Chicago and London.

Hugo, Victor. [1845]. [anon., trans.], *Hans of Iceland; or, the Demon Dwarf.* London.

Hull, Eleanor. 1913. *The Northmen in Britain.* London.

Johnstone, James. 1782. *The Norwegian Account of Haco's Expedition against Scotland, A.D. 1263.* [Copenhagen].

Kalinke, Marianne. 1990. *Bridal-Quest Romance in Medieval Iceland.* Ithaca, N.Y.

Karlsson, Sven Olof. 1992. *Frihetens Källa.* Stockholm.

Kålund, Kr., ed. 1916. Arne Magnússon, *Brevveksling med Torfæus.* København.

Kelvin, Norman, ed. 1984. *The Collected Letters of William Morris. I 1848-80.* Princeton, N.J.

Ker, W.P. 1896. *Epic and Romance.* London.

Keyser, Rudolf. 1854. Barclay Peacock, trans., *The Religion of the Northmen.* New York and London.

Kvaran, Guðrún and Sigurður Jónsson. 1991. *Nöfn Íslendinga.* Reykjavík.

Laing, Samuel. 1854. *Journal of a Residence in Norway during the Years 1834, 1835, and 1836.* Fourth edition; first edition 1836. London.

———. 1839. *A Tour in Sweden in 1838.* London.

———, trans. 1844. *The Heimskringla; or, Chronicle of the Kings of Norway.* 3 vols. London.

———, trans. 1889. *The Heimskringla; or, The Saga of the Norse Kings.* 4 vols. (Revised edition by Rasmus B. Anderson). London.

Latham, Robert Gordon, trans. 1838. *Frithiof, A Norwegian Story.* London.

———. 1840. *Norway and the Norwegians.* 2 vols. London.

———. 1862. *The English Language.* Fifth edition. London.

Larsson, Ludwig, ed. 1893. *Sagan ock Rimorna om Friðþjófr hinn frækni.* Samfund til Udgivelse af Gammel Nordsk Litteratur 22. København.

Larsson, Ludwig, ed. 1901. *Friðþjófs saga ins frækna.* Altnordische Saga-Bibliothek 9. Halle.

Leach, Henry Goddard. 1921. *Angevin Britain and Scandinavia.* Cambridge, Mass.

Locock, C.D., trans. 1924. *Fritiof's saga.* New York and London.

Longfellow, Henry Wadsworth. 1886. *Works.* 11 vols. London.

Lyall, Edna. 1889. *A Hardy Norseman.* London.

Malling, Ove. 1807. Andreas Feldborg, trans., *Great and Good Deeds of Danes, Norwegians and Holsteiners.* London.

Marschall, Birgit. 1991. *Reisen und Regieren: Die Nordlandfahrten Kaiser Wilhelms II.* Heidelberg.

Metcalfe, Frederick. 1856. *The Oxonian in Norway, 1854–5.* London.

———. 1880. *The Englishman and the Scandinavian.* 2 vols. London.

Milford, John. 1842. *Norway and her Laplanders in 1841.* London.

Miller, John B., trans. 1905. *Frithiofs saga.* Chicago.

Miller, Olive Beaupré, ed. 1920. *From the Tower Window*, vol. 5 of *My Bookhouse*, 6 vols. Chicago.

Mitchell, Stephen A. 1991. *Heroic Sagas and Ballads: Myth and Poetics.* Ithaca.

Mjöberg, Jöran. 1967. *Drömmen om Sagatiden.* Stockholm.

Morris, William. 1910–1915. *The Collected Works of William Morris.* 24 vols. London.

Morris, William, [and Eiríkur Magnússon], trans. 1871. 'The Story of Frithiof the Bold', *The Dark Blue* 1, 42–58, 176–182.

Morris, William, and Eiríkur Magnússon, trans. 1875. *Three Northern Love Stories.* London.

———, trans. 1900. 'The Story of Frithiof the Bold', *Poet-Lore* 12, 353–384.

———, trans. 1970. *The Story of Kormak, the Son of Ogmund.* [Introduction by Grace J. Calder]. London.

Mucklestone, R., trans. 1862. *The Frithiof Saga. A poem.* London.

Müller, Peter E. 1817–1820. *Sagabibliothek.* 3 vols. København.

Nielsen, Jørgen-Erik. 1986. 'Andreas Andersen Feldborg. In Denmark English and in England Danish', *Angles on the English Speaking World* 2, 51–63.

ODQ 1980 = *Oxford Dictionary of Quotations,* Third edition. London.

Paijkull, C.W. 1868. M.R. Barnard, trans., *A Summer in Iceland.* London.

Phillpotts, Bertha. 1931. *Edda and Saga.* London.

Pope, Alexander. 1966. Herbert Davis, ed., *Pope: Poetical Works.* London.

Pope, Rev. Alexander. 1866. *Ancient History of Orkney, Caithness and the North.* Wick.

Powell, George E. J. and Eiríkur Magnússon, trans. 1864. *Icelandic Legends, Collected by Jón Árnason.* [A second series of legends was published under the same title in 1866]. London.

Power, Rosemary. 1984. 'Journeys to the North in the Icelandic *Fornaldar-sögur*', *Arv* 40, 7–26.

Ragozin, Zenaide A., trans. 1899. *Frithiof—The Viking of Norway*. New York and London.

R[igg], J.M. 1892. 'Samuel Laing'. *Dictionary of National Biography* 31, 404–406.

Rowntree, George. 1875. *Iceland. A Poem which obtained the Chancellor's Medal at the Cambridge Commencement, MDCCCLXXV*. Cambridge.

Schlauch, Margaret, trans. 1928. *Medieval Narratives, A Book of Translations*. New York.

———. 1934. *Romance in Iceland*. London.

Sephton, John, trans. 1894. 'A Translation of the Saga of Frithiof the Fearless', *Proceedings of the Liverpool Literary and Philosophical Society* 48, 69–97.

Shaw, Clement B., trans. 1908. *Frithiof's saga, A Legend of Ancient Norway*. Chicago and London.

Sherman, L.A., trans. 1877. *Frithiofs Saga, A Legend of Ancient Norway*. Boston.

Slingsby, C.W. 1904. *Norway the Northern Playground*. Edinburgh.

Spalding, H., trans. 1872. *The Tale of Frithiof*. London.

Stefán Einarsson. 1957. *A History of Icelandic Literature*. New York.

Stephens, George. 1839. *Fridthiofs Saga of Esaias Tegnér, A Legend of the North*. Stockholm and London.

———. 1878. *Thunor the Thunderer carved on a Scandinavian Font of about the Year 1000*. London.

———. 1883. *Studies on Northern Mythology shortly examined*. London and Edinburgh.

———. 1884. *Handbook of the Old-Northern Runic Monuments of Scandinavia and England*. Copenhagen.

———. 1890. *Er Engelsk et tysk sprog*. Copenhagen.

Stone, Olivia M. 1882. *Norway in June*. London.

Strong, W., trans. 1833. *Frithiof's Saga: A Scandinavian Legend of Royal Love*. London.

Thomsen, Grímur. 1859. 'The Northmen in Iceland', *Société Royale des Antiquaires du Nord: Séance annuelle du 14 mai 1859*, 4–16. Copenhagen. [Review of Dasent 1858].

Thomson, William P.L. 1985. 'The Udal League', *Orkney View* 2, 15–17.

Thorkelín, Grímur Jónsson. 1788. *Fragments of English and Irish History in the Ninth and Tenth Century*. London

Tomlinson, Henry. 1930. *Great Sea Stories of All Nations*. London.

Townsend, J.A.B. 1992. 'The Viking Society: A Centenary History', *Saga-Book* 23/4, 180–212.

Tudsbery, Francis. 1907. *Brunanburh. A.D. 937*. London and Chester.

Tulinius, Torfi. 1992. *'La Matière du Nord' dans la littérature du XIIIe siecle islandais*. Doctoral dissertation, University of Paris.

Upton, George, trans. 1907. *The Frithiof Saga*. Chicago.

Veblen, Thorstein, trans. 1925. *The Laxdæla Saga*. New York.

Wagner, Félix, ed. 1904. *La saga de Fridthjof le fort*. Louvain.

Watson, Margaret. 1897. 'Frithjof's Saga', *Dublin Review* 121, 30–40.

Wawn, Andrew. 1981. 'John Thomas Stanley and Iceland: the Sense and Sensibility of an Eighteenth-Century Explorer', *Scandinavian Studies* 53, 52–76.

———. 1982. *'Gunnlaugs saga ormstungu* and the Theatre Royal, Edinburgh: Melodrama, Mineralogy and Sir George Mackenzie', *Scandinavica* 28, 5–16.

———. 1985. 'Hundadagadrottningin', *Saga* 23, 97–133.

———. 1987. *The Iceland Journal of Henry Holland 1810*. London.

———. 1990. 'Henry Sweet, Guðbrandur Vigfússon and "Runic Lore"', *Henry Sweet Society Newsletter* 15, 4–10.

———. 1991a. *The Anglo Man. Þorleifur Repp, Philology and Nineteenth-Century Britain*. Studia Islandica 49. Reykjavík.

———. 1991b. 'The Assistance of Icelanders to George Webbe Dasent', *Landsbókasafn Íslands: Árbók 1989*, nýr flokkur 14, 73–92.

———. 1992a. 'The Victorians and the Vikings: George Webbe Dasent and *Jómsvíkinga saga*', in Janet Garton, ed., *Proceedings of the Ninth Biennial Conference of the British Association of Scandinavian Studies, April 1991*, pp. 301–315. Norwich.

———. 1992b. 'The Spirit of 1992: Sagas, Saga-steads and Victorian Philology', *Saga-Book* 23/4, 213–252.

———. 1994a. 'Shrieks at the Stones: the Vikings, the Orkneys and the Scottish Enlightenment', in Colleen Batey, Judith Jesch, and Christopher D. Morris, eds, *The Viking Age in Caithness, Orkney and the North Atlantic*, pp. 408–422. Edinburgh.

———. 1994b. 'Óðinn, Ossian and Iceland', in Gísli Sigurðsson et al., eds, *Sagnaþing helgað Jónasi Kristjánssyni sjötugum 10. apríl 1994*, 2 vols., II 829–840. Reykjavík.

Wenz, Gustav, ed. 1914. *Die Friðþjófssaga*. Halle

Wiesener, Anthon M. 1913. *Katalog over Bergens Museums manuskriptsamling*. Bergen.

Worsaae, J.J.A. 1846. *The Antiquities of Ireland and Denmark*. Dublin.

———. 1849. *The Primeval Antiquities of Denmark*. London.

11

'The North begins inside': Auden, Ancestry and Iceland

SVEINN HARALDSSON

In my childhood dreams Iceland was holy ground; when, at the age
of twenty-nine, I saw it for the first time, the reality verified my
dream; at fifty-seven it was holy ground still, with the most magical
light of anywhere on earth. (Auden 1967, 10)

This quotation from W.H. Auden's foreword to *Letters from Iceland*
shows what a central role Iceland played in Auden's imagination all
through his life. As Valentine Cunningham puts it:

A mythic north compelled the grown-up Auden as it had Auden the
little boy, both conscious of their Icelandic roots. (Cunningham 1989,
166)

In this article I intend to shed some light on Auden's 'Icelandic roots',
the background to his interest in Iceland and things Icelandic, and show
how they formed a part of his identity.

I

Strangely enough, apart from occasional references to Old Norse
literature and a few metrical experiments, there are few direct references
to Iceland in Auden's poetry. There is, it is true, a discernible influence
from Germanic poetic metres, but this can be attributed more to Anglo-
Saxon than Old Norse literary models. Auden's earliest poetry has a
Norse flavour to it and is set in an imagined world which is recognisably
Northern, but the general lack of references to Iceland in Auden's
favourite literary medium is puzzling. There is nothing comparable to the
other great icon of Anglo-Old Norse literary relations, the Victorian poet
William Morris, half of whose *Collected Works* are translations of sagas,
poems based on Old Norse literature, romances derived from Icelandic
sources or travel literature about Iceland. Auden was a very different kind
of poet who 'restored to poetry an encyclopedic fullness of subject matter
and style' (Mendelson 1981, xxi). Such a poet could not be fettered by
the literary forms and themes of a long gone age. Instead he mined

Icelandic literature and culture and then used what he found in his own idiosyncratic way.

There is rather more evidence of Auden's interest in Iceland in his prose writings. Two of his plays are permeated by a saga atmosphere, there is an essay on the sagas, and there are references in various reviews, interviews and letters. His translations of Eddic poetry are also important in this respect. They form, along with the travel book, Auden's most extensive work dealing with Iceland or Old Norse literature.

Although the old literature of Iceland was not a central influence on Auden's poetry there are a surprising number of instances where Auden's 'Northernness', as I would like to term it, is referred to, either by himself or by his contemporaries. One of Auden's friends from school was John Pudney. He remembered Auden in his autobiography, *Home and Away* (Pudney 1960, 45) as 'a Nordic, sagacious, heavy-footed boy in another house'. The fact that Auden is referred to as 'Nordic' at such an early age suggests that he was already identifying himself as such. One of Auden's contemporaries at Christ Church, Oxford, was A.L. Rowse. He (1987, 15) describes Auden as being 'Nordic, flaxen-haired with fair skin, a blond'. Later on, when this is repeated, Nordic becomes synonymous with 'Aryan':

> July to September Auden spent in Iceland, a holiday from Europe. But he did run into the brother of the egregious Goering with a party there. They 'exchanged politenesses at breakfast. Rosenberg is coming too.' He was the 'philosopher' of the Nazi movement, expounder of their Aryan racial rubbish and Nordic cult. [...] 'The Nazis have a theory that Iceland is a cradle of the Germanic culture [*sic*].' Wystan travelled in a bus with these asses, who talked incessantly about the Aryan qualities of the Icelanders: [...] He qualified as Nordic, with his fair skin and flaxen-coloured hair; his father was passionately devoted to Icelandic sagas and Northern mythology, and had brought his boy up on them. (Rowse 1987, 41–42)

In this passage from his book on Auden, Rowse quotes (slightly incorrectly) from Auden and MacNeice's *Letters from Iceland* (1937, 119, 136). There the beginning of Auden's interest in the 'North' is attributed to his upbringing by his father. The comparison or equation of 'Nordic' with the racially charged term 'Aryan' is also made by Auden himself in a stanza in his 'Letter to Lord Byron' part IV. This was, in fact, removed from the second edition of *Letters from Iceland* when Auden edited it for re-publication in 1965 (the date of the 'Foreword'):

> My name occurs in several of the sagas,
>   Is common over Iceland still. Down under
> Where Das Volk order sausages and lagers
>   I ought to be the prize, the living wonder,
>   The really pure from any Rassenschander,

In fact I am the great big white barbarian,
The Nordic type, the too too truly Aryan.

(1937, 201)

Apparently Auden thought that this would no longer strike people as comic anymore in a post-holocaust world, hence the deletion.

Auden has two characteristics which can be connected to the term 'Aryan'. In an earlier stanza he muses on the way he looks, describing his hair as 'fair (it's tow-like)' in a rather iconoclastic manner. And Auden's intent gaze was a trait which his contemporaries comment upon as being 'Nordic'. Interestingly enough the description of this feature is in both cases accompanied by a reference to Auden's haircolour. The first passage comes from Christopher Isherwood's *Lions and Shadows*, an autobiographical account with the names of his friends changed to pseudonyms. Wystan Hugh Auden becomes Hugh Weston:

> At my preparatory school, during the last two years of the War, there had been a boy named Hugh Weston. Weston—nicknamed 'Dodo Minor' because of the solemn and somewhat birdlike appearance of his bespectacled elder brother—was a sturdy, podgy little boy, whose normal expression was the misleadingly ferocious frown common to people with very short sight. Both the brothers had hair like bleached straw and thick coarse-looking, curiously white flesh, as though every drop of blood had been pumped out of their bodies—their family was of Icelandic descent. (Isherwood 1985, 112)

Cyril Connolly's version makes the connection between the frown/glare and the haircolour more explicit:

> He was tall and slim, with a mole on his upper lip, rather untidy tow-coloured hair in a loop over his forehead with extraordinary greenish eyes suggesting that iceberg glare he liked to claim from his Norse ancestors. (Connolly 1975, 70)

There are three references to the 'Nordic glare' in *Letters from Iceland*. One, 'The Arctic Stare', is a caption for a photograph of a boy staring into the lens (facing 144). The other two are both quotations from Richard Burton's less than complimentary book on his travels in Iceland, *Ultima Thule*. Auden gives the first of these references the heading 'Concerning their [the Icelanders'] eyes':

> A very characteristic feature of the race is the eye, dure and cold as a pebble—the mesmerist would despair at the first sight. (1937, 63)

The second one is headed 'The translator of the Arabian Nights gets the raspberry':

> Among the gentler sex a soft look is uncommonly rare, and the aspect ranges from a stony stare to a sharp glance rendered fiercer by the habitual frown. (1937, 73–74)

Why would Wystan Auden claim that his way of staring at people had anything to do with his 'ancestry'? Why did he refer to this specific 'Nordic glare' three times in his travel book on Iceland? The answer is probably connected with his aspiring to be 'Icelandic'. Even though his hair was fair his eyes, as he describes them in 'Letter to Lord Byron', were not Aryan blue but hazel (201). To compensate for the lack of Nordic credentials in this respect he referred to his frown as 'Nordic' in order to 'Aryanise' his eyes.

Stephen Spender's version of this habit of Auden's is much less complimentary and more clinical, precisely because of the lack of accompanying signifiers. When the description of Auden's way of scrutinizing people is not linked to any reference to his 'ancestry' it loses all its positive aspects. Auden's glance is merely 'myopic' and the description of him unflattering:

> He had almost albino hair and weakly pigmented eyes set closely together, so that they gave the impression of watchfully squinting. (Spender 1951, 50)

So much for his 'Iceberg glare'!

Auden's biographers and some of his critics do not elaborate on Auden's claim that he was Icelandic. Either they cite this as a fact or they refer to it as a quirk of Auden's, that he *liked to think* of himself as being so. None of them questions his assumption or tries to delve into what lies behind it. Edward Mendelson, Auden's literary executor, when discussing the 1936 journey to Iceland (1981, 194), says that he 'had personal reasons for going North. His family traced its origins to Iceland, and his childhood had been nourished on sagas.' These were all claims made by Auden at some point. That it is uncertain if the family's claim to Icelandic ancestry is actually true does not alter the fact that they believed it to be true. Another critic who leaves the point unresolved is Monroe K. Spears. He deduces (Spears 1963, 13) that 'since Auden is Northern in background, affinities, and tastes' it follows that 'his fantasies were of the North'. There is no attempt made to verify the first statement. The most recent example is Anthony Hecht. He refers to Auden's journey to Iceland as

> the chance to visit a wholly different and alien landscape with which Auden identified his Nordic ancestors. (Hecht 1993, 171)

This last example shows that it is accepted now amongst Auden's critics that he had Scandinavian ancestors of some sort, preferably connected with Iceland.

It is interesting to note how this is commonly agreed upon by Auden's critics, given the reluctance of his biographers to believe it. Carpenter and Osborne do not accept Auden's Nordic credentials as a given fact, but they nevertheless refuse to examine them further. Charles Osborne is deliberately indefinite:

> As a young man, Wystan Hugh Auden was described by his contemporaries as Nordic, and in later years he liked to refer to himself as a creature of the north. [...] In any case, the family is said to have come originally from Iceland. (Osborne 1980, 9)

The choice of words, 'was described as', 'liked to refer to', 'is said to have', seems carefully and even deliberately evasive. The matter is intentionally left unclear. What cannot be authenticated must not be probed into. Carpenter describes Auden's feelings on the matter and leaves it at that. At least he has examined some of the material on which the claims to Icelandic ancestry were based—and dismissed them—before he reaches this point:

> Whatever the truth about his ancestry, Wystan Auden enjoyed believing that he was Norse by descent—not just on his father's side but his mother's as well. [...] So it was that Wystan Auden could describe himself whimsically as 'pure Nordic'. (Carpenter 1981, 8)

The context of this assertion of Auden's is a section called 'Heredity' in Auden's review of autobiographical works by Evelyn Waugh and Leonard Woolf (1973, 496). Auden's claim to be 'Nordic' on his mother's side came from the tradition that her ancestors had come over from Normandy after the conquest of England by the Normans and that by virtue of being Normans they were of Scandinavian descent. Carpenter emphasises what is surely the most important aspect of this whole genealogical debate—namely, that Auden's actual ancestry does not matter; it is the ancestry that Auden believed in which counts. Carpenter's reference to Auden as being 'whimsical' indicates that he believed Auden enjoyed making these claims, without really believing in them.

There is some indication that Carpenter is correct in this belief. The question is—did Auden play out this charade consciously all his life or was this a belief which he discarded somewhere along the way? What is clear is that when Auden gave an interview with Michael Newman in 1972 his views on this vexed topic had sobered up considerably. As an answer to the question 'Where did you pick up your interest in the Icelandic Sagas?' Auden gives the following answer:

> My father brought me up on them. His family originated in an area which once served as headquarters for the Viking army. The name *Auden* is common in the Sagas, usually spelled *Audun*. But we have no family trees or anything like that. My mother came from Normandy—which means that she was half Nordic, as the Normans were. (Newman 1977, 263)

The tone is non-committal. The denial—'no family trees'—puts the discussion on a different level. There may be a connection, and Auden gives the names as an example, but he does not insist. It is left in the air as a conceivable possibility. In stark contrast to this indefiniteness, we find Auden's explicit claim that his mother came from Normandy, which makes her 'half Nordic'. There is nothing to indicate that this really only refers to a family tradition according to which some of her ancestors came from Normandy more than eight hundred years before she was born. These inconsistencies—if they are not due to the editing of the interviewer—leave us, firstly, with the feeling that Auden was aware by now that his earlier identification with things Nordic had been a personal myth, created by himself out of raw materials given to him by his father; but, secondly, with the sense that he still very much wanted the myth to be true, which would explain the claim about his mother.

Auden's closest colleagues Spender and Isherwood, who together with him make up the trinity or triumvirate of thirties literature in Britain, have the last word on what his contemporaries thought of him. Their views date from different ends of the spectrum of Auden's career and highlight different aspects of what I would like to refer to as Auden's Northernness. Spender's contribution is very late. It is from an address delivered by him a few days after Auden's death at a memorial service in Christ Church Cathedral, Oxford:

> He found symptons everywhere. *Symptomatic* was his key word. But in his very strange poetry he transmogrified these symptoms into figures in a landscape of mountains, passes, streams, heroes, horses, eagles, feuds and runes of Norse sagas. He was a poet of an unantici-pated kind—a different race from ourselves—and also a diagnostician of literary, social and individual psychosomatic situations, who mixed his Iceland imagery with Freudian dream symbolism. Not in the least a leader, but, rather, a clinical-minded oracle with a voice that could sound as depersonalized as a Norn's in a Norse saga. (Spender 1973, 5)

Auden's Northernness has here been integrated into his character and his work. Spender is not discussing this aspect specifically but he manages to use the adjectives 'Icelandic' or 'Norse' three times in this short passage. He is of course referring to the start of Auden's career, in the knowledge of all that had changed in between. Isherwood's piece, from which the following extract is taken was first published in the 'Auden Double Number' of the periodical *New Verse* which helped in establish-ing Auden's critical reputation during the thirties. The tone is defiant and self-assured, permeated by the certainty of youth:

If I were told to introduce a reader to the poetry of W. H. Auden, I should begin by asking him to remember three things.

First that Auden is essentially a scientist: [...]

Second, that Auden is a musician and a ritualist. [...]

Third, that Auden is a Scandinavian. The Auden family came originally from Iceland. Auden himself was brought up on the sagas, and their influence upon his work has been profound. (Isherwood 1937, 4)

This was the official line at the time—this is what we have to work from. Auden used his perceived Icelandic background to build himself an 'Icelandic' identity. Even though his use of the word does not conform to our ideas of its meaning—limited as we are by our belief in historical veracity—we cannot dismiss his claim as false. What follows in this essay is an exploration of some of the different questions which arise when this aspect of Auden is examined; in particular, where did he get this idea from, and what empirical data do we have which bear on this discussion?

II

All of Auden's biographers mention the wide range of intellectual interests displayed by his father, George Augustus Auden. One of the areas of interest handed down from father to son was, as mentioned earlier, Norse literature and myth. Auden refers to this in *Letters from Iceland*, which is dedicated to his father.

Few English people take an interest in Iceland, but in those few the interest is passionate. My father, for example, is such a one, and some of the most vivid recollections of my childhood are hearing him read to me Icelandic folk-tales and sagas, and I know more about Northern mythology than Greek. (1937, 214)

When describing his childhood in 'Letter to Lord Byron' (Part IV) the wording suggests an almost deliberate conversion of Wystan Auden to 'Northern interests' (Gosse's phrase) by his father:

With northern myths my little brain was laden,
    With deeds of Thor and Loki and such scenes
                                        (1937, 205)

Whatever the circumstances of this conversion, its effects were to last a lifetime.

George A. Auden was born in 1872 in Repton in Derbyshire and educated at the public school of the same name. He read Natural Science at Christ's College in Cambridge (and took a first class degree) as preparation for studying medicine, and later went to London as an intern at St Bartholomew's Hospital, where he met Constance Rosalie Bicknell, whom he married in 1899. He moved to York, where he practised medicine and where his three sons were born. In 1908, the year after the birth of the youngest, Wystan Hugh, the family moved to Birmingham, where Dr Auden, true to the family ethic of undertaking public service, became a School Medical Officer, the first in the city, and a post which offered less financial benefit than his former private practice in York. He also served as Sanitary Adviser to the Governors of Rugby School and honorary psychologist to the Birmingham Children's Hospital. In 1941 he became Professor of Public Health at the University of Birmingham. He was later to lecture on the same subject with the Ontario Board of Education, at Columbia University in New York and at the University of Michigan. He joined the Royal Army Medical Corps in World War I and served in the Eastern Mediterranean and in France (Osborne 1980, 10; Mendelson 1981, xxi; Callan 1983, 26).

Dr Auden seems to have been extremely versatile in his scholarly pursuits. Mendelson (1981, xxii) mentions not only his stable and gentle character but also his exceptionally wide learning including natural sciences from his Cambridge days and expertise in archaeology and classics. His published contributions in the field of public health were important and he 'was one of the first officials in his field to make use of Freudian psychology'. According to Osborne (1980, 11) he was 'a voracious reader and also a published writer and translator of archaeological and psychological articles'. Carpenter calls him a 'factually-minded man, and widely read' (1981, 8). Amongst the languages he mastered were of course Latin and Greek; he was for many years Honorary Secretary of the local Classical Association in Birmingham and published papers on the medical aspects of classical literature. He was also a Fellow of the Society of Antiquaries (Callan 1983, 27). Carpenter (1981, 8) mentions that his knowledge of German and Danish was good enough for him to translate works on antiquities and archaeology from these languages into English.

The *National Union Catalog* (1969, 25, 517) lists three books by Dr George Augustus Auden. The first one is a translation of Dr Fredrich Rathgen's *The Preservation of Antiquities: A Handbook for Curators*, published by the Cambridge University Press in 1905, which shows Dr Auden's dedication to that subject. It is translated from German and we may assume that more of the responsibility for the translation lies with Dr Auden's co-translator, his brother Harold A. Auden, who held a degree from Tübingen in Germany, than with Dr Auden himself. The other two volumes listed are collections of articles which Dr Auden edited for the British Association for the Advancement of Science. The first one was edited for its 75th meeting in York in 1906, when he was still living in the city. It was originally published in York for the purposes of the meeting as *A Handbook to York and District*, and then, with a different title page in London for the general reader as *Historical and Scientific Survey of York and District*. Seven years later, in 1913 when the British Association held its 83rd annual meeting in Birmingham, where Dr Auden was then living, he again edited the handbook for that city and neighbourhood. In addition to editing the two *Handbooks* and the translation of Rathgen's *Preservation of Antiquities*, Callan mentions that Dr Auden also translated the official *Guide to the Prehistoric Collection* of the National Museum of Copenhagen ([1908]), presumably from Danish (Callan 1983, 27).

Besides editing the 1906 collection for the British Association, he also wrote the preface and the first article, on 'Pre-Historic Archæology', where he gives a scholarly overview of the archaeological findings in York and surrounding districts from the time of the first signs of human occupation until Roman times. For the 1913 collection, in addition to editing the volume and writing the preface, he wrote a similar article to the one on York, this time discussing the 'Pre-History of the Neighbourhood' of the city of Birmingham. In this case the history is continued up to the time of the Norman Conquest and Dr Auden could make use of documentary evidence. In the York Collection the only reference he could make to the Vikings was when describing the geography of the area. There he could mention that the existence of a certain geographical feature helped explain the route taken by the armies on their way to Stamford Bridge in 1066, elaborating on one of the many points where his twin interests of Scandinavian and English history come in contact with each other (Auden 1906, 3n).

By this time Dr Auden had for two years been an active member of the Viking Club, as it was then known (Townsend 1992). He joined in 1904 at the same time as his brother, Harold (*Saga-Book* 1907, 5/1, 4), in a year that saw a large increase in membership, according to Dr J.G. Garson, the president of the club (*Saga-Book* 1906, 4/2, 268). He had become the honorary district secretary for York by 1906 (*ibid.*, 408). The then recent translation of *The Preservation of Antiquities* by the two brothers was presented to the club library (*ibid.*, 264) by Dr Auden and conscientiously reviewed by Albany F. Major in the same volume of the *Saga-Book* that notes the gift. Major has only the highest praise for the brothers' endeavours:

> This is a book which should be invaluable to all curators of museums
> or collectors of antiquities, and the translators deserve their gratitude
> for the work they have undertaken. (Major 1906, 479)

In the same volume of the *Saga-Book* there is an account by the reviewer of a lecture given by Dr Auden to the Yorkshire Philosophical Society on 'The Remains of Danish Sculpture in Yorkshire and Derbyshire'. Not only does Dr Auden seem to have made some interesting discoveries about the distribution of Scandinavian remains in the area; he also uses the opportunity to invite his fellow Vikings to come and look at them:

> He pointed out that, besides the strong Danish element in York, the Danish monuments in Yorkshire were found to a very large extent within a radius of twenty miles round Leeds, Ilkley, Collingham, Thornhill and Dewsbury. This year the British Association is visiting York, and Dr. Auden has suggested to us that another year we might, with advantage, make it the object of an excursion. (*Saga-Book* 1906, 4/2, 408)

He was of course editing the handbook for the meeting of the British Association himself this year as mentioned above. This handbook is in turn reviewed by Albany Major in the next volume of the *Saga-Book* where again he has only the most laudatory remarks to make about the volume and its editor:

> This book is fully worthy of the occasion which produced it, dealing with its subject on a scientific plan that leaves little to be desired. The prehistoric archæology of the district is handled by the editor in a brilliant and comprehensive sketch, where all the results of scientific research are combined to illuminate the dark pages before the dawn of history. (Major 1907, 195)

Dr Auden seems to have begun a correspondence with another member of the Viking Club around the same time. John Romilly Allen (1847–1907) was one of the earliest members of the club and its first editor. He was a Fellow of the Society of Antiquaries of Scotland and editor of *Archæologia Cambrensis* and *The Reliquary and Illustrated Archæologist*. One of the first papers read to the Viking Club was his 'Scandinavian Art in Great Britain', and he wrote an article for the first volume of the *Saga-Book* on the 'Prehistoric Art of the North' (1895, 54–73). His obituary in the fifth volume of the *Saga-Book* describes his scholarly erudition and reputation (1908, 5/2, 404). It was in connection with early art that Dr Auden wrote to Romilly Allen. In the Romilly Allen Collection in the British Library there is a bound volume (LXV) marked 'Scandinavian Art in Great Britain'. Romilly Allen may have been planning a book on the subject as the volume contains a long lecture, a collection of articles and discussion of finds—541 pages in all. Amongst these documents are four letters from Dr Auden dated 1905–1907. In these he discusses Scandinavian finds from York and sends photographs of the objects (BL Add. MS 37,603, LXV, 166–167, 471–476). Romilly Allen died less than four months after receiving the last letter. One can only wonder whether he had time to read and edit Dr Auden's article on the 'Pre-Conquest Cross at Rolleston, Staffordshire' that appeared in *The Reliquary and Illustrated Archæologist* in January 1908.

Although his brother Harold only remained a member of the Viking Club for a few years, Dr George A. Auden continued to be a very literate and active Viking. In 1907 he submitted a lengthy report to the *Saga-Book* as District Secretary for York on recent finds in the city. In it his own photographs of the objects are described.[1] It is clear that he had travelled in Norway recently and that he was reading Norwegian works on history and antiquities as he quotes some in his report (1907–1908, 55–59). There is also another report from York (247–250), with photographs which had already appeared in *The Reliquary*, and more quotations from Norwegian sources. Finally, there is discussion (397) of his article in *The Reliquary*, and Dr Auden is also mentioned several times (175, 178, 202–204) in the same volume. Not only does Dr Auden seem to be one of the most illustrious members of the Club, it seems to have been in danger of being taken over by him!

The next volume (6, 1909–1910) of the *Saga-Book* includes an article written by Dr Auden on his then apparently favourite subject 'Antiquities Dating from the Danish Occupation of York' (including seven photographs) which was an abstract of a paper read to the club (with lantern illustrations) on 22 January 1909 (Auden 1910a). There was a discussion afterwards (163). One of the members who took part was the president of the club, W.P. Ker. He gave up the presidency later the same year, and was succeeded by Sir Israel Gollancz, Professor of English at King's College, London. Sir Israel's nephew, Victor Gollancz, was twenty-three years later to commission a travel book from Dr Auden's son, W.H. Auden, and thus enable him to travel to Iceland. This lecture was recycled for an audience of members of the Yorkshire Philosophical Society in the same year (*Year Book of the Viking Club* 2, 1909–1910, 44). Dr Auden had already moved to Birmingham with his family by then and soon his time-consuming new duties there meant that he had to give up some of his former interests. The last contributions Dr Auden made to the Viking Club were two reviews printed in that same *Year Book* (1910b, 54–55; 1910c, 69).

The last mention of Dr Auden in the publications of the Viking Club

---

[1]Dr Auden not only took photographs of objects for his own articles; he also seems to have lent a helping hand to Jón Stefánsson when he was obtaining photographs for his *Saga-Book* article (1906, 309) on 'The Oldest Known List of Scandinavian Names'.

is in the *Year Book* for 1911–1912. His name is not included in the list of members (105), but is mentioned as one of members 'inadvertently omitted' (113), probably because of late payment of fees. By the publication of the next *Year Book* in 1913 another member has become Honorary District Secretary of Yorkshire and George A. Auden is no longer listed as a member. Dr Auden was to be away from England for the duration of the war and when he returned to the country the Viking Club, soon to be termed the Viking Society, had lost many members and was slow to recover (Townsend 1992, 196). There is little evidence that Dr Auden maintained his former ties with Norse studies, now that his hands were full with his career and the difficulties of financing the private education of three boys. There is only one indication that the flame of his old interest was not totally extinguished. In 1923 he travelled to Iceland to stay with somebody with whom he shared an interest in psychology and had corresponded, Dr Þórður Sveinsson of the Lunatic Asylum at Kleppur in Reykjavík.[2] Wystan Auden was to spend a night there thirteen years later during his stay in Iceland (Carpenter 1981, 202).

III

One factor connecting Auden and Iceland that needs careful consideration is his family name. Apparently the family thought that it derived from Iceland. It is a point worth examining more closely. Both of Auden's biographers mention this connection. Charles Osborne (1980, 9) says that 'in any case, the family is said to have come originally from Iceland', which is rather vague and fails to refer to the source of this information. Humphrey Carpenter (1981, 7), on the other hand, is more sceptical when he states that Auden's father 'believed that his own family name, Auden, showed that he himself was of Icelandic descent.' Edward Mendelson, in his book about Auden's early literary output, says without any further explanation that Auden's father 'traced his ancestry to Iceland' and seems not to doubt the veracity of this (1981, xxii). There are two letters in the National Library of Iceland which might throw some light on the matter. I think it is best first to print them in full and then to discuss them

[2]Information given to the author by Þórður Sveinsson's son, Agnar Þórðarson, in private conversation in Reykjavík, 6 August 1992.

together below. The first (Lbs. 2186a 4to, 28 May 1904)[3] is from Auden's father to Eiríkur Magnússon, an Icelandic scholar who translated sagas with William Morris; he was a fellow of Trinity College and a librarian at the University Library in Cambridge.

Dear Sir

A couple of years ago you most kindly discussed with me the derivation of the Norse name Audun and its possible relationship with my own name, Auden, which by family tradition has always been thought to be of Danish origin.

When in Copenhagen a few weeks ago it was pointed out to me in the Royal Library there that Oehlenschläger in his Hakon Jarl makes Odin when in disguise assume the name Auden.

I should be deeply interested if you could give me any information or theory how the poet came to make use of this particular name as a *nome de plume*. I see that Grimm (*Teutonic Mythology* Vol. IV p. 1326) raises the question whether Audun does not stand for Odin; but I was unable to find any evidence in Denmark of the use of Auden as a personal name. Can you tell me whether the name still exists in any form in Iceland, as I believe Audin is still found in Norway.

With apologies for thus troubling you
Believe me
Yours faithfully
George A. Auden

[3]Eiríkur Magnússon played host, on exactly that date, to an excursion of fifty people who visited Cambridge under the auspices of the Viking Club. Eiríkur, who was then vice-president of the club, 'exhibited some rare manuscripts of the Sagas, early printed Sagas, and other treasures of the [University] library, and gave a brief discourse on Danish and other Scandinavian palæography,' according to the *Saga-Book* (1905, 4/1, 9). It is obvious that Dr Auden was not a member of this group of visitors if he was writing to Eiríkur from York at the time. His thoughts may indeed have been with the group and he may have longed to join them, thus perhaps explaining his writing to Eiríkur on exactly that day. It is likely that he was unable to go because of medical duties in York; as the letterhead on his letter to Eiríkur Magnússon indicates, his surgery hours were between 2 and 3 pm every day but Wednesday (and presumably Sunday); and 28 May 1904 was a Saturday. As an alumnus of Cambridge Dr Auden may have already been familiar with the manuscripts and early printed books mentioned. He may even have come across Eiríkur Magnússon during his student days.

The second letter (Lbs. 2181a 4to, 2 June 1904)[4] is a draft reply to Dr Auden's inquiries. The surprising thing about it is its curtness. Eiríkur was no doubt often plagued by queries from dilettante amateurs with an obsession for all things Norse, but this still seems unnecessarily direct:

> Dear Sir,
>
> Oehlenschläger's freak to give the name of Auden to Odin in disguise has no historical precedent to lean on. He had, no doubt, read in Snorri's Ynglinga saga that the personal name Audunn was derived from Odin—a fanciful remark of Snorri's without any etymological authority—and so considered the form Auden good enough for doing service as Odin's *nom de guerre*. I am not in [a] position to say whether Auden is a name found in Denmark; I have never come across it. In Norway it does not seem to exist.

It is impossible now to identify the occasion on which, according to his letter, George A. Auden met Eiríkur Magnússon. Dr Auden did not become a member of the Viking Club until 1904, the year in which the letter was written, so it is unlikely that their meeting 'a couple of years ago' was in connection with club activities although it does indicate that Auden's interest in Norse things predated his joining the club.

Another interesting feature of the letter is Dr Auden's claim that there is a family tradition of the name being Danish. It is difficult to say whether this is correct or whether Auden is here influenced by the fact that Scandinavians in this part of England (Dr Auden was born in Repton in Derbyshire and at the time of writing the letter lived in York, both locations within the area of the ancient Danelaw) were generally referred to as 'Danes'. Nor is it possible to know whether Dr Auden travelled to Denmark in the spring of 1904 on business or if he went there as a tourist to get to know better the archaeology and history of the country. It is possible that he was there in connection with one of the 'Visits to Denmark', which are mentioned in the *Saga-Book* (4/1, 241–242 and 4/2, 407) for 1905–1906. These were arranged by a certain Miss F.M. Butlin,

---

[4]The date of the draft is in Icelandic, '2. júní, 1904', which shows that Eiríkur Magnússon was still thinking in his native language, even after nearly forty-two years abroad. There is a note at the top of the sheet in pencil, in all likelihood by Stefán Einarsson, Eiríkur's biographer: 'Svar við fyrirspurn frá e-m George A. Auden, sem vill vita um uppruna nafns síns' [A reply to an inquiry made by a George A. Auden, who wants to know about the origin of his [family] name]. Stefán Einarsson had no way of knowing when he started going through Eiríkur's letters in 1924 that this George A. Auden's son had inherited his father's interest in Iceland and was on his way to becoming the most influential English poet of his generation.

who also organised a 'Visit to Sweden' around the same time.

The 'Oehlenschläger' reference is to Adam Gottlob Oehlenschläger (1779–1850), an influential Danish dramatist and poet who was especially interested in Norse literature and mythology. His drama (1807) *Hakon Jarl hin Rige* was the first of his great 'Northern' tragedies. It is based on Snorri's account of the hero in *Ólafs saga Tryggvasonar* in the *Heimskringla*.

Snorri Sturluson's 'fanciful remark' is in *Ynglinga saga* in *Heims-kringla* in a chapter called by some editors 'Frá íþróttum Óðins': 'Eptir Óðins nafni var kallaðr Auðun ok hétu menn svá sonu sína' (Bjarni Aðalbjarnarson 1941, 20). The edition adds in a footnote that one manuscript spells the name *Auðon*, and that the two names *Óðinn* and *Auðun(n)* are unrelated. In Morris and Magnússon's archaically flavoured translation in *The Saga Library* the chapter is called 'Of Odin's Crafts' and the translation is as follows:

> Folk are called Audun after Odin's name, as men were wont so to call their sons. (1893, 19)

In Magnússon's fourth and accompanying volume to the *Heimskringla* translation 'Audun (Auðunn)' is explained in an identical way as a 'personal name that Snorri, playing at etymology, derives from the name of Odin' (1905, 15).

Jakob Grimm mentions the name *Audun* in his *Teutonic Mythology*. Dr Auden quotes the English translation by James Stallybrass from 1888, which used the fourth edition of the German original (1875–1878). After pointing out some different variants of *'Óðinn'* Grimm asks the question 'Does Audun in Norw. docs. stand for Oðin?' but he does not provide an answer (1888, IV 1326). This question, first put forward by Grimm in 1835, had already been answered by late nineteenth-century philologists long before Dr Auden came upon it. Hence Eiríkur Magnússon's impatience with him.

Eiríkur Magnússon subtly corrects Dr Auden's French terminology when referring to Odin's pseudonym as his *nom de plume* (and misspelling it) meaning 'a name assumed by a writer' and substitutes in his reply the correct *nom de guerre*, which means 'a name assumed by, or assigned to, a person engaged in some action or enterprise' (*OED*). This unac-knowledged correction adds to the condescending tone established elsewhere in the letter: we note the vocabulary used—'freak' suggesting that Oehlenschläger's methods were philologically unsound; 'no histor-ical precedent' implying that Oehlenschläger was no scholar; 'no doubt' indicating that of course Oehlenschläger's source was the most obvious one, and that he could not have done any detailed research; 'fanciful' meaning that even though Snorri was a renowned historian in his day he would not be regarded as on a par with modern scholars; 'without any etymological authority' indicating that of course Eiríkur Magnússon had examined the matter carefully, making use of the most recent philological theories, and found Dr Auden's claims to be without any scientific foundation; 'good enough' implying that it does not really 'do service' for anything else. The last three short sentences project the message with staccato clarity: please do not bother me with any more trivial, inconsequential, amateur inquiries. And, furthermore, Eiríkur does not answer that part of the query to which he must have known the answer (unless it was included in some later incarnation of the note), namely, whether the name still existed in Iceland. It does, as Wystan Auden found out later as is shown by the quotation from his 'Letter to Lord Byron' poem noted above. Although Eiríkur Magnússon may have been tired of, as Andrew Wawn puts it, 'daily dealings with a lunatic (or at best wearisome) fringe of correspondents' (1992, 214), this was no way to treat a fellow Viking.

It is obvious that Dr Auden was already interested in the origin of his family name around the turn of the century. I think it is likely that he decided, in view of the curt reply from Eiríkur Magnússon, to annoy him no further but to continue with his own research on the problem. The fact that Eiríkur had dismissed the theory of *Auðun* and *Óðinn* being cognate forms apparently did not drive the idea out of Dr Auden's mind, for he seems to have handed it down to his youngest son. A.L. Rowse remembers Auden mentioning that his family name 'was synonymous with Odin' (1987, 43). As a scholar Rowse adds that even though Auden may have believed this to be true, the name 'may have an Anglian rather than Norse derivation'. This may indeed be so, although it would be very difficult to distinguish between possible Norse or Old English claims. Ásgeir Blöndal Magnússon points out in his Icelandic Etymological Dictionary that the Old Norse and Modern Icelandic name *Auðun(n)* is cognate with the Old English name *Ēdwine*, both being derived from the nouns meaning 'wealth' and 'friend' in the respective languages (1989, 31).

Both of Auden's biographers discuss the possible origin of his family name. Osborne (1980, 9) mentions it briefly, and comes to the conclusion that

> 'Auden' is probably an Anglo-Scandinavian corruption, 'Healfdene' or 'half Dane', though it could also be the old English 'Aelfwyne', 'elf-friend'.

Carpenter (1981, 7–8) refutes the 'Ælfwine' theory and says that it is based on a misreading. He analyses the evidence at length and cites experts on English surnames as his authority for claiming that Auden is 'just a variant of "Alden" or "Aldwyn", or perhaps "Edwin"', being 'ultimately derived from Anglo-Saxon *Healfdene*, "half Dane", or from *Ealdwine*, "old friend", or possibly from *Eadwine*, "rich friend"'. There the discussion comes full circle, as *Eadwine* has the same meaning and origin as *Auðunn*, as was mentioned earlier. It is obvious that Carpenter's specialists include P.H. Reaney in his *A Dictionary of English Surnames* (1991, 19), the same authority misquoted by Osborne. The name is not mentioned in Reaney's *The Origin of English Surnames* (1967).

Carpenter points out an interesting possibility concerning Auden's ancestry:

> The Auden ancestors might have been migrants from Iceland to Britain, possibly as a result of the fishing trade in waters between the two countries. (1981, 7)

A number of Icelanders settled in England in the fifteenth century during a period of English predominance in trade with Iceland. It is possible that the Auden family ancestor could have been one of these Icelandic immigrants or that he was an English merchant trading with Iceland and that the family tradition was garbled.[5] These possibilities seem less likely than that one of Auden's forefathers was a Scandinavian settler in the Danelaw and that the family named is formed from a later pronunciation of his name or his patronymic. As the adjective used for the origin of the family name in Dr Auden's letter to Eiríkur Magnússon is Danish and as Auden mentions in the interview from 1972, a year before his death, the belief that his father's family originally came from an area that had served as headquarters for a Viking army (both above), the conclusion must be that the family tradition points to a Danish rather than an Icelandic origin.

Humphrey Carpenter comes to the same conclusion:

> More probable, however, is the explanation that the Audens of England and the Auðuns of Iceland had only a remote connection, more than a thousand years ago, in a common Scandinavian origin, before the settlement of Iceland or the Viking invasions of Britain. And even this does not seem very likely. (1981, 7)

I would contest Carpenter's final words on the matter. I think it is at least

---

[5]On Icelanders settling in England see Björn Þorsteinsson (1969, 19; 1970, 102); Carus Wilson (1933, 166–167); *DI* 16 (236, 282–283, 365, 427, 439, 553). On English merchants involved in the Iceland trade having names that could be an earlier form of Auden see *DI* 16 (12, 17, 33, 408, 722). See also Carpenter (1981, 8n) citing P.H. Reaney (1991, 5, 19) on 'Aldine' being an earlier form of 'Auden' in support of the latter theory.

as likely that Auden is of Old Norse as of Old English derivation. It is obvious from medieval records that names, probably of Old Norse derivation, resembling the modern family name were in use in the Danelaw long after the Scandinavian settlement.[6] This, when added to the family tradition, which might be genuine, leaves the case open to interpretation. A conclusive argument cannot be put forward given the lack of evidence either positive or negative. We have to look at the material as it is and draw our own conclusion. This cannot be done with absolute objectivity, as there is always a tendency to support one side or another from the beginning based on one's initial assumptions and inclinations. In this we are joined by Auden himself, and it was obvious on which side he stood. His first name, Wystan, was the name of an Anglo-Saxon martyr. We should claim Norse ancestry for his family name, as he did throughout his life in different ways.

IV

There is a curious note in Humphrey Carpenter's biography of Auden (1981, 7) about Dr Auden's view on the origin of his family name:

> Dr Auden [...] also believed that his own family name, Auden, showed that he himself was of Icelandic descent. He believed this because 'Auden' resembles the Icelandic name Auðun or Auðunn [...], which is often found in early Norse literature and has survived as a modern Icelandic surname. George Auden apparently believed that his family was descended from or related to, a certain Auðun Skökull, who is recorded as one of the first Norse settlers in Iceland in the ninth century; and he told Wystan that before the settlement the Audens' remote ancestors had lived on the coast of the Vík, the bay to the north of modern Denmark from which the Vikings had sailed.

The 'family tradition' that the name was of Danish origin has apparently been cast aside in favour of the possibility of its being Icelandic. Maybe Eiríkur Magnússon's claim that he had never come across any such name in Denmark had something to do with this change of view. The fact is that Danish in the English Midlands tradition means anything connected with the Vikings; it is virtually impossible to decide with certainty whether a name is Danish, Norwegian or even Swedish, given the shared culture and language of these countries around the time of the Scandina-

---

[6]See list of 'Old Norse Personal Names' in Barber (1903, 18); Baring-Gould (1910, 191–198); Jón Stefánsson (1906, 296–311); see Feilitzen (1937, 18–20) for names that are similar to Auden either orthographically or phonetically.

vian settlements in England, albeit that the settlers in that part of the country were predominantly Danish. Denmark, being closest to the more developed countries in the heart of Europe, was more heavily influenced by their common Christian culture early on and thus retained less of the distinctly 'Viking' heritage. Iceland, on the contrary, was geographically furthest away from the rest of Europe and developed a unique literary tradition. The idiosyncratic 'Viking' flavour of medieval Icelandic and the abundance of literary sources, which has turned genealogy into an Icelandic national pastime, also made it a better option for nineteenth-century Englishmen searching for their Viking ancestors. The possibilities of the name Auden being of Norwegian or Danish derivation, which were on Dr Auden's mind in 1904, had apparently not been confirmed and it is as if the choice had been made to go for the more romantic appeal of the 'Saga Isle'. It goes without saying that this would be most uncharacteristic of the scientifically minded Dr George Auden, MD, MA, FSA. Either Dr Auden allowed himself to improvise on this one point—or more likely we can attribute this improvisation to his son, who was of a very different disposition, and liked to fantasise about his family origins.

The connection with Auðunn skökull is, to say the least, extremely fanciful. There is some indication that Auden really did think that the family was in some way connected with this ninth-century settler. He is mentioned frequently in the *Landnámabók*, in fact more often than all but one of his ten namesakes, according to the index to Finnur Jónsson's edition of the main manuscripts (1900, 330). The name is indeed fairly frequent in Old Icelandic literature; there are nine Auðunns mentioned in *Sturlunga saga* but only three in *Heimskringla*, including the use of the name as Óðinn's pseudonym as was mentioned above. There were two versions of the *Landnámabók* that would have been available for the scrutiny of the eager Dr Auden: the Rev. Thomas Ellwood's translation (1898), and the more recently published version by Guðbrandur Vigfússon and Frederick York Powell (1905).

> Hunda-Steinar was the name of an Earl in England. He had for wife Alof, the daughter of Ragnar Lodbrog; their children were these: Bjorn, the father of Audun Skokul and Eric, the father of Sigurd Bjod-Skalli, and Isgerd, whom Earl Thorir in Vermaländ had for wife. Audun 'Skokul' went to Iceland and settled Vididale, and dwelt at Audunstead; with him came out Thorgil gjallandi (yelling), his fellow, the father of Thorarin the 'godi.' Audun 'Skokul' was the father of Thora 'Moshals's' ('Mewsneck') the mother of Ulfhlid, the mother of Asta, the mother of St. Olave the King. (Ellwood 1898, 112–113)

This translation by Ellwood is full of printing errors, translation mistakes and inconsistencies. Auðunn skökull is referred to earlier on as 'Audun

Skokil' and the use of quotation marks around his nickname is inconsistent; moreover, unlike some of the others, this nickname is not translated. But although this translation is inadequate, I prefer it to the Vigfússon-York Powell bilingual edition in *Origines Islandicae*. The main drawback there is the metamorphosis of the Norse names into Old English equivalents. Thus poor Auðunn skökull (in Vigfússon and York Powell's diplomatic Icelandic text *Auðunn Skœkoll*) becomes the hopelessly inappropriate 'Eadwine Shackle'—the questionable fruits of Rev. Ellwood's spare-time labours seem preferable.

The ancestry of Auðunn skökull is traced back to England. Whether Hunda-Steinarr[7] is Norse or Anglo-Saxon is not mentioned. His maternal great-grandfather is the hero Ragnarr loðbrók who is the subject of one of the legendary sagas. Auðunn's grandmother Álöf Ragnarsdóttir is not mentioned in *Ragnars saga loðbrókar*, but presumably she was the daughter of his second wife Áslaug, the only issue of Sigurðr Fáfnisbani and Brynhildr Buðladóttir. Auden would have been delighted to know that his ancestor Auðunn skökull had a great-great-grandfather in Wagner's Siegfried, thus making Auden one of the Volsungs. It is possible to trace his ancestry even further back. According to *Völsunga saga* the great-great-great-grandfather of Sigurðr is none other than Óðinn himself.[8] Sadly there it is no record anywhere of Auden's having been

---

[7]In *Melabók* Lunda-Steinar.

[8](1) Auðunn skökull is, according to *Landnámabók* (Jakob Benediktsson, 1968), the settler of Auðunarstaðir in Víðidalr; (2) His father was Björn; (3) Björn's parents were Hunda-Steinarr 'jarl í Englandi' and Álöf; (4) Her father was Ragnarr loðbrók. Ragnarr had, according to *Ragnars saga loðbrókar* (Guðni Jónsson 1954, 231, 239), sons by two women. As no daughters are mentioned we can choose either one of his two wives as the mother of Álöf. For the purpose of our argument we of course choose his second wife Áslaug/Kráka/Randalín; (5) Áslaug's parents were the famed Sigurðr Fáfnisbani and Brynhildr Buðladóttir (221, 244); (6) Sigurðr's parents were Sigmundr and Hjördís Eylimadóttir, according to *Völsunga saga* (Guðni Jónsson 1954, 135-40); (7) Sigmundr's parents were Völsungr and Hljóð Hrímnisdóttir (112); (8) Völsungr's father was Rerir (110–112); (9) Rerir's father was Sigi (110); (10) Sigi's father was Óðinn (109).

Since writing this I have found out that the name of Álöf's mother is given in two genealogies, both printed by Guðbrandur Vigfússon and York Powell in *Origines Islandicae*. In these sources, *Bergsbók* and an appendix to one of the *Landnámabók* manuscripts, Þóra Borgarhjörtr, the daughter of Herruðr jarl in Gautland, is said to be Álöf's mother (1905 I 247, 271).

Sigurður A. Magnússon mentions that there is a genealogy from 1949 linking Auðunn skökull to Queen Elizabeth II: 'His great-granddaughter was the mother

aware of his divine ancestry: he would hardly have kept it quiet had he known.

Later on in *Landnámabók,* Auðunn skökull is named as one of the nine noblest (*göfgastir*) settlers in the Northern quarter of Iceland in the *Hauksbók* manuscript of *Landnáma* (Finnur Jónsson 1900, 125/4). In the two other manuscripts, *Sturlubók* (Finnur Jónsson 1900, 202/18) and *Melabók* (Finnur Jónsson 1921, 125/1), he is indeed named first of the best (*ágætastir*) men in his quarter. He is the great-great-grandfather of King Olaf the Saint and the great-great-great-grandfather of Gizurr, the second bishop of Iceland. It is also clear that the name Auðunn was handed down in the family, as two of Auðunn skökull's descendants are named after him. Carpenter's claim (above) that the name has survived in Iceland as a family name is of course a misunderstanding. As a general rule modern Icelanders do not use family names but use the traditional patronymic system. The family name *Auðuns* is of course a twentieth-century coinage from the patronymic *Auðunsson.*

Iceland also has very different traditions connected with this ancient custom. In the rest of Europe the tradition of the 'family' tends to be strongest amongst those that share a common family name. These are not the norm in Iceland and consequently the Icelandic concept of what constitutes a 'family' is somewhat different. As Icelandic women keep their patronymic after they marry, the family tradition can be as strong on the female side as on the male side. When Icelanders trace their family line back to the heroes of the Saga Age they can trace through their ancestors of either sex, although it is considered more prestigious to be descended from Egill Skallagrímsson 'í beinan karllegg' [in the direct male line] or from Auðr djúpúðga 'í beinan kvenlegg' [in the direct female line], as the attributes of these half-mythological heroes would be better carried from one generation to another down the line through members of the same sex.

There is no mention of Auðunn skökull having come from 'the coast of the Vík' (above) in any Old Norse source. I think that this is a garbled version of the fact that one possible explanation of the term 'Viking' was presumed to be (and still is) 'man from the Vík district' (Ásgeir Blöndal Magnússon 1989, 1135; see also Smyth 1977, 34; but not in Cleasby and

of St Ólaf, King of Norway (d. 1030), whose daughter married Ordulf, duke of Saxony, who died in 1074. From him there was an unbroken line of German dukes down to Ernst August, the first electoral prince of Hanover and the father of King George I of Great Britain (reigned 1714–27)' (1977, 76n).

On the accuracy of these genealogies see Jakob Benediktsson (1968, cxxx, cxxxn, 215n).

Gudbrand Vigfusson 1874, 716). It is most likely that Dr Auden would have come across the term in the *Saga-Book of the Viking Club*, where its meaning was discussed in 1904–1906 (3/3, 470-471; 4/1, 242). Even if the term 'Viking' derives from the place-name, it does not mean that these marauders preferred to sail from that particular location rather than from others in or around Scandinavia. There is also no record of Auðunn skökull having been one of the first Norse settlers. It seems unlikely, given that the *landnám* of the early settlers tended to be huge areas, later divided up amongst their followers, whereas Auðunn skökull is said only to have settled Víðidalur.

Carpenter's claim (above) that Dr Auden believed himself to be 'descended from or related to' Auðunn skökull is questionable. It seems to be out of character for a man who was so meticulously scientific in all other respects to yield to such flights of fancy. Wystan Auden indeed explained the differences between his parents in the following way:

> I don't know if it is a universal habit of children, but everybody whom I have asked about the matter tells me that he classified his parents as I did: one parent stood for stability, common sense, reality, the other for surprise, eccentricity, fantasy. In my case, it was Father who stood for the first, Mother for the second. (1973, 499)

and describing their respective families:

> On the whole, the members of my father's family were phlegmatic, earnest, rather slow, inclined to be miserly, and endowed with excellent health; my mother's were quick, short-tempered, generous, and liable to physical ill health, hysteria, and neuroticism. Except in the matter of physical ill health, I take after them. (499)

It is indeed likely that Dr Auden pointed out the similarity between the name of this fabled 'ancestor' and the family name to his young son, and possibly suggested a connection. Auden did not see his father between the ages of seven and twelve and a half because of his serving in World War I (500). Any tidbits about the family origin told to a seven year old would be stored away securely in his memory and treasured, taking on added significance as the years of separation grew longer. Wystan Hugh Auden had, according to himself, a character that was the complete opposite of his father's, taking more after his mother. His childish romantic imagination, fuelled by the Old Norse myths, Icelandic legends, and tales from the sagas, wanted to identify with them *and* establish and maintain a link with the absent father and the 'family tradition'. By the time his father returned from the war and was in a position to clarify the matter with the now adolescent Wystan, it had already become a part of his personal mythology. In an interview in Iceland during his second sojourn in that country (Matthías Johannessen 1977, 225), Auden mentions that he did not start reading things about Iceland until the age of eleven. His father had been absent for several years and it is therefore unlikely to have been at his instigation that Auden turned to Norse literature. Maybe the little boy found comfort in reading about things which he knew his father approved of in an attempt to identify with him in some way, however intangible.

In 'Letter to Lord Byron', Part I (1936, 17–24) Auden discusses his shortcomings as a traveller and a writer:

> The shades of Asquith and of Auden Skökull
> Turn in their coffins a three-quarter circle
> To see their son, upon whose help they reckoned,
> Being as frivolous as Charles the Second.
>
> (1937, 23)

The reference to 'Auden Skökull' in the poem has been taken to refer to his presumed ancestry. I think this assumption is based on a misunderstanding. The two names 'Asquith' and 'Auden Skökull' are supposed to exemplify the opposites in Auden's background and character. Asquith refers to Herbert Henry Asquith (1852–1928), the Liberal Prime Minister (1908–1916).[9] Asquith symbolises dreary stability in Auden's mind, those English attributes which Auden inherited from his professional middle class background: in Mendelson's words (1981, xxi) 'religious observance and public obligation'. 'Auden Skökull' seems to refer to Auden's other self, the pagan Icelandic side which he seems to have associated in his mind with those aspects of his character which did not conform to middle-class morality: the surprise, eccentricity, fantasy element he inherited from his mother. Who could signify these things better than a Viking? Auden has blurred the distinction between himself and his chosen 'ancestor' by changing the spelling from 'Audun' to 'Auden'.

Humphrey Carpenter points out in a footnote (1982, 7) that 'the name "Skökull" means "carriage-pole", and seems also to have been used as slang for "penis".' He does not elaborate any further on these connota-

---

[9]Asquith is referred to in the *Encyclopaedia Britannica* as 'a competent statesman, but not a great one. He had no original or innovating genius and lacked the sense of the dramatic needed to convince Britain that it was in good hands in a time of national crisis.' The official biography was written by J.A. Spender, an uncle of Auden's friend Stephen Spender. A quotation from Mendelson (1981, 28) may make this Asquith reference in the poem clearer: 'By the time he [Auden] went up to Oxford in 1925 he had made plain his rejection of the family ethic of public service. Politicians, he told his friends, were lackeys who ought to be ignored.'

tions. In a chapter on 'Letter to Lord Byron' Anthony Hecht (1993, 185), after quoting Carpenter, comments that 'in this way Auden contrived to insinuate the erotic into the close as well as the opening of the First Part [of the Poem]'. He does not say, however, what role the erotic has in the poem. Hecht asks himself what buried reason there may be for Auden identifying with Byron and hints that the connection is homosexual (180). I think we can take a step further and state that Auden identified with Byron because of their shared status as sexual outlaws. This can be traced back to the position of the character of Don Juan in European literature; Auden borrowed the verse form for his 'Letter to Lord Byron' and its chatty tone from Byron's *Letter to Don Juan*. There are three erotic references in the first part of 'Letter to Lord Byron'. In the first, Auden is discussing the nature of the imaginary 'fan-mail' which Byron is receiving, his own offering being one of these letters:

> Sometimes sly hints at a platonic pash,
> And sometimes, though I think this rather crude,
> The correspondent's photo in the rude.
>
> (1937, 17)

This opens the erotic discourse of this part of the poem. The next reference is more overtly homosexual:

> But still confession is a human want,
>> So Englishmen must make theirs now by post
>> And authors hear them over breakfast toast.
> For, failing them, there's nothing but the wall
> Of public lavatories on which to scrawl.

Auden is referring to the role of the 'cottage' (public toilets) as a meeting-place or sanctuary for homosexuals. He scrawls his confession to Byron (a fellow 'deviant') on the toilet wall—a space which is usually reserved for more purposeful messages.

This finally brings us to the reference to 'Auden Skökull'. I think the hidden link to which Hecht refers is not so much literary as psychological. Auden, having compared himself to Byron, establishes his ancestry/background by introducing 'Asquith' and 'Auden Skökull', the binary opposites, the two contradictory sides of himself: one representing respectability and the other outlawry. In the Cleasby-Vigfússon *Icelandic-English Dictionary* (565), the probable source of Carpenter's version above, the first definition given for *skökull* is 'the pole of a cart' or 'carriage'. The second one is euphemistically rendered as 'a horse-yard', a horse's penis (this meaning of 'yard' is deemed obsolete by the *OED*). We may surely draw the conclusion that Auðunn skökull's nickname was not due to his having a close resemblance to the first explanation of the term. George Auden may have been blissfully unaware of the probable meaning of his chosen ancestor's nickname, for the alternative dictionary which he may have used, Sveinbjörn Egilsson's *Lexicon Poeticum* (first published in 1860), gives the second meaning as (Danish) *buk*, 'billy goat' (1913-1916, 516). Auden is obviously aware of the real meaning of *skökull* as a nickname and revels in this information. His identification of his 'bad side' is completed by changing the name for it from 'Audun' to 'Auden'. 'Auden Skökull' combines risqué sexuality and Auden's identification with Iceland and makes this third 'erotic' reference in the poem the conclusive element in forging the psychological link with Byron and, more remotely, with Don Juan.[10]

V

Geoffrey Grigson sums up many of the aspects of Auden's ancestry, real or imaginary, and how one side contributes to the other:

> What kind of name was *Auden*? In the early Auden years I liked to think this name of his must be Old Norse, proper for a poet who knew about trolls running along the edges of the mind, liked Morris's *Sigurd the Volsung*, read the sagas, and visited (I had been there before him, impelled, I suppose, by the same kind of reading) the 'sterile, immature', cindery landscape of Icelandic dales and plains—the great plains 'forever where the cold fish is hunted'. The surname dictionary says Auden could be Anglo-Scandinavian, *Healfdene*, 'half Dane'. That would do. But it could also be English, from *Ælfwine* 'elf-friend'. That, too, would serve for this Wystan Auden, the elf-friend, the magician, allowing that there are good and bad elves, good and bad magicians. (1975, 14–15)

There is no denying that Iceland, both its literature, culture and history, and imaginary ideas based on all these and mixed with other elements to form a mythical cosmos of the 'North', greatly influenced Wystan Auden, both in his work and in his life. This forms an integral part of his imaginary world throughout his career, but especially in the early years. This fact has been more or less overlooked by his critics, mainly because they have lacked the prerequisite knowledge of Icelandic culture, literature and language needed to examine the question.

Let us end with the words of Louis MacNeice, Auden's fellow traveller in Iceland, taken from his poem 'Epilogue', dedicated to Auden, and

---

[10]It is interesting to note in this context that the man who served as prototype for Tirso de Molina's Don Juan de Tenorio was homosexual according to Robert Stradling (1993, 16).

appended to *Letters from Iceland*. These few lines explain as well as any words in what way Auden was Icelandic. He was not a scholar of Icelandic literature; he spoke only a few words of the language and read the literature in translation; he never lived in the country and made only two short trips there; and his ancestral links with Iceland are very tenuous. But the fact that Auden identified with Iceland from an early age to his dying day cannot be denied:

> And the don in me set forth
> How the landscape of the north
> Had educed the saga style
> Plodding forward mile by mile
>
> And the don in you replied
> That the North begins inside
>
> (1937, 259)

BIBLIOGRAPHY

[Author unknown]. 1908. Obituary of J.R. Allen, *Saga-Book of the Viking Club* 5/2, 404.

Allen, J. Romilly. 1895. 'Prehistoric Art of the North', *Saga-Book of the Viking Club* 1/1, 54–73.

Ásgeir Blöndal Magnússon. 1989. *Íslenzk orðsifjabók*. Reykjavík.

Auden, George Augustus. 1904. Letter to Eiríkur Magnússon: 28 May 1904 (Lbs. 2186a 4to).

―――. 1905–1907. Letters to John Romilly Allen: 27 October 1905; 10 November 1905; 30 October 1906; 12 March 1907 (BL Add. MS 37,603, No. LXV, 166–167, 471–476).

―――, ed. 1906. *Historical and Scientific Survey of York and District*. [Also published as *A Handbook to York and District*]. Prepared for the 75th meeting of the British Association. York.

―――. 1907. 'York', in 'Reports of District Secretaries', *Saga-Book of the Viking Club* 5/1, 55–59.

―――. 1908a. 'York', in 'Reports of District Secretaries', *Saga-Book of the Viking Club* 5/2, 247–250.

―――. 1908b. 'Pre-conquest Cross at Rolleston, Staffordshire', *The Reliquary and Illustrated Archæology* [January].

―――. 1910a. 'Abstract of a Paper on Antiquities Dating from the Danish Occupation of York', *Saga-Book of the Viking Club* 6/2, 169–179.

―――. 1910b. [Signed G.A.A.] 'Review of *York in English History* by J.L. Brockbank and W.M. Holmes', *Year Book of the Viking Club* 2, 54–55.

————. 1910c. [Signed G.A.A.] 'Review of *Proceedings of the Barrow Natural History Field Club and Literary and Scientific Society* Vol. XVII', *Year Book of the Viking Club* 2, 69.

————, ed. 1913. *A Handbook for Birmingham and Neighbourhood.* Prepared for the 83rd Annual Meeting of the British Association for the Advancement of Science. Birmingham.

[Auden, George Augustus.] [1908]. *Guide for Visitors: The Danish Collection, Prehistoric Period.* [The National Museum]. Copenhagen.

Auden, George Augustus and Harold A. Auden, trans. 1906. Fredrich Rathgen, *The Preservation of Antiquities: A Handbook for Curators.* Cambridge.

Auden, Wystan Hugh. 1963. *The Dyer's Hand and Other Essays.* London.

————. 1967. Foreword, in W.H. Auden and Louis MacNeice, *Letters from Iceland*, 2nd ed., pp. 9–11. London.

————. 1971. *A Certain World: A Commonplace Book.* London.

————. 1973. *Forewords and Afterwords* [Selected by Edward Mendelson]. London.

Auden, Wystan Hugh and MacNeice, Louis. 1937. *Letters from Iceland.* London.

Barber, Henry. 1903. *British Family-Names; Their Origin and Meaning: With Lists of Scandinavian, Frisian, Anglo-Saxon, and Norman Names* (2nd ed., enlarged). London.

Bardsley, Charles Wareing. 1897. *English Surnames, Their Sources and Significations.* 5th ed. London.

————. 1901. *A Dictionary of English and Welsh Surnames* (with special American instances). London.

Baring-Gould, Sabine. 1910. *Family Names and Their Story.* London.

Bjarni Aðalbjarnarson, ed. 1941. Snorri Sturluson, *Heimskringla.* Reykjavík.

Björn Þorsteinsson. 1969. *Enskar heimildir um sögu Íslendinga á 15. og 16. öld.* Reykjavík.

————. 1970. *Enska öldin í sögu Íslendinga.* Reykjavík.

Burton, Richard, Sir. 1975. *Ultima Thule: or, A Summer in Iceland.* 2 vols. London.

Callan, Edward. 1983. *Auden: A Carnival of Intellect.* Oxford.

Carpenter, Humphrey. 1981. *W.H. Auden: A Biography.* London.

Carus Wilson, E.M. 1933. 'The Iceland Trade', in Eileen Power and M.M. Postan, eds, *The Iceland Trade. Studies in English Trade in the Fifteenth Century*, pp. 155–182. London.

Cleasby, Richard and Gudbrand Vigfusson. 1874. *An Icelandic–English Dictionary.* Oxford.

Connolly, Cyril. 1975. 'Some Memories', in Stephen Spender, ed., *W.H. Auden: A Tribute*, pp. 68–73. London.

Collingwood, William Gershom. 1907. 'Some Illustrations of the Archaeology of the Viking Age in England', *Saga-Book of the Viking Club* 5/1, 111-141.

———. 1908. 'Anglian and Anglo-Danish Sculpture in the North Riding of Yorkshire', *Saga-Book of the Viking Club* 5/2, 410–411.

———. 1989. 'Northumbrian Crosses of the Pre-Norman Age.' (Reduced facsimile of the 1927 ed.). Lampeter.

Cunningham, Valentine D. 1989. *British Writers of the Thirties*. Oxford.

DI = *Diplomatarium Islandicum: Íslenzkt fornbréfasafn* 16. 1952–1959. Reykjavík.

Eiríkur Magnússon. 1904. Letter to George Augustus Auden: 2 June 1904 (Lbs. 2181a 4to).

———. 1905. *Heimskringla* 4 (The Saga Library, 6). [A biography of Snorri Sturluson and indexes]. London.

Eiríkur Magnússon and Morris, William, trans. 1893. Snorri Sturluson, *Heimskringla* 1 (The Saga Library, 3). London.

Ellwood, Rev. T., trans. 1898. *The Book of Settlement of Iceland*. Kendal.

Feilitzen, Olof von. 1937. *The Pre-Conquest Personal Names of Domesday Book* (Nomina Germanica: Arkiv för Germansk Namnforskning, 3). Uppsala.

Finnur Jónsson, ed. 1900. *Landnámabók* (Hauksbók, Sturlubók, Melabók). Copenhagen.

———, ed. 1921. *Landnámabók* (Melabók (Þórðarbók)). Copenhagen.

Grigson, Geoffrey. 1975. 'A Meaning of Auden', in Stephen Spender, ed., *W.H. Auden: A Tribute*, pp. 13–16, 25. London.

Grimm, Jakob. 1888. James Steven Stallybrass, trans., *Teutonic Mythology*. 4 vols. London.

Guðbrandur Vigfússon and York Powell, Frederick, eds and trans. 1905. *Origines Islandicae*. 2 vols. Oxford.

Guðni Jónsson, ed. 1954. *Fornaldarsögur Norðurlanda* 1. (Includes *Völsunga saga* and *Ragnars saga loðbrókar*). Reykjavík.

Hanks, Patrick and Hodges, Flavia. 1988. *A Dictionary of Surnames*. Oxford.

Hecht, Anthony. 1993. *The Hidden Law: The Poetry of W.H. Auden*. London.

Isherwood, Christopher. 1937. 'Some Notes on Auden's Early Poetry', in *New Verse* 26–27, 4–9.

———. 1985. *Lions and Shadows: An Education in the Twenties*. (First ed. 1938). London.

Jakob Benediktsson, ed. 1968. *Íslendingabók—Landnámabók*. Íslenzk fornrit 1. 2 vols. Reykjavík.

Jón Espólín. 1821–1855. *Íslands árbækur í sögu-formi*. Copenhagen.

Jón Stefánsson. 1906. 'The Oldest Known List of Scandinavian Names', *Saga-Book of the Viking Club*, 4/2, 296–311.

Lbs. = Landsbókasafn Íslands, The National Library of Iceland

MacNeice, Louis. 1965. E.R. Dodds, ed., *The Strings Are False: An Unfinished Autobiography*. London.

Major, Albany F. 1906. 'Review of Dr. Fredrich Rathgen's *The Preservation of Antiquities: A Handbook for Curators*, translated by G.A. Auden and Harold A. Auden', *Saga-Book of the Viking Club* 4/2, 479.

———. 1907. 'Review of G.A. Auden's *A Handbook to York and District*', *Saga-Book of the Viking Club* 5/1, 195.

Matthías Johannessen. 1977. 'Maður má ekki ljúga í ljóði: W.H. Auden', *M: Samtöl* 1, 224–234.

Mendelson, Edward. 1981. *Early Auden*. London.

The National Union Catalog Pre-1956 Imprints, 25. 1969. London.

Newman, Michael. 1977. 'W.H. Auden', in George Plimpton, ed., *Writers at Work: The Paris Review Interviews* 4, pp. 243-269. London.

Oehlenschläger, Adam Gottlob. 1840. *Hakon Jarl: A Tragedy in Five Acts, and Poems after Various Authors* (translator not named). London.

———. 1849. 'Hakon Jarl'. *Oehlenschläger's Tragødier* III 115–246. Copenhagen.

———. 1857. John Chapman, trans., *Hakon Jarl: A Tragedy in Five Acts*. London.

———. 1874. F.C. Lascelles, trans., *Earl Hakon the Mighty*. London.

———. 1911. Frederick Strange Kolle, trans., *Hakon Jarl: An Historical Tragedy*. New York.

Osborne, Charles. 1980. *W.H. Auden: The Life of a Poet*. London.

Pudney, John. 1960. *Home and Away: An Autobiographical Gambit*. London.

Ragnars saga loðbrókar. See Guðni Jónsson.

Reaney, P.H., 1967. *The Origin of English Surnames*. London.

———. 1991. *A Dictionary of English Surnames*. 3rd ed. with corr. and add. by R.M. Wilson. London.

Rowse, A.L. 1987. *The Poet Auden: A Personal Memoir*. London.

Sigurður A. Magnússon. 1977. *Northern Sphinx: Iceland and the Icelanders from the Settlement to the Present*. London.

Smith, A.H. 1936. 'Early Northern Nick-names and Surnames', *Saga-Book* 10 [1928–1936], 30–60.

Smyth, Alfred P. 1977. *Scandinavian Kings in the British Isles 850–880*. Oxford.

Spears, Monroe K. 1963. *The Poetry of W.H. Auden: The Disenchanted Island*. New York.

Spender, Stephen. 1951. *World Within World*. London.

———. 1973. *W.H. Auden: A Memorial Address*. London.

————, ed. 1975. *W.H. Auden: A Tribute*. London.

Stradling, Robert. 1993. 'The Death of Don Juan: Murder, Myth and Mayhem in Madrid', *History Today* 43, 11–17.

Sveinbjörn Egilsson. 1913–1916. *Lexicon Poeticum antiquæ linguæ septentrionalis*. Copenhagen.

Völsunga saga. See Guðni Jónsson.

Townsend, J.A.B. 1992. 'The Viking Society: A Centenary History', *Saga-Book* 23/4, 180–212.

Wawn, Andrew. 1992. 'The Spirit of 1892: Sagas, Saga-Steads and Victorian Philology', *Saga-Book* 23/4, 213–252.

12

The English Translations of *Völsunga Saga*

JOHN KENNEDY

I

It has become a cliché in the study of translations that the translator is necessarily an interpreter of the text he or she is translating, particularly if it is a literary text. A translation of a literary text cannot fail to reveal something of the translator's attitude to the source language, the target language, and the cultures associated with them, and something of how he or she regards the task of translation. But translations also reflect the period in which they are produced, and if a text is significant enough to have been translated several times into a certain language over an extended time span, comparison of the translations may reveal something of the varying reception of the text in the cultural history of the users of that target language.

There are several reasons why *Völsunga saga* seems to offer a suitable focus for comparative study, at least for someone interested in English translations. Leaving out of consideration the practice of summarising or paraphrasing the saga, which began in 1806 with William Herbert's summary in his *Select Icelandic Poetry* and seems to have enjoyed its greatest popularity on both sides of the Atlantic in the four decades before 1914, and also passing over Jacqueline Simpson's translation of extracts from the saga in *Beowulf and its Analogues,* first published in 1968 by her and G.N. Garmonsway, *Völsunga saga* has appeared in complete English translation the manageable number of five times from when Eiríkur Magnússon and William Morris first presented their version to the public in 1870. As the second translation (by Margaret Schlauch) appeared in 1930, the third (R.G. Finch) in 1965, the fourth (G.K. Anderson) in 1982, and the fifth (Jesse Byock) in 1990,[1] the intervals between them form a rough geometrical progression, though it would probably be unwise to attach great significance to this or to expect that the appearance of future translations of the saga will continue the pattern

---

[1]See Herbert 1804–06, II 20–33; Garmonsway and Simpson 1968, 252–264, 276–279; Eiríkur Magnússon and Morris 1870, facsimile repr. 1980; Schlauch 1930; Finch 1965; Anderson 1982; Byock 1990. Quotations from the five complete translations of *Völsunga saga* are drawn from the editions listed here.

of reducing the interval by half! It should be noted, however, that a *Völsunga saga* translation by Haukur Böðvarsson and Kaaren Grimstad was announced some years ago, and that although Haukur has died Professor Grimstad intends to complete the project.[2] All five complete published translations are likely to be quite readily accessible. After being republished in several British and American editions before 1914,[3] the Eiríkur Magnússon-William Morris version reappeared in 1962 in a cheap paperback edition, with an introduction by Robert W. Gutman, and this was reprinted at least twice, in 1967 and 1971 (Morris 1962). That the intended primary market was not a scholarly one is clearly indicated by such details as the disappearance of Eiríkur Magnússon's name from the title page, the splendid horned helmet worn by the figure on the 1967 cover, and by the assurance on the first page of the book that 'From the mist-shrouded world of the Norsemen come these marvellous tales of adventure, vibrant with life and imagination'. A facsimile reprint of the original 1870 version came out in 1980. Schlauch's 1930 version has had a more subdued bibliographic career, but the American-Scandinavian Foundation republished it in 1949 and 1964, and AMS Press brought out a reprint in 1976. To judge from the 1992-1993 edition of the US listing *Books in Print*, and the May 1993 CD-ROM version of the British listing *Whitaker's Bookbank* only the Finch version is completely out of print.[4]

Though all five versions seem to differ somewhat as to the editions of the Old Norse text on which they are based, the task of comparison is simplified by the relatively straightforward manuscript situation. *Völsunga saga* exists in only one medieval manuscript (Ny kgl. Saml. 1824b 4to), dated to about 1400, and in paper versions from the seventeenth to nineteenth centuries which all directly or indirectly derive from the medieval vellum, though they provide readings of varying degrees of usefulness when the medieval manuscript is illegible as a result of deterioration.

A further reason for concentrating on *Völsunga saga* is the fact that it is generally classified as one of the *fornaldarsögur*, a genre which usually receives far less attention in considerations of English translations from

[2]Kaaren Grimstad, letter to the writer, 24 September 1990.

[3]See Halldór Hermannsson 1912, 44–47; 1937, 64–65; Fry 1980, 104–105. Bibliographical information about English language translations, paraphrases, and summaries can be found in these works and Acker 1993, 102.

[4]Hisarlik Press has published Byock's translation in an unaltered reprint, which is actually dated 1993 although *Bookbank* incorrectly lists the date of publication as November 1992.

the Old Norse than the *Íslendingasögur* and *konungasögur*. Though *Völsunga saga* is an unusual *fornaldarsaga* (and indeed an unusual Icelandic saga) in that many of its principal characters and situations are likely to be quite familiar to educated readers of English encountering it for the first time, thanks largely to Richard Wagner,[5] it may be of interest to observe the extent to which an awareness of the *fornaldarsögur* as works different from the other genres emerges from the translations.

II

The modern reader who picks up *Völsunga Saga: The Story of the Volsungs & Niblungs,* as Eiríkur Magnússon and William Morris called their version, will immediately become aware of the markedly archaic quality of the writing. It is full of words, phrases, and syntactic constructions no longer in general use: particularly striking is the frequent appearance in dialogue of the obsolete second person singular pronouns 'thou' and 'thee' and of the second person singular verbal inflection '–est'. This impression of archaism owes of course almost nothing to the passage of more than a hundred and twenty years since the translation was first published: an anonymous reviewer in *The Athenæum* (11 June 1870, 764) described the translation as 'too elaborately and obtrusively archaic'.

But though never universally accepted, the approach adopted by Eiríkur Magnússon and William Morris reflected an attitude to translating ancient and medieval texts which was widespread at that time. An archaic style was felt to add dignity to a translation, to demonstrate proper respect for the text being translated. More importantly, it was felt to emphasise the remoteness in time of the text's composition, and to replicate in some degree the experience which a fluent reader of the source language in modern times would experience in confronting the original. Writing in 1902 W.G. Collingwood and Jón Stefánsson summed up the approach by means of an analogy:

> Now in copying an old picture one may try to restore it,—to make it look
> as it did to contemporaries when the colours were fresh; or one may take
> it as we find it now. It is always dangerous to restore. We have not the
> contemporaries' eyes to see it with, even if we were successful in

---

[5]The extent of Wagner's knowledge of *Völsunga saga*, and when he acquired this knowledge, are not straightforward matters. See Magee 1990, esp. 13, 18–19, 30, 44–49, 56, 60–61, 153–154.

reproducing the old-fashioned handiwork. So in translating a Saga, we cannot hear it read or said by the ancient Saga-teller, nor put ourselves in the place of his mediaeval audience. It is impossible to treat it as a contemporary narration. Part of the charm they found in it is gone; another charm has come to it from its faded age and coated varnish of antiquity, through which the human nature still shines, attracting us to our kin of long ago. (Collingwood and Jón Stefánsson 1902, 21)

'Our kin of long ago' is significant here, for there was an additional argument for using old vocabulary and old grammar when translating the Icelandic sagas that did not apply to Greek and Latin texts, and of this William Morris and his disciples were very aware. Old English was far more similar to Old Norse than Modern English is, and by imitating older forms of English and using where possible Germanic words rather than their Romance equivalents the translator could stress the ancient link between the English-speaking peoples and the Scandinavians. One could also take over into English far more of the vocabulary and the grammatical constructions to be found in the sagas, arguably thus giving the English-speaking reader a better idea of what the Icelandic text was like. Writing after Morris's death Eiríkur Magnússon stressed this point:

> As to the *style* of Morris little need be said except this that it is a strange misunderstanding to describe all terms in his translations which are not familiar to the reading public as 'pseudo-Middle-English'. Anyone in a position to collate the Icelandic text with the translation will see at a glance that in the overwhelming majority of cases these terms are literal translations of the Icel. originals, e.g. by-men—býjar-menn = town's people. (Eiríkur Magnússon 1893–1905, IV vii–viii)

In his 'Introduction' to the 1962 reprint Robert Gutman offered as part of his defence of the translation the argument that it was a characteristic product of its era:

> His [Morris's] language, rich and varied, was Victorian, of an age that in general admired the opulent, the intricate, and the ornate, as witness the great creations in architecture of Pugin and the full-voiced diapason of Ruskin's almost Biblical prose. Is Morris to be reproved because he spoke in the accents of his era? The forms he chose accord with the subject matter; the archaisms he introduced help achieve tone. The old Norse poets sought atmosphere by the very same means; it is interesting to observe in the ancient skaldic lays the use of already obsolete words. (Gutman in Morris 1962, 79)

William Morris might not joyfully have accepted every point in this defence, but doubtless he did believe that his choice of vocabulary accorded with the subject matter, and that the archaisms helped establish an appropriate tone. It is worth stressing, however, that similar methods were used in the many other translations from the Old Icelandic on which he and Eiríkur Magnússon collaborated, including their versions of *Heimskringla* and such *Íslendingasögur* as *Bandamanna saga, Eyrbyggja saga* and *Heiðarvíga saga* (Eiríkur Magnússon and Morris 1891, 1892). Indeed their *Völsunga saga* translation, an early work, probably presents a comparatively mild example of their style. There is no evidence that they saw an archaic style as especially appropriate to a saga of heroes and supernatural beings set in a very remote past. The same style was considered appropriate for accounts of eleventh-century Icelandic farmers and twelfth-century Norwegian kings.

Victorian translators of Old Norse material frequently provided copious editorial material, but here Eiríkur Magnússon and Morris were sparing in this regard: the 'Preface' runs to only six pages, and there are less than two pages of notes. The edition, they claim, is directed 'to the lover of poetry and nature, rather than to the student' (Eiríkur Magnússon and Morris 1870, v). They do, however, provide an extensive selection of translations from the *Poetic Edda*, most of them treating of subject matter dealt with in the saga, though at least two pieces won inclusion primarily because they appealed to the translators (Eiríkur Magnússon and Morris 1870, vii, x). Some of this verse is inserted in the body of the saga translation where, of course, it joins translations of verse found in the medieval saga manuscript. Like many other Victorian editors and translators they did not have the reverence for the integrity of the manuscript versions of medieval texts which has dominated much twentieth-century scholarship.

The 1870 translation was in every sense a pioneering effort, published just before the 1874 Cleasby-Vigfússon *An Icelandic–English Dictionary*. It contains a number of inaccuracies, turgid and obscure passages, and passages which bring an inappropriate smile to the modern face ('Why art thou so bare of bliss? this manner of thine grieveth us thy friends; why then wilt thou not hold to thy gleesome ways?', ch. 24, 82). But the reader can sense that this rendition of 'the best tale pity every wrought' was a labour of love, and indeed the performance of a sacred duty, 'for this is the Great Story of the North, which should be to all our race what the Tale of Troy was to the Greeks' (Eiríkur Magnússon and Morris 1870, xx, xi).

III

Margaret Schlauch published her *The Saga of the Volsungs* in 1930, soon after the midpoint of that twenty year interval between the World Wars which seems to have yielded only a modest crop of major English translations from the Old Norse. Archaism still had its supporters: E.R. Eddison argued quite passionately in favour of old-fashioned language in an essay, 'Some Principles of Translation', appended to his translation of *Egils saga Skalla-Grímssonar*, published that same year (Eddison 1930). But an alternative view urging that the sagas be translated into an unadorned contemporary prose was gaining ground, having been strikingly exemplified in 1925 by the *Laxdæla saga* translation of the noted economist Thorstein Veblen (Veblen 1925).

Whilst proclaiming her admiration for the Eiríkur Magnússon-William Morris translation and declaring it 'essentially accurate', Schlauch complained that 'the excessively archaic language he [Morris] chose to employ, out of very respect for his original, is unfortunately all but incomprehensible in places'. Her declared response was to employ a 'slightly archaic style', attempting 'to avoid any expressions not immediately understandable to a modern reader', and she adds: 'I have confined most archaic locutions to the dialogue' (Schlauch 1930, xxx–xxxi).

The result is a translation which often does have a decidedly archaic flavour, particularly in its direct speech (for example, 'Who art thou that ridest into this burg, where none may enter save by the leave of my sons?': ch. 26, 121). It is a style markedly in contrast to that for which Schlauch herself argued forcibly twenty years later when she translated *Bandamanna saga* and *Droplaugarsona saga*, and moreover one which she at least partly rejected in reviewing the Finch translation of *Völsunga saga* in 1967: 'I may say that I now question the Biblical archaisms (morphological rather than lexicographical) which I introduced into my own translation of the saga back in 1930' (Schlauch 1967, 208, a review of Finch 1965; also Schlauch in Scargill and Schlauch 1950, 54).

The reason for the use of archaisms in 1930 was Schlauch's conviction that 'even to the Sagaman it [*Völsunga saga*] was a tale of remote, ancient days, of gods and demigods and half mythical kings' (Schlauch 1930, xxxi). A very similar attitude was held at that time by E.V. Gordon, probably England's most distinguished Old Norse scholar then active. In introducing Stella Mills's 1933 translation of another of the *fornaldarsögur, Hrólfs saga kraka*, he remarked:

> One considerable risk was taken by the translator, but she is justified
> by the result. The translation includes many archaic forms and idioms,
> though it is free from any taint of Wardour Street, where so many
> false antiques were sold. The habit of heavy archaism has in the past
> given a very misleading impression of Icelandic style. Saga-tellers
> and saga-writers had nothing equivalent: they used the language of
> their own time, almost the language of everyday use. In this transla-
> tion the mild archaism is not misleading. Hrolf's saga tells of events
> of ancient days (the sixth century), and the fourteenth century author
> was fully conscious of the antiquity of his matter. The flavour of
> archaism is just what is needed to express this consciousness.
> (Gordon in Mills 1933, xii)

In 1950 Schlauch was still prepared to state that an archaic translation
style might be defensible for the 'mythical-heroic sagas', that is, the
fornaldarsögur (Schlauch in Scargill and Schlauch 1950, 54).

Like the 1870 translation, that of Margaret Schlauch does not seem
directed towards the student. There is an informative but non-technical
introduction, and a very brief bibliography, but no indexes or notes on
the translation text. The volume does usefully provide what is still the
only complete English translation of *Ragnars saga loðbrókar,* a work
appearing virtually as a continuation of *Völsunga saga* in the medieval
manuscript, though only tenuously linked to it in its characters and
subject matter. There is also a verse translation of the relatively short
Krákumál.

IV

The third translation of *Völsunga saga*, by R.G. Finch, appeared facing
the normalised Old Icelandic text in one of the few volumes published
in the brave but short-lived series Nelson's Icelandic Texts. Despite what
one might expect, however, the translation was not a minor part of the
edition, or a literal and unliterary crib designed to assist students make
sense of the Icelandic. Professor Finch's version reads fluently: indeed
one reviewer complained that occasionally it 'sacrificed accuracy for
fluency, and that is a step along the primrose path' (Page 1967, 280).

Finch attempts 'to provide an English version as free as possible from
unnecessary archaisms'. While accepting Schlauch's argument that 'even
to the Sagaman it was a tale of remote ancient days', he rejected the view
that it was appropriate to signal this by self-consciously old fashioned
language: 'there can be little doubt that the legendary heroes were as real
to the people of the mediaeval North as those of the more immediate
past, and the compiler of *Völsunga saga* aims at presenting his poetic

material in straightforward saga style and language' (Finch 1965, xxxix).

It would be hard to argue that in adopting a fluent, modern, slightly colloquial prose style Finch was not in accord with the translating spirit of the times, or at least a major strand within it. The aim of the enormously popular Penguin Classics series (which produced four volumes of Icelandic saga translations as part of its large output in the 1960s) was to provide the reader with translations which lowered the barriers of time and place, rendering even poetic texts like *The Iliad* and *The Aeneid* into prose which could be read almost as easily as a conventional twentieth-century novel. Whereas Victorian translators like Morris had tended to emphasise the 'otherness' of what was being translated, the aim now often was to make it as accessible and enjoyable as scholarly integrity permitted.

There were dissenters, of course. Hedin Bronner harshly denounced the 1960 translation of *Brennu-Njáls saga*, by Magnus Magnusson and Hermann Pálsson, stating that the translation

> simply is not a saga. The terseness, the dignity, the stylistic range between fire and ice, have been replaced by a chatty and pedestrian prose [...]. And when *allmikill lögmaðr* (great lawman) is rendered as 'outstanding lawyer', it is a Hollywood courtroom melodrama rather than the Alþing tragedy that looms before us. (Bronner 1962, 318)

Perhaps fortunate in that he was working on a less exalted original Finch did not encounter criticism of this severity, though it is certainly possible to point to occasions when the tone of middle class modernity jars. One example comes toward the end of the saga, when King Atli reproaches his wife Guðrún, who after slaughtering their children and serving them to him as food has now taken part in fatally wounding him. The Icelandic reads (in Finch's own edition): 'ok þína sværu léztu opt með gráti sitja' (ch. 40, 73). It may not be a particularly successful touch in the original, but Finch's 'and you often had your mother-in-law in tears' (p. 73) seems to strike the wrong note of bourgeois domesticity. Even Eiríkur Magnússon and Morris's 'and thy mother-in-law full oft thou lettest sit a-weeping' (ch. 39, 153) and Schlauch's 'and thou hast oft given my mother cause to sit weeping' (ch. 38, 173) seem less incongruous.

Notwithstanding its very readable translation Finch's volume is provided with the kind of apparatus traditionally associated with scholarly editions of medieval texts, and seems directed at an academic rather than a popular audience. The level of the material suggests an attempt to meet the needs of serious students who have been studying Old Norse for a year or two, rather than those of experienced Old Norse specialists who could doubtless produce their own translation.

V

It has been suggested in examining the first three translations of *Völsunga saga* that they were in large measure products of their times. With George K. Anderson's 1982 translation the situation is somewhat different. It is a posthumous publication, having been seen through the press by Geoffrey Russom after Professor Anderson's death in January 1980 at the age of seventy-eight. George Anderson had a long and distinguished career as a specialist in Old and Middle English literature, and according to T.M. Andersson, he 'developed a strong interest in Norse literature toward the end of his life' (Andersson 1983, 841; also Russom in Anderson 1982, 9).

The George Anderson volume is indeed marked by characteristics one is inclined to associate with a labour of love compiled when the pressures of a professional scholarly career have been lifted. It is in fact far more than just a translation of *Völsunga saga*. Also included are a 'Genealogical Table', 'Notes on the Pronunciation of Old Norse Words', a 'Specimen of Old Norse, with English Translation', an 'Introduction' to *Völsunga saga*, 167 often lengthy notes on the translation, an extract from *Skáldskaparmál* with introduction and notes, an extract from *Norna-Gests þáttr* with introduction and notes, an extended précis of the *Nibelungenlied*, a short essay entitled 'Two Views of the *Nibelungenlied*', a 'Synopsis of the *Thridrekssaga*', a 'Glossary of Minor Characters', a 155 item annotated bibliography, and an Index. We often move far from the text of *Völsunga saga*; and the commentary often has a chatty, uninhibited quality avoided by most academic writers in their scholarly publications: 'Müllenhof's approach—for the time and for his country only moderately arrogant—indicates that only professional scholars can know; therefore let amateurs keep away' (Anderson 1982, 246).

But while Anderson sometimes seems inclined to re-fight battles of earlier decades his *Völsunga saga* translation is, despite some inconsistencies and obscure passages, in a generally clear modern style. Unfortunately, however, it is very often not accurate: T.M. Andersson reported finding twenty-five translation errors in a sample of five pages (Andersson 1983, 841), and anyone comparing the translation with the original text is likely frequently to be dissatisfied by its response to the more difficult passages in the Icelandic.

The reviewers were divided in their reactions to the Anderson volume when it appeared in 1982. It was both praised as making a 'decided contribution to the study of medieval Germanic literature' (Mitchell 1984,

174), and dismissed as 'the bequest of a learned and spirited colleague' which 'will not find a place in our scholarly libraries' (Andersson 1983, 841). Many errors of detail were noted, and there was an understandable uncertainty as to the audience for which this relatively expensive volume was intended: Russom in his 'Foreword' had rather unhelpfully suggested a mixed audience of 'scholars, students and general readers'. Stephen A. Mitchell in *Scandinavian Studies* concluded his review by observing: 'the sad truth is, we still need a reliable, inexpensive translation of *V[ölsunga] s[aga]*' (Mitchell 1984, 174).

VI

Jesse Byock's 1990 translation, available in paperback as well as in hardcover, is clearly an attempt to provide what Mitchell considered desirable. It is the only one of the five translation volumes to focus on presenting an English version of *Völsunga saga*, without also providing extensive translations from other works or an edition of the Icelandic text. Byock's book should not intimidate the non-specialist reader as, for different reasons, Finch's and Anderson's are in danger of doing: his introduction is clear and non-technical, and though there are 110 notes on the text, 85 of these are three lines or less in length.

Byock announces in his 'Note on the Translation' that he has consulted the four earlier translations of the saga, and he acknowledges: 'Although frequently disagreeing with their interpretations of the text, I have found all four works useful in the preparation of this translation' (Byock 1990, 31-32). One suspects that most competent translators follow a similar procedure, though only rarely is it acknowledged as openly as here. It is hard not to be in broad agreement with the remarks of Donald Frame, the distinguished translator from the French who died in 1991:

> I strongly favor regarding translation, like scholarship, as a cumulative undertaking, and therefore borrowing—or stealing—whenever you see that you own best solution to a problem is clearly inferior to someone else's.

Before translating for publication, of course, the translator must have grounds for believing that he or she 'can markedly improve on all existing translations, and do that without anthologising (combining everyone else's best parts)' (Frame 1989, 82–83).

Byock could not be accused of being an anthologist: his translation, though in a clear, generally modern idiom like those of Finch and Anderson, is clearly his own. He does not wholly eschew archaisms—

there are some quite striking examples, such as Sigurðr's salutation of Brynhildr: 'Be greeted, lady. And how do you fare?' (ch. 25, 74). M.J. Driscoll, though identifying some possibly questionable usages, refers in his review of the translation to its 'nice balance between the archaic and the conversational' (Driscoll 1992, 306). Most students and 'general readers' will probably find it the most useful and accessible English version of the saga, and it seems in general very accurate, though someone attempting to understand the Icelandic may welcome having available also a copy of Finch's translation, which is sometimes more literal.

VII

In this short essay detailed comparison of the five translations must necessarily confine itself to a few short passages, albeit that this carries the risk of unfairness in selection and injustice to one or more translators. In an attempt to exhibit the range of each of the five translations four different kinds of passage have been chosen here: a narrative passage, a descriptive passage, a sample of direct speech, and a stanza of verse. The Icelandic text in each case is quoted from Finch's edition (with the substitution of ö for the older form of the letter, in accordance with the practice throughout this volume). The chosen passages are not cases in which translators are likely to have used significantly different versions.

Towards the end of chapter 8 the circumstances surrounding the birth of the hero Helgi Sigmundarson are described in narrative prose which is syntactically quite straightforward but raises questions as to how place names should be treated and what assistance should be provided by way of explanatory notes:

> Ok er Helgi var fœddr, kómu til nornir ok veittu honum formála ok mæltu at hann skyldi verða allra konunga frægastr. Sigmundr var þá kominn frá orrustu ok gekk með einum lauk í mót syni sínum, ok hér með gefr hann honum Helga nafn ok þetta at nafnfesti: Hringstaði ok Sólfjöll ok sverð, ok bað hann vel fremjask ok verða í ætt Völsunga. (ch. 8, p. 14)

Eiríkur Magnússon and William Morris provide fully Anglicised versions of the place names in accordance with their normal practice in their many translations, and add a fine alliterative epithet for the sword without any authorisation from the original. They expect the reader to know who the Norns were, eliminate the puzzling *laukr* and paraphrase *nafnfestr*. Characteristically, their translation has an archaic flavour, and it offers somewhat misleading renditions of 'veittu honum formála' and 'bað hann vel fremjask':

> And when Helgi was born, Norns came to him, and spake over him, and said that he should be in time to come the most renowned of all kings. Even therewith was Sigmund come home from the wars, and so therewith he gives him the name of Helgi, and these matters as tokens thereof, Land of Rings, Sun-litten Hill, and Sharp-shearing Sword, and withal prayed that he might grow of great fame, and like unto the kin of the Volsungs. (ch. 8, 25–26)

It will be noticed that this translation preserves the tense variations of the original. Margaret Schlauch standardises all forms into the past tense (as do the other three translators of the passage), and she opts for a partial Anglicisation of the place names. She offers no help to the reader likely to be puzzled by the Norns or the leek. Her version is accurate and significantly less archaic in style than that of Eiríkur Magnússon and Morris:

> But when Helgi was born the Norns came and prophesied, and said that he would be most famous of all kings. Sigmund was at that time returned from war, and he went to see his son bearing a leek, and therewith he gave him the name Helgi, and likewise these gifts with the naming: Hringstead and Solfell and a sword; and he bade him grow great and be one of the Volsung race. (ch. 8, 66)

In marked contrast to the first two translators Finch offers five explanatory footnotes to his translation of the passage. The reader is invited to consult his 'Glossary' for *nornir* and *nafnfestr*; the meaning and significance of *laukr* are discussed; Helgi's role in other literary sources is briefly outlined; and the possibility of identifying Hringstaðir and Solfjöll is considered. Finch's Anglicisation of the names is confined to the replacement of *-fjöll* by *fell*; rather inconsistently, he does not deal correspondingly with *staðir*. Finch permits himself considerable freedom with the original syntax, replacing co-ordinate clauses with subordinate constructions. His style is modern—perhaps jarringly so in 'get on in life':

> And when Helgi was born, the Norns appeared, and they granted him knowledge of his destiny, saying that of all kings he would be the most famous. Sigmund had just returned from battle, and taking with him some garlic he went to see his son, and thereupon gave him the name of Helgi, and his gifts for the occasion were Hringstaðir and Solfell and a sword, and he told him he must get on in life, and be a real Volsung. (ch. 8, 14)

Anderson offers three notes, on 'Norns', 'leek', and 'natal feast'—the last term, and the note referring to it, seem to reflect a misunderstanding of *nafnfestr,* which could literally be translated 'name-fastening'. He does not discuss the place names and, apart from substituting *d* for *ð*, leaves them as they are in the original. This involves use of a form based on the accusative case of *Hringstaðir,* a practice not repeated when he translates *Grindum*, the dative case of the place name Grindir, a few pages later (Finch, ch. 9, 17; Anderson, ch. 9, 71). The style of the translation is modern (apart from 'therewith') but more faithful to the Norse syntax than is Finch's version:

> When Helgi was born, the Norns came and made him a prophecy. They said he would become most famous of all kings. Sigmund had come home from a battle and went to see his son with a leek, and therewith he gave him the name Helgi and these gifts at his natal feast: Hringstadi and Solfjöll and a sword. He bade him have good success and grow as one of the Völsung family. (ch. 8, 69)

Byock provides notes on 'Norns', 'leek', and the place names, which he renders in the same way as Schlauch, while pointing out in his notes that *Solfjöll* literally is a plural meaning 'mountains of the sun' (p. 115). His style too is modern, apart perhaps from 'bid':

> And when Helgi was born, Norns came and set his destiny, saying that he would become the most famous of all kings. Sigmund had returned from battle and went with a leek to meet his son. He gave the boy the name Helgi, and as gifts for this name fastening he granted Hringstead, Solfell, and a sword. He bid the child advance himself well and to take after the race of the Volsungs. (ch. 8, 47)

VIII

The practices of the translators in dealing with passages of description are probably best exemplified by examining part of the eulogy to Sigurðr Sigmundarson, the saga's pre-eminent hero:

> Hár hans var brúnt at lit ok fagrt at líta ok fór í stórlokka. Skeggit var þykkt ok skammt ok með sama lit. Hánefjaðr var hann ok hafði breitt andlit ok stórbeinótt. Augu hans váru svá snör at fár einn þorði at líta undir hans brún. (ch. 23, 41)

Eiríkur Magnússon and Morris lend their version a somewhat heightened, 'poetic' quality which is attractive here. The version is accurate, though the other translators have understandably preferred a more restrained substitute for 'golden-red of hue':

> Now the hair of this Sigurd was golden-red of hue, fair of fashion, and falling down in great locks; thick and short was his beard, and of no other colour; high-nosed he was, broad and high-boned of face; so keen were his eyes that few durst gaze up under the brows of him. (ch. 22, 78–79)

Schlauch's version lacks this exuberance but is admirably clear, modern, and direct:

> His hair was light brown and fair to look upon, and it grew in long curls; his beard was thick and short and of the same color. His nose stood high, and his face was broad and large boned; his eyes were so keen, that few men dared look direct beneath his brows. (ch. 22, 110)

Finch also employs a clear modern idiom, but he is a little freer in rendering syntax and meaning than is Schlauch:

> His hair, which fell in long locks, was brown and handsome to look on. His beard was short and thick and of the same colour. He had a high-bridged nose and broad, large-boned features. His eyes were so piercing that few dared look him in the face. (ch. 23, 41)

Anderson's version is quite similar to Schlauch's:

> His hair was brown in color and fair to look at and grew in long locks; his beard was thick and short and of the same color. His nose was high; he had a broad face and was large-boned. His eyes were so keen that few dared look under his brows. (ch. 22, 94)

Though stylistically quite different from the Eiríkur Magnússon-Morris version, that of Byock resembles it in allowing itself a few rhetorical flourishes which might be justified as capturing the spirit of the piece better than a more strictly literal translation:

> Sigurd's hair was brown and splendid to see. It fell in long locks. His beard, of the same color, was thick and short. His nose was high and he had a broad, chiseled face. His eyes flashed so piercingly that few dared look beneath his brow. (ch. 23, 72)

IX

The following piece of direct speech is spoken to Helgi Sigmundarson by his future wife Sigrún Högnadóttir during their first meeting:

> 'Högni konungr hefir heitit mik Hoddbroddi, syni Granmars konungs, en ek hefi því heitit at ek vil eigi eiga hann heldr en einn krákuunga. En þó mun þetta fram fara, nema þú bannir honum ok komir í mót honum með her ok nemir mik á brott, því at með engum konungi vilda ek heldr setr búa en með þér.' (ch. 9, 15)

The Eiríkur Magnússon-William Morris version is predictably archaic and verbose, and it is difficult to know what prompted the rather startling alliterative phrase at the end:

> 'King Hogni has promised me to Hodbrod the son of King Granmar,
> but I have vowed a vow that I will have him to my husband no more
> than if he were a crow's son and not a king's; and yet will the thing
> come to pass, but and if thou standest in the way thereof, and goest
> against him with an army, and takest me away withal; for verily with
> no king would I rather bide on bolster than with thee.' (ch. 9, 28)

Schlauch's version, while still displaying archaisms, is markedly simpler
and more direct than that provided in 1870:

> 'King Hogni has promised me to Hoddbrod, son of King Gunnar
> [*sic*], but I have sworn that I will no sooner have him than a raven;
> and yet it will come to pass unless thou ban him and do battle against
> him with thy host and take me away with thee, for with no king
> would I rather abide than with thee.' (ch. 9, 68)

Finch's version, while accurate, tends in characteristic fashion to combine
slightly formal and slightly colloquial elements:

> 'King Hogni [...] has promised me in marriage to Hoddbrodd, King
> Granmar's son, but I have vowed to have him no more than I'd have
> a fledgling crow as a husband—but it will none the less come to that,
> unless you stop him and come against him with an army and take me
> away, for there is no king I would rather make a home with than with
> you.' (ch. 9, 15)

Whilst not obviously distorting the sense of the passage Anderson is a
good deal more free:

> 'King Högni has promised me to Hoddbrod, son of King Granmar,
> but I have sworn that I would as soon marry a young crow as marry
> him, and yet this will come to pass unless you can prevent him by
> going against him with warriors and then taking me away, for I have
> no wish to live with any other king than you.' (ch. 9, 69–70)

Byock allows himself significant freedom with the original syntax—
probably more than is usual in his translation. He nevertheless seems
faithfully to reproduce the sense of the passage:

> 'King Hogni has promised me to Hodbrodd, the son of King
> Granmar. But I have sworn that I would no sooner have him than a
> young crow. Yet the marriage will take place unless you stop
> Hodbrodd. Fight him with your army and take me away, because
> there is no king with whom I would rather dwell than with you.' (ch.
> 9, 48)

X

Some thirty stanzas are embedded in the text of *Völsunga saga*. One of the most famous describes Sigurðr's ride through the wall of flames to win Brynhildr for his brother-in-law Gunnarr:

> Sigurðr Grana
> sverði keyrði.
> Eldr sloknaði
> fyrir öðlingi,
> logi allr lægðisk
> fyrir lofgjörnum
> Bliku reiði
> er Reginn átti. (ch. 29, 49)

Though taking some metrical liberties Eiríkur Magnússon and Morris attempt to suggest the original alliteration, and their archaic touches do not seem discordant in a rendition of what seems so clearly 'heroic' verse. One might, however, question the translation of *öðlingr* by 'king':

> Then Sigurd smote
> Grani with sword,
> And the flame was slaked
> Before the king;
> Low lay the flames
> Before the fain of fame;
> Bright gleamed the array
> That Regin erst owned. (ch. 27, 96)

By contrast, Schlauch abandons alliteration and introduces end-rhyme. Her version is the most free of the five translations of the stanza, probably as a consequence of her decision to use rhyme. The stanza retains some power but is in danger of degenerating into doggerel:

> Sigurd smote Grani with the touch of his sword;
> The fire grew slaked and dim;
> The flames burnt low, but the harness gleamed
> That Regin had given him. (ch. 27, 126)

Finch elects for alliteration and quite successfully imitates the original in a more modern idiom than that of the 1870 translators:

> With sword did Sigurd
> spur Grani onwards.
> Before the prince
> the fire then died.
> The flames all ceased

for the seeker of glory,
resplendent the harness
Regin had owned. (ch. 29, 49)

Anderson employs neither alliteration nor rhyme in a version which seems to concentrate simply on conveying the meaning of the stanza in modern English:

Sigurd urged on Grani with point of sword,
The flames slackened before the prince,
All the fire dropped before him eager for praise,
His harness glistened, with Regin has owned. (ch. 27, 104)

Byock, finally, provides another stanza marked by use of alliteration. His achievement at this point is broadly similar to Finch's:

Sigurd with his sword
Spurred Grani on.
The flames expired
Before the prince,
The fire all fell back
Before the fame-hungry one.
The harness was radiant
Which Regin had owned. (ch. 29, 81)

XI

There may be earlier translations of other sagas which have been totally superseded by more adequate versions and deserve to languish in almost total obscurity. *Völsunga saga*, however, seems to have been better served across the years by those publishing English versions of it. Though Anderson's work may be best entrusted only to those with enough knowledge to identify its shortcomings as well as its merits, all five versions have positive qualities, and all are readable. Each reflects an interestingly different approach to saga translation, and with the partial exception of the somewhat anachronistic Anderson version all shed light on the translation philosophy of the period in which they first appeared.

A reader of the five complete translations will find that, with the exception (to a limited extent) of those by Eiríkur Magnússon-Morris and Byock, the English versions eliminate the apparently arbitrary oscillations between present and preterite which are such a characteristic feature of saga narrative. Though no one is likely to propose a wholesale revival of archaism in saga translation, there is today what seems to be a growing belief that features of saga style such as this tense variation and a syntax which tends to avoid subordinate clauses in favour of series of independent ones should be retained in English translations, even if the price is a kind of sometimes jagged English prose which reads rather oddly on first acquaintance. Its supporters believe that such an approach can provide a freshness and energy missing from translations into more conventional English, and that any other approach is likely to destroy important information on the 'world-view' of those who created the sagas (Durrenberger and Durrenberger 1992; also Acker 1988, 212). Again, as in Victorian times, there is concern that readers of translations should not readily forget the distance which separates us from medieval Iceland. Though both the economics of publishing and the achievements of the first five versions must severely limit the market for new versions of *Völsunga saga* in the years immediately ahead, it seems possible to perceive at least one direction likely to be taken by future translators in their task of interpretation.

BIBLIOGRAPHY

Acker, Paul. 1988. '*Valla-Ljóts saga*: Translated with an Introduction and Notes', *Comparative Criticism* 10, 207–235.

———. 1993. 'Norse Sagas Translated into English: A Supplement', *Scandinavian Studies* 65, 66–102.

[anon.] 1870. Review of Eiríkur Magnússon and Morris 1870, *The Athenæum* 2224 (11 June), 763–764.

Anderson, George K., trans. 1982. *The Saga of the Völsungs, Together with Excerpts from the Nornageststháttr and Three Chapters from the Prose Edda*. Newark and London.

Andersson, Theodore M. 1983. Review of Anderson 1982, *Speculum* 58, 841.

Bronner, Hedin. 1962. Review of Magnus Magnusson and Hermann Pálsson, trans., *Njál's saga*, *The American Scandinavian Review* 50, 317–318.

Byock, Jesse L., trans. 1990. *The Saga of the Volsungs: The Norse Epic of Sigurd the Dragon Slayer*. Berkeley.

Collingwood, W.G. and Jón Stefánsson, trans. 1902. *The Life and Death of Cormac the Skald*. Ulverston.

Driscoll, M.J. 1992. Review of Byock 1990, *Journal of English and Germanic Philology* 91, 303–306.

Durrenberger, E. Paul and Dorothy, trans. 1992. *The Saga of Gunnlaugur Snake's Tongue, with an Essay on the Structure and Translation of the Saga*. Rutherford and London.

Eddison, E.R., trans. 1930. *Egil's Saga*. Cambridge.

Eiríkur Magnússon and Morris, William, trans. 1870. *Völsunga saga: The Story of the Volsungs & Niblungs, with Certain Songs from the Poetic Edda.* London. Facsimile repr. London and Totowa, NJ, 1980.

———. trans. 1891. *The Story of Howard the Halt; The Story of the Banded Men; The Story of Hen Thorer.* London.

———. trans. 1892. *The Story of the Ere-Dwellers with the Story of the Heath-Slayings as Appendix.* London.

———. trans. 1893–1905. *The Story of the Kings of Norway Called the Round of the World (Heimskringla), by Snorri Sturluson.* 4 vols. London.

Finch, R.G., ed. and trans. 1965. *The Saga of the Volsungs.* London.

Frame, Donald. 1989. 'Pleasures and Problems of Translation', in John Biguenet and Rainer Schulte, eds, *The Craft of Translation*, pp. 70-92. Chicago.

Fry, Donald K. 1980. *Norse Sagas Translated into English: A Bibliography.* New York.

Garmonsway, G.N. and Simpson, Jacqueline. 1968. *Beowulf and its Analogues.* London and New York.

Halldór Hermannsson. 1912. *Bibliography of the Mythical-Heroic Sagas,* Islandica 5. Ithaca, NY.

———. 1937. *The Sagas of the Kings (Konunga sögur) and the Mythical-Heroic Sagas (Fornaldar sögur): Two Bibliographical Supplements,* Islandica 26. Ithaca, NY.

Herbert, William. 1804–1806. *Select Icelandic Poetry,* 2 vols. London.

Magee, Elizabeth. 1990. *Richard Wagner and the Nibelungs.* Oxford.

Mills, Stella M., trans. 1933. *The Saga of Hrolf Kraki.* Intro. by E.V. Gordon. Oxford.

Mitchell, Stephen A. 1984. Review of Anderson 1982, *Scandinavian Studies* 56, 172–174.

Morris, William, trans. 1962. *Völsunga saga: The Story of the Volsungs and Niblungs.* Intro. by Robert W. Gutman. New York.

Page, R.I. 1967. Review of Finch 1965, *Notes and Queries* n.s. 14, 280.

Scargill, H.M. and Schlauch, Margaret, trans. 1950. *Three Icelandic Sagas.* Princeton and London.

Schlauch, Margaret, trans. 1930. *The Saga of Volsungs.* New York.

———. 1967. Review of Finch 1965, *Medium Ævum* 36, 207–209.

Veblen, Thorstein, trans. 1925. *The Laxdœla Saga.* New York.

13

George Mackay Brown and
Orkneyinga saga

JULIAN MELDON D'ARCY

George Mackay Brown is Orkney's best known and most successful living writer. His books of poetry, plays, novels and collections of short stories dealing predominantly with the ordinary farmers and fishermen of Orkney from ancient times until the present day have captivated a growing number of readers with their simplicity and sincerity. His artistic versatility is evident in the variety of literary forms he is willing to use, though whether writing poems, plays or stories he has a very distinctive style, employing a deceptively simple but exact diction with mythic and symbolic overtones. His work has a very special ambience, a distinct blend of folklore and religious mysticism. Moreover his insistence on stressing the values of the elemental forces of life, as opposed to those of modern technology, has struck a resonant chord in the late twentieth century with its increasing social and ecological problems. His readership and reputation now extends well beyond the Orkney Isles to Europe and the wider world.

One of the most notable features of Mackay Brown's increasingly popular poetry and fiction is the influence of Old Norse literature on his work, a direct result of his love and admiration for the sagas and skaldic poetry of medieval Scandinavia. This is not only apparent in his spare and sometimes laconic prose style, so reminiscent of the Icelandic sagas, and in his experimentation with his so-called 'rune' poems and modern versions of 'kennings' or skaldic metaphors (Murray 1986; D'Arcy 1990), but also in the sheer number of his poems and stories based on Viking history and literature. Virtually every novel and collection of short stories or poems by Mackay Brown contains subject matter from the Viking Age.[1]

Mackay Brown's interest in Old Norse literature should come as no great surprise, bearing in mind that Orkney has an immense Norse heritage; indeed for three centuries medieval Orkney was an important

---

[1]The only major exception would appear to be *The Sun's Net* (1976), a collection of short stories.

geopolitical pivotal point in the western Norse world of Scandinavia, Iceland and the British Isles. Moreover Orkney was a vibrant centre of Old Norse literature, the home or base of important skalds such as Arnor Jarlaskald and Earl Rognvald Kolson (Mackay Brown's spellings of Norse names are used throughout this essay) who produced important work and even influenced the form of Old Norse poetry (Olsen 1932; Holtsmark 1937). The major literary achievement associated with Orkney, however, is undoubtedly *Orkneyinga saga*, the history of the Orkney Isles (and indeed often of Caithness, Sutherland and the Hebrides) from the late ninth to the early twelfth century. The saga was written around 1200, probably by an Icelander with Orcadian connections (Pálsson and Edwards 1982, 13), though there are claims for a pure Orcadian provenance, possibly involving Bjarni Kolbeinson, Bishop of Orkney from 1188 to 1222 (Holtsmark 1937; Macrae-Gibson 1989). The important point for our purposes is that although Mackay Brown has read extensively in Old Norse literature (in translation) and has claimed *Njal's saga* to be his 'greatest treasure' (*Letters from Hamnavoe* 86), it is *Orkneyinga saga* which has consistently proved to be the major source for many of his poems and stories, in particular his lyrical book on Orkney, *An Orkney Tapestry* (1969), the Viking and skaldic poems in *Winterfold* (1976), the play *The Loom of Light* (1972), and his two historical novels *Magnus* (1973) and *Vinland* (1992).

What makes Mackay Brown's use of this source interesting and worthy of detailed study is the fact that he does not simply ransack it to re-tell various incidents from Orkney's history—he attempts to re-interpret and, in some cases, even reformulate the saga. The inspiration for Mackay Brown's new renderings of *Orkneyinga saga* is clearly his profound sense of religious faith. Becoming a Roman Catholic in 1961, his vision of the necessity and relevance of Christian faith is evident throughout his poetry and fiction, especially in his liturgical and biblical imagery, in his frequent use of regular and secular clergy, and in those of his stories obviously intended as modern parables. As far as his Norse-inspired work is concerned, Mackay Brown's Christianity has made him take a hard look at the Vikings and present their pagan fatalism and predilection for violence in a highly critical and often ironic manner.

Mackay Brown's stance is immediately apparent in the three chapters, 'Warrior', 'Martyr' and 'Crusader', in *An Orkney Tapestry*, his first major rendering of parts of *Orkneyinga saga*. The section called 'Warrior' (55–68), for example, relates some of the life and adventures of Earl Sigurd of Orkney, culminating in his death at the Battle of Clontarf in 1014, and it is here that Mackay Brown first presents the heroic values which dominated the Norse world:

Of only a few abstract qualities could a man be sure—of courage, for
example, and of loyalty, and of generosity. These were the jewels that
a man could save out of the flux. If you were lucky, perhaps some
sagaman would set your actions in the horn and silver of his prose;
that was the only kind of immortality a man could hope for.

(Orkney Tapestry 56)

It was thus only natural that Earl Sigurd should fight at Clontarf as he
'wanted nothing but the centre of the battle and a place in the story', and
Mackay Brown pays tribute to his 'courage, loyalty, generosity' (60).
Nonetheless, Mackay Brown makes it clear that, in his opinion, the
Norsemen were doomed to adhere to these values simply because they
were ignorant of any others: 'Christ's charity meant nothing as yet to
Earl Sigurd' (57). The Battle of Clontarf was thus a battle 'between
Christ and Odin for the soul of Ireland' (62). Mackay Brown ends the
chapter by quoting Thomas Gray's 'The Fatal Sisters', claiming it as a
savage mockery of so-called heroes who were, in fact, no more than
'servants of Valkyries' embroiling nations in carnage and war.[2] In terms
of bloodshed Earl Sigurd was thus simply a 'small-time huckster'
(66–68). In the following two sections, 'Martyr' (69–101) and 'Crusader'
(102–123), Sigurd's apparently ignominious death at Clontarf is
contrasted with the martyrdom of St Magnus and the magnanimity of
Earl Rognvald, whilst Earl Sigurd's pagan banner and the Norns'
weaving of the Web of Fate are starkly contrasted with the 'seamless
garment' of Christ's love metaphorically woven for and worn by St
Magnus. Mackay Brown thus clearly sees the sections of *Orkneyinga
saga* from the death of Earl Sigurd (1014) to the pilgrimage of Earl
Rognvald to Jerusalem (*c.* 1151) as portraying an important period of
spiritual progress.

A further example of this kind of presentation of the saga can be found
in the short story 'The Fires of Christmas' (*Hawkfall* 59–65) in which
Mackay Brown re-tells two other incidents from Orkney's history, Earl
Thorfinn's burning of Rognvald Brusison in 1046, and the killing of
Sweyn Breastrope by Sweyn Asleifson in 1135 (*Orkneyinga saga* chs 29
and 66). At the end of these two accounts Mackay Brown adds a
paragraph in which he simply states that, although there had been eighty-
nine years between the events:

[2]'The Fatal Sisters', Thomas Gray's English version of a Latin translation
of *Darraðarljóð*, was composed in 1761, though not published until 1768. It
marks the beginning of the late eighteenth-century fascination with so-called
'runic' poetry: see Farley 1903, 33–36.

> in the meantime the blood of Saint Magnus had been shed. The
> second drama is not so dark and hopeless as the first. Fate had given
> way, to some extent at least, to grace. (*Hawkfall* 65)

Even a convinced Christian familiar with *Orkneyinga saga* must find
Mackay Brown's argument rather difficult to accept. The first killing was
both a self-defensive act of revenge (Rognvald had previously attempted
to burn Earl Thorfinn to death in his hall) and an unfortunate necessity
to ensure that Rognvald would never again treacherously disturb the
peace and prosperity of Orkney. Moreover Thorfinn's burning of
Rognvald at Paplay was scrupulously conducted according to the
conventions of the time: women, children, and unarmed men were
allowed out of the burning building. The murder of Sweyn Breastrope,
Earl Paul's retainer, on the other hand, was carried out by a guest of Earl
Paul's in his own homestead, and was the result of stupid and drunken
jealousy. One cannot deny, of course, that both killings were brutal and
unpleasant, but the Thorfinn/Rognvald confrontation had a weighty
justification behind it, whereas the incident involving the two Sweyns
seems petty and despicable. Indeed, in the latter instance, a careful
reading of the saga (ch. 66) clearly shows that the murder was connived
at and stage-managed by Eyvind Melbrigdason for reasons unknown. So
it seems hard to see how exactly Mackay Brown perceives these events
as illustrating any distinct advance in human moral progress.

It is important to note, however, that in both these examples the facts
of the saga remain unchanged in the modern re-telling; Mackay Brown's
interpretation is presented either by direct comment or in the way that he
emphasises certain aspects of the incidents. Readers are left to choose for
themselves whether or not they agree with the author's evaluation. In
other renderings of the events of *Orkneyinga saga*, however, Mackay
Brown seems no longer satisfied with this method of presenting saga
events; in order to emphasise his Christian interpretation of history, he
sometimes actually alters, usually unobtrusively, the very saga itself. The
best way to see and evaluate this is to examine his fiction and poetry
dealing with the two Norse saints of Orkney, Magnus Erlendson and
Rognvald Kolson.

The story of the earl and saint, Magnus Erlendson, is perhaps the most
famous episode in Orkney's history (*Orkneyinga saga* chs 39–52).
Renowned for his religious sensibility and celibate marriage, Magnus
ruled Orkney jointly with his cousin Earl Hakon Paulsson in peace and
co-operation during the early part of the twelfth century. Rival supporters
of the two earls gradually stirred up animosity between the cousins,
however, and faced with outright civil war the two factions met fully
armed at the Orkney Thing where armed conflict was averted by a peace

treaty to be ratified on the isle of Egilsay on Easter Sunday 1116 or 1117. Magnus duly arrived at Egilsay with two warships, as agreed, but Hakon arrived with eight, a clear indication of his treacherous intentions. Faced with the inevitable, Magnus at first tried to come to terms with Hakon and made three offers: firstly, that he, Magnus, would go on a pilgrimage to Jerusalem and then remain in permanent exile from Orkney; secondly, he would retire to a monastery and take no further part in political life; and thirdly, he would submit to mutilation and permanent imprisonment. Hakon refused the first two offers, but was willing to accept the third. His men, however, would hear of no compromise and insisted on the death of one of the two earls. '"Better kill him then," said Hakon. "I don't want an early death; I much prefer ruling over people and places"' (*Orkneyinga saga* ch. 49). None of Hakon's men would actually do the deed and he was forced to order his cook, Lifolf, to carry out the execution. Magnus knelt in prayer before being killed by a single blow of an axe to the head. Shortly after Magnus had been interred at Birsay, miracles began to happen at his tomb and he was canonised as a martyr *c.* 1137, or twenty years after his death.

The story of Magnus has inspired Mackay Brown all his creative life, and implicit and explicit references to the life and death of St Magnus can be found throughout his poems, plays and stories right up until the present day. In one five-year period Mackay Brown produced three important renderings of the St Magnus story: the 'Martyr' section of *An Orkney Tapestry,* mentioned above, the play *The Loom of Light* and the novel *Magnus.* The notable feature of these works is that Mackay Brown gradually expands and changes his material over the period, and an examination of this development reveals several interesting facets of the author's vision of the saint and his martyrdom.

In 'Martyr', Mackay Brown presents a relatively straightforward re-telling of the saga events with additional literary embellishments such as a fictional one-act drama concerning two Orkney tinkers, Jock and Blind Mary, the latter regaining her sight as a result of Jock's prayers at Magnus's tomb. Although admitting that Magnus's monkish biographers were biased in their presentation of the saint's life, Mackay Brown nonetheless argues that: 'The events that gather about him are so extraordinary, and were witnessed by so many people, and were enacted in such a hard light, that there is no faking of the record' (72). He also adds his own personal slant to the story by presenting Earl Hakon as a religious as well as a political rival, for 'fame in history was probably the only kind of immortality this young Norseman believed in: a resurrection of the word' (71). Hakon is thus clearly associated with the Old Norse pagan values which Mackay Brown has already condemned in the earlier 'Warrior' section on Earl Sigurd. Hakon's repentance over the slaying of

Magnus and his pilgrimage to the Holy Land can consequently be seen
as the ultimate victory of Magnus's Christian faith.

Near the end of 'Martyr', Mackay Brown writes: 'The story of Magnus
and Hakon unfolds like a drama. Some day a play will be written about
it; I have not the ability myself' (87). He evidently changed his mind
soon after, however, for in 1972 his play *The Loom of Light* was
produced in Kirkwall. Scene 1 opens with two Orkney peasants, Mans
and Hild, struggling to plough their field whilst across the water on
Birsay Earl Paul is marrying Thora, the future mother of Magnus. Scene
2, set ten years later, presents Magnus and Hakon as schoolboys on
Birsay; Hakon is already aggressive and wilful, whereas Magnus is
significantly concerned over a wounded seal on the beach. Scene 3
presents one of the most famous incidents in Magnus's career: his refusal
to fight alongside King Magnus against the Welsh in the Menai Strait.
Whilst the sea-battle rages Magnus steadfastly reads aloud from his
psalter, ignoring the king's disapproval and Hakon's taunts of cowardice.
At the end of hostilities, Magnus binds the wounds of Mans, who is now
one of the longship's oarsmen. In Scene 4, seventeen years later, we
return to Mans and Hild who are desperately trying to save their land
from the depredations of both Hakon's and Magnus's men; the whole of
Orkney is aflame in civil war. In Scene 5 the leading men of both
factions approach the bishop on Birsay in an attempt to involve him in
negotiations for peace. The bishop declines the invitation, ominously
commenting: 'What is desperately needed in Orkney this Easter is
something more in the nature of a sacrifice: the true immaculate death of
the dove' (*Three Plays* 32). Scene 6 presents the confrontation on
Egilsay. Here Mackay Brown makes an important change from the saga,
for it is now Hakon who makes the proposals (here reduced from three
to two) to his men; Magnus is not even present and only appears after the
decision to kill him has been taken. The significance of this change will
be discussed below in connection with the novel *Magnus*. The final scene
of the play is an expanded version of the one-act drama from 'Martyr',
the tinkers Jock and Mary begging for food from Mans and Hild before
continuing on their journey to St Magnus's tomb and experiencing the
miracle.

Mackay Brown's dramatisation of the saga events seems primarily
aimed at underlining both the ritual necessity of sacrifice and the fact that
it was Magnus who was specifically *chosen* for the Christ-like role.
Nonetheless Mackay Brown seems unconvinced that he had done full
justice to this vision, for as he explained in the preface to his plays:
'Some writers are never content to leave well alone. On to the stark
framework of the play I rigged the novel *Magnus*' (*Three Plays* ix). This
novel is indeed the culmination of Mackay Brown's study and interpreta-

tion of the Orkney saint's life. Its first three chapters are greatly expanded prose versions of the first three scenes of the play with Mackay Brown naturally 'making as full use as possible of the more varied techniques at the novelist's disposal' (*Three Plays* x). Effective additions in the novel include details of the wedding and nuptial night of Magnus's parents which underline the ploughing and sowing symbolism already hinted at through the parallel of Mans' and Hild's working in the fields.

The fourth chapter, 'The Temptations', is a completely new and ambitious addition to the story, for here Mackay Brown introduces the Keeper of the Loom or Magnus's guardian angel who appears to him and informs him of the weaving of a seamless garment in preparation for his being bidden to a marriage feast. He is also warned to beware the Tempter, and indeed for the remainder of the chapter we see Magnus resisting the varying temptations of lust, power, war and resignation from life. This section of the novel, with its pervasive biblical and religious motifs, is often the most difficult for readers to understand.

The fifth chapter, 'Scarecrow', contains the same material as Scene 4 of the play, but this time with more harrowing scenes of pillage and murder as the earls' factions ride roughshod over the rights of the Orcadians in their military struggle for power. The sixth chapter, 'Prelude to the Invocation of the Dove', is centred on the leading men's appeal to the bishop (cf. Scene 5 of the play), but has an additional section in which the bishop composes a homily, 'Concerning the Two Coats, of Caesar and of God, that cover Adam's Shame', which reiterates the garment symbolism prevalent throughout Mackay Brown's renderings of the Magnus story. As in the play, the chapter ends with the bishop's premonition of the necessity of a blood sacrifice.

The seventh chapter, 'The Killing', takes place on Egilsay, only the proposals concerning Magnus's fate (again reduced to two) are now mooted by Magnus's leading men, Finn Thorkelson and Hold Ragnarson (*Magnus* 147–162). Hakon's men rudely reject them and Magnus is condemned to death, once more in his absence. The chapter also contains a long digression on the nature and meaning of sacrifice and the Catholic mass, and the startling introduction of Brechtian *Verfremdungseffekte*. Mackay Brown not only has twentieth-century journalists reporting on the events on Egilsay, he also relocates the execution scene in a Nazi concentration camp; the victim is now not Magnus, but Dietrich Bonhoeffer, the Lutheran priest who was a steadfast opponent of Hitler's regime and was hanged on 8 April 1945. The executioner, still called Lifolf, is now the camp butcher, and Hakon is the Commandant, his leading men SS officers of varying rank. Mackay Brown clearly uses this technique to imply that martyrdom is still relevant in the twentieth century. It is certainly a startling innovation in what purports to be an historical novel set in medieval Orkney.

The final chapter, 'Harvest', once again returns to the twelfth century and the pattern established in *An Orkney Tapestry* and *The Loom of Light*: the tinkers Jock and Mary are on their way to Birsay and begging from Mans and Hild, now enjoying the peace and prosperity of Hakon's reign, the 'harvest' made possible by the spilling of Magnus's blood.

Magnus is an ambitious novel, and critical evaluations of it have varied. Elizabeth Huberman asserts that it is 'a novel which transforms a suspect genre and an unfashionable subject into a true and timeless work of the imagination' (Huberman 1981, 133) whilst Alan Bold views it more harshly as 'a theological discourse with fictional asides' (Bold 1978, 101). An anonymous reviewer sees both positive and negative aspects of the novel, summing up *Magnus* as 'a collection of magnificent pieces which do not quite fit together to achieve the desired unity' (*Times Literary Supplement* September 1973, 1101). There are quite clearly both strengths and weaknesses in the novel. For religious readers it must provide a poignant and dramatic affirmation of faith in Christ's death and resurrection. Stylistically, too, some of its scenes, especially those concerning the peasants Mans and Hild and the tinkers Jock and Mary contain some of Mackay Brown's finest writing and reveal his deep compassion for ordinary folk struggling against the vicissitudes of life. The callous scenes in the civil war section provide a very effective condemnation of the pointlessness and barbarity of violence. The use of *Verfremdungseffekte* may disturb the unity of the novel for some readers, but on the whole it is imaginative and daring, and at the very least displays a measure of stylistic virtuosity.

Two of the main flaws in the novel, as Bold has pointed out, are the rather nebulous characterisation of the eponymous hero and the long sections of liturgical imagery and theological moralising which may well prove somewhat irksome, if not incomprehensible, to non-Roman Catholic readers. Bold particularly criticises Mackay Brown for tacitly assuming 'that the martyrdom was ordained by God' and for 'dogmatically accepting' the sanctity of Magnus. By making Magnus 'a particular chosen seed, a summoned one' (*Magnus* 26) and by giving him a guardian angel who foretells his fate, Mackay Brown 'deprives Magnus of a free will' and removes all dramatic tension from the novel. Bold is also unimpressed with Mackay Brown's introduction of the Dietrich Bonhoeffer parallel, pointing out that the passive martyrdom of Magnus bears no comparison with the active anti-Nazi resistance of the Lutheran pastor (Bold 1978, 100–108).

One other feature of *Magnus*, however, apparently overlooked or ignored by the critics, needs further consideration. This concerns Mackay Brown's unobtrusive manipulation of Old Norse history, mentioned earlier. Most critics, and presumably most readers, tacitly assume that apart from the obvious fictional embellishments, the story of Magnus is that of the saga. A careful study of *Orkneyinga saga* (and Mackay Brown's other major source, John Mooney's *St. Magnus: Earl of Orkney* [1935]), however, reveals that this is not the case. In three specific incidents Mackay Brown has changed the saga facts to suit his own purposes. The first is in Magnus's relations with his namesake King Magnus Barelegs of Norway both before and during the sea-battle in the Menai Strait. In both *The Loom of Light* (*Three Plays* 20) and *Magnus* (62–63) Mackay Brown has King Magnus confirm the fathers of Magnus and Hakon as joint earls of Orkney. This is a total contradiction of the saga in which King Magnus actually *deposes* Earls Paul and Erlend (sending them into exile in Norway where they die) and proclaims his own son as overlord of the Northern Isles (*Orkneyinga Saga* ch. 39; see also Mooney 1935, 83 and Thomson 1987, 55). Mackay Brown does in fact give the saga version in *An Orkney Tapestry* (70), but why does he depart from the saga in the play and the novel?

The answer would seem to be that, contrary to one critic's claims (Huberman 1981, 122–127), he wishes to remove all ambiguity from Magnus's actions; in Bold's words, Mackay Brown must 'scan the saga account of Magnus's life and isolate the quality of saintliness' (Bold 1978, 101). Thus Magnus's refusal to fight King Magnus's Welsh enemies, for example, must be seen as a specific act of Christian non-belligerence and not as a political protest against the king's disinheriting his father (and ultimately himself) of the Orkney earldom. Furthermore, the supposition that Magnus's intentions were in actuality more worldly than religious gains further credence when possible political links between Magnus and the Welsh are taken into account (Thomson 1987, 56–57 is very persuasive on this point). Moreover Mackay Brown's claims for the uniqueness of Magnus's action (*Orkney Tapestry* 74) are also inaccurate; although unusual, a refusal to fight was not without precedent in the Norse world. King Brian Boru refused to bear arms at the Battle of Clontarf on Good Friday in 1014 (*Njal's Saga* ch. 157), and in another famous incident Kjartan Olafsson threw down his sword and accepted death at the hands of his cousin Bolli rather than kill the latter himself (*Laxdœla Saga* ch. 49).

A second important instance of Mackay Brown's deviation from the saga concerns the civil war between the earls Magnus and Hakon. In *An Orkney Tapestry* Mackay Brown stresses that Orkney 'had been torn and bloodied with centuries of civil strife' and that all the earls 'had given most of their wealth and energy to war' (77). In *The Loom of Light* and *Magnus* Mackay Brown therefore presents the reader with vivid portrayals of the rapine and looting of Magnus's and Hakon's men. Most critics seem to take these scenes at face value (Huberman 1981, 127–128 and Bold 1978, 105), but they are completely at variance with the facts. The latter part of Earl Thorfinn's reign was blessed with peace and splendour and Earls Paul and Erlend (the fathers of Hakon and Magnus) had ruled jointly and harmoniously for decades, only finally becoming alienated by the rivalry of their sons. Even then, however, the Orkney magnates always brought about reconciliations through turbulent but non-violent negotiations. There may have been an occasional brawl between rival supporters of Hakon and Magnus, but there was never open war between them; the last major conflict between two Orkney earls, Thorfinn and Rognvald Brusison, had been in 1046. In other words Orkney had enjoyed relative peace and security for almost three generations before the Hakon–Magnus confrontation ended in murder in *c.* 1117 (Thomson 1987, 45–46, 54–55). Mackay Brown's aim in creating a fictitious war between Hakon and Magnus seems clear, for it gives far greater meaning to Magnus's death if it ended a vicious civil war rather than simply averted one. Within the terms of novelistic license this is perhaps perfectly justifiable in that civil war *would* almost certainly have broken out had the earls both continued to live in dispute. Nonetheless it underlines Mackay Brown's assiduous, if not anxious, concern to magnify the relevance of Magnus's martyrdom—even if it meant modifying the saga.

The final incident revolves around the proposals mooted on Egilsay in an attempt to avoid bloodshed. In *An Orkney Tapestry* (81) Mackay Brown faithfully presents the saga version of the incident, with Magnus making the three offers to Hakon. In the play and novel, however, as previously mentioned, these proposals are reduced in number and put forward either by Hakon or Magnus's men, in each case with Magnus absent. Why does Mackay Brown make this important change from the saga? Again, the answer seems to be that he is trying to make Magnus as unworldly as possible. In the saga, Magnus's attempts to come to terms with Hakon and save his own life are perfectly natural and reveal a normal and fallible human being. By removing Magnus from the negotiations altogether, Mackay Brown also removes this worldly blemish from his martyrdom and underlines the pre-ordained nature of his fate. This interpretation supports Bold's assertion that 'Magnus is conspicuous by his corporeal absence' and helps explain the rather nebulous character-isation of Magnus (Bold 1978, 109).

All these divergences from the saga show that Mackay Brown is determined to play down the fallible and human aspects of Magnus and to emphasise his saintliness. The modification of historical fact for purposes of narrative fiction is not unknown, of course; indeed in the

Scottish tradition itself Sir Walter Scott set a notable precedent, and Mackay Brown is justified in presenting his vision of St Magnus in whatever form he feels most effective.[3] Nonetheless, when such literary refractions and rearrangements are noted by readers with a knowledge of *Orkneyinga saga*, the result may be a greater wariness and scepticism towards Mackay Brown's intentions, especially if these seem overtly didactic. In this sense, Mackay Brown's manipulation of the saga could defeat his own ends.

As all the above comments suggest, understanding and evaluating *Magnus* is a complex process involving shifting historical, religious and artistic viewpoints. Indeed that complexity is at the heart of the work's achievement; the reader is confronted with a powerful and intriguing fictional experience. This is particularly notable in that a reader with no particular knowledge of Roman Catholicism or *Orkneyinga saga* can nonetheless engage deeply with the novel. The identification of Magnus's fate with that of Bonhoeffer can be read as a poignant and explicit statement of '*la condition humaine*' in which justice does not always triumph and truly good men of all ages and races are often mercilessly destroyed in the unscrupulous pursuit of political power and ideological hegemony. As Huberman has argued: 'The choices presented in archaic terms to the twelfth-century Magnus are suddenly the choices presented to us in the conflicts of conscience of this century' (Huberman 1981, 132).

Mackay Brown's fondness for altering the substance of the *Orkneyinga saga* text is also apparent in his treatment of the skaldic poems of Earl Rognvald Kali Kolson. It is not surprising that Mackay Brown should be drawn to Earl Rognvald (1136–1158) as he is beyond doubt one of the most attractive characters in the saga (chs 64–104). A brave and resourceful man, patient and magnanimous to his enemies, his greatest achievement was the founding of St Magnus Cathedral in 1137. Mackay Brown reveals his admiration for Rognvald in his eulogistic 'Crusader' section of *An Orkney Tapestry* (102–123) in which he lovingly re-tells the saga story of Rognvald, dwelling especially on his pilgrimage to Jerusalem, including the romantic interlude with Princess Ermengarde in Narbonne, the defeat of a tyrant in Galicia, and the sinking of a dromond in the Mediterranean. Mackay Brown ends his account with an entirely fictitious description of Rognvald and his men participating in the Stations of the Cross in the Church of the Holy Sepulchre in Jerusalem.

Besides being a crusader, cathedral-builder, and canonised saint (1192),

---

[3]Scott, however, usually added copious notes to his works outlining what the real historical facts were and why he had changed them.

Rognvald was bound to excite the sympathy and imagination of Mackay Brown as a highly accomplished medieval poet who attracted other skalds to his Orkney court, and in *An Orkney Tapestry* and *Winterfold* Mackay Brown makes a serious attempt to present modern versions of the earl's skaldic verses. These verses are not translations as Mackay Brown knows no Old Norse,[4] but modern responses to the strophes in A.B. Taylor's 1938 translation of *Orkneyinga saga*. As Mackay Brown himself explains:

> I have had to wrench skaldic verse into a shape acceptable to modern readers. Any attempt to reproduce something like the original is impossibly difficult [...]. I expect no delight at all for my very free paraphrase; only that perhaps it is more in accord with modern taste. (*Orkney Tapestry* 2–3)

Skaldic verse is indeed notoriously difficult to understand, let alone translate.[5] Nonetheless, translating such poetry is only *impossibly* difficult for those who have no knowledge of Old Norse; a very good attempt has been made to reproduce both the style (notably the alliterative patterning) and the meaning of *Orkneyinga saga*'s skaldic verses in the recent translation by Pálsson and Edwards. Mackay Brown's versions of Earl Rognvald's and his skalds' strophes must be judged on their own terms, therefore: as modern responses to Taylor's translations. A comparison between the two writers' renderings is revealing.

In general terms Taylor's translations are accurate versions of the meanings of the verses, but although they give some hint of the original style, they are not very striking as poetry. Mackay Brown's versions, paying less attention to the Norse fondness for alliteration, are much more concise, compressed and effective. Compare for example the two versions of a strophe by one of Rognvald's skalds (Armod) on a sexually frustrated seaman on watch:

Taylor (1938, 298)	*An Orkney Tapestry* (p.117):
We watch o'er the sea-steed	Night. Sheets of salt.
When o'er the stout gunwale	Armod on watch.

---

[4]In a conversation in August 1987, Mackay Brown informed me that he had intended studying Old Norse under Hermann Pálsson at the University of Edinburgh, but the proposed text book proved too expensive!

[5]To appreciate the problems involved in translating skaldic verse, one need only read a recent study of Rognvald's poetry (with English paraphrases) in which all the strophes are analysed in detail, revealing the intricacies and opacity of Old Norse kennings (Bibire 1988, 208–240).

The billow breaks wildly.	A heave and wash of lights
Thus duty is done.	from the island.
While the lazy land-lubber	The lads of Crete
Sleeps by some maiden	Toss in hot tumbled linen.
Soft-skinned and kind,	This poet on watch
Over my shoulder	Cold, burning, unkissed.
I gaze towards Crete.	

Mackay Brown's jagged paratactic syntax is much more successful than Taylor's clausal subordination in drawing out the mood of taut awareness and sexual frustration of the man on watch. Similarly, Mackay Brown's version of Armod's strophe on the stormy coast of Northumberland (*Orkney Tapestry* 104; Taylor 1938, 285) captures much more succinctly the sarcasm of the sailor towards those safe on dry land. Mackay Brown's artistry is most strikingly apparent, however, in his invariably effective use of imagery. Feeling unable to mimic all the linguistic patterns of skaldic poetry in modern verse forms, he cleverly seizes on implied images in the strophes and uses them as structural matrixes, often contrapuntally. Thus in a strophe in *An Orkney Tapestry* (104–105) the images of drinking and horse-riding in the first half are turned into metaphors in the second half through the mention of 'hogsheads of salt' as the earl 'spurs the ship'. Similarly the red wine and silver-white hair of Ermengarde are contrasted with the redness of blood and the 'sharp whiteness' of swords (*Orkney Tapestry* 109; Taylor 1938, 290); in another strophe Sigmund thinks of his lover's spinning wheel in Orkney whilst he himself is involved in the 'red wheel of war' (*Orkney Tapestry* 110; Taylor 1938, 291).

Other notable comparisons can be made between Mackay Brown's own different versions of Rognvald's strophes, for although two of them are repeated from *Orkneyinga saga* with very minor and insignificant changes in *Winterfold*, two others are re-written with very different nuances. Compare, for example, the two versions below (Taylor 1938, 286):

An Orkney Tapestry (106):	*Winterfold* (23):
Golden one,	Your hair, lady
Tall one,	Is long, a bright waterfall.
Moving in perfume and onyx,	You move through the warriors
Witty one,	Rich and tall as starlight.
You with the shoulders	What can I give
Lapped in long silken hair	For the cup and kisses brought
Listen: because of me	to my mouth ?
The eagle has a red claw.	Nothing.
	This red hand, a death-dealer.

Here we can see a distinct shift in emphasis; in the earlier version the 'red claw' of Rognvald is clearly meant to impress the princess, whereas in the later version the earl has become more demure and unsure of himself. There are further differences in the following strophes, also translations of compositions by Rognvald (Taylor 1938, 287):

An Orkney Tapestry (111):	*Winterfold* (23):
The small mouth of Ermengarde	The summer mouth of Ermengarde
Commands two things—	Commands two things—
A sea strewn with wreckage	A sea of saga-stuff, wreckage, gold,
As far as Jordan,	As far as Jordan,
And later, in autumn	And later, at leaf-fall,
With other migrant wings	On patched homing wings
A returned prow.	A sun-dark hero.

In the earlier version the 'small mouth of Ermengarde' has implicit sexual undertones reinforced by 'a returned prow'. In the later version, however, the 'summer mouth of Ermengarde' removes all sensuality from the verse and the earl will return as a conventional 'sun-dark hero' rather than a lover. Mackay Brown clearly wishes to present a gentler, more chivalrous crusader in *Winterfold* than the more aggressive earl in *An Orkney Tapestry,* probably reflecting Mackay Brown's increasing interest in the religious rather than military aspects of Rognvald's life. Indeed, Mackay Brown's concern with presenting Rognvald and his men as true Christians in *An Orkney Tapestry* and *Winterfold* often seems to result in his creating meanings and nuances completely at variance with the original Old Norse versions. In one instance, for example, the monks of Westray are ironically described by Rognvald (in translation) as 'sixteen young women [...] bevies of maidens with heads bald and bare' (Taylor 1938, 252; for another version, see Bibire 1988, 22), but Mackay Brown presents them as 'sixteen walkers' with heads 'bare as stone', and only in the last line does he add 'Demure and harmless as girls' (*Winterfold*, 21). Rognvald's implied sarcasm and amusing metaphor is completely removed by Mackay Brown, who replaces it with a very tame simile; again perhaps his own religious sensitivity prevents him from re-telling Rognvald's irreverent jest. Yet Mackay Brown's determination to emphasise Rognvald's Christianity produces even greater divergences from the text; he changes completely the last few lines of the earl's strophe on the latter's departure from the Holy Land for Constantinople and the Byzantine court:

Taylor (1938, 301):	*An Orkney Tapestry* (122):
Let us take the bounty	We will be the Emperor's husbandmen,
Of the mighty Monarch	Winnowing chaff from the holy grain

Push on to clash of sword,	Redden the wolf's jaws,
May we be worthy at last	For the glory of Christ the King
And honour the King.	To break bread in the white churches.

Seeking plunder and fame in the service of the Byzantine Emperor is thus turned into a statement of religious fervour, with the worldly 'King' of the original becoming 'Christ the King' in Mackay Brown's version. He changes the strophe still further in *Winterfold* (24), now introducing a laudatory chant from the Mass:

Sin darkens the grain-hold.
We have branded their coasts with rage and lust,
The old dragon-breath.
No end of sorrow, soultroth, seeking, still.
Kyrie, Christe, Kyrie eleison
The Golden Harvester
Comes out to grace, with robe and ring, the swineherd.

There is at least some mention of violence here, but in tones of guilt and regret which are simply not present in Earl Rognvald's original strophe. Indeed Mackay Brown has completely transformed Rognvald's verse from a traditional expression of Norse expectations of battle and honour into what amounts to a confessional homily. Mackay Brown's apparent need to mute the earl's more violent history and foreground his Christian sensibility has resulted in a substantial re-writing of the earl's poems, which now sometimes bear little resemblance to the *Orkneyinga saga* originals.

Mackay Brown does not always feel the need overtly to re-formulate the saga text, however, for in his most recent novel, *Vinland*, he adopts yet another approach in presenting material from *Orkneyinga saga* to convey what he sees as an important Christian truth. In this instance he neither simply re-tells nor manipulates the saga, but instead, in the more traditional way of historical novelists, he creates a fictional hero whose story interweaves with or runs parallel to specific saga events.[6]

Vinland relates the life and times of the fictional Orcadian Norseman Ranald Sigmundson. As a boy of twelve he deserts his bullying father on a trading expedition in Iceland and stows away on the ship of Leif Ericson, thus becoming one of the Vikings who first land in America, or Vinland as it was known in the Norse world. After the failure of attempts to come to peaceful terms with the natives and make a settlement there,

---

[6]The main sources for the Norse discovery of America are *Grænlendinga saga* and *Eiríks saga rauða*, often referred to as the Vinland sagas. This is indeed the title of the translation of these sagas by Magnús Magnússon and Hermann Pálsson; see bibliography.

he returns to Greenland with Leif and wins a famous horse race. On visiting Norway he is entertained by King Olaf, who is anxious for news of the new continent, and on returning to Orkney he outwits Earl Sigurd's treasurer in the payment for the cargo his ship is carrying. He then successfully reclaims his inherited land at Breckness and becomes a prosperous and influential farmer, a member of the Orkney Thing, and privy to the Earl's family and political machinations. Thus in 1014 he accompanies the Earl to Ireland and takes part in the famous battle at Clontarf, and some five years later is present at the feast where Earl Einar is murdered. He lives to see the struggle for power between Earls Thorfinn and Rognvald Brusison, which ends with the latter's death at the Burning of Paplay. He finally dies as the victorious Thorfinn is about to set off for Rome with the Scottish king, Macbeth, around the year 1050.

As this brief summary of *Vinland* illustrates, Ranald Sigmundson's life encompasses some of the most stirring events in the Norse world in the first half of the eleventh century. Indeed, his journey to Vinland, meeting with King Olaf, participation at Clontarf, and his relations and dealings with some of the most famous Norsemen of his time, all at first suggest that Ranald will have an illustrious career as a typical Viking. Half way through the novel, however, a dramatic change takes place in Ranald's role and attitude. He is so appalled by the treachery and bloodshed at Clontarf that he is reluctant to talk about his experiences there and his distaste for the crudity and barbarity of Orcadian intrigues reaches a climax with the murder of Earl Einar by Thorkel, after which Ranald rejects his former friendship with Thorkel and quite literally resigns from public life, never again attending the Thing or the earls' conferences, and resolutely minding his own business. He later explains to his grandchildren how

> a deep disgust had entered into his heart at human folly and cruelty, his own included; and how he had seen that power drives men mad, and how Earl Einar of the Twisted Mouth had fallen into his own web-of-treachery at Skaill in Sandwick; and how he had decided to wash his hands of politics and violence and attend only to the farm of Breckness. (*Vinland* 226)

For the rest of his life Ranald tends to shun the company of the wealthy and powerful and seeks instead the company of lowly fishermen, boat-builders and peasants. He provides loans on generous terms for other farmers in difficulty and gives away food and clothing to beggars. The death of his favourite child, Margaret, makes him even more reclusive and he hands over the running of Breckness to his son Sumarlid and eventually moves to a dilapidated hovel on a nearby hill. He becomes increasingly devout, especially after talks with the monk Fergus and the abbot Peter, and plans to set sail again for Vinland in a boat being built for him by his friend Lodd, long since dead. However he dies, significantly on an Easter Monday, before he can make this impossible dream come true. In Mackay Brown's view, Ranald Sigmundson thus redeems himself to become a true Norse hero: a once typical Viking who in the pride of life rejects the vanities of this world to live a simple, honest Christian life by trying to be at peace with all men, the world of nature and his God. But how successful is this new approach now that Mackay Brown has used a fictional secular saint instead of an historically canonised one?

As might be expected, *Orkneyinga saga* is the source for most of the historical events of the novel; as only eleven of the novel's 232 pages are actually concerned with the first Norse attempt to establish a settlement in America, Mackay Brown only uses the relevant Vinland sagas very briefly. For the most part he remains faithful to them, though he does conflate the various versions of the discovery of Vinland into one simplified story: though the historical Leif never saw any natives, Mackay Brown has him trade and later fight with them, and the famous grapes are given to the Norsemen by the Indians themselves. This imaginative conflation of the sources is perfectly acceptable within the artistic structure of the novel for, as we shall see, the exact details of the Norse discovery of Vinland are subordinate to its symbolic significance for the character of Ranald.

When it comes to *Orkneyinga saga,* however, Mackay Brown is faced with a structural problem, for although in this instance he remains true to his source he is confronted with a technical difficulty as regards the novel's narrative structure. The story is related entirely from Ranald's point of view, but, as the plot synopsis above reveals, about half way through the novel Ranald completely retires from public life. In order to justify this, however, and make this gesture seem valid, the reader must still be able to witness the treacherous and bloody events of Thorfinn's struggle to become the sole earl in Orkney as recorded in the saga (chs 13–32) even though Ranald no longer takes part in Orcadian politics. Mackay Brown's solution to this is to have news of all the relevant incidents in the saga brought to Ranald (and thus the reader) by those who had apparently seen or heard of these events, for example: 'these matters Ranald of Breckness learned from the men who came to visit him...' (*Vinland* 138) and 'news of the earls' quarrels and manoeuvrings was brought to him from time to time...' (*Vinland* 162). His informants are merchants, skippers and other farmers, and later on his son Sumarlid and son-in-law Ramir (*Vinland* 165, 179, 193, 217, 225, 198, 204).

There are two main drawbacks with this device; firstly, the 'news came to Ranald' formula occurs more than a dozen times and thus becomes a very repetitive, if not distancing form of narrative, and secondly, there is a danger that the reader will begin to experience the novel as a simple re-telling of the *Orkneyinga saga* after all, and not as an independent work of fiction. To be fair to Mackay Brown, though, it is hard to see how else he could have surmounted this narrative problem; the reader *must* see the bloody events of *Orkneyinga saga* as they enfold while Ranald *must* remain on his farm in silent, peaceful protest, for any poignant contrast to be made. Moreover Mackay Brown does at least avoid another possible weakness concerning an inactive main protagonist: although Ranald takes no part in the politics of Orkney he is always shown doing small acts of piety, kindness and friendship in between the bloody scenes of intrigue. He thus never becomes as nebulous a character as some readers find the eponymous hero of *Magnus*.

Despite these narrative problems and a few minor anachronisms, *Vinland* remains a gripping, thought-provoking, and ultimately moving fiction. This is a result of Mackay Brown's skilful weaving together of two major themes: a telling and persuasive contrast of Norse fatalism and Christian free will, and the powerful and unifying symbol of Vinland itself.

As has been previously noted, Mackay Brown had criticised the Norse concept of fate in part of his *An Orkney Tapestry*. In *Vinland*, however, this subject provides the central debate of the novel. Throughout his life, Ranald is troubled by the 'riddle of fate and freedom' (*Vinland* 227) and he neatly summarises how a belief in fatalism can give a man an apparent sense of free will:

> 'Believing this—it is in the very marrow of our bones, it is carved deep in our hearts—bestows a kind of wild freedom. Let us wring what we can out of the tight fist of fate. Then we can go down with a certain carelessness, even with laughter, into the invisible dust [...]'. (*Vinland* 185)

But events in Ranald's life gradually undermine this belief. Earl Sigurd, for example, would '"rather fish in the burn for trout or shoot grouse on Greenay hill"' (*Vinland* 85), but fear of society's contempt, and his mother's sarcastic tongue, drive him to go a-Viking in Ireland. True to the fate his mother had prophesied, he dies in battle at Clontarf and 'earns his place in the story'. Essentially, however, the impression is gained that Sigurd is in reality a hen-pecked man and a slave to conformity. He had little real choice in going to Clontarf, and his death, in practical terms, achieves absolutely nothing. The careers of Earls Einar and Rognvald Brusison can also be seen in this light. They certainly achieve fame but in reality their deaths are rather ignominious: Sigurd dies wrapped in his own banner because no one else will carry it; Einar's

Viking raids always fail and his head is split with an axe while drunk; and the handsome and dashing Rognvald is butchered in a boathouse, betrayed by his own dog. Even the brave and resolute Thorfinn, with his many admirable qualities, can be guilty of appalling acts of cold-blooded murder to achieve his ends (*Vinland* 210). In other words, Mackay Brown seems to imply that a belief in fate provides no reassurance when confronted with the vicissitudes of life: it actually encourages ruthless ambition and anarchic violence. As Ranald's mother Thora comments:

> 'There is still too much talk of fate and the old gods here in the north. It has made men hard and bitter and cruel [...]. I hope I will hear no more talk of the inexorable workings of fate, for only cruelty and rage and ugliness come out of such a belief' (*Vinland* 112–113)

There are hints throughout the novel that fate is not as inexorable as medieval Norsemen believed. Earl Sigurd's mother, Eithne, had woven a magic Raven banner which would guarantee victory though its bearer would die. Sigurd duly dies literally wearing the banner—but on the losing side, a point on which the author of *Orkneyinga saga* remains curiously silent. Moreover Eithne's prophecies concerning Ranald turn out to be inaccurate. She admittedly predicts years of prosperity and happiness (and even his wife, Ragna), but then she also states:

> 'The worst thing that can happen to a man [...] is to grow old in stupidity and complacency. The silver hairs come into his beard. He gets aches in his joints, his breath comes short, his children pay no attention to his advice and go here and there about their own affairs [...]. He thinks people are mocking him behind his back—and so they are, most like, and little wonder [...]. That, Ranald Sigmundsson, is the kind of death that men seem to want nowadays. But it won't happen to you, I'm glad to say.' (*Vinland* 87–88)

Ironically, of course, this is more or less exactly how Ranald *does* die (he is referred to as an 'old dottled farmer', for example: *Vinland* 183), but the important point is that this is because Ranald *chooses* to die this way: Ranald takes his fate into his own hands and makes what he wants of his life, in this case a dedication to pacifism and a contemplation of the real meaning of existence. He successfully refuses to conform to the dictates of the prevailing ethos of his time. Ranald gains neither gold nor glory, but his death, though non-violent, is really much more dignified than those of the earls mentioned previously. The values Ranald lives for are summarised in a long lyrical speech made by the abbot Peter:

> '[...] always, at night, a good man may lie down at peace with himself and sleep.
> 'Yet, even so, he may think, searching his conscience before

sleep, "I have wrought no evil on earth today as far as I know, and I have helped my neighbour in this small matter and that, but does it matter in the end? This sleep that will soon fall on me at midnight is a foreshadowing of death, the last endless sleep. Then it will be as if a poor crofter or fisherman like me had never lived. I might indeed have lived more comfortable nowadays with my wife and children if I had gone viking in the days of my strength, and gotten fame and gold[....]" But the good man knows indeed that, though he is poor, it is a better treasure to lie down at night with an unburdened heart[…].

'The piece of the light that we tend and trim in our hearts will outlast the darkness and the dust of death[…].

'And so, dear children of the light, go out in peace to your fields and your fishing-boats.' (*Vinland* 189–190)

This simple, but beautifully expressed view of the positive and uplifting values of Christian pacifism seems a more positive achievement than the death and destruction which follow in the wake of the earls' greed for fame and is placed in stark contrast to the aggressive ways of contemporary Norsemen. This vision of humility and non-aggression is succinctly and effectively symbolised by the emotional impact of the most memorable event of Ranald's life: his participation in the discovery of Vinland.

It can come as a surprise after a first reading of *Vinland* to realise just how little of the novel actually deals with the Viking discovery of America, but short-lived though it may be, this adventure is to have an enduring influence on the twelve-year old Ranald's imagination, and Vinland eventually becomes a convincing and unifying symbol for all his beliefs and aspirations. Two things in particular make a great impression on him: the vision of harmony between man and nature as portrayed in the lifestyle of the Indians (the 'web of creation', so often referred to in Mackay Brown's works), and a sense of the lost opportunity of creating a lasting and friendly relationship with the natives of the new continent. The 'skraelingar', as the Norsemen call them, greet Leif Ericson and his men peacefully and courteously and attempt to communicate and trade with them. Ranald himself strikes up a sort of friendship with a young boy of his own age, the two of them happily splashing each other with water down on the beach. Unfortunately, however, the Norsemen give the Indians alcohol, which they have never drunk before, and one of them, making a boisterous gesture is misunderstood by a quick-tempered Norseman who instantly kills him. A fight ensues and from then on relations between the two groups are marked by suspicion, fear and violence; Ranald himself is struck by a stone thrown by the Indian boy. Constantly besieged and outnumbered, the Greenlanders eventually give up their attempt at settlement and return home.

For the rest of his life Ranald always remembers his transient friendship with the Indian boy. What haunts him most is the sense of a missed opportunity: the *promise*, the *possibility* of two races previously unknown to each other meeting, communicating and living together in mutual respect and understanding in an integrated community; a possibility which, by analogy, also extends to all peoples at all times. Thus, in his old age, yearning for a world of peace and reconciliation instead of violence and confrontation, Ranald talks of building a boat and sailing to Vinland to try and renew his friendship with the Indian. He knows, of course, that in reality this is impossible, but the projected return to Vinland is an inspiring dream to uplift his last frail years; it neatly represents all that he has learnt and valued in his life.

The symbolic meaning of Vinland is cleverly reinforced by the parallel Celtic legend of a magic land far to the west. Ranald is especially impressed by the monk Fergus's tale of Saint Brandon who found an 'unutterably delightful' earthly paradise in the Atlantic, where everyone is young, but was nonetheless informed by one of the inhabitants that 'heaven was further west still' (*Vinland* 180). This is part of the same Celtic tradition which embraces the fantastic sea-journey of Mael Duin and the Gaelic Otherworld of Tir-nan-Og, the Land of Everlasting Youth, all far to the west.[7] As the title of the last chapter 'Tir-nan-Og' suggests, Mackay Brown has synthesised pagan and Christian myths and Norse and Celtic sagas and legends to provide a perfect symbol for Ranald's aspirations and the duality of man's nature: the search for a new, peaceful and *real* world where men could live together in harmony (Vinland), and a visionary *ideal* world of complete perfection and immortality (Tir-nan-Og/Heaven).

What ultimately makes the duality of this symbol convincing and effective is the character of Ranald himself. It is always difficult for an author to create a truly good character without making him or her seem implausible or priggish, but in Ranald Sigmundson Mackay Brown has presented a convincing portrayal of a man who tries to be benevolent and sincere while remaining strikingly human and credible. Throughout all the turbulent events of his lifetime, the young Viking and aging recluse remains constant in his basic integrity. He may die a disreputable 'straw death' in contemporary Norse terms, but in the eyes of a modern reader

[7]Details of this Celtic mythology are outside the scope of this essay, see Meyer 1895; also Mackay Brown's play, *The Voyage of Saint Brandon* (*Three Plays* 81–150); on Tir-nan-Og see McNeill 1989, 104–107; on the historical background to Brendan's explorations see Jones 1986, 33–34.

he can be seen as an ordinary and fallible human being who, against the many odds of his time and society, managed to live a life of basic honesty and decency which is inspiring in its humility and dignity. As Ranald once says to his son Somarlid:

> 'Who knows how many saints there are among those poor humble men? Not only in the little churches either, but in the crofts and fishing-bothies there are men and women of great goodness, though their lives are often hard.' (*Vinland* 195)

As the whole of *Vinland* implies, Ranald Sigmundson is indeed one of these saints and his character one of Mackay Brown's most appealing representatives of his Christian faith.

As this essay has sought to show, *Orkneyinga saga* has been a central and vital inspiration for George Mackay Brown throughout his career as poet and novelist. The saga has proved especially alluring to him not only because it is the most detailed historical source for early Orcadian history, but also because it provides important and striking examples, in Mackay Brown's view, of the conversion of Orkney (and Scandinavia) from fatalism and paganism to optimism and Christianity. Whether or not readers are sympathetic to Mackay Brown's Christian vision of the saga, two impressive claims can be made about the Orcadian novelist's achievement. Firstly, Mackay Brown's persistent imaginative engagement with *Orkneyinga saga* has produced several strikingly lyrical and moving works of modern literary art; secondly, his fictions and poetry have brought *Orkneyinga saga* to a much wider modern audience than the saga would otherwise have reached. In George Mackay Brown's hands a masterpiece of Old Icelandic narrative art has found renewed and fruitful life.

BIBLIOGRAPHY

Bibire, Paul. 1988. 'The Poetry of Earl Rognvaldr's Court', in Crawford 1988, pp. 208–240. Aberdeen.

Bold, Alan. 1978. *George Mackay Brown*. Edinburgh.

Brown, George Mackay. 1975. *Letters from Hamnavoe*. Edinburgh.

———. 1976. *The Sun's Net*. London.

———. 1976. *Winterfold*. London.

———. 1978. *An Orkney Tapestry* (1969). London.

———. 1983. *Hawkfall* (1974). London.

———. 1984. *Three plays: The Loom of Light, The Well* and *The Voyage of Saint Brandon*. London.

————. 1987. *Magnus* (1973). Glasgow.

————. 1992. *Vinland*. London.

Crawford, Barbara E., ed. 1988. *St Magnus Cathedral and Orkney's Twelfth-Century Renaissance*. Aberdeen.

D'Arcy, Julian Meldon. 1990. 'On Certain Aspects of Old Norse Influence on Modern Scottish Literature.' Unpublished doctoral dissertation, University of Aberdeen.

Farley, Frank Edgar. 1903. *Scandinavian Influences in the English Romantic Movement*. Boston.

Holtsmark, Anne. 1937. 'Bjarne Kolbeinsson og hans forfatterskap', *Edda* 37/1, 1-17.

Huberman, Elizabeth. 1981. 'George Mackay Brown's *Magnus*', *Studies in Scottish Literature* 16, 122–134.

Jones, Gwyn. 1986. *The Norse Atlantic Saga*. Second revised edition. Oxford.

Laxdæla saga. 1969. Trans. Magnus Magnusson and Hermann Pálsson. Harmondsworth.

McNeill, Marian F. 1989. *The Silver Bough, Vol. I. Scottish Folk-Lore and Folk-Belief* (1957). Edinburgh.

Macrae-Gibson, O.D. 1989. 'The Other Scottish Language—*Orkneyinga Saga*', in J. Derrick McClure and Michael Spiller, eds, *Bryght Lanternis: Essays on the Language and Literature of Medieval and Renaissance Scotland*, pp. 420–428. Aberdeen.

Meyer, Kuno, trans. 1895. *The Voyage of Bran*. London.

Mooney, John. 1935. *St. Magnus: Earl of Orkney*. Kirkwall.

Murray, Rowena. 1986. 'The Influence of Norse Literature on the Twentieth-Century Writer George Mackay Brown', in Dietrich Strauss and Horst W. Drescher, eds, *Scottish Language and Literature, Medieval and Renaissance*, Scottish Studies IV, pp. 547–557. Frankfurt am Main.

Njal's saga. 1960. Trans. Magnus Magnusson and Hermann Pálsson. Harmondsworth.

Olsen, Magnus. 1932. 'Orknø-Norn og Norrøn Diktning paa Orknøene', *Maal og Minne*, 139–153.

Orkneyinga saga. 1982. Trans. and introd. by Hermann Pálsson and Paul Edwards (originally published 1978). Harmondsworth.

Taylor, A.B., trans. 1938. *Orkneyinga saga*. Edinburgh and London.

Thomson, William P.L. 1987. *History of Orkney*. Edinburgh.

Times Literary Supplement. Anonymous review of *Magnus*. Sept. 1973, p. 1101.

The Vinland Sagas: The Norse Discovery of America [*Grænlendinga saga* and *Eiríks saga rauða*]. 1965. Trans. Magnus Magnusson and Hermann Pálsson. Harmondsworth.

Part IV:

Afterword

14

The Gloss

Ian Duhig, Leeds

Our conquering heroes grasped too late
the stout resistance they had not met,
the fires guiding them to safe harbour
past submarine hulks off Scarborough.
Ashore their winged helmets and dripping furs
stirred folks' envies more often than their fears.
Boys hung on every word they said. A
landlord laid on Karaoke Edda.
Inland, monasteries were signposted
in Esperanto, Geat and Old High Norse,
listing hours monks would be available
for visitors to disembowel.
In time they drove on to the Dales,
their tattoos peeling in the clement gales—
a bad one blew away both man and horse.
None could hear if they still spoke Old High Norse.
After their first excursion in spring rain
they never saw their testicles again.
They held down their fields with dry stone walls.
The harvest of their fields was dry stone walls.
They carved homes and chesspieces from these stones
and never lost their hatred of these stones.
All of them were broken by the work.
The berserkers were constantly berserk,
dying so and shipless for their bones
to prop up epitaphs in these stones—
with dates wrong and misspellings of their names
moaned the red-haired pedants on pub quiz teams.
The last of these would die in our village,
asked to gloss the Old High Norse for pillage.

Index